Jackie

Jackie

PUBLIC,

PRIVATE,

SECRET

◇◇◇◇◇◇◇◇◇◇

J. RANDY TARABORRELLI

ST. MARTIN'S PRESS
NEW YORK

First published in the United States by St. Martin's Press, an imprint of St. Martin's Publishing Group

JACKIE. Copyright © 2023 by Rose Books, Inc. All rights reserved. Printed in the United States of America. For information, address St. Martin's Publishing Group, 120 Broadway, New York, NY 10271.

www.stmartins.com

Designed by Gabriel Guma

Library of Congress Cataloging-in-Publication Data

Names: Taraborrelli, J. Randy, author.
Title: Jackie : public, private, secret / J. Randy Taraborrelli.
Description: First edition. | New York : St. Martin's Press, 2023. |
    Includes index.
Identifiers: LCCN 2023009379 | ISBN 9781250276216 (hardcover) |
    ISBN 9781250276223 (ebook)
Subjects: LCSH: Onassis, Jacqueline Kennedy, 1929-1994. |
    Celebrities—United States—Biography. | Presidents' spouses—
    United States—Biography.
Classification: LCC CT275.O552 T368 2023 | DDC 973.922092
    [B]—dc23/eng/20230228
LC record available at https://lccn.loc.gov/2023009379

Our books may be purchased in bulk for promotional, educational, or business use. Please contact your local bookseller or the Macmillan Corporate and Premium Sales Department at 1-800-221-7945, extension 5442, or by email at MacmillanSpecialMarkets@macmillan.com.

First Edition: 2023

10 9 8 7 6 5

For all those who have faced the darkest trauma of their lives
and struggled to move through, or move on,
and for the peace that may come one day after the crucible,
in the light
of a path toward acceptance.

I have been through a lot and I have suffered a great deal, but I've had lots of happy moments, as well. I have come to the conclusion that we must not expect too much from life. We must give to life at least as much as we receive from it. Every moment one lives is different from the other, the good, the bad, the hardship, the joy, the tragedy, love, and happiness are all interwoven into one single indescribable whole that is called life.

—JACQUELINE KENNEDY ONASSIS,
TO MARYAM KHARAZMI, *KAYHAN* NEWSPAPER, IRAN, MAY 1972

Oh, Jack, you know me. I have three lives. Public, private, and secret.

—JACQUELINE KENNEDY ONASSIS,
TO JOHN CARL WARNECKE, 1989

CONTENTS

⬦⬦⬦⬦⬦⬦⬦⬦⬦⬦⬦⬦⬦⬦

BOOK II: THE TRAGIC HEROINE

BOOK III: REBIRTH

BOOK IV: DECISIONS AND CONSEQUENCES

BOOK V: NEW HORIZONS

BOOK VI: CHALLENGES

BOOK VII: A SAD FAREWELL

W hat's the point of biography if it doesn't reveal secrets?"

That was the question posed by Jacqueline Kennedy Onassis to me in January 1983 when she was an editor at Doubleday & Company in New York. I was a young newspaper reporter at the time who'd just been signed to write a biography of Diana Ross, a book whose publication Jackie had championed. I was sitting in her office, which was small and cluttered with just one window. My eyes scanned her desk. There was a square, crystal container holding different colored pencils, all efficiently sharpened. An ashtray overflowing with cigarette butts. A stack of art books and a couple about dance. Two empty foam coffee cups, two unfinished pastries. A silver-framed picture of her children, Caroline and John, with her mother, Janet Auchincloss. On the wall, just a poster of famed ballet dancer Rudolph Nureyev. I searched the room for her husbands, President John F. Kennedy or Aristotle Onassis, but there were no pictures of either.

"I just adore Diana Ross," she told me. "She's so . . . what's the word I'm looking for?" She gazed at me for a moment before it came to her. ". . . *enigmatic*. Speaking of which," she added, "do you know Michael Jackson?" I told her he was a friend. "Then, we should definitely talk about him one day," she said. She was interested in acquiring books by or about public figures who had private lives readers would find unusual or surprising. "Like it or not, a person's secrets are what makes any biography worthwhile," she concluded. "Otherwise, what's the point?"

How ironic, coming from a woman known for guarding her own secrets, especially since Jackie had so much trouble with biographies about herself. There was the first one by Mary Van Rensselaer Thayer in 1960, which caused a rift between Jackie and her mother (a matter I explore in this book for the first time). There was one by William Manchester in 1967, which resulted in litigation. There was Kitty Kelley's in 1978, which caused a dispute between Jackie and her half brother, Jamie Auchincloss. Many dozens of others were published without her approval. Maybe that's why Jackie had trouble balancing her own editorial mandate to demystify celebrities with her more natural instinct to protect them. That's what she ended up doing for Diana Ross with my first of two books about her, *Diana Ross: A Celebration of Her Life and Career,* published by Doubleday in 1985. Four years later, in 1989, I authored another book about her, *Call Her Miss Ross.* Whereas the Doubleday book was not successful in the marketplace, the second became a *New York Times* bestseller.

About a month after the publication of *Call Her Miss Ross,* I was having lunch with its editor, Hillel Black, at the Lotos Club in New York, one of the oldest private literary clubs in the country. Jackie happened by and joined us. As we chatted, she compared the two Diana Ross books. "Obviously, the reason the second one worked so well," she observed, "is because, unlike the first one we published, this one is very revealing." Hillel and I glanced at each other. I wanted to say, "The other one was, too, before it was edited." I didn't have to, though, because she came to it on her own. "Doubleday did an ambitious edit on that first book, didn't we?" she asked. I nodded. "Well, that explains it," she concluded. "That was our big mistake."

Jackie then confirmed a story I already knew. In February 1983, she and Doubleday's president, Sam Vaughan, had a meeting with Diana Ross and her literary agent, Irving "Swifty" Lazar. Fiercely protective of her privacy, Miss Ross sought to stop publication of my first book. In its place, she offered Jackie her autobiography, but with one caveat: it would "include no personal details, whatsoever." Being gracious, Jackie said she'd give the odd proposition some thought. Before leaving, Diana asked what Doubleday intended to do about my book. Jackie told her not to worry about it.

A month later, Jackie passed on Diana's book. She did offer, however, to send an advance copy of mine to Diana and Swifty for their review. They were given permission to cut anything they didn't like. I knew nothing about this arrangement until sometime later. When the manuscript finally came to me for my own review, a lot of it was edited. To this day, I don't know if that was Diana Ross's doing or Swifty Lazar's. Obviously, I wasn't happy about it, but I was young, and it was my first book so . . . what did I know?

Years later, with a glint in her eye, Jackie concluded, "So, in the end, it was *your* book that ended up with no personal details whatsoever, and you see where that got us." She smiled and added, "Congratulations on finally doing it the right way. I can't wait to read it."

Her surprising deal with Diana Ross makes sense when one considers how diligently Jackie worked to maintain her own privacy. Other than the few interviews she gave after the assassination of her husband, President John F. Kennedy, in 1963, she had always been careful not to reveal much about herself. She never did the introspective Barbara Walters interview. She never wrote the insightful memoir.

Like most people, I had many questions when I first met her. As she spoke, I couldn't help but wonder who she really was and how she viewed herself. Her life had been filled with as much trauma as reward, all of it playing out before the whole world. After everything she went through, where did she draw her strength from, her confidence, her wisdom? There she sat before me, one of the most famous women of all time, open, candid, and available. It wasn't her grace, charm, or intelligence that surprised me— one would certainly expect that of Jackie—it was her trusting nature. She made me feel as if I could ask her anything. There was just one problem: I wouldn't dare. It somehow felt unconscionable. How could I take advantage of her by returning her to any dark time in her life? Looking back all these years later, I think her great secret weapon was her basic trust in humanity. She believed people to be essentially good and had faith that no one would ever be so unkind as to quiz her about her painful past. It's how she survived in New York all those years, walking freely, trying to be "normal" while being stalked by photographers though rarely stopped by passersby. Maybe it was also one of the reasons she was able to maintain her aura of mystery. Perhaps she got away with never talking about her life simply because no one could bear to ask her about it.

Though I've written four previous books related to Jackie and her families, the Bouviers, Auchinclosses, and Kennedys, this is my first full-scale biography of her. When I started it three years ago, I had to wonder if there was more to report given all of the previous books. In the end, I found that the biggest surprises had to do with placing well-known stories into their proper context. For instance, I often reported on her marriage to Aristotle

Onassis, but not until this book did I understand its purely transactional nature and the reasons Jackie allowed him to continue his love affair with Maria Callas. Also, I knew she'd quit her job at Viking Press due to disagreement over a book. Not until this research did I understand that her departure also had to do with prioritizing family over career, primarily the care of her mother. I also never understood, until now, her unusual relationship with Maurice Tempelsman. I now recognize that she made the same choices with him that her mother had made with her second husband, Hugh Auchincloss. Speaking of Jackie's "Uncle Hughdie," this is the first book to delve into her close relationship with him, one so important he gave her away at both her weddings.

Jackie's half brother, Jamie—Hugh was his father—told me, "Our mother used to say, 'Sometimes it feels to me like Jacqueline is completely unknowable.' At the same time, a paradox about her was that she could occasionally be too revealing, such as after the assassination, when she couldn't stop talking about it and repeatedly told the same stories. We all knew, though, that this was her trauma speaking." Indeed, it also wasn't until researching this book that I fully grasped Jackie's continued suffering over what happened to her husband, the president. Obviously, she went on with her life, but she never got past his murder, or so she confessed to her former lover, John Warnecke, in the weeks before her death.

I've written about the Kennedys for the better part of the last twenty-five years. In doing so, I've conducted many hundreds of interviews with family members, friends, and other associates who are now gone, some for many years. You'll find many of their memories of Jackie memorialized in this book. I felt a responsibility to them to go back over decades' worth of tape recordings and transcripts in order to tell their stories as accurately as possible. I also reviewed many letters from family sources invaluable to me over the years, clarifying stories and verifying information, as well as diaries, calendars, and other important mementos. I was also able to interview many intimates who now feel much freer to talk about Jackie, almost thirty years after her death in 1994.

I'm honored to have known Jacqueline Bouvier Kennedy Onassis in the small way I did, certainly not as a friend but just as someone whose path somehow managed to cross my own. I hope this book brings you a bit closer to this remarkable woman, especially those rare instances when she's maybe not her best self, when she falls prey to anger or insecurity or jealousy. It's in those unguarded moments we can recognize that she really was just human like the rest of us, not that she ever tried to be anything else. It's we who were guilty of trying to make her something she wasn't and never wanted to be—not a mere mortal but, rather, some sort of mythological figure.

John Warnecke told me that, in 1989, about a week before her sixtieth birthday, Jackie observed, "I have three lives. Public, private, and secret," thus, the title of this book. While she didn't elaborate, it seems obvious that "public" was the life people thought they knew; "private" was the one about which they gossiped; and "secret" was the one about which they had absolutely no idea. To a certain extent, though, isn't that true of all of us? No one of us is an open book. We're all mysterious in our own ways with the same three lives—public, private, and secret. Where Jackie is concerned, I strove to make this book primarily about that last one, the "secret" one. If my job as a biographer is to invade the privacy of my subjects—and I feel certain, based on our conversations, that Jackie would agree with this mandate—then, hopefully, in these pages, you'll learn a few things about her you didn't know, maybe even a secret or two. After all, as the lady herself so aptly put it, "What's the point of biography if it doesn't reveal secrets?"

J. Randy Taraborrelli

January 2023

Foreword

⟨⟨⟨⟨⟨⟨⟨⟨⟨⟨⟨⟩⟩⟩⟩⟩⟩⟩⟩⟩⟩

HOW REMARKABLE

I t was nightfall as John Warnecke walked to the towering limestone building at 1040 Fifth Avenue in New York to visit his close friend and former
lover, Jacqueline Kennedy Onassis.

After checking in with lobby security, he was escorted up the elevator to the fifteenth floor. The doors parted and opened into Jackie's foyer.
Behind a glass door was a gallery of black-and-white marble. Beyond that,
a large entryway from which the other rooms in the sprawling apartment
flowed. It was a real showplace, stylishly furnished with French antiques, oil
paintings, and other works of fine art. The views from tall french windows
were all spectacular—Central Park; the Hudson River in the distance; the
Metropolitan Museum of Art down Fifth Avenue; the reservoir that ran
from Fifth to Ninety-Sixth, from east to west, with its path for horses and
dog walkers.

Usually, Jackie's chef and companion, Marta Sgubin, greeted visitors,
but tonight she was nowhere to be found. The apartment was dark and
quiet. John Warnecke—better known to loved ones like Jackie as "Jack"—
noticed a telescope in the corner. Jackie had once told him she often gazed
into it to see how the other half lived as they walked about the park. Be they
tourists or native New Yorkers, how lucky they were to be able to move so
freely about without being bothered. It was a luxury that had eluded her for
at least the last forty years.

John Warnecke, tall, balding, and distinguished-looking at seventy-five,
had been close to Jackie for nearly thirty years. In 1964, while he was designing the John F. Kennedy Eternal Flame memorial grave site at Arlington

National Cemetery, they became lovers. He now lived in San Francisco. While visiting New York, he'd been inspired on Valentine's Day to send Jackie a note reaffirming his affection for her. Rarely out of his thoughts, he wrote, she was one of the most special women he'd ever known. It wasn't the first time he'd expressed his love for her, of course, but so moved was she by it she asked to see him.

Jack crossed the flowing space past an antique gilt mirror and Chinese porcelain vases filled with branches and flowers. On the other side, he noticed light from one of the rooms. It was the library. He went to the doorway and peeked inside to a room lit only by a soft orange glow shimmering off red-papered walls.

Jackie's back was to him. Wearing a pink chenille sweater over white silk pajamas with a matching headwrap, she was seated in an upholstered chair close to the fireplace. There was a small blaze. She looked up, noticed Jack, and gave him a smile, as beguiling as ever. She motioned to a chair next to her. A cup of hot tea awaited on a small glass end table.

She was leaner, her glowing complexion now dulled. It wasn't the passing of the years that had taken such a toll. It was cancer.

A little more than a month earlier, Jackie had been diagnosed with aggressive non-Hodgkin's lymphoma. The cure, as is often the case, seemed somehow worse than the disease. Yet, while chemotherapy had begun to rob her of her looks and sap her of her energy, it didn't diminish her presence. There remained an imperiousness in the way she held her head, her dark brown eyes still full of enormous power as she gazed up at Jack and beckoned him to sit.

After he was seated, Jackie asked Jack to not reveal to anyone what was about to happen, not while either of them was alive, anyway. He would relate details in interviews in 1998 and again in 2007 but with the proviso that the story not be told until ten years after his death. He died in 2010 at the age of ninety-one.

In the 1998 interview, Jack said, "As I took my seat, Jackie handed me a stack of envelopes neatly tied together with yarn. She explained it was correspondence from friends, family, and in some cases, dignitaries, all of it treasured. My presence that evening was part of a ritual having to do with these mementos. Every night that week, she told me, she was inviting a trusted friend or family member to her home to take part in it. Last night, it had been her longtime personal secretary Nancy Tuckerman. Tomorrow night, she said she was thinking of asking her stepbrother, Yusha Auchincloss. She asked Lady Bird Johnson to fly up from Texas, but said she feared it might be too much for her."

Jackie untied the yarn and took a letter from the stack. She read it before placing it into the fire. She took another envelope, opened it, scanned it quickly, and handed it to Jack. He put it in the flames. He recalled, "There were letters from Jackie's children, John and Caroline; from her mother, Janet Auchincloss; her stepfather, Hugh Auchincloss; birthday cards from her sister, Lee Radziwill; her half brother, Jamie; her half sister, Janet, and from Yusha. There were also letters from Jack Kennedy, Aristotle Onassis, her father, Jack Bouvier, and even a few from me."

Jack knew not to read any of the letters. He was there to participate in a ceremony, not invade Jackie's privacy. He had to wonder, though, how she squared her love of history with the destruction of it. She explained that these letters had a distinction: they weren't written by her but to her. It wasn't fair, she said, that friends and loved ones should have their private words made public after her death. Hers to them? Yes. She was used to that, but not theirs to her. She knew she'd have no way to protect their privacy once she was gone. Therefore, she decided to take matters into her own hands while she was still able to do so.

Locked in moments of prolonged silence, Jack and Jackie saw to their task. One by one, she examined each note and each card and then leaned in to gently place it on the fire, after which she'd hand another to Jack for the same purpose. There, the keepsake slowly burned until nothing remained of it but orange embers and gray ash.

After about an hour, Jackie was tired. Jack felt he should leave, but there were still many stacks of letters. When he offered to return, she said no. Again, someone else would join her tomorrow night.

As Jack rose, he caught their reflection in an enormous, Louis XV– style, giltwood mirror hanging above the fireplace. It had been a gift to her from her stepfather, Hugh, thirty years earlier when she moved from a Georgetown home to this apartment. It hadn't hung in this spot until recently, Jackie said. It was usually in one of the guest rooms next to a large, framed poster of President Kennedy, the only one displayed in the apartment. Jackie moved it to this more prominent place, above the fireplace and tilted slightly downward so, as she explained, she could see and maybe in some way even honor her changed reflection. Jack stood back and regarded it for a moment, nodding to himself in appreciation of its elegance, its beauty.

Meanwhile, Jackie pulled a manila envelope from the stack. There was no writing on it. She peeked inside, found a note, and read it. Then, turning to Jack and motioning to the mirror, she said, "Uncle Hughdie wrote this to me when he gave that to me."

Jack read the note: "To live in prison is to live without mirrors. XO Uncle Hughdie. 7/64."

It had been appropriate. Hugh always seemed to have the ideal quote for every occasion, and this one from Margaret Atwood—at the time, a lecturer in English at the University of British Columbia in Vancouver—was just perfect. The reason Jackie had left the Georgetown house was because she felt so imprisoned by pressing crowds that gathered daily for just a glimpse of her after the assassination of her husband.

Jack smiled and handed the note back to Jackie. She tilted the manila envelope, and a few photographs fell to her lap. There was a picture of her as an infant, one of her mother riding a horse, her graduation picture from Miss Porter's, and one of her sister standing in front of the Eiffel Tower. She held another of the photographs and stared at it. It was her and Jack Kennedy on the momentous day of his inauguration in Washington. Jackie smiled to herself while returning it and the others, along with the note from Hugh, to its envelope. Reaching out, she leaned forward to place it on one of the logs. But, then, she hesitated. "Keep this for me, will you?" she asked, handing the envelope to Jack.

"Of course I will," he said.

As she gazed at the flames, Jackie said she was never the type to look back. There was no point to it. It was why she had no interest in writing her autobiography. With a chuckle, she recalled her father once telling her, "Never look backward or you'll fall down the stairs." It was a quote from the English journalist Rudyard Kipling. Staring at the fire, she then began reciting his most significant poem, "If—" in a soft, almost hypnotic voice:

If you can keep your head when all about you are losing theirs and blaming it on you

If you can trust yourself when all men doubt you but make allowance for doubting too

If you can wait and not be tired of waiting, or being lied about, don't deal in lies

Or being hated, don't give way to hating

And yet don't look too good, nor talk too wise.

She turned back to Jack and noted that the poem ends with Kipling stating that if a person could do everything as he described, "yours is the earth and everything that's in it and, which is more, you'll be a man, my son." However, she said that when her father used to recite it to her, he'd always replace the last line with: "And which is more, you'll be the woman you've always been meant to be, my darling daughter."

"How remarkable is that?" Jackie asked reflectively, almost to herself. "How truly remarkable is that?"

BOOK I

Becoming Jackie

"NOBODY KNOWS THE REAL JACKIE"

∞∞∞∞∞∞∞∞

NOVEMBER 22, 1963

Every time we got off the plane that day, three times they gave me the yellow roses of Texas. But in Dallas, they gave me red roses. I thought, how funny, red roses. The seat was full of blood and red roses.

S ome said it sounded like a crack. Others, a pop or a firecracker. Maybe a cherry bomb. Jackie Kennedy thought it was the backfire of a motorcycle. Confused, she watched as Jack grabbed his throat and lurched to the left. Then, there was another bang, and another.

Rifle shots, all. Three in the course of less than five seconds.

Jack turned and I turned back, so neatly, his last expression was so neat. He had his hand out. I could see a piece of his skull coming off. It was flesh-colored, not white. He was holding out his hand and I can see this perfectly clean piece detaching from his head. Then, he slumped in my lap. His blood and brains were in my lap.

JANUARY 20, 1961

She was so proud, it was as if she could feel her heart swell.

In the long history of the world, only a few generations have been granted the role of defending freedom in its hour of maximum danger. I do not shrink from this responsibility, I welcome it. I do not believe that any of us would exchange places with any other people or any other generation. The energy, the faith, the devotion which we bring to this endeavor will light our country and all who serve it—and the glow from that fire can truly light the world.

America's new First Lady, Jacqueline Bouvier Kennedy, sat serene and beautiful between Mamie Eisenhower and Lady Bird Johnson as she watched President John Fitzgerald Kennedy address the nation for the first time, its thirty-fifth president.

And so, my fellow Americans: ask not what your country can do for you, ask what you can do for your country. My fellow citizens of the world, ask not what America will do for you, but what together we can do for the freedom of man.

Jackie thought it had been a magnificent speech. "I had heard it in bits and pieces many times while he was working on it in Florida," she later said. "There were piles of yellow paper covered with his notes all over our bedroom floor. That day, when I heard it as a whole for the first time, it was so pure, beautiful, and soaring that I knew I was hearing something great. And now I know that it will go down in history as one of the most moving speeches ever uttered—with Pericles' Funeral Oration and the Gettysburg Address."

At forty-three, Jack Kennedy would be the youngest president in American history, and also the first Roman Catholic. His election felt like a new beginning, a fresh and exciting start after the staid Eisenhower years. Square-jawed, handsome, and bursting with vitality, he looked impeccable in his formal day dress and striped trousers. Though he didn't wear it for the oath, a top hat completed the look—an Inauguration Day tradition for U.S. presidents such as Franklin D. Roosevelt and Harry Truman. With Jackie at his side, Jack had been sworn in taking his oath on a Catholic Douai Bible that had belonged to his maternal grandfather, John Francis "Honey Fitz" Fitzgerald.

For this important day, Jackie had her designer, Oleg Cassini, create a long, fawn-colored wool coat with a sable collar and matching sable muff for her hands. Completing the outfit would be the fur-trimmed, beige pillbox hat designed by Halston—a look she would popularize in the States and abroad; still to this day when people think of pillbox hats, they think of Jackie.

Looking back, it's hard to believe how young she was. She was just thirty-one, and the eyes of the whole world were on her. Maybe Jackie wasn't beautiful in the conventional sense—her teeth weren't perfectly aligned, for instance—but she was so vital and engaging she gave the impression of rare beauty. Her face was clear and luminous though a bit fuller after just having given birth less than two months earlier. Without makeup, people were always astonished at how girlish she seemed. "But all dolled up," her doting father, Jack Bouvier, used to say, "no one can beat my Jackie in the looks department." Her eyes were probably her most spectacular feature, large and intelligent, soulful and deeply brown. Tall and slender, she always moved with unaffected grace. "She just has a way," her stepfather, Hugh Auchincloss, would say. "Jackie's way."

Even given her youth, Jackie had already lived a rarified kind of life, especially in the last seven years as the wife of a senator and then president. She never could have imagined herself as a public person—"I'm actually not fond of the public," she had said—but while stumping for Jack in his campaigns, she learned a lot about herself. She was tougher than she knew, and more charismatic, too. People gravitated to her, and, much to her surprise, she welcomed it. Even though she had reservations about what the future would hold for her and her family, she was ready to steel herself for the challenges ahead as First Lady. "As frightened as I was, I was exhilarated, too," she would tell her friend Joan Braden many years later. "You know how it is when you're on a roller coaster? You're scared, but excited too and apprehensive and you feel as if what's about to happen will be fun and unforgettable. That's how I felt when Jack was inaugurated. I felt like as worried as I was and as nervous as I was about what would happen to my family, my children, I was excited in equal measure. I was happy for Jack, too," she concluded, "because, my God, how he deserved it. How he deserved every bit of it."

She was ready to commit to her new endeavor—that is, if she could just feel like her old self.

Jackie still wasn't well after giving birth to her and Jack's second child, John Jr. Bone-tired and headachy, she was in a sort of daze after having taken heavy doses of Dexedrine for her nerves. Her mother-in-law, the ever-stoic Kennedy matriarch Rose Fitzgerald Kennedy, was overheard saying Jackie was taking too long to recover. She'd had nine children, she proudly noted, and bounced back quickly after each one. "But have you ever had a Cesarean delivery?" Jackie's mother, Janet Auchincloss, wanted to know. Rose was taken aback by the personal question. The answer was no. "Then, you don't know what it's like, do you?" Janet asked. "So perhaps it would be best if you didn't have an opinion about it." It was often tense between the mothers-in-law, even though Rose did try to keep the peace. Her son's was a political marriage, after all, and Rose knew it only served the Kennedys to have a good rapport with the Auchinclosses. It's just that the Kennedys had political ambitions and the Auchinclosses didn't, so Janet wasn't quite as motivated.

"Family tensions aren't unusual in heightened moments," wrote Jackie's stepbrother, Yusha Auchincloss, later. He added that when the stakes are as great as they had been on that day, it was only natural that nerves would be frayed.

Confusion about the seating arrangements for Jackie's mother and stepfather at the inauguration didn't help.

Jackie's half brother, Jamie Auchincloss—twelve at the time—watched the inaugural proceedings seated directly in front of his brother-in-law, the new president. Next to him was his sister, Janet Jr., his stepbrother, Yusha, as well as other Auchinclosses and Bouviers. All of them were in choice seats near Eleanor Roosevelt and Adlai Stevenson, all of them except for Jamie's parents, Jackie's mother and stepfather. When he searched the crowd for them, he found them out in the distance facing him and, thus, the back of the president. Surely, this was a mistake. "I had a sinking feeling," he recalled, "because there was my mother, sitting up impatiently way out there, and even from that distance I could see she was fuming. It was especially embarrassing since she'd just hosted a luncheon for the Kennedy, Bouvier, and Auchicnloss families. Many people who may not have been familiar with her before now knew she was the incoming First Lady's mother. Some were pointing, as if surprised."

Adora Rule, Janet's assistant, who attended the inauguration and was seated with the Auchinclosses behind the president, recalled, "After the inauguration, as we left the Capitol, Mr. A. made a beeline to me. 'Where's Tish?' he asked. 'We need to speak to Tish.' He was asking about Jackie's new social secretary, Letitia Baldrige. She was already at work, I told him. The White House changed hands at exactly noon, and Tish was making sure there were no snafus. Mr. A. looked at me with concern and said, 'Mrs. Auchincloss is saddened by our seating. She's practically in tears. How could that have happened?' I had no idea. Then, on the bus headed to the

Mayflower Hotel for the buffet luncheon, which was to be hosted by the Kennedys, he leaned in and whispered in my ear, 'Jackie did it on purpose.' I was surprised. 'That can't be true,' I told him."

Adora had known Jackie since she was hired in 1953 to assist with arrangements of her and Jack Kennedy's wedding reception at the family's homestead, Hammersmith Farm. While she had witnessed many tense and argumentative moments over the years, what Jackie was being accused of now was more spiteful than Adora could ever have imagined.

When one considers the tragic way the Kennedy administration would culminate in a little more than a thousand days, it seems ironic that it would commence with bruised feelings over something that, in light of later tragic events, might seem trivial. But, at the time, it felt hurtful, at least to Jackie's mother and stepfather. After all, though they certainly had their differences, from the day her daughter was born, Janet had been Jackie's biggest champion. "She was my heart," is how Janet later put it, "no matter how much we fought, and boy did we ever fight." For her to be stripped of the privilege of looking at Jackie's shining face as she became the nation's third-youngest First Lady seemed unfair. Maybe Jackie felt she had good reason to slight her, but to also deprive Hugh? All he'd ever done since the time she was twelve and moved into his home after he married her mother was to care deeply for her. Thanks to him, she'd enjoyed a rich, privileged life. He thought of her as his own, and his pride in her was equaled only by her mother's. It all seemed wrong. How had things spiraled so out of control?

"I know Jackie," Adora stated with confidence, "and she'd never do anything like that."

Hugh couldn't help but chuckle at her naivete. As much as he loved Jackie, and felt he had a rapport with her, he was still often completely baffled by her behavior. She was a woman of contrasts. Her life had always been one of great highs and lows, and her responses often unpredictable. She was like her mother—a total enigma. "Kiddo, you may think you know Jackie," Hugh told Adora, "but take it from me, nobody knows the real Jackie."

"THAT BOOK"

◇◇◇◇◇◇◇◇◇◇◇◇◇◇

don't want this damn book to come out," Jackie was saying, "and I mean it." It was a little late. She now held in her hands samples of the book's first excerpts, which would appear in six weeks' time in *Ladies' Home Journal.*

The book in question had been Janet's idea. After her son-in-law announced his candidacy, she suspected there'd be many books written about her daughter that would be penned by authors over whom the family would have no control. She thought of a trusted friend, Mary Van Rensselaer Thayer—known as Molly—who was a journalist. Molly had often been a guest at Auchincloss Christmases and Thanksgivings, where she'd provide the dinner from her turkey farm in Virginia. It was Janet's idea that Molly write a book that would be positive about her daughter and perhaps even repeat some of the fanciful embellishments she and Jackie's father, Jack Bouvier, had dreamed up about themselves over the years. They always made their families sound much nobler and more aristocratic than they really were.

Jackie wasn't in favor of it. She cherished her privacy and, as a former journalist, understood that a book would only have value if it was revealing. Despite her reservations, she reluctantly agreed. She then spent a few weeks with Molly, cherry-picking which stories she felt comfortable seeing in print. She found the process a difficult one. Her memories were private, especially of her beloved late father, Jack Bouvier. The more Molly asked about him, the more she shut down. Being asked about her competitive sister, Lee, made her feel no better, and trying to sugarcoat her conflicted feelings for her mother was real work. Having to share her memories of moving into Hugh Auchincloss's massive estates, Merrywood and Hammersmith Farm, felt intrusive. She needed to be at her husband's side as he campaigned for high office, and that commitment had to be her priority.

Campaigning with Jack had been such grueling work, and Jackie really had to rise to the occasion. "For an entire year, she was busy on the campaign trail," Jack's brother Ted Kennedy recalled during a symposium at the John Fitzgerald Kennedy Library, "traveling with him on the campaign jet called *Caroline* [purchased by their father Joseph Kennedy for $350,000] to dozens of cities, speaking Spanish when it was called for, French, Italian and Polish, too, for taped radio messages. She also did many television interviews. She was marvelous, a real asset to Jack. She never complained and, believe me, it was very hard work.

"What I remember most," Ted continued, "was how low expectations were for Jackie and how well she exceeded them. You have to remember, this was a time when women were just beginning to get out there to campaign for their husbands. His opponent, Nixon's wife, Pat, was a different kind of woman than Jackie. She was more practiced, I guess you could say, but rather unexciting. Though Jackie was soft-spoken, there was something authentic there which people responded to, something fun and positive and thrilling, even, and glamorous, too, which was important. I always said that much of Jack's success was due to Jackie's appeal."

After Eleanor Roosevelt, Bess Truman, and Mamie Eisenhower, the time definitely seemed right for a younger, more effervescent First Lady, someone stylish, a modern American woman who could represent the country in a different way. Everywhere Jackie went, she dazzled. It did take a toll, however, and she had no patience for anything extra—like a book about her life.

"Frustrated by Jackie's unavailability, Molly Thayer went to Mummy and complained that she was having trouble finishing the book," recalled Jamie Auchincloss. "Mummy spoke to Jack about it, and he suggested that she work with the author herself. She then spent many months helping Molly fashion a manuscript. She gave her private correspondence from Jackie to relatives, poems Jackie had written, rare family photos, and even letters to her by her grandfathers. When Jackie eventually heard about all of this, she was very unhappy about it and told her secretary Mary Barelli Gallagher to call Mummy and tell her to knock it off."

It was too late. The book was finished.

When Molly offered Jackie the opportunity to review the completed manuscript, she declined, saying she was too busy. She just wanted it canceled. However, Molly had a contract with Harper & Row and fully intended to honor it. The book went into production with First Serial sold to *Ladies' Home Journal* for $150,000, about $1.5 million in today's money and a huge amount for book extracts. Now, a year after the book was conceived, and with Jack president-elect, it was ready to be published. Janet was sure Jackie would approve once she heard a few selections. As Jackie gazed steadily at her, Janet read:

> *While Jacqueline does like her privacy, she also likes people to know about her and she and her family have let down their guard for these special excerpts.*

Already, Jackie objected. First, she didn't want it stated so forthrightly that she liked her privacy. Even though it was true, it made her sound snobbish. "And this part about me letting my guard down, I don't like that, either," she said. It made her sound "empty headed and silly." She grabbed the papers from her mother and flipped to a section about her first meeting with Jack Kennedy:

> *The evening they had been introduced Jacqueline looked into Jack's laughingly aroused, intelligently inquisitive face and knew instantly that he would have a profound, perhaps a disturbing influence on her life. In a flash of inner perception she realized that here was a man who did not want to marry. She was frightened. Jacqueline, in this revealing moment, envisaged heartbreak, but just as swiftly determined such heartbreak would be worth the pain.*

A look of astonishment crossed Jackie's face. "Really, Mummy?" she asked. "This is all right with you? My heartbreak would be worth the pain? I don't even know what that means?"

Janet had to admit, it was a bit much, and she wasn't quite sure what it meant, either. However, she said the excerpts were already scheduled for release, followed by the book. None of it could be stopped.

Already under stress because of the planning involved for moving into the White House, Jackie was perhaps more emotional than usual. "The one thing I prize more than anything is discretion," she said, and certainly that was true of her, and everyone knew it. How had this thing gotten so out of hand? When Jackie accused her mother of betraying her, Janet said she'd actually protected her. For instance, she pointed out, she'd excised any mention of Jackie's first fiancé, a man no one ever heard of named John Husted. He was erased from history in this version of her life. Jackie didn't care. "I can't believe how you've botched this up," she exclaimed.

Jamie, who was present as the argument took place, knew it wasn't wise to take that tone with their mother. "How dare you speak to me that way, Jacqueline?" Janet demanded, her eyes narrowing. "I was trying to help."

"No," Jackie said. "You were trying to be in control."

The book excerpt appeared in *Ladies' Home Journal*'s February 1961 issue, which went on sale for thirty-five cents a few days before the inauguration. Jackie was on the cover, about age five, posing with her dog. The headline read: "First Years of the First Lady—Jacqueline Kennedy—An Exclusive Look into Her Private Picture Albums by Mary Van Rensselaer Thayer."

Jamie recalled, "The book was symbolic of Jackie's growing lack of control over things. She was a very private woman now being forced into a very public life. It was done, though. The excerpt was out and the book would follow. I figured there wasn't much Jackie could do about it."

∞∞∞∞∞∞∞∞∞∞∞∞∞∞∞∞∞∞

After the inauguration, Jackie claimed to be mortified by the unfortunate seating arrangement and vowed to get to the bottom of it. Janet didn't believe her and felt there was no way it had been an innocent mistake. For her, the fact that Jackie wouldn't just admit what she'd done somehow made it all the more hurtful. Still, trying to take her at her word, she noted that if such a snafu could occur on an important day like the inauguration, it suggested that Jackie wasn't up for the job at hand. She'd have to work harder to make sure this kind of breach never again occurred on her watch as First Lady. It was a pointed criticism, as usual, and just as usual, Jackie hated being criticized. She didn't have much moral ground on which to stand, however.

"Mummy knew the truth," Jamie said. "We all did. It had been purposeful. Jackie was upset about the book and lashed out. It ruined the day for Mummy, not so much for Daddy, though." Indeed, Hugh apparently wouldn't let the unfortunate situation taint his memory of the inauguration. In his diary, under the date of January 20, 1961, he simply wrote: "Wow!"

Three years later, in 1964, Jackie wasn't willing to discuss the seating snafu when it came up between her and Jamie as they reviewed photographs from that momentous day. It was in the past, she said, and didn't matter. In fact, it now felt like "silliness" to her, "and I can only wish we, today, had concerns so trivial. A great injustice, a real tragedy not just for the nation but for her family, had put all of it into jarring perspective. "How did we not realize how lucky we were?" she asked.

Certainly, Jackie Kennedy's life hadn't turned out the way she'd hoped while she sat watching her husband speak on that promising morning in 1961. Now, she couldn't even look at photographs of the day without feeling pain. "What I've learned," she told her half brother, "is that we take for granted how incredibly lucky we are until the terrible day it's thrown in our faces how incredibly *unlucky* we are. That day came," she concluded, "when I lost Jack."

JACK KENNEDY

◇◇◇◇◇◇◇◇◇◇◇◇◇◇

John Fitzgerald Kennedy—Jack—was born on May 29, 1917, in Brook-line, Massachusetts, the second of nine children. Kennedy was descended from Irish forebears who'd immigrated to Boston. His paternal grandfather, Patrick J. Kennedy, was a saloonkeeper who went on to become a politician in Boston. His son, Joseph Patrick Kennedy, was a Harvard graduate who'd been a bank president at twenty-five before marrying Rose Fitzgerald, the daughter of John Francis "Honey Fitz" Fitzgerald, mayor of Boston.

The Kennedys, at first, lived modestly in Brookline, but as Joseph's fortunes grew as a result of his success in the stock market, they soon moved to bigger homes and, eventually, to New York. Jack, who attended private schools, had been in the shadow of his older brother, Joe, the father's favorite, who had been expected to go far in politics. However, after Joe was killed during World War II, his father turned his attention to Jack. He would be the first to become a politician, running for the U.S. House of Representatives in 1946, which he won by a large majority. He went on to become a senator in 1952 and president in 1960.

Jack was two weeks shy of his thirty-first birthday when Jackie first met him in 1948. "It was surprising that he wasn't married given that men and women usually married much earlier," recalled his friend and journalist Charles Bartlett. "He'd had a full life already; he'd fought in the war, written a successful book, *Why England Slept*, was now the congressman from the Eleventh District of Massachusetts."

It sometimes seemed the odds were stacked against JFK because of his health issues, especially his bad back, a consequence of injuries he suffered at sea in 1943 on the now historic PT-109 as well as from college football days. Also, he was afflicted with Addison's disease, which had affected his adrenal glands and made him appear very sickly. He never complained, though, despite being close to death several times. "He lived every moment to its fullest as though he was in a race against time," recalled Charles.

Jackie's courtship with Jack had a few starts and stops. It started in 1948 when Charles became fascinated by Jackie after meeting her at a Washington party. Jackie wasn't interested in him, though, feeling he was, as she later put it, "too buttoned up." While he was cerebral, a trait Jackie admired in a man, Charles wasn't much fun. He ended up marrying Martha Buck in 1951. Even after his marriage, he remained fascinated with Jackie. "I would invite her to the house for drinks, conversation," he said. "Martha didn't much like it."

At one point, Martha called her father to ask his opinion of a husband who so often invited to their home a woman with whom he was so clearly smitten. If she really wanted to solve the problem, her father said, Martha should find someone else for Jackie. Betsy Walker, daughter of Martha's close friend Antoinette Walker, recalled, "Kennedy history has it that Charles introduced Jackie to Jack, that he invited them both to a party and that this is how they got together. That's not how my mother remembered it, though. She said Martha was the one who invited Jackie because she knew Charles had invited JFK. Martha's plan was to introduce the two and hope for the best. Much to her delight, they hit it off."

Jack would later say he felt Jackie was more intellectual than women with whom he was usually set up and that this was why he was so immediately interested. But time passed, and they didn't see each other again. Jackie and Lee were off to Europe in June 1951 for the summer—London, Paris, Venice, Rome, and Florence. Jackie was twenty-two at the time, and this would be her second time in Europe. Lee was seventeen.

THE FIRST FIANCÉ

◇◇◇◇◇◇◇◇◇◇◇◇

Janet and Hugh Auchincloss met John Husted in the spring of 1951 at a party in New York. At twenty-five, he was good-looking with dark hair and deep brown eyes. His father was a friend of Hugh's and a partner at Brown Shipley, the British division of Brown Brothers Harriman stock brokerage. He attended Summerfields School in Hastings, England, St. Paul's School in Concord, New Hampshire, and Yale University, class of 1949. He was also a vet, having served with the American Field Service attached to British forces in Europe. For the last two years, he'd been working for Dominick & Dominick on Wall Street. In speaking to John, Janet realized she knew his mother well; the two had cohosted a Red Cross benefit a year earlier at Merrywood, the Auchincloss estate. John was intelligent and witty, and Janet was impressed. She wanted him to meet Jackie.

Jackie soon began seeing John, and while he was nice enough, she found him dull. She needed more passion. Every time they got close to having sex, he backed off. He'd later say his hesitation wasn't about Jackie as much as it was about her mother. His close friend John Glover (not the actor) recalled, "John was conservative, not the type to just jump into bed with a girl. But he was tempted to do so with Jackie. However, he feared that if he did and her mother found out about it, it would end any future he'd have with her, and he did want one."

Finally, as if to make good on the promise of a future sexual relationship with her, John proposed to Jackie in December 1951. While Jackie wanted to go to bed with him, she definitely didn't want to marry him. She said she needed to think it over. When she told Janet about it, Janet wanted

Jackie to accept. Her goal was to get Jackie married off by the time she was twenty-one, and she was already a year behind. "You need to be settled," she told her, "and there's nothing wrong with this man. Do yourself a favor and say yes." Jackie usually did what her mother wanted her to do, but she often wasn't happy about it, and this time was no exception. She told John she would marry him, but her heart wasn't in it.

Besides the question of her age, there was another reason Janet wanted Jackie to get "settled." She'd need the money. Janet's husband, Hugh, was rich, but he had children from his previous two marriages—Yusha, Tommy, and Nina—as well as the two he had with Janet—Janet Jr. and Jamie. Jackie wasn't in line to inherit anything from him, and neither was Lee. Moreover, their own father's financial situation was precarious at best. Janet's father, James T. Lee, was wealthy, but he was such a skinflint that Janet felt she'd be lucky to inherit anything, and was sure her daughters would not. Their paternal grandfather was far less wealthy. Therefore, Janet's goal was for Jackie and Lee to both marry well

The wedding announcement was published in local papers in January 1952 with a portrait of Jackie, her brunette hair cascading down her back: "Jacqueline Lee Bouvier Engaged to J G Husted, Jr., Wedding Set for June."

In February of 1952, Janet hosted an engagement party for Jackie at Merrywood. Just prior to it, though, she began hearing rumors that John wasn't as well off as she'd thought. When she confronted him, he said he made $17,000 a year, not bad—$160,000 in today's money—but not enough for Janet's taste.

At the same time questions arose over John's finances, Janet befriended Charles Bartlett's wife, Martha. The two belonged to the same charity groups, one of which had recently held the fundraiser at the Auchinclosses' second estate, Hammersmith Farm. At that event, Janet confided in Martha about Husted's financial deficiency. She asked Martha if she might try once again to set Jackie up with Jack Kennedy. "I have to tell you," Martha told her, "I heard from my husband that he's quite the ladies' man. I'm not so sure he would be a good husband."

Janet had heard the same rumors about Kennedy, but she now pre-ferred him over Husted. Not only did the Kennedys have money, everyone knew they were powerful. By this time, JFK was preparing to run against Republican incumbent Henry Cabot Lodge for his seat in the Senate. "Janet liked the idea of Jackie being with a senator," Charles Bartlett said, "so this plan was cooked up by my wife and Jackie's mother to get Jack and Jackie together again for another go-round. Though I've been given credit for it over the years, it really wasn't me. It was the two of them."

At Janet's behest, Martha invited Jackie and Lee to join the Bartletts at a party at the Palm Beach home of the Kennedys. It was a festive party where everyone looked beautiful and affluent. Because the Bouvier sisters were the newcomers, the focus was on them. Jack Kennedy seemed much more interested in Lee than he did Jackie. Although Lee was barely eighteen while he was in his early thirties, there was real chemistry.

As Jackie watched them interact, she figured her sister would end up with him. While Lee rarely smiled and could seem glum and depressed as if burdened by the weight of the world, she seemed brighter when talking to Jack. The day after the party, when Lee talked about him, it was as if she was reliving a perfect moment in her life and all she wanted to do was savor it. If Jack Kennedy could bring that out in her sister, Jackie was happy for her. After all, she was already engaged to John Husted.

The next day, Martha called Janet long distance to tell her that while she wasn't sure about the congressman for Jackie, he and Lee were obviously a very good match. Janet was surprised. She had only sent Lee with Jackie to keep her company, and now Jack was interested in her?

"So, what happened in Palm Beach?" she asked Jackie the next day.

Jackie told her mother that while she hadn't hit it off with Kennedy, Lee seemed to have a connection with him. "But did you really try?" Janet asked. Janet knew Jackie could be a little cold and aloof at times, not easy to know. She was worried about her, she said, because she wondered if she'd ever really fall in love. Years later, in 1964, when she gave an oral history to the Kennedy Library, Janet admitted, "You know, Jackie is a bit cold." Then, she stopped herself. "Oh, that's awful. Take that out," she said. "I should never have told you that." Family friend Joan Braden, who was interviewing her, said, "No, that's good, Janet. It's honest." But Janet disagreed, saying, "It's a little too honest."

Jackie admitted that she didn't do much to interest Jack. When she saw that he liked Lee, she decided not to pursue him at all. "That was a big mistake," Janet told her. "You're older. You need to get settled now, Jacqueline, not later."

"Make up your mind, Mummy," Jackie exclaimed. "I thought you wanted me to be with John Husted."

First of all, Janet told her, she should watch her tone. Secondly: "I changed my mind. *I'm allowed!*"

WHAT IF . . . ?

◇◇◇◇◇◇◇◇◇◇◇◇◇◇

On a crisp February morning in 1952 at the Auchinclosses' Merry-wood estate in McLean, Virginia, Jackie Bouvier sat on a straight-backed wooden chair in the hallway outside her mother's bedroom. While thumbing through a fashion magazine, she took a deep drag off her Lucky Strike.

Next to Jackie sat her sister, Lee, eighteen, and her stepbrother, Yusha, twenty-four, both also smoking and reading magazines. Sitting beside them was their half sister, Janet, six, and half brother, Jamie, who would turn five in a month.

"Each chair in the hallway was positioned against the wall," Jamie would recall many years later, "and next to each was a small table upon which was neatly stacked the latest magazines. There were ashtrays—as on just about every table in our home—and boxes of Lucky Strike.

"This was our family's morning ritual. Every day at about nine o'clock, we'd gather in this hallway, a makeshift waiting room of sorts on the second floor. There, we'd wait for an audience with the woman in charge—Mummy, of course."

Many years later, Yusha would remember this particular morning with clarity to his friend Cybil Wright, to whom he was introduced by the woman who'd become his wife, Alice Emily Lyon.

"Yusha told me Jackie and Lee had returned from the party in Palm Beach about a week earlier," recalled Cybil. "Lee had a crush on Jack Kennedy. 'Do you think he liked me?' she asked her sister. Jackie said she had a feeling he liked all the girls at the party. When Lee said he'd called and left a message for her, Jackie wanted to know if she'd returned the call. Lee said she wanted to wait until she spoke to their mother about it."

A door in the hallway opened, and the family's English nursemaid, Mamie Stratton—who was primarily responsible for Jamie and Janet Jr.'s care—came out and walked over to Jackie. "Mummy will see you now," she said. Jackie smiled, put down her magazine, and went to the doorway. Gazing inside the room, she saw Janet reclining on the bed in her silk robe, a breakfast tray before her with toast, coffee, and a single red rose in a vase. A telephone was extended by its cord onto the tray and, next it, a lined yellow notepad. "Close the door, please," Janet told her.

"Every morning, Mummy would welcome each of us into her room to discuss whatever was going on in our lives," recalled Jamie. "Decisions were made. Usually, they were insignificant, such as how to best entertain a guest for lunch or what outfit might be appropriate for dinner. Was there a new art exhibit in the city? Should we go? Would there be a swimming lesson or tennis? Usually, these judgments were of little consequence. Once in a while, however, a decision would be rendered with an outcome so profound, it could really alter the course of things."

After about fifteen minutes, Jackie emerged, leaving the door open. "How is she?" Lee asked as her sister lit another cigarette. "Same," she answered. "She's anxious to finish with us so she can see her massage therapist."

From inside the room came the voice: "Lee, I'm ready to receive you now." Lee looked at Jackie, and Yusha and Jamie and rolled her eyes at her mother's silly, old-world formality. She rose, walked into Janet's chamber, and closed the door.

Ten minutes later, the door flew open, and Lee bolted from the room. Dabbing her eyes, she was upset.

"I hope you're satisfied," she said, glaring at Jackie.

"Lee, wait," Jackie said as Lee began down the hall. "Don't be ridiculous," she added as Lee began to descend the winding staircase. "You can have the next one."

"What about John Husted, your *fiancé*?" Lee shouted up the stairs.

"What about him?" Jackie answered.

Janet had firmed up her decision that Jackie, not Lee, should be with Jack Kennedy, and, despite what she felt earlier, Jackie wholeheartedly agreed. It was a calculation based on two factors. First of all, Kennedy had more money and better earning potential than Husted. Secondly, Jackie was older, and it was time for her to get "settled." Lee had more time. While they didn't know it at the time, this decision would lay the whole world at the feet of the older sister and condemn the younger one to a life of wondering, "What if . . . ?"

"Janet," came the familiar voice. "I'm ready to receive you now." The little girl rose and walked to the doorway. She caught Jackie's eye and scowled. "Wait until you're older," Jackie told her, "and you'll understand."

That afternoon, Janet called Martha Bartlett to tell her of her decision. The next day, Martha invited Jackie—without Lee—to another dinner at which Jack would be a guest. This time, it went very well. The two hit it off, probably because Jackie actually worked at it. Jack pretty much forgot all about Lee as he and Jackie went on a few dates.

One weekend soon after Jackie started dating Jack, John Husted was invited to dinner at Merrywood. They had a pleasant evening together, dinner with the family. The next morning, Jackie took him to the airport, but she was quiet and distant. She didn't explain and didn't have to; he already knew. Before he boarded his plane, she took off her engagement ring and slipped it into his vest pocket. "Please don't do this," he told her, but it was too late. It was already done. When she got back to the house, Janet asked her how it went. "How do you think it went?" was Jackie's response. Janet ignored her tone. "Fine," she said. "Now, call Jack Kennedy."

Many people believe that Jackie Bouvier and Jack Kennedy had a whirlwind romance. Supposedly, Jack—who at thirty-four was twelve years older than Jackie—was swept away by her, as was his entire family. Many also believe that Jackie was just as enamored of him. In truth, neither was the head-over-heels type, despite public statements they'd both make in years to come in an effort to put a romantic spin on things. They were both raised by pragmatic parents to weigh each decision with hard-eyed practicality.

Later, Jackie said she found Jack to be "staggeringly handsome." Studying photographs from this time, it's easy to see why. He had high cheekbones, a wide brow, a straight nose, and generous mouth. His unruly brownish-red hair and twinkling blue eyes completed the picture. But he was also extremely thin and had a yellow pallor from his Addison's disease. Janet and Hugh actually thought he'd had malaria somewhere along the way and hadn't fully recovered!

As practical as his parents, Jack knew he needed to marry well if he was going to one day run for high office, and that was definitely the plan—first congressman, then senator, then president. "Thus began the little dance," Yusha Auchincloss would recall, "him getting to know her, she him, the families meeting, all a delicate little dance that could either end successfully or in heartbreak all around. Happily, it ended with Jackie and Jack together and, therefore, altering forever the trajectory of our family and, I daresay, the entire country."

JACKIE FINDS HER PURPOSE

<><><><><><><><><><>

A s the nation's new First Lady, Jacqueline Kennedy, walked through one of the corridors in the private quarters of the White House, she stopped and turned to her personal decorator, Sister Parish. "My God. How did it ever come to this?" she wondered. Sister shook her head in dismay. "Just look at this wallpaper," Jackie said as she ran her hand across a badly chipped blue wall with decorative white border. She flicked a piece of paper with her fingernail, and it went flying.

"These family rooms will be easy to do over," Sister offered. "It's the common rooms downstairs, the most historical of rooms, that'll be a lot tougher. The furniture down there is a hodgepodge. Who the heck knows where it came from?"

"Sister" was a nickname by which the noted decorator Parish was known to all; her real name was Dorothy Kinnicutt Parish. She and Jackie had to laugh because, when Jack was elected, some newspapers erroneously reported that Jackie had hired a nun to help her restore the White House!

The women sat at the kitchen table before a large binder with photographs of all 132 rooms in the White House, provided by its chief usher, J. B. West. While thumbing through it, Jackie looked up at Sister with a gleam in her eye. "What a great challenge this is for us," she whispered. "Do you realize we could make history here?" Then, after a beat, she added, "This is why I'm here, isn't it? I mean, this is my . . . purpose, isn't it?" Sister had to agree.

Though Jackie had been curious to see the inner sanctum of the White House, nothing could've prepared her for what the outgoing First Lady,

Mamie Eisenhower, showed her during their walk-through a couple of weeks earlier. "Jackie told me it was awful," recalled Jamie Auchincloss, "with fake flowers, cheap reproductions of furniture, and plastic fans in front of the fireplaces. It was small, dark, and cramped. Jackie could tell Mamie couldn't wait to end the visit. She didn't even offer her a cup of tea."

By the time Jackie got back to the home she and Jack shared in Georgetown on N Street, she was crying. Already emotionally overwrought since giving birth to John, the unfortunate tour put her right over the edge. "I absolutely hate it," she said to Janet and Hugh, who awaited her, "and, I'm sorry, but I refuse to live there."

"Her face looked wan," added Adora Rule, who had been present. "She had lines of fatigue and dark circles under her eyes. She was overreacting, but ever since having John, she was really at loose ends. Looking back, she must have been suffering from postpartum, as had her sister. For some reason, we didn't pinpoint it at that time, though, which maybe shows how hectic things were for everyone after Jack was elected.

"Mrs. A. swallowed hard and tried to adapt a cheerful tone. 'It can't be that bad, dear,' she said. 'After all, Mrs. Eisenhower has such very good taste.' Mr. A. said, 'We'll buy some new pieces, hang a few paintings on the walls. We'll help you, Jackie. It's the White House. How bad can it be?' To which Jackie said, 'How bad? It looks like a Holiday Inn decorated with wholesale furniture obtained by some suburban woman during a clearance sale. That's how bad.'"

Hugh had to chuckle.

"It's not funny, Uncle Hughdie!" Jackie exclaimed, but even she had a difficult time suppressing a smile.

Going into problem-solving mode, Hugh wondered if there might be some way for his stepdaughter to avoid moving into the White House until some changes were made. What if, he suggested, she was just there during the day "for work" and spent her evenings at one of the two Auchincloss estates, probably Merrywood, which was closer? Then, after she had a chance to fix things, she could move in on a more permanent basis. Jackie's face lit up. Was this even an option? She picked up the telephone right away to call Jack.

While Jackie was on the phone with her husband, Janet shook her head. The idea wasn't feasible. The First Lady had a duty and responsibility to the country and needed to be at the White House at the president's side. It's what the American people expected of her. When Janet looked at Hugh, he knew what she was thinking.

Jackie hung up the phone. "Jack said no," she said. "It figures," she added. "Why would he ever do anything to make me happy?"

"Stop it, Jacqueline!" Janet exclaimed. "This is beneath you."

According to Adora, Janet went to her daughter and held her firmly by the shoulders. "Listen to me," she said, "you are a Lee!" she told her, referencing her own maiden name. "And I want you to start acting like one."

Janet acknowledged that things had lately been tense. However, Jackie was now America's First Lady, and Janet cautioned, "You must stop with all this handwringing. You can't fall apart every time something doesn't go your way." She said it didn't matter what the White House looked like; Jackie's challenge would be to restore it to decency and decorum as the home of the American people. "Why don't you think about how to do *that*," Janet said, "and stop whining about whether or not it's pretty enough to live there.'"

Jackie was taken aback. She began to defend herself, but Janet wasn't interested. "I'm disappointed in you right now," she said as she left the room.

"Mummy's right," Hugh said once Janet had departed. "You can fix it, Jackie. Be open to it. I'll just bet you and Jack can be happy there."

She smiled at him. Her stepfather always knew exactly the right thing to say.

◊◊◊◊◊◊◊◊◊◊◊◊◊◊◊◊◊◊◊◊

told Jackie that in order for us to do what we needed to do, which was basically redo the entire White House, we'd need the cooperation of several committees," said Sister Parish in an interview in 1990. "Otherwise, we'd never get it done in four years and maybe not eight. So, the Fine Arts committees were formed—the major committee chaired by Henry du Pont, a wealthy collector and someone with an understanding of American antiques. The others selected were all tops in their fields of décor and also, importantly, in American history. We went to work right away, room by room, with Jackie on top of every decision."

So much has been written about Jackie's historical renovation of the White House—entire volumes have been produced on the subject—and many dozens of her handwritten notes and letters have been published revealing her thoughts about the furniture, fabrics, carpeting, and other elements of the restoration. She also worked to save the federal architecture of nearby Lafayette Square, which the Eisenhower administration had planned to completely demolish, across the street from the White House on Pennsylvania Avenue. What is often missing from the many years of analysis of her work in this regard, however, is how vitally important it all was to Jackie's state of mind. Her cousin John Davis once put it this way: "Jackie knew what America needed in its First Lady and she wanted to be that woman. Bigger than that, though, her marriage was . . . well, we all knew it wasn't the best. Jack had his extracurricular activities, and everyone knew it. Her restoration of the White House was her salvation, her way of turning her pain into purpose."

"Both Jack and Jackie had an enormous sense of their own presence," observed presidential historian Doris Kearns Goodwin, "and they, together, created this image of this handsome couple—attractive, well-dressed, well-mannered, funny. It was partly true, but partly not true at all because of his other life, what was going on privately. She knew if she obsessed about the other women every day, it would destroy herself and even destroy her marriage. So, she became, she created *Jackie Kennedy,* something quite apart from Jack Kennedy."

"I think the White House should show the wonderful heritage that this country has," Jackie said at the time. "We had such a wonderful flowering in the late eighteenth century. And the restoration is so fascinating—every day you see a letter that has come in from the great-great-grandson of a president. It was such a surprise to come here and find so little that had association and memory. I'd feel terribly if I lived here for four years and hadn't done anything for the house."

"Jackie was able to call upon her education abroad, her love of art, her personal taste, and her interest in the finer things of life to make changes in the White House that would endure for many years," said James Roe Ketchum, the White House curator who worked closely with Jackie every day. "I don't think I ever saw her as the symbol of elegance the rest of the world saw," he said, "but rather she would be wearing jeans and a pullover and looked like anyone you might see in the street of a suburban community. She liked to just roll up her sleeves and get to work. She was the most energetic First Lady I ever knew, and I worked with three presidential spouses. She also had a wicked sense of humor, which played a vital role in her being able to survive the slings and arrows that come the way of every First Family."

"She drew from a wide spectrum of experiences," Jamie Auchincloss said, "some of it personal to our family."

Jamie recalled his father and Jack Kennedy having conversations about the painter George Catlin, known for his portraits of American Indians, when Jack was at Merrywood recovering from back surgery in 1955. "My mother had gifted my father with a book of paintings by Catlin, which Jack found in the bedroom," said Jamie. "Six years later when he became president, he remembered the book and those talks. He mentioned it to Jackie, and she checked with the Smithsonian to see if they had any other Catlin paintings. It turned out they had the only authentic collection in the world. She selected a number of them and hung them in the White House's private quarters, thereby turning Catlin overnight into one of the most well-known artists in the world. Daddy loved that he had a little something to do with that.

"Jackie could be fastidious, and it made sense that she'd bring that aesthetic to the White House just as she did to everything else she touched," he added. He recalled that even as a young girl, she was concerned with color schemes. He remembered, "When she was a teenager, she decreed that all our family pets be black. The walls at Hammersmith were white and the carpeting was red, so only black dogs would do in that color scheme. So, her Bouvier des Flandres, Caprice, was black; Lee's poodle, General de Gaulle, was black; Mummy's Scotty, Corkscrew, was black, and on and on it went."

Every detail mattered. "I was just wondering if Mrs. Roosevelt's portrait outside the East Room didn't bring the 20th Century in so much," Jackie wrote to Lady Bird Johnson, "that it really jars the unity of that whole floor—which, except for the portraits lost on the walls of Green and Fed Rooms is completely restored to our earliest days. The problem one runs into is always this—one admires and reveres Mrs. Roosevelt—so she should have a place of honor—why not there? But then later people of different administrations will start according to places of honor to their own heroes, and the whole harmony of the early years of the White House will be lost."

"I remember once when she was painting in the Deck Room at Hammersmith and Mummy and I had 'The Grand Canyon Suite' by Ferde Grofé playing in the background," Jamie recalled. "She loved it and asked what it was. I showed her the album cover, and we had a conversation about it. A month later, I was at boarding school and read in *Time* that Jackie had Grofé perform 'The Grand Canyon Suite' at the White House at one of her parties. The next week, this record which I'd paid two dollars for had become one of the biggest-selling albums in the country, and all because Jackie had heard it while she was water-coloring in the Deck Room."

In years to come, Jackie was determined to not only restore the White House but to bring accomplished musicians in to play at formal events, of which there would be many. Joan Braden attended the night Margot Fonteyn and Rudolf Nureyev performed at a state dinner. "What a night to remember," she wrote in a letter in 1990. "The Kennedys revolutionized the White House and brought class and style to it. It was fun, glamorous, memorable. There'd never been anything like it. Since then, other administrations have done similar things, but it was because the Kennedys showed them how it should be done and, as far as I was concerned, that was all Jackie."

"VIVE JAC-QUI. VIVE JAC-QUI."

⬦⬦⬦⬦⬦⬦⬦⬦⬦⬦⬦⬦⬦

On the morning of May 31, 1961, the Kennedys arrived in Air Force One at Orly Airport in Paris for their first trip to Europe since Jack's inauguration. There had been a great deal of speculation as to how Charles de Gaulle might treat Jack, who was so much younger and—in de Gaulle's eyes, anyway—lacking in experience.

It didn't help that Jack suffered his first major setback as president, indeed of his entire political career up until that point, when 1,400 Cuban exiles trained by the CIA stormed the south coast of Cuba in a territory known as the Bay of Pigs. Apparently, as was later discovered, the Soviets learned about the invasion in advance and came in, slaughtering everyone in sight. The United States was left to clean up the mess and get as many invaders out as possible. In the end, only fourteen were rescued. More than a thousand had surrendered to Castro. It was a disaster, the weight of which the president knew he had to shoulder. "There's an old saying," JFK said, "that victory has a hundred fathers and defeat is an orphan. I am the responsible officer of this government."

"It was an awful time," Jackie recalled later in her oral history, "and he [Jack] really looked awful. We had to go to the Greek dinner that night [at the Greek embassy on the nineteenth, accompanied by Rose Kennedy] and they were so nice, the Greeks. They were almost our first visitors [at the White House]. But I remember so well when it happened . . . and he came back . . . to the White House to his bedroom and he started to cry, just with me. He put his head in his hands and sort of wept."

"She was always asking how the Pentagon worked and about the relationship between the Joint Chiefs of Staff and civilian officials," recalled Roswell Gilpatric, JFK's deputy secretary of defense. "When I wrote about the duplication in the armed forces, she responded that she hoped recommendations for change would be followed. She worried about the incompetence at the Defense Department, the CIA—and who should be removed and what military personalities were irresponsible, and how to implore the president to remove them."

"It was good for Jack and Jackie to get out of the country, and to France of all places, the country Jackie loved so much in her youth," Janet Auchincloss said. This time, though, she wouldn't be free to enjoy France as she saw fit, not with the press corps following her everywhere she went.

Jackie had really had it with the intrusive press by this time, especially the female reporters, whom she felt, even more than their male counterparts, should empathize with her frustration of constantly being photographed and bombarded with questions. It was a job requirement, of course, but that didn't mean Jackie had to like it. "Oh, she hated us," said Helen Thomas. "She called us harpies and thought the White House should use their bayonets on us." Thomas was the long-serving member of the White House press corps covering for UPI. "Once, Frances Levine, of Jewish descent (with the Associated Press) and I, of Arab descent, were sitting on the steps of the church she went to in Palm Beach and she told the Secret Service, 'Two Spanish types are following me.' Of course, she knew who we were by this time. She just didn't want us around. And yes, incidentally, we *were* following her."

Clint Hill recalled, "There was press everywhere as more than two hundred thousand Parisians lined the streets, most of them waving little American flags. There were people hanging out of windows and packed on balconies, eager to catch a glimpse and snap a photo. All along the route people held up welcoming signs and cheered, '*Vive le président Kennedy.*' But more frequently you would hear the voices in the crowd yelling, '*Vive Jac-qui. Vive Jac-qui.*' Jackie was a real sensation by this time, a global sensation, and everyone just wanted to see her even if from afar and in a fleeting moment."

While Jack had his own duties, Jackie also had meetings with diplomats and other officials and visits to hospitals as well as many interviews with the media. Also on this adventure, in addition to Lee, were Rose Kennedy and Eunice Kennedy Shriver. A humorous moment occurred when Jackie was about to make an appearance and Rose leaned in and whispered, "Your skirt's too short, dear." Without breaking her smile, Jackie said, "I know. But I can't pull it down now, can I?"

A white tie dinner at Versailles was the high point of a trip full of memorable moments for Jackie. Wearing a sleeveless gown hand embroidered with pastel flowers, she looked radiant as she stood next to de Gaulle at Versailles, a diamond hair clip giving her just the right royal look. De Gaulle seemed enchanted by her as the two conversed in French. After dinner was a ballet performance, which, for Jackie, was the perfect end of a magnificent evening.

"People were mesmerized by her," said Letitia Baldrige, who was on the trip. "This was when I saw her come into her own. She was surrounded by the things she loved most—art, culture . . . French cuisine, intelligent conversation. She became a star on this trip. There was a luncheon and the president started off by mentioning his wife." Actually, Kennedy's words, which are well known by now, were: "I do not think it altogether inappropriate to introduce myself, I am the man who accompanied Jacqueline Kennedy to Paris. And I have enjoyed it."

On June 2, the Kennedys left Paris en route to Vienna and then off to London, a stopover for the christening of Lee's daughter, Tina. (Lee and Polish aristocrat Prince Stanislaw "Stas" Radziwill were married on March 19, 1959.) After the ceremony, Jackie was scheduled to go to Greece with the Radziwills, her first foreign trip without the president.

ONASSIS

<<<<<<<<<<<<<

Prior to Jackie's important trip abroad, word began circulating in some circles that her sister, Lee, was having an affair with the Greek shipping mogul Aristotle Onassis. Jack and Bobby Kennedy found the rumor a little troubling.

Onassis, who was fifty-five in 1961, was a unique character, a bon vivant who had made a fortune in shipping by always operating just outside the law. He'd been under investigation by the FBI and, six years earlier, fined $7 million by the government for the illegal operation of war supply ships. As far as the Kennedy brothers were concerned, this man was a criminal. They felt it was just a matter of time before he'd slip up and be brought to justice. Meanwhile, Onassis continued living the good life all over the world in the best hotels or aboard his famous 315-foot yacht called *Christina* (the name of his daughter). He also had holdings in Monaco and, it was said, owned about a third of the principality.

"Jack and Jackie had sailed with Onassis on his yacht, *Christina,* during both the summers of 1955 and 1959," recalled John Davis. "JFK had no personal ax to grind with him other than his judgment of possible criminal activity. Bobby, though, was more emotional about him. He'd actually met Onassis earlier than Jack, at the Plaza Hotel in the spring of 1953 during a cocktail party hosted by the English socialite Pamela Churchill. Bobby was twenty-seven, Onassis forty-seven and, for the two of them, it was hate at first sight.

"One reason for Ari's disdain was that, as part of his job with the Department of Justice, Bobby was investigating hundreds of ships owned by

Greek shipping families doing trade with the People's Republic of China," added John Davis. "He said at the time, 'It doesn't make sense our major allies whom we're aiding financially should trade with the communists who are killing GIs.' While Ari didn't have ships involved in that investigation, he still didn't like Bobby nosing around in his business."

Six months later, a federal grand jury handed down a sealed indictment against Aristotle Onassis on other charges. Now, his ships were being seized all over the world and their revenues impounded. From 1953 until his death in '68, RFK would continue to investigate Onassis, from tobacco insurance scams to illegal arms shipping to all manner of underhanded dealings with the Saudis. He could never nail him, though, and the way Onassis always managed to slip through the legal system infuriated him.

How would it look if the First Lady's sister was involved with an international criminal? Cheating on her husband, Stas, was bad enough, but with Onassis? Even though Stas was a prince in name only—a Polish refugee allowed to use the title by the Queen of England—the public was confused enough in thinking he was true royalty, which made the idea of his wife having an affair all the more controversial.

One day in the summer of '61, Jack asked Hugh Auchincloss to see him at the White House. Early that morning, Hugh dressed in his baggy tweeds, a well-worn sweater, and a shapeless tweed hat. When Janet saw what he was wearing, she made him go back to his room and change into a suit. "It's the White House, not the clubhouse," she told him.

When Hugh got to the White House, Evelyn Lincoln, the president's secretary, escorted him to the Oval Office, where Jack and Bobby awaited. He took a seat opposite the Resolute Desk. Jack got right to the point. He wanted to know what Hugh knew about Lee and Aristotle Onassis. He knew nothing. Hugh asked if Lee was somehow involved with Onassis. They said that's what they wanted to find out. When Hugh offered to ask Janet about it, the president said, "Fine, get back to us." They shook hands, and that was the end of it. The meeting lasted five minutes. "I could've just worn my tweeds and no one would've known the difference," he later said.

When Hugh asked Janet about Onassis, she became worried. Was Lee in danger? When Janet called her, Lee insisted she had nothing at all to do with Onassis.

In fact, Lee really was having an affair with Onassis. However, she was always one to keep the family at arm's length. Feeling judged and compared unfavorably to Jackie, she never allowed herself to be vulnerable or honest with any of them. Janet and Hugh could only do so much to reach her, and the same held true for Jackie. There was no way Lee was going to be candid about Onassis. She just lied and said she had nothing to do with him.

At this same time, the president called Jackie's Secret Service agent Clint Hill and asked to see him. Clint had never before been summoned by the president. Jackie was his protectee, and Jack pretty much left him alone to take care of her the way he saw fit. Bobby was in the office with Jack when Clint arrived.

The upcoming trip to Athens would be Jackie's first trip overseas on her own, Jack reminded Clint. "The attorney general and I want to make one thing clear," he said. "Whatever you do in Greece, don't let Mrs. Kennedy cross paths with Aristotle Onassis." Clint didn't understand, and the Kennedys didn't elaborate. "Yes, sir, Mr. President," was the agent's quick response. "Fine," Jack said. "Have a safe trip. That'll be all."

As it happened, Jackie's trip to Greece went off without a hitch. Lee was accompanied by Stas, and Onassis wasn't a problem. There were meetings with officials, sightseeing adventures at the Parthenon and the Acropolis, and tours of ancient and historic ruins—like Delos where, it's been said, Apollo was born. Of course, there was also pandemonium wherever the popular First Lady ventured forth. Jackie even had the opportunity to water-ski in the Aegean Sea.

On June 15, Jackie and her entourage took a commercial flight back to Washington. Her sister and brother-in-law went back to England. After all the concern and hubbub, Aristotle Onassis never even showed up in Athens. However, the interest in him and concern about him from the president and attorney general were just a harbinger of things to come.

"WHAT A LIFE WE'RE HAVING"

‹‹‹‹‹‹‹‹‹‹‹‹‹‹‹‹‹‹‹

Jackie spent much of the summer of 1961 at both her home in Cape Cod and at the Auchinclosses' estate in Newport. When she arrived in Hyannis on June 30, it was the first time she'd been there since the inauguration, and the compound was swarming with Secret Service agents. Of course, they had to have a strong presence given that the president was also present; the American flag flew high in front of his parents' home whenever he was in residence.

The focal point of the Kennedys' enclave was the Big House, Rose and Joseph's enormous, three-story, Cape Cod–style beach house with its wraparound porch. Jack and Jackie had a home close by, as did Bobby and Ethel. Ted and Joan were on Squaw Island, a peninsula about a mile away. Jack's sister Eunice and her husband, Sargent Shriver, also lived nearby. Other assorted Kennedys would rent homes with relatives coming and going throughout the summer. Jackie was close to some of them—Ethel and Joan in particular. Joan said she liked to think of them as "outlaws as much as in-laws."

One of the bigger events of the summer was the July 11 state dinner Jackie planned for Mohammad Ayub Khan of Pakistan, which Jackie decided shouldn't be at the White House, where state dinners were usually held, but at Mount Vernon, the home of George Washington. Planning an event such as this one was a major task. Just getting the food from the White House to Mount Vernon in military vehicles was a major feat—but Jackie pulled it off. Members of the Kennedy family were present as well as the Auchinclosses and many of Jackie's Bouvier relatives. It was an opportunity for a family reunion as much as it was a moment to host a foreign dignitary. "I want it to be fun," Jackie said. "As a family, we don't see each other enough."

The rest of 1961 proved to be a chaotic time in America. As a considerate wife, Jackie devoted herself to making it as easy as possible for JFK to deal with a myriad of national issues, such as racial tensions, which were at an all-time high. Cuba was always a problem, especially after the Bay of Pigs. Vietnam was also becoming problematic. Because there were almost three hundred thousand American soldiers in Europe at this time, the resumption of nuclear testing by the Soviet Union was also worrying. The question facing the president was whether the United States should do the same. "I remember him being so worried at the time about our resuming," Jackie said. "That was terrible. There was nothing that worried him more than all that testing.

"I think the job of the First Lady has to be to give the president a place of comfort," she also said. "He doesn't want to discuss the world crisis at the end of his day. He wants to be with his wife and his children, his family, his parents and siblings, my parents. We all try to find ways to be a family first no matter what other things are going on in the country. There will always be something for the president to handle, that's the job. My job is to give him a relaxation break from all of that."

This may have been less her personal view than what she felt Jack's public wanted to hear. It was 1961, and many women felt their place in society was "just" as homemakers. It was clear that Jackie wanted to be known more for her accomplishments as a First Lady than simply as the wife JFK came home to. It was the reason she devoted herself so completely and so passionately to her White House restoration. When her mother told her early on that her job should be to return the White House to grandeur, she took that mandate seriously.

On September 19, there was a state dinner for President Don Manuel Prado of Peru. A week later, on the twenty-fourth, Jackie watched as Jack spoke to the United Nations in New York. The next day, they were off to Hammersmith for downtime, where the highlight of each day was a lunchtime cruise on the *Honey Fitz*, the yacht named after Jack's maternal grandfather, John F. "Honey Fitz" Fitzgerald, who'd served as a U.S. representative and mayor of Boston.

The Kennedys were back at the White House on October 27, but just for a week before they returned to Squaw Island. In November, Jackie once again visited the Auchincloses at Hammersmith in Newport before returning to the White House to greet the visiting prime minister of India, Jawaharlal Nehru, and his daughter, Indira Gandhi.

During that visit, JFK and Jackie brought the prime minister to Hammersmith for several days. The Auchincloses were unnerved by the fact that Nehru had a security guard sitting on the floor, his back to the bedroom door, the entire night. "It was just such heavy going," Jackie said of spending time with Nehru. "Just that real Hindu thing—you learn it in India, that they don't look on social gatherings as a time to speak. I don't know if they're contemplating . . . but I also say it's just damned spoiled brattishness because you should make an effort when other people are trying."

The next day, as Hugh, Jack, and Nehru helicoptered over the great estates and yachts, Jack cracked, "I just wanted you to see how the average American family lives." Nehru was barely amused.

On November 13, after a state dinner for Governor Luis Muñoz Marín and his wife, Inés, Jackie hosted a special concert at the White House. Performing was renowned cellist, eighty-four-year-old Pablo Casals, who hadn't played in the States for more than thirty years. Letitia Baldrige wrote, "That night was the most special. We had such a guest list, Lenny Bernstein, Aaron Copland . . . Teddy Roosevelt's daughter, Alice, was there and she had seen Casals perform in the White House back in 1904. I thought, what a life this is . . . what a world we're living in. The way Jack and Jackie looked at each other that night, I thought, my God, they're like a King and Queen who adore one another. Such magic."

Jackie sent Rose Kennedy a note after that night: "Dearest Belle Mere," it read, "You were so sweet to stay up with the Casals so late last night. It made such a difference to have you stay. You added immeasurable luster to our gayest weekend of the year. So many thanks. Love XO J."

On November 17, after that state dinner and concert, Jackie was off to Glen Ora to ride her horse, Bit of Irish, at the Hunt Club. Dressed in her equestrian outfit, she galloped along, relaxed and happy and about to jump a rail fence when a photographer suddenly appeared and started snapping photos. In doing so, he frightened the horse, it stopped short, and Jackie went flying over the fence headfirst. It was a shocking moment, and of course the photographer was able to capture it. Jackie, who was wearing a helmet, broke the fall with her arms and hands, brushed herself off, jumped back on the horse, and galloped away as if nothing had occurred.

There were two Thanksgiving dinners the year John turned one on November 25 and Caroline, four, on the twenty-seventh. The first was at Rose and Joe's home with the rest of the Kennedys on the actual holiday, November 23, the first of the holidays with their son as president.

The holidays were Jackie's favorite time of the year, and her friends knew that she still showed such girlhood excitement when offered a pleasing gift. "A black pearl was always the most romantic, exotic piece of jewelry," she wrote to Lady Bird that year when LBJ's wife presented her with the jewel, which, she wrote, she never imagined she'd ever be fortunate enough to own. She said she would wear it on her pinkie finger.

"That Thanksgiving at Grandma and Grandpa's was the one during which Jackie taught us how to do the Twist," Joan Kennedy recalled. "She had on a pink slacks suit designed by Schiaparelli. I was playing the piano while she taught Teddy to twist. Everyone then started dancing to rock and roll records and what a fun time it was—brothers dancing with sisters, husbands with sisters-in-law. It was so marvelous and the president sitting there smoking his cigar, taking it all in."

The second Thanksgiving was a couple of days later at the Auchincloses' Merrywood estate. Getting the family together was always very important to Janet and Hugh. "We are not much without each other," Hugh always said. Times had been very stressful of late, making it all the more important, Hugh said, for everyone to check in with each other at the holiday dinner table.

"As head of the family, Daddy stood and raised his glass," recalled Jamie Auchincloss. "Beaming at Jack, he toasted the fact that he'd gotten through the first year of his presidency. 'Fine. Can we just stop now?' Jackie asked, kidding. 'No,' Daddy told her. 'You still have a few more years.' Jack smiled at her and said, 'Then four more after that? Right?' She nodded eagerly, and just by the way she glowed, she really and truly meant it. No matter what problems they had, I could tell, at least in my own, little fourteen-year-old mind, that she loved him and he loved her back."

Jack raised his glass to Jackie. "To my wife," he said. She clinked it. "To my husband," she told him. "What a life we're having, right?" he asked. She smiled and agreed, "Yes, Jack. What a life we're having."

JACKIE'S EARLY DAYS

◇◇◇◇◇◇◇◇◇◇◇◇◇

I lived in New York City until I was thirteen and spent the summers in the country," Jacqueline Kennedy Onassis once recalled. "I hated dolls, loved horses and dogs, and had skinned knees and braces on my teeth for what must have seemed an interminable length of time to my family. I read a lot when I was little, much of which was too old for me. There were Chekhov and Shaw in the room where I had to take naps and I never slept but sat on the windowsill reading, then scrubbed the soles of my feet so the nurse would not see I had been out of bed. My heroes were Byron, Mowgli, Robin Hood, Little Lord Fauntleroy's grandfather, and Scarlett O'Hara."

It was no wonder the Kennedys were so taken by her when she started dating JFK. She was intelligent, well-educated, cultured, and gorgeous. Her childhood was nothing less than privileged and exceptional. Her parents, not just Janet but her father, Jack Bouvier, too, had made sure of it.

Jackie was an excellent equestrian from an early age, taking after Janet, who put her on a horse at the age of two. By the time Jackie was five, mother and daughter took third prize in an East Hampton show. In 1935, after a year at Miss Yates's kindergarten, Jackie enrolled in Miss Chapin's School on East End Avenue in Manhattan for grades one to seven. Meanwhile, Janet made sure she took ballet lessons and encouraged her interest in reading and wanted to be sure she could speak French. On her own, Jackie decided she wanted to speak German, too, and started taking lessons from her Swiss governess.

The Bouvier sisters were close when they were young, with Jackie being protective of Lee. Janet encouraged it. However, she also inadvertently fostered the sisters' lifelong competition, with Lee almost always the loser. It started early on when Janet would take Jackie to the city to shop or for high tea at the Plaza, leaving Lee behind. "First, my father preferred Jackie because she was such a good [horse] rider," Lee recalled in 2012. "I couldn't compete. I was too young. Soon, I realized my mother preferred her, as well. I would walk into a room and there they would be painting their nails and talking, with me just on the outside. I lived with it. In a strange way, I understood it. Jackie was special. I wasn't.

"The childhood days were when we were closest. Her nickname for me was Pekes. I called her Jacks. We loved each other without condition. Everything was simple then. Complication, confusion, wounds, suffering, none of it had entered our lives."

Maybe Lee had romanticized things a bit. In fact, it was often tense at home, partly because just as Janet preferred Jackie, the two sisters favored their father to their mother. Janet, hurt by their preference, would often lash out at them. "There was a period of time, when they were young, where the sisters had a lot of animosity for their mother," said their cousin and author John Davis. "Jackie was so fixated on her father, it was no wonder it grew to be a problem for Janet."

Chronically nervous and upset, Janet chain-smoked and bit her nails to the quick, habits she'd hand down to both daughters. In fits of anger, she'd often slap the girls, first with the palm of her hand and then with the back of the same hand. It was shocking, no matter how many times she did it. She would hit Jackie more than she did Lee, and some speculated that was because she was more focused on Jackie and on whatever Jackie did or said. Maybe in that respect, Lee was better off because Jackie was Janet's focus.

After a violent episode, Janet would be filled with regret and try to coddle them. The girls wouldn't have it, though; they were just too hurt and upset. Janet would wait a few more hours and then call them into the kitchen where she'd prepared a snack for them, always the same one because she knew they loved it.

Though she wasn't skilled in the kitchen—that's what chefs were for—Janet could make a decent butterscotch pudding from scratch with milk, eggs, butter, and brown sugar. When she was growing up, her mother used to make it for her and her sisters. Now she did the same for her own daughters. She'd allow the girls to squirt Quip Whipped Cream from the can onto their own treats; Jackie would always do the honors to her mother's. This tradition almost always took place, Lee once recalled, "after she had just completely lost her mind and regretted it."

From 1942 to 1944, Jackie attended the Holton-Arms School in northwest Washington and then, from 1944 to 1947, Miss Porter's School in Farmington, Connecticut, where she graduated in the top of her class. Hugh's sister Annie had gone to Miss Porter's, and her husband was on the board of trustees, which was how Jackie got into the school. She thought her stockbroker father was paying for it. He wasn't. With his brokerage suffering so many losses, Jack Bouvier couldn't be counted on for the money. He did manage to send her and Lee an allowance of $50 a month, $600 each in today's dollars. Hugh, an incredibly decent man, paid the rest of the bills but insisted to Janet that she allow Jackie to think it was her father; it was Hugh's way of protecting Jackie's relationship with her biological father.

In August of 1947, Jackie made her debut to high society with a festive gala at Merrywood. The Auchinclosses invited three hundred guests to Hammersmith for a tea, a reception, and dancing, the event later described by the *New York Daily News* as "a grand evening with Clifford Hall, pianist from the Clambake Club, playing at the sumptuous estate of her parents [*sic*], Hugh and Janet Auchincloss."

That was also the year Jackie's half brother, Jamie, was born. She shared the spotlight with the five-month-old infant at the coming-out party, both acknowledged on the engraved invitation, Jamie as "Master James Auchincloss." He'd just been christened that same afternoon at Trinity Church, with the dean of the Virginia Theological Seminary officiating.

In an odd touch, Janet proudly showed off her newborn by placing him in a silver bowl in the middle of the buffet table, one that had just been used the prior Christmas for eggnog. Guests admired the sleeping infant, resplendent in his long christening robe, while loading their plates up with culinary delights. "No, I cannot explain it," he says today with a chuckle. "I, of course, was a cute baby, but Jackie was the focus of attention in her coming-out gown. Igor Cassini [brother of Oleg, who'd go on to design Jackie's White House wardrobe] later named her 'Debutante of the Year.'"

In the fall of 1947, Jackie enrolled at Vassar College in Poughkeepsie, New York, where she was, again, a good student, though not fond of the school. She later said it was "all just so pretentious and ridiculous." She belonged to arts and drama clubs and also wrote for the newspaper there. Thanks to Hugh's largesse, along with a study-abroad program through Smith

College, she was able to spend her junior year at the University of Grenoble in Grenoble, France, and at the Sorbonne in Paris.

Her stepbrother, Yusha Auchincloss—Hugh's son—joined her in Paris. He'd had a crush on Jackie since the day she and her mother and sister showed up at his father's home, Merrywood, in 1941. At that time, Jackie was twelve, and he was fourteen. Late in his life, Yusha told his good friend Robert Westover (who, as an "honorary member of the family," called him "Uncle Yusha") that he gave Jackie her first kiss. "We were driving along the—Narragansett Bay," Robert remembered, "and as we passed the big house of Hammersmith, Yusha pointed up and said, 'See those two rooms up there, the windows at the end? My bedroom was the one with the curved windows and Jackie's was right next to it. Late one night, she came into my room and said, "Yush,"—she called him Yush, not Yusha—"I have such big lips, no man is ever going to want to kiss my big lips." I said to her, "But I want to kiss you, Jackie. I want to kiss you right now." She said, "You do?" And I just leaned in and kissed her. She said that was her first kiss, and it was mine, as well.'"

Now, six years later, he had a chance to be with her in the City of Lights. For him, it was "the most glorious time of my life," or so he later said. For Jackie, as she later wrote, Paris was "all glamour, glitter and rush. It was heaven," she recalled.

Later, Jackie and Yusha would travel to Ireland and Scotland and end up sailing home together on the *Liberté* cruise liner. "This made him fall even deeper in love," said Robert. "It was torture for him. He loved her so much and just wanted to be in her presence, wherever she was in the world. 'So close yet so far,' was how he put it more than thirty years later."

For her part, Jackie returned home from Europe feeling as if she'd really grown. "Being away from home gave me a chance to look at myself with a jaundiced eye. I learned not to be ashamed of a real hunger for knowledge, something I had always tried to hide, and I came home glad to start in here again but with a love for Europe that I am afraid will never leave me."

Once home, Jackie transferred out of Vassar to George Washington University in Washington, D.C., and, in 1951, graduated with a bachelor of arts degree in French literature.

It was while she was at George Washington that Janet encouraged her to enter *Vogue*'s annual Prix de Paris competition. The grand prize was as a junior editor for six months in the Paris office and then six months in New

York. Jackie's essays about fashion and art won the prize, beating out 1,280 entries from 225 colleges!

After having a chance to think about it—and after talking to her socialite friends—Janet called Jackie into her bedroom from her hallway "waiting room" one morning to tell her she'd decided Jackie shouldn't accept the honor. She didn't want Jackie surrounded by what she assumed would be a predominately female staff. Jackie wasn't going to meet her husband that way. Maybe that was a factor, but a bigger one for Janet was that she feared that if Jackie spent six months in Paris, she'd love it so much she'd never return. She imagined a future with her daughter married to a Frenchman, raising her grandchildren three thousand miles away, and she had no intention of moving to France to be with them. Therefore, she vetoed the job.

Jackie, who now thought of herself as old enough to make her own decisions, wanted to take the job and, in fact, said she *was* going to take the job. She had this sense that she wanted to do something for herself, free of any societal restrictions that would force her into "just marriage." She said, "I want above all to become a working girl who earns her own living."

"I don't care what you say, I'm accepting the prize," Jackie told her. That little show of bravado earned her two of Janet's sharp slaps, first with the palm of her hand and then with the back of it.

At this same time, the Bouvier sisters had another trip to Europe planned, a graduation gift for Lee. Janet suggested Jackie think about the *Vogue* job while she was abroad and was sure that when she returned she would make the right decision. This vacation was a thrill for the Bouvier sisters, which would later be memorialized in a book they eventually published called *One Special Summer.* "We did the book for Mummy, really," Jackie said, "as a thank-you. It features many of our poems and little thoughts and dreams, and some of my perhaps amateurish drawings. It's a sweet book and brings back memory."

Jackie returned from Europe saying she'd decided not to take the job. She wanted to go to New York, however, and turn it down in person. Though Janet felt she really just wanted to go into the city and explore, she allowed it. In discussing the job with a *Vogue* editor named Carol Phillips, Jackie was told that her mother was probably right; she'd likely never get settled working in a mostly female environment. That editor suggested she go to Washington and find a job there in a city of politicians (i.e., wealthy men).

Jamie Auchincloss said, "Daddy knew Arthur Krock, bureau chief of

The New York Times, who knew Frank Waldrop, the editor of the *Washington Times-Herald.* The next thing we knew, Jackie was a columnist for the *Times-Herald* called the 'Inquiring Camera Girl.' She was paid something like forty dollars a week to ask strangers questions about a range of topics personal and political. Should women have joint accounts with their husbands? Should women hold political office? Should spouses criticize each other? Should you live with your in-laws? Do candidates' looks affect the way you vote? In its own way, it had feminist leanings, though that wasn't the intent. It was human interest, and with each answer there'd be a photo of the respondent taken by Jackie. Mummy and Daddy were so proud. Jackie's life had really taken off."

Jackie landed the job with the *Washington Times-Herald* in the fall of 1951. Within a year, she'd break off her engagement to John Husted and would begin dating Jack Kennedy, and the rest, of course, would be history—*American* history.

JOE'S STROKE

As every year, the president and First Lady would spend the Christmas holiday with Jack's family in Palm Beach, Florida. Back in Virginia at Merrywood, it was the same story every year. Janet would line up everyone by age, even the adults present, with the oldest getting to talk to Jack and Jackie over the phone first. "Now, hurry up," she'd say, "and don't talk too long. He's the most important person in the world, so don't dillydally."

The youngest, Jamie, would stand at the back of the line. As the others talked, he tried to think of something intelligent to say to the leader of the free world, a little witticism that might make him sound smart. Before finally handing him the phone, Janet would tell him, "Make it snappy. You have five seconds." Jamie would then say something like, "Merry Christmas and goodbye." This year, the fourteen-year-old stole the Marx Brothers line, "Hello. I must be going." JFK would always get a kick out of him.

This one turned out to be a very sad holiday because, on December 19, the Kennedy family patriarch, Joseph Kennedy, suffered a stroke. It was so critical, doctors even suggested turning off life support. However, Bobby refused, saying he and his siblings wanted their father to have a fighting chance to recover. In years to come, Jackie would question that decision. Joe was never the same, and, in her mind, it was debatable as to whether or not his life was even worth living. With the right side of his body paralyzed, he'd end up confined to a wheelchair and unable to speak, which was a cruel twist of fate for a man who'd been such a vital force in the family. He'd live another eight long and painful years, requiring round-the-clock nursing.

In the summer of 1962, after months of rehabilitation, Joseph was finally able to take a few unsteady steps on his own. On the day he was to take those first steps, Jackie presented him with a black-and-silver walking cane. The engraving said, "To Grandpa, with love, Jackie." She reached down to help him rise from his chair. He struggled, but he made it. "Come on, Grandpa," she whispered as she held on to him tightly. "Let's take a walk."

MONEY FOR A BABY?

<><><><><><><><><><><>

Jackie and her father-in-law, Joe Kennedy, were always close, going all the way back to when Jackie suffered the agony of a stillbirth in 1956.

At that time, Jackie had only been married to Jack Kennedy for three years, but already the marriage was in trouble because of his chronic infidelity. Priscilla McMillan, who was a researcher for Kennedy when he was a senator, recalled, "One day I said to him, 'Jack, when you're straining every gasket to one day perhaps be elected president, why do you endanger it yourself by going out with women?' I put it just like that. He looked at me a long second and said, 'Because I can't help it.'"

"I'm just not enough for him," Jackie tearfully told her mother. "You *are* enough," Janet told her. "*He's* not enough." While Janet could be hypercritical of her children, she wouldn't abide self-condemnation. She blamed herself for Jackie's marriage and felt she shouldn't have pushed so hard for JFK. Now her daughter was stuck in the same kind of marriage Janet had with Jack Bouvier. Apparently, infidelity ran in both families, because Joe Kennedy had cheated on Rose for years, and everyone knew it. Many affluent women of this time felt it was just what men did—they cheated, period. Acknowledging it, though, didn't make it hurt any less.

When Jackie was pregnant in 1956, she'd already suffered one miscarriage. She and Janet both hoped that if she carried the next baby to term, it would help solidify her marriage. However, the baby—whom Jackie unofficially named Arabella—was stillborn on August 23. Making things even worse, Jack happened to be on a cruise off the coast of Italy having fun with his friends, among them a few women. When he decided not to return after

Jackie's miscarriage, everyone was appalled. His brother Bobby stepped in at Ethel's behest to comfort Jackie. He and Janet then went to the cemetery after arranging Arabella's burial.

For Janet, the final nail in Jack's coffin was when Jackie later tearfully confided in her mother that she'd suffered from the sexually transmitted infection chlamydia during the first few weeks of her pregnancy. This stunning revelation was more than Janet could bear. "Obviously, Jack got it from one of his whores and gave it to you," she exclaimed. She was livid. Downplaying its long-lasting severity, Jackie said the infection had already been cured with antibiotics. However, she wondered if it had been the reason Arabella had been stillborn. They didn't know the answer to that question, and doctors weren't sure, either. Janet would always hold it against Jack. She knew she'd never be able to get past it. "I want you to divorce him and never think about him again," was her advice to her daughter, and Jackie wholeheartedly agreed. She was done with him.

When Hugh contacted a lawyer for Jackie, the three of them met in the Deck Room at Hammersmith to discuss how the Kennedy fortune might be divided. There was no prenup, however, nothing that guaranteed Jackie anything. Making things even more complex, she had no idea of the extent of the Kennedys' wealth. "You're on the horns of a dilemma," Hugh told Jackie, "and the only solution is to get smarter. Learn about your husband's assets."

Five days after Arabella's death, Jack finally returned. Naturally, he wanted to stay at Hammersmith with the family, but Hugh thought it best to keep him away from his mother-in-law. The senator was banished to a small servant's bedroom over the garage.

At about this same time, Jackie had an emotional conversation with Ethel Kennedy, during which she said she no longer wanted to be married to Jack. Ethel, ever the Kennedy loyalist, went straight to her father-in-law to clue him in.

Divorce was the last thing Joe Kennedy wanted for Jack. The whole point of Jackie being in his son's life was to burnish his image as a stable politician. He'd only just begun his career, which Joe was certain would culminate with the presidency. Joe asked to see Jackie for lunch at Le Pavillon, a French restaurant in New York, to sort things out.

The persistent rumor in the family after this luncheon and for many years after was that Joe offered Jackie $1 million for any child she would have with Jack. The story was even published in *Time* in 1960 and described as "an unverified arrangement but still described by relatives as likely." However, according to a lawyer who worked for the Auchincloss family from 1950 to 1960, the offer was actually $100,000, and only for the first child. That amount makes more sense: $100,000 at that time was worth about $1 million in today's money, whereas $1 million would be worth about $10 million today. It seems unfathomable that Joe would ever offer Jackie that much money. It can now be confidently reported that he offered to pay her $100,000 for a first child Jackie would carry to term, that last part—"to term"—being hurtful since the implication was that he wasn't paying for any more miscarriages or stillbirths.

According to the family's history, Jackie didn't know how to respond. When she told her mother and stepfather about it, Janet was angry. "You don't pay a woman to have your grandchild!" she said. Hugh didn't think it was such a bad arrangement. He'd just gone over Jackie's finances, he reminded Janet, and she had no assets. Considering the hell she'd gone through with Jack thus far in their marriage, why shouldn't she be compensated?

Jackie reminded her mother that for as long as she could remember, Janet had stressed to her and Lee that "the secret to happiness is money and power." Now, she argued, a great deal of money was being offered to her by a very powerful man. She couldn't understand the opposition.

No one had more appreciation for the value of money than Janet Auchincloss. However, she feared the prospect of Jackie getting pregnant again was loaded with emotion because of her previous history. To add a financial incentive to the equation was, she believed, a recipe for disaster. "How many miscarriages are you willing to endure before you finally cash in?" she asked her. Maybe it was an indelicate way to put it, but she had a point. Also, Janet knew that if Jackie carried a baby to term, she'd never leave her marriage. She'd never break up her home, no matter how unhappy she was with Jack, and Janet really did want her to divorce him. Ultimately, though, she conceded that it had to be Jackie's decision.

Many years later, Janet told her son, Jamie, "Look, she wanted children. She'd always wanted children. She said, 'Why shouldn't I get paid to have a baby if I'm going to have one anyway?' She looked at it as a financial opportunity. I was against it, but maybe she was right. Maybe she deserved it."

"The Auchincloss attorney—not Jackie—called Joseph and told him to have the papers drawn up," Adora Rule stated. "She signed a contract about a week later." Adora didn't learn of the arrangement until almost twenty years later, when Janet told her about it in 1976 after Hugh died and the lawyer responsible for paperwork showed up at his funeral.

"It wasn't conventional," Jamie Auchincloss said, "but we, as a family, had accepted that nothing about the Kennedys was traditional. Jackie had accepted it, too. She would often say they were not your typical couple. It troubled her at first, but she began to accept it.

"Jack used to worry when Jackie would go off without him because it gave her too much time to wonder about their marriage," Jamie added. "She'd come home feeling differently about things, and not in a way more warmly toward him. He would just as soon she not have too much time to think about things. But, in fact, it was during those times alone that she was able to come to terms with the marriage. It did her, and him, a lot of good when they had space from one another."

Jamie's observation is supported by a three-page letter Jackie wrote to her husband in 1957 when she was on a holiday without him. She wrote, in part, "We are so different . . . I was thinking this trip that every other time I've been away, you would write 'don't ponder our relation too much' etc.— and [you would say] 'You are an atypical husband'—and you are increasingly so in one way or another every year since we've been married." She wrote that she felt she was "an atypical wife" and that they both would've been unhappy with "the normal kind" of marriage. She added that she couldn't write in that letter the true depth of her feeling for him, "but I will show you when I am with you—and I think you must know." She closed saying that she no longer tried to figure out their marriage, "as one doesn't ponder anything that is a part of you." By the spring of 1957, Jackie was pregnant again. On November 27, she gave birth to her and Jack's first child, Caroline Bouvier Kennedy. The next day, Joseph made good on his promise. He opened an account in her name and deposited $100,000.

"DON'T LET THAT BE ME"

⬦⬦⬦⬦⬦⬦⬦⬦⬦⬦⬦⬦⬦

A couple of weeks after Joseph Kennedy was released from the Horizon rehabilitation facility in the summer of 1962 and was back home at the Cape, Jackie's side of the family, the Auchinclosses, went to visit him.

Jackie had previously explained to Rose Kennedy that Hugh had been very upset about Joseph's stroke. Coming to terms with the fact that such a vital man now had crippling infirmities had a profound effect on him. Rose understood. "Any time someone around your stepfather's age falls sick, it reminds him of his own mortality," she said. "It's a fact of life, though," she added in her own pragmatic way. "We get sick. We die."

At seventy-three, Joseph Kennedy was nine years older than Hugh Auchincloss. The two patriarchs had often enjoyed lively conversations about politics. Hugh admired Joseph for the way he'd raised his family, particularly his sons. One was president, the other attorney general, and Ted would become a member of the Senate in November.

On the day Janet, Jamie, and Janet Jr. accompanied Hugh to the Cape for a visit, the place was swarming with Secret Service agents. "It was chaos," recalled agent Joseph Paolella. "There were probably a dozen kids playing with barking dogs while their nannies watched over them and their parents tossed a football around on the front lawn—a typical day in the so-called compound."

Jackie walked with Hugh up to the Big House. There was Joseph, on the porch in his wheelchair, wearing a white linen shirt with a blanket on his lap. "Grandpa, look who's here," she exclaimed. Joseph looked at Hugh and managed a crooked smile.

For a moment, Hugh was stunned by Joseph's feebleness. He walked up to the porch and sat next to him. As he did so, Joseph pulled out the pillow he was resting on and showed it to Hugh. The embroidery said: "You're dipping into your Capitol!" His lips curled into a smile. Hugh had to laugh. "Okay, we'll be fine here," he told Jackie.

Rose came out to greet them. She and Janet embraced and walked into the house. Jackie followed with Jamie, Janet Jr., Caroline, and John.

"Later that day, an army of Kennedys, young and old, gathered on the expansive green lawn for a rowdy game of touch football, as was their well-known custom," recalled Paolella.

Janet and Rose sat in rocking chairs on the porch, drinking iced tea and whispering to one another. Occasionally, they'd stop to take in the action, laugh, and comment about it.

On the other side of the terrace sat Joseph and Hugh—with Caroline on his lap—in their own rocking chairs, also watching the game. Occasionally, Jackie's stepfather would point something out, and Jack's father would nod his approval. He'd try to speak, but it wasn't worth the effort. Instead, he'd put his good hand on Hugh's arm and squeeze hard.

Jack stared at him sadly from the doorway. "Don't ever let that be me," he said.

"Never," Jackie promised.

JACKIE'S TOUR OF THE WHITE HOUSE

◇◇◇◇◇◇◇◇◇◇◇◇◇

The Kennedys stayed in Palm Beach until the end of January 1962 so that they could be close to Joseph. Once back in Washington, Jack gave his State of the Union address; Jackie sat in the gallery with Helen Sullivan O'Donnell, wife of Jack's special assistant Kenny O'Donnell, and Martha Buck Bartlett, wife of Chares Bartlett. Behind her sat Bobby's wife, Ethel. The president, quite popular at this time, with an approval rating hovering around 70 percent, spoke about education, tax cuts, and more support for Medicare. "He is a leader with vision," is how the Associated Press put it. "Some feel his wife should spend less time on fashion choices, however."

Like many public figures, Jackie enjoyed attention if she could control it. When Blair Clark—vice president of CBS's news division, who'd known JFK since Harvard—contacted her in October 1961 to suggest a televised tour of the White House to show off her restoration, she wanted to do it. However, she was concerned about her lack of experience in front of cameras. At the Cape Cod house during the 1961 Christmas holiday, Jackie and members of both families, Auchinclosses and Kennedys, debated the pros and cons of such an appearance.

Most of the family was against it. It was felt that an experienced female news anchor should go room to room with Jackie and ask her questions. The fear was that Jackie on her own would appear stiff and inexperienced. "None of us are entertainers," Yusha cautioned her. The CBS correspondent Nancy Dickerson, a personal friend of Hugh's, was his choice to do the talking.

Janet disagreed. She felt it was Jackie's duty to do the tour herself and that she could make it work. Actually, it was never the network's intention that Jackie just deliver speeches. The plan was always for her to be interviewed by the network's Charles Collingwood.

One evening during a visit at the Big House at the Cape, Ethel suggested to Jackie, "Stand here now and tell us something about the White House. Let's see how you do." Jackie stood awkwardly before Jack and his brothers, Bobby and Ted, and their wives, Ethel and Joan, and said a few words about one of the rooms. When she finished, Jack said, "Very nice, Jackie." Joan agreed. Ethel didn't. "Why's she talking like that?" she asked.

Perhaps it was nerves, but Jackie had adopted a tone that didn't sound like her. Ethel turned to the others and asked, "Who does she sound like? I can't put my finger on it." Bobby thought it over, snapped his fingers, and said, "Marilyn," to which Ethel said, "Yes. That's it. Marilyn Monroe." Jackie was dismayed. "I do not sound like Marilyn Monroe," she exclaimed. Seeing that she was upset, Ethel then assured her she'd be fine on camera, "as long as you don't talk like that."

Jackie, bewildered by the impromptu audition, fled the room. Ethel and Bobby had been critical at a moment she really needed support. More than that, she was already reluctant to do the broadcast, afraid she'd come off as boasting about her restoration work. While she was proud of it, she wasn't sure she should tout it. The Kennedys' critique, which really sounded more like ridicule than constructive criticism, felt to Jackie like another roadblock.

Ethel and Bobby were immediately contrite. The next day, Ethel slipped a note of apology under Jackie's door at her home. Jackie didn't respond, causing Ethel to ask Rose Kennedy, "Don't you think she needs a thicker skin, Grandma? People can be mean. That's not news." Rose's pithy response: "*You* can be mean, Ethel. *That's* what's not news."

It took Jackie a few days to decide what to do about the show. "She decided, 'Yes, I can do this,'" recalled Jamie Auchincloss. "'And damn it, I'm going to do a good job, too.' If you knew our family and the way we were raised, you'd know that standing in front of a TV camera full of confidence was not who we were. In that respect, my sister had nerves of steel, because this was really a stretch for us."

After CBS agreed to donate $100,000 to Jackie's restoration project, the deal with the network was finalized for a one-hour special. On the day of taping, January 15, 1962, Jackie was dressed in pearls with a bright red suit—which didn't much matter since the show would be televised in black and white—and ready for what she imagined would be a few hours' work. It took all day.

"I thought she was a total professional," said producer Perry Wolff. "There weren't people cueing her. She was prepared, going room to room with Charles Collingwood and describing the décor while also mentioning the names of private donors. I found her sophisticated yet, at the same time, childlike. Off camera, she smoked a lot. But watching her, I thought America would love her, and of course, America did."

When the show was broadcast on February 14, 1962, on both CBS and NBC—with no commercials—more than forty-six million people watched and enjoyed it. That was almost 75 percent of a total viewing audience. (ABC would broadcast the show the following Sunday, which added ten million more viewers.) Jackie's voice did surprise some people.

Jackie had been on television in the past, such as in a statewide Massachusetts morning program show called *At Home with the Kennedys* in 1952 and again in 1958. That program featured Rose and other Kennedy women. During the '58 broadcast, Rose talked about how lucky Jack was to have found someone like "Jack-leen" (pronounced just as Janet liked it). Jackie couldn't have been stiffer or more robotic as she spoke about the recent campaign. Her voice, naturally soft and whispery, took on more mannered nuances on television; her accent distinctly upper-class New York, as in: "This is a *rawther mahvelous* piece."

Astronaut and former senator John Glenn, who knew the Kennedys well, once put it this way: "When she was placed in a formal situation as the center of attention, her voice, and the way she acted, was a retreat from herself, more formal as, perhaps, a defense mechanism. She was careful what she did, careful about every word she said. But in private, she sounded different—relaxed, easy." Or, as White House curator James Ketchum put it, "She simply didn't record well. You weren't nearly as aware of her vocal mannerisms when you were one on one with her, or even on the phone with her, as you were when she was being recorded. That's when she always sounded sort of fascinated or surprised. Part of that was a mode she shifted into when she saw the red light on a camera."

About twenty years later, when Jackie was an editor at Doubleday, a colleague asked her about the broadcast and what she thought of it. Jackie said that she still couldn't believe she went through with it. "That was a real leap," she said. "For the times? For women? To do something like that?" She smiled and concluded, "Even I have to admit, that was really something."

MARILYN

∞∞∞∞∞∞∞∞∞∞

I t was ironic that Bobby and Ethel thought Jackie sounded like Marilyn Monroe, given what would be the movie star's prominence in Kennedy history. There had been so many women in her husband's life, but Jackie opted not to think about them, keeping herself focused on family matters and the White House restoration. Once in the White House, she realized Jack's infidelity was not an anomaly.

Senator George Smathers said in 1999, "When you go back and look at the personal lives of presidents, the only ones I knew—and I shook hands with eleven presidents—who were totally one hundred percent faithful to their wives were Truman and Nixon. Those were the only two. Jackie knew that, too. She dealt with it."

Priscilla McMillan, who worked for Kennedy when he was a senator, added, "Jack Kennedy lived his life in compartments. There was one compartment having to do with his love life, one for his marriage, and one for his family. I think ambition was the glue which held all of these life compartments together."

There was one woman who seemed to affect Jackie in a way the others in Jack's life hadn't, and that was Marilyn Monroe. It's not hyperbolic to say that JFK's "affair" with her is the stuff of legends. There's been so much reportage about it over the last fifty-plus years, it's difficult to separate fact from fiction. In fact, they were together sexually for just one weekend, beginning on March 24, 1962, at the Palm Springs home of Bing Crosby. That was it. Two nights. No affair. "Jack and I talked about her," recalled Senator George Smathers. "He thought she was beautiful, but maybe not the smartest girl in the world. He liked her sense of humor and her playfulness.

He said Jackie was more serious, and it was fun being with a girl who was just . . . not."

While Jack and Marilyn were in Palm Springs, he received an urgent telegram from Jackie in Pakistan. The First Lady was scheduled abroad for most of the month of March 1962—four days in Rome, seventeen in India, five in Pakistan, and three more in London. Her sister, Lee, and friend Joan Braden went with her to keep her company. On their last day in Pakistan, Jackie and Lee hiked themselves atop a camel—sitting sidesaddle in skirts and high heels. As they rode on it, Lee in front of her sister, both looked delighted. Photographs of that fun moment made it all around the world and, still today, remain popular images of the Bouvier sisters.

The high point of the trip for Jackie, though, was the presentation to her by President Mohammad Ayub Khan of a horse named Sardar, a descendant from the horses of Agha Khan. Sardar, however, had to be quarantined in New York for thirty days. "It seems so rude to Pakistanis to suggest that their beautiful horse has hoof-and-mouth disease when obviously he hasn't a germ in the world," said Jackie's telegram. She added that she "cannot bear to be parted from him" for the thirty days and that such exile would be "cruel and inhumane." She asked Jack to have a New York veterinarian examine the animal and give him a clean bill of health, thus making quarantine unnecessary. "It would be like leaving Lee in quarantine to part with him," she said—and one wonders how Lee might've felt about the equivalency. In a final effort to convince Jack to give the horse a break, Jackie wrote that if he didn't do so, "You will lose ASPCA vote forever." She signed the telegram, "Love, Jackie."

The fact that Jack received this telegram from his wife while he was entertaining Marilyn Monroe shows how different their priorities were that weekend. The president did as the First Lady suggested.

WHEN MARILYN CALLS

◇◇◇◇◇◇◇◇◇◇◇◇

In April of 1962, Jackie was in Hyannis Port when the phone rang in her bedroom, she picked it up, and the breathy voice on the other end asked, "Is Jack home?" Jackie said he wasn't home and asked who was calling. "Marilyn Monroe," came back the answer. "Is this Jackie?" she asked. When Jackie identified herself, Marilyn asked if she'd tell the president she'd called. Jackie asked what it was regarding. Marilyn said it was nothing in particular; she just wanted to say hello. A little stunned, Jackie said she'd pass on the message and hung up.

According to family members, this call was the extent of Jackie Kennedy's communication with Marilyn Monroe.

Jackie found the call off-putting. She told her mother the voice was haunting and sad and had an ethereal, little-girl-lost quality, which she found disturbing.

Earlier, Jackie had begun hearing rumors about the weekend Jack and Marilyn spent at Bing Crosby's. She wasn't sure if she believed them. Lee, who knew Marilyn socially, told her there was also a lot of chatter about Marilyn and Bobby Kennedy. Lee also said Marilyn was addicted to certain medications and seeing a psychiatrist almost daily. Jackie didn't like the sound of any of it and told Jack she didn't want him to continue whatever relationship he had with Marilyn Monroe. Jack's response was that he and the actress were just friends but, still, he agreed. Then the telephone call happened.

Jackie had to wonder if it was a prank. How could she know if it were really Marilyn? It did come in on the Kennedys' private number, though.

The Secret Service had the phones wired in the Kennedys' home in such a way that all calls went through agents who monitored them, with the exception of those made to the bedroom's private number. The only people who had that number were a few Kennedys and Janet and Hugh. Lee didn't even have it. Would Jack give it to Marilyn? It seemed unlikely.

As the family began to buzz about the call, it became a topic of discussion. "Jackie called Mrs. A. to ask if Jamie, who was quite the little prankster back then, had played a practical joke on her," recalled Adora Rule. "Mrs. A. said she'd find out, but then asked me, 'How am I supposed to ask my son if he imitated Marilyn Monroe to play a joke on Jackie? That's too much, even for this family.' As far as I know, she didn't ask. I did, however, hear her tell Jackie that Jamie said it wasn't him."

Today, Jamie laughs as he says, "I can assure you, never did I imitate Marilyn Monroe to play a joke on my sister, though that does sound like something my fourteen-year-old self might've done."

When Jackie passed Marilyn's message on to Jack, he said it had to be a crank call given that it had come in on their private line. Why, he asked, would she ever think he'd ever give that number to Marilyn? He told her she was being silly. But was he telling the truth? Had it really been Marilyn?

If Elizabeth Taylor had called, would everyone have been wondering if it were really her? But Marilyn was such an enigma and such a subject of controversy and intrigue, Jackie and those around her simply couldn't believe it was her on the phone.

THE MADISON SQUARE GARDEN
DILEMMA

⬦⬦⬦⬦⬦⬦⬦⬦⬦⬦⬦⬦

I n the spring of 1962, Marilyn Monroe was invited to sing at President Kennedy's forty-fifth birthday celebration at Madison Square Garden on Saturday, May 19. His actual birthday was May 29. Jackie was well aware that Marilyn had been scheduled to perform and couldn't shake the feeling that whatever was being planned would be embarrassing. She didn't want to be present for it. The weekend before the gala, she polled her family as to how to proceed.

Larry Newman and Joseph Paolella, two of Jack's Secret Service agents, were both assigned to Jackie that week when Clint Hill had another duty. They were at Hammersmith with her and the Auchinclosses.

Larry Newman remembered, "Mrs. Kennedy, Mrs. Radziwill, Mr. and Mrs. Auchincloss, and young Janet were lunching on the stone porch. Jamie was away at school. The hot sun was shining and the bay water glistening. It was a gorgeous day. 'If I don't go, how will it look?' Jackie asked everyone at the table. 'How will it look if you *do* go?' was Janet Jr.'s response. Their mother felt Jackie should attend. 'As the First Lady, you can't be driven by emotion,' she told her. 'You must rise above it. You don't need the Kennedys' approval, but you do need their respect.'"

Joseph Paolella said Janet felt that not facing the Marilyn situation head-on would only serve to feed the rumor mill, and then, as she put it, "the lie becomes the truth."

Jackie, Lee, and Janet Jr. walked down a flight of stone steps into the lush sunken garden and then talked things over in front of the large fountain, inside of which swam koi and goldfish. Meanwhile, the Auchinclosses

sat awaiting their return while chatting with the Secret Service. Finally, after a half hour, the sisters walked toward the house. Once they were seated,
Janet turned to Jackie: "So?"

Jackie said, "I'm not going. I think it's just asking for trouble."

Janet wasn't happy about it. "This decision's not noble," she told her.
"It's selfish." Jackie's mind was made up, however. Hugh gave his wife a
look that told her to drop it. Janet then asked if Jackie intended to stay at
Hammersmith with them. No, Jackie said, she thought they'd have a better
time at Glen Ora. "We can have some wonderful family time there, and you
know how much you like that, Mummy," she said.

By this time, Jackie was spending as many as four days a week away
from the White House at Glen Ora, her and Jack's rented country estate
about forty miles and two hours from Washington, outside of Middleburg,
Virginia. Their friend Bill Walton had found it for them, and Jackie started
going as soon as she became First Lady, her first visit barely a week after the
inauguration. At Glen Ora, she enjoyed riding her horses on four hundred
acres, as far away from her White House duties as possible. Jack would usually chopper over on Saturdays and leave the next day.

"Fine," Janet said. "But all of this over Marilyn Monroe? You're the
First Lady. *And* you're a Lee! What is she? A Hollywood actress? Don't be
stupid, Jacqueline."

Jackie shot her a look, shocked but also hurt.

Realizing how much the insult cut, Janet seemed to instantly regret it.
Mother and daughter stared at each other for a tense moment before Jackie
rose and left the table. The moment hung awkwardly and painfully before
Janet, too, excused herself.

"I REFUSED TO RAISE
WEAK DAUGHTERS"

◇◇◇◇◇◇◇◇◇◇◇◇◇◇◇

When Janet Auchincloss would sit in front of the mirror of her vanity and comb her hair, Jackie—at about the age of seven—would stand behind her and just stare.

"What are you looking at?" Janet would ask with a knowing smile.

"You, Mummy," was her daughter's answer. "You're just so pretty."

Janet would just shake her head. "Oh, please, I am not," she'd say.

"But you are," Jackie would insist, "and I want to be just like you, Mummy."

As an older woman, Janet would say the compliment filled her heart, "and there was nothing like it for me in this world."

Janet would apply her expensive French perfume, Dana's Tabu—which smelled of patchouli, carnation, and vanilla—to her wrists, rub them together, and offer them to her daughter. Jackie would take in the scent and never forget it. When she was older, it would be one of her favorite fragrances. "I thought she was elegant and wonderful," Jackie said of her mother, "and strong. I guess that's what I admired most about her, her strength."

"I loved being a mother," Janet Auchincloss said in a 1976 interview. "I agonized over it, though. I was afraid of cocking it up. After my divorce, I was a single mother. I had a nurse named Bertha Newey, and the temptation was to have her do the hard work. I had to force myself, lest I feel like less a mother. As the girls grew, I was critical," Janet admitted, "but it was because they needed to be strong to make it in what female libbers today call a 'man's world'—and how I hate the phrase. They couldn't be weak, though. I'm sorry, but I refused to raise weak daughters. If they took issue with that, and they sometimes did, fine. I knew they'd thank me later." She then added a flourish that even she probably laughed at when she later read it: "I wouldn't dream of telling them what to do, however."

Janet Norton Lee was born on December 3, 1907, in New York City, the daughter of the wildly successful banker and eventually real estate developer James Thomas Aloysius Lee, the son of Irish-Catholic immigrants, known as "Jim."

Jim married Margaret Ann Merritt, Janet's mother, in 1903. Also of Irish descent, Margaret came from hardworking parents; her father was a grocer. She was raised in vastly different circumstances than her new husband in a Lower East Side tenement of New York City. Educated at Sacred Heart, she eventually went on to become a teacher.

Jim, a good friend of President Herbert Hoover's, earned his first $2 million before turning thirty. After his marriage, he lost his money in 1907 when the economy crashed. He got it back, though, and more. In fact, in 1926, *The New York Times* estimated his worth to be over $35 million— about $400 million by today's standards. At around this same time, he spearheaded the building of the Shelton, the first postwar skyscraper and tallest hotel in the world, with its modern art deco design. He'd go on to win many awards for his designs in New York, some of which still today stand tall and proud, such as the art deco nineteen-story 740 Park Avenue, on the west side of Park Avenue in the Lenox Hill neighborhood. Jackie would often credit him with her avid interest in architecture and restoration.

Jim wasn't an easy man. He treated his family with the same manner he did those with whom he did business—coldly and ruthlessly. His wife, Margaret, was emotionally abused by him throughout Janet's childhood. He never allowed her an opinion about anything. It wasn't that he underestimated her intelligence as much as he was certain she had none.

"It was a cold and distant household," Janet's son, Jamie, said. "Basically, my grandparents were separated but living in the same house on different floors. There had been no divorce in the family yet, and they definitely weren't going to be the first."

By her example, Margaret taught Janet and her sisters, Marion and Winifred, how *not* to be in a marriage. They'd watch daily as their father lorded over their mother and, worse yet in their eyes, even *her* mother, their beloved grandmother, Maria Merritt. She lived with the family but had been banished to a guest room because of her thick Irish brogue. Guests were told she was the maid.

As a grown woman, Janet rejected the kind of weakness her mother and grandmother represented in her life, so much so that there'd be no photographs of them in her homes. Not only was she ashamed of them, she was ashamed of the way she, too, had acted. She once recalled that when she was a young girl and a friend came to visit, she parroted her father's behavior by telling that friend of her grandmother, "Oh, don't pay any attention to her. She's just the maid." Janet's son, Jamie, didn't even know what his great-grandmother looked like until he saw a vintage black-and-white photograph of her at the opening of the JFK Library in 1979, when he was thirty-two. Transfixed by it, he put his camera up to the display and took a picture of Maria Merritt for posterity.

Janet also sought to deny her Irish background. Jamie says he didn't even know she had Irish blood in her until, as an adult, he started reading books about his famous sister. "Jackie called one day, and I said, 'Jackie, I've been reading that Mummy is Irish Catholic. I thought she was *English* Catholic and that her family had settled in Maryland and that she was somehow related to the Lees of Virginia.' She said, 'Jamie! Please! *None* of that is true. She's Irish Catholic and has no lineage to the Lees of Maryland. She made all that up years ago.' Here, I had fancied myself the family historian and had it all wrong."

Despite her unhappy homelife, Janet was still a cheerful, smart girl. She studied languages, knew world history, and spoke fluent French thanks to a French governess; she took dance classes at the Plaza Hotel and the Colony Club, attended Miss Spence's private school in New York City, Sweet Briar College in Virginia, and Barnard College of Columbia University in New York, though she didn't graduate from the latter.

Janet was thin and angular, her short brown hair styled simply. Her mother described her as "handsome," which didn't seem like much of a compliment, but that was only because Janet didn't work hard at her appearance or, more accurately, didn't feel the need to. By the time she was twenty, for instance, she never wore makeup, and when her sisters encouraged her to do so, she always rejected the idea. "For what?" she asked. "To get a man?" If all he was interested in was what she looked like and not what she thought or felt or who she was on the inside, he wasn't the man for her.

"HAPPY BIRTHDAY, MR. PRESIDENT"

◇◇◇◇◇◇◇◇◇◇◇◇◇

The weekend in 1962 Marilyn Monroe was scheduled to sing "Happy Birthday" to the president, the First Lady and her family went to Glen Ora. With them were a host of other family members as well as Secret Service agents.

As soon as they got there, Pat Kennedy Lawford—JFK's sister, married to the actor Peter Lawford—called Jackie to tell her that any concern about Marilyn was blown way out of proportion. She explained that what was being planned was nothing more than "a harmless prank." Though one might think it odd under the circumstance, Pat was actually one of Marilyn's best friends. She said she'd never allow her to do anything to embarrass Jackie. According to what Jackie later told a relative, she asked Pat, "Exactly what's going on with her and Jack?" to which Pat responded, "Nothing, Jackie. I swear it."

The Saturday night of the Madison Square Garden show, May 19, the Auchinclosses and some of their staff enjoyed a family cookout. Jackie was in good spirits, though she did stay clear of her mother. She was protected by Joseph Paolella and Larry Newman while Bob Foster and Lynn Meredith watched over John and Caroline. "Maybe some people were whispering about Marilyn, but she wasn't a main topic of discussion," said Larry Newman. "However, there was definitely an anti-Kennedy sentiment." Jackie was overheard telling Hugh, "Our family is family in a way the Kennedys will never understand family.'"

The next day, Sunday, Jackie participated in the Loudoun Hunt Horse Show as planned. Billed as a "surprise entrant," she competed in several classes and took a third-place ribbon with her horse, Ninbrano. A photograph of her and the entire family posing with Ninbrano would hang in Hugh's office for years to come.

Marilyn Monroe's performance at JFK's birthday—"Happy Birthday, Mr. President"—remains, all these years later, iconic. The Jean Louis design she wore, a sheath of flesh-colored soufflé gauze encrusted with 1,200 rhinestone beads and sequins, was sewn onto her body. It was so tight and revealing, it almost appeared as if she were nude. Almost sixty years later, Kim Kardashian wore this gown at the Met Gala in 2022, having leased it from the museum where it had been stored. Though her fashion choice was met with no small amount of dismay by Marilyn aficionados and historical fashion connoisseurs, the controversy definitely brought the dress back into focus for a lot of people. The dress had cost Marilyn $12,000, almost $100,000 in today's money.

While Jack and Bobby were delighted about Marilyn's act, others in the family felt uneasy about it. Ethel called Jackie at Glen Ora to tell her she felt the performance was "very disconcerting." She said she couldn't understand why Jack authorized it. Jackie responded, "The attorney general is the troublemaker here. Not the president." She said it was Bobby she was most annoyed with, not her husband.

More than sixty years later, what are we to make of this story? Had Jackie overreacted?

Marilyn's breathless performance lasted all of two minutes. Viewing it today, it seems more self-parody than erotic. But Jackie didn't know what to expect. With Marilyn—always as unpredictable as she was gorgeous—anything was possible. In hindsight, the First Lady could probably have just been seated next to the president, with a bemused expression playing on her face, and the world would have dismissed it as harmless fun. It's worth noting that her absence really didn't raise many eyebrows. Times are different now. If a major birthday celebration for the president was planned today at Madison Square Garden with stars the caliber of Marilyn performing, and the First Lady decided not to attend, it would generate major headlines. In 1962, however, the media just took Jackie Kennedy at her word that she had other plans.

◇◇◇◇◇◇◇◇◇◇◇◇◇◇◇◇◇◇

Marilyn Monroe died on Saturday night, August 4, 1962, of an overdose at the age of just thirty-six. Jackie was at Hyannis Port when

Letitia Baldrige called with the news on Sunday morning when Marilyn's body was found.

Certainly, President Kennedy had his hands full with racial tensions and violence escalating in American cities, especially in the South. Globally, there was great concern about the resumption of atmospheric testing of nuclear weapons. Tensions with the Soviet Union continued to frighten Americans. But Marilyn's death was still front-page news.

Jackie made a statement that was less than fulsome: "She will go on eternally."

FEELING OF DREAD

◇◇◇◇◇◇◇◇◇◇◇◇◇◇

Jackie bundled herself up in a warm, beige raincoat and wrapped a scarf around her hair. "Where are you going, dear?" Rose Kennedy asked. Jackie said she needed time alone. "Be careful," Rose told her. "Don't trip." She suggested maybe someone should go with her. "Then, I wouldn't be alone, Grandma, would I?" Jackie asked with a smile.

As the Kennedys' family photographer Jacques Lowe documented every moment, Jackie walked out onto the veranda of the Big House, down its wooden stairs, and out onto the expansive, green lawn. She passed a few Kennedys and friends as they played football. Ethel smiled at her. "Want some company?" she asked. No, Jackie said, she was fine. Ethel then leaped into the air to catch the football. Jackie had to laugh; no one was more athletic than her sister-in-law.

The breeze coming in from the Nantucket Sound was crisp and bracing. As Jackie walked along, she wrapped her arms around herself to stay warm. Turning around, she saw that she was being followed by Clint Hill, her Secret Service agent, in his dark business suit with a black tie. He looked hopelessly incongruous on the beach.

Hearing the chopping sounds of a helicopter above her, Jackie stopped and tilted her head back. Smiling to herself, she shook her head in resignation as if asking herself, *Whose life is this, anyway?*

"We going to Italy, Mrs. Kennedy?" he asked.

"No," she said. "I've decided against it."

He nodded. "I think you'll change your mind," he said with a smile.

"Nope," she said as she kept walking.

Jackie had a trip planned to Ravello, Italy, with her sister, Lee. It was described by the White House as a "private vacation." The Radziwills had rented a large, sixteenth-century villa called Villa Episcopio (the house of the bishop) from the Duca Riccardo di Sangro, one of the founders of the Corviglia Club at St. Moritz. The villa was situated high atop a cliff about twenty-five miles south of Naples, near Amalfi in the Gulf of Salerno. It had once been inhabited by the last king of Italy, Victor Emmanuel III, and his wife, Elena. Stas loved the place, having once stayed there with his first wife, Grace, in 1955.

The sisters planned to stay in Ravello for two weeks, after which Jackie would then spend the rest of the summer with the Auchinclosses in New-port. The problem for Jackie was that after Marilyn's death, she was in no mood for a vacation. She couldn't shake a feeling of dread, especially given that disturbing telephone call, which may or may not have been Marilyn. "There's a big difference between wanting to die and running out of reasons to live," she told one friend. She also didn't want to be with Jack. She wanted to skip Ravello and go straight to Hammersmith Farm and spend the sum-mer with Janet and Hugh.

When Jackie called Lee early on the morning of Tuesday, August 7, to cancel, Lee was already at Villa Episcopio getting things ready and beside herself. "She was frantic," is how Annunziata Lisi, Lee's friend who lived in Ravello and helped her organize the trip, recalled, "mostly because of Onassis." When he pushed for an invite to Ravello, Lee had no choice but to discourage him because Stas and the children were going. Feeling over-whelmed, she telephoned Annunziata in tears.

"By the time Lee called me, Marilyn's death was a big story," recalled Annunziata. "Lee said Jackie didn't want to leave the States. She just wanted to go back to her country home in Virginia. She called back a half hour later and, this time, said John-John was coming down with the flu and that Jackie was definitely canceling. 'But she needs this trip, and so do I,' she told me, 'so I'm going to make it happen. I'll convince her, don't worry.'"

Lee somehow did manage to change Jackie's mind.

The next morning, Wednesday, August 8, Jackie informed Clint Hill that she was, indeed, going to Italy after all and leaving that night. He was used to these last-minute decisions and had already planned the trip with advance agents just in case.

Hours later, Jackie wrote Joseph Kennedy a note. "You were taking a nap when I left," she wrote. She promised to see him as soon as she returned, "& bring you marvelous presents." She enclosed a picture of her, Jack, Caroline, and John and asked him to put it "right by your favorite chair where Eunice will see it—& nail it down so she can't take it away and put Timmy there, instead." (Timmy was Eunice and Sarge's three-year-old, their youngest at the time.) She signed it, "I love you—Jackie."

Jackie, Caroline, Clint Hill, and Jackie's personal assistant, Providencia (Provi) Paredes left Idlewild Airport in New York on a Pan American World Airways red-eye for Rome. (The ailing John stayed behind with Jackie's mother.) The four sat in first class, reserving all the seats in that section so that Jackie wouldn't be bothered. They landed in Rome the next morning and then took a private plane to Salerno, where they met Lee, Stas, and their children. Another of Jackie's agents, Paul Rundle, was there to greet them. They all then drove the ten miles to Ravello.

THE TROUBLE WITH LEE

E arly one morning as the sun rose, Lee Radziwill and Annunziata Lisi stood on one of the balconies of the grand Villa Episcopio, chiseled into a rocky hillside eleven hundred feet above the Mediterranean with spectacular views of the Amalfi coast. As they gazed down to the many turrets and ancient stone landings, and then even farther below to a small strip of beach, they spotted a woman facing the rolling ocean. She wore a white, diaphanous cover-up over a scarlet bathing suit, her dark hair wrapped in an elegant white scarf. Taking in the salty air and crisp breeze, she seemed contented. Noticing three men in shorts and T-shirts approaching, she turned and extended her hand in a motion that was clear: "Back up." Lee smiled and said, "Jackie has a love-hate relationship with those guys."

Just moments earlier, Lee and Annunziata had made a game of trying to spot Secret Service agents hiding on the property. "There's one," Annunziata said, "and there's another. And yet another." Out in the distance, two police boats patrolled the coast. "Does all the attention your sister gets bother you?" she asked Lee.

"I'm used to being overlooked," was Lee's unsmiling answer.

"How did she get down there?" Annunziata asked as she watched Jackie on the beach. It seemed impossible to get from the villa to the sandy landing. If there were stairs, they'd have to be old, crumbled, and dangerous. "I'd kill myself trying," Lee said. "Jackie's the athletic one. You'd have to carry me on your back." As she stared down at her sister, she sighed. "That's so like her to be down there by herself with just the Secret Service. My poor sister. She has it all, but thinks she has nothing."

Annunziata recalled, "Lee said a misconception about her and Jackie was that people thought she [Lee] was the mixed-up one. In fact, she said, Jackie was the more confused. 'I accept who I am *not*,' Lee said, 'whereas Jackie cannot accept who she is. She just thinks she's being used by Jack. I'd rather be used than not needed at all.'"

As if her life were not complicated enough, Lee revealed to Annunziata that she'd just been released from a Swiss clinic—which she called "the nervous hospital"—for treatment of the eating disorder anorexia nervosa.

Terrance Landow, a friend of Lee's from England, recalled, "She told me she stopped eating around the time she arrived at Jackie's alma mater, Farmington, in 1947, at fourteen, the year Jackie graduated. She couldn't compete with the impression Jackie had made there and felt out of control of everything. 'Now, I get to control when I eat and when I don't eat,' she told me, 'which is the only thing I can control.' Classic anorexic mindset. She said Onassis's sister Artemis had told her she was too fat—which was so untrue!—and her solution was for Lee to sit and stare at her plate of food for five minutes before eating. 'Then,' she said, 'you'll eat much less.' Lee said, 'She's nuts. I need to eat more, not less.' I once confronted Jackie and said, 'You know your sister is anorexic, right?' She said, 'Don't be silly. Lee eats when she feels like it, and she never feels like it.' She added that Oleg [Cassini] told her she couldn't even gain five pounds or she wouldn't fit into her wardrobe and everything would then have to be refitted. 'So, I never eat either,' she said.

"When I asked if Jackie knew she'd been in the clinic," recalled Annunziata, "she said, 'No, and I'm not telling her.' I asked why, and she said, 'Because I don't need her or Mummy holding that over my head for the rest of my life. Only Stas knows,' she said, 'and I intend to keep it that way.' She made me promise not to say anything. As it happened, Jackie was in no mood to hear this kind of news, anyway."

"HOPE IS THE LAST THING TO DIE"

◇◇◇◇◇◇◇◇◇◇◇◇

Throughout the next two weeks, Annunziata Lisi found Jackie Kennedy to be, as she put it, "sort of a downer, very melancholy. Before I met her, I thought she'd just radiate charisma. She did not. She was just blue.

"One evening we went sailing on Gianni Agnelli's yacht, the *Agneta*. [Gianni Agnelli was an Italian industrialist whose grandfather founded the Fiat corporation. In four years, Agnelli would become its chairman.] It was Gianni, his wife, Marella, the legendary photographer Benno Graziani—who was a very good friend of the Kennedys—and his wife, Nicole, me, and several other friends, along with Lee and Stas and a little entourage Stas had with him. We were on the Tyrrhenian Sea on our way to Capri where we were to have dinner with the designer Princess Irene Galitzine and her husband, Silvio Medici de' Menezes.

"After dinner, Princess Irene wanted to return to the villa. We all got back on the *Agneta*. Gianni's chef prepared spaghetti and piccata, but since we'd all had such a big dinner, no one touched it. Instead, we sipped negronis—Campari with sweet vermouth garnished with a slice of orange. At one point, everyone started talking about Marilyn's death and how tragic it was while Jackie smoked and Lee looked at her, worried. Finally, Jackie said, 'Isn't it tragic enough without our gossiping about it under the stars?' which shut everyone up. Gianni raised his glass and said, '*La speranza è l'ultima a morire.*' Jackie asked, 'What does that mean, Gianni?' He answered, 'Hope is the last thing to die.' We all then repeated it: *La speranza è l'ultima a morire.*"

Annunziata also recalled a telling conversation she, Nicole, and Lee had with Jackie the next day while baking under the hot sun. In the distance could be seen photographers, snapping away. Occasionally, their cries of "Jackie! Jackie! Look over here!" could be heard above the din of ocean waves crashing into rocks. Through it all, Jackie was pensive, gazing up at the blue sky. She turned to Nicole and asked, "Do you and Benno fight?" Nicole said they argued on occasion, but she wouldn't use the word "fight."

She asked, "What about you and Jack?"

Jackie thought it over and said, "I wouldn't think to fight with him because, in our marriage, he's always right."

Lee put down her book and looked at Jackie with bewilderment. "He's *not* always right," Lee exclaimed. "No man is always right, Jackie. What's wrong with you? That's not how we were raised."

Jackie shook her head. "Well," she said, "Jack is."

Obviously, Jackie was anything but a feminist. It was an ironic turn of events considering that when she was seventeen and graduated from Farmington in 1947, under "Ambition" in her yearbook entry, she wrote: "Never to be a housewife." Twelve years later, in 1964, in her oral history, she would say, "Someone [during an interview] asked, 'Where do you get your opinions?' And I said, 'I get all my opinions from my husband.' Which is true. How could I have any political opinions? His were going to be the best and I could never conceive of not voting for whoever my husband was for. I mean, it was really a rather terribly Victorian or Asiatic relationship we had, which I think's the best."

If a ten-page letter Jackie wrote to Jack from Ravello is any indication, she was content in what she saw as her role as his wife. While she was conflicted about her marriage when she left the States, once she had time to think about things, she, apparently, began to long for her husband. She began the letter writing, "Dearest Jack," and wrote, in part, "I miss you very much, which is nice though it is also a bit sad—because it is always best to leave someone when you are happy & this was such a lovely summer." Obviously feeling nostalgic and maybe even romanticizing things a bit, she wrote that she felt "lucky" to miss Jack because, in her view, their marriage was more special than any other she had known. "I know I exaggerate everything," she wrote, "but I feel sorry for everyone else who is married." She added, "I am having something you can never have, the absence of tension—no newspapers every day to make me mad. I wish so much I could give you that—I never realized till I got to another country how the tension is—But

I can't give you that. So I give you every day while I think of you—the only thing I have to give & I hope it matters to you."

Gilbert "Benno" Graziani, along with his wife, Nicole, remained with Jackie for the Ravello vacation. He had known her since her days at the *Washington Times-Herald*. He recalled in 2009, "Jackie's feelings for her husband never abated despite everything she knew or thought she knew about his other life. She still loved him. He felt the same.

"The president attempted to call her several times in Ravello and was frustrated by the complications caused by the small town's switchboard," said Graziani. "He did manage to reach her several times in the middle of the night. Their marriage was not black and white. It was complicated. Like most relationships, it had many shades of gray and could only truly be understood by the two people in it."

Jackie spent the remainder of the two weeks in Ravello gathering her strength to go back to her husband and resume her duties in the United States as its First Lady. She had been emotionally bowed by all that had happened, but not beaten. She and Lee had such a relaxing time, in fact, they decided to extend their vacation by almost two weeks. It actually turned out to be a very happy time for them. "These magical days drifted serenely from one to the next," Lee recalled. "Perhaps part of what made one enjoy them so deeply was knowing how special and carefree they were." In fact, Lee, in her eponymous book of photographs of her life and times, recalled their time in Ravello as "the happiest summer of my life."

On the final day of their vacation, Jackie and Lee strolled on the beach, arm in arm. They ambled up a steep sand dune until reaching a huge rock against which waves crashed, spraying water all over them. Jackie turned and asked one of the ever-present Secret Service agents for a penknife. He searched his airline travel bag but came up empty. However, Lee noticed a shard of glass on the sand. Jackie picked it up, much to the consternation of the agent, who worried she'd cut herself. She then began to carve into the rock, working on it for about five minutes. When she finished, she, Lee, and the agent stood back and stared at it, Lee resting her head on Jackie's shoulder.

It said: "JLB & CLB x JVB," honoring, forever, the man who'd meant the world to Jackie Lee Bouvier and Caroline Lee Bouvier—their beloved father, Jack Vernou Bouvier.

"BLACK JACK"

∗∗∗∗∗∗∗∗∗∗∗∗∗∗

John Vernou Bouvier III—better known as Jack, or "Black Jack" because of his perpetual tan—was born in 1891 in East Hampton, New York. His father, John Bouvier Jr., would later fashion his own version of Bouvier history in a self-published book called *Our Forebears* in 1940. In it, he falsely claimed that the Bouviers were nobles related to French patriots and aristocrats. Janet would much later tell the Kennedys that the Bouviers were descended from French aristocracy; she even repeated this fiction in the newspaper's engagement announcement. In fact, Jackie was only one-eighth French, three-eighths English, and half Irish, which is what she mostly had in common with the Kennedys.

"The truth," Jack Bouvier used to say, "has never done anyone a bit of good." In his case, though, it really wasn't that bad. His great-grandfather Michel Bouvier was a master carpenter and cabinetmaker from the South of France who settled in Philadelphia in 1815 after fighting in the Napoleonic Wars. In addition to his woodwork, he eventually began a business distributing firewood and, to support that venture, went into real estate. It was in that business that he had exceedingly good fortune, making millions.

When Michel died, he left much of his fortune to his son, grandson John Vernou Bouvier, and great-grandson John Jr. John Jr. then married Maude Frances Sargeant and had five children, of whom John Vernou Bouvier III—Jackie's father, Jack—was the oldest.

Jack Bouvier graduated from Yale in 1914 and went on to work as a stockbroker at his father and uncle's firm. He had always been a real ladies' man, someone who could walk into a room and own it. Good-looking with piercing brown eyes and the same head of wavy black hair as his father, he also had had his manner, gregarious and outgoing. In fact, he was even more vital and more ambitious. Always dressed in the finest clothes, he was intelligent and motivated to have the best of the best.

Jack's father—known by the family as "the Major"—owned a beautiful estate called Lasata ("place of peace" in a Native American language) on Further Lane in East Hampton. It was a meeting place for Bouviers of many generations and walks of life, and Jack made sure Jackie enjoyed many summers of nature and horseback riding there.

It was a spring evening in 1927 when Jack first laid eyes on Janet Lee. He was standing in a corner of a club in East Hampton called the Maidstone, checking out the pretty girls as they walked by while trying to decide which one he'd go home with that night. He spotted one young lady sitting alone at a table, nursing a soft drink. Their eyes met and, to hear him tell it years later, "That was it. I was a goner."

Though she could appear remote and chilly, once she was in conversation with him, Jack realized that Janet was full of charisma. She said she loved riding horses, and when she talked about doing so, her eyes lit up. When she talked about her family, it wasn't in the most glowing terms, but her candor intrigued him. He really was captivated.

After a few dates, Janet thought Jack was upwardly mobile, a man who could make things happen in his life. He was clever, driven, and determined to be a success, or so she thought. In that respect, he reminded her of her father except, unlike Jim, he wasn't a big brute. He had a soft side, and Janet felt there was no way he'd ever treat her the way her father had treated her mother and grandmother.

They had sex right away. He was surprised because she seemed, at first blush, to be so buttoned-up and conservative. After having his way with her, he wasn't even sure she'd been a virgin. She seemed to have experience and was fearless, as if she couldn't get enough of him. In a matter of weeks, it turned into love for them, and they wanted to marry. When Jack told his father about it, his response was less than enthusiastic. He felt his son could do a lot better. However, after asking around about Janet's family, he learned they were wealthy. It was all her father's money, though, and he was anything but generous.

Janet's father was even less enthused about Jack Bouvier. That was surprising to Janet because, by this time, Jack was making about $100,000 a year, good money for the times, about $1.5 million today. The Bouviers were known in Manhattan for their big lifestyle. The problem was that when James T. Lee looked into Jack's background, all he could find was, as Jack's nephew John Davis put it, "debt, debt, and more debt. His wealth was an illusion. Sometimes, he had money, sometimes he didn't. He'd profit from a good deal, then he'd lose more because of a bad one."

When Jim forbade the wedding, Janet's mother suggested that she move forward without his blessing. She wanted her to get out of the house as soon as possible. Janet wasn't sure. Could she make it on her own? She was just twenty, and all she knew was life with her family, as mixed up and ruined as it was. She knew she wanted out; she just didn't know how to do it.

It was Jack who gave her courage. "Don't become your mother," he said, "and, for God's sake, don't become your grandmother." He told her she was strong, self-reliant, and needed to break out on her own and be her own woman. No one had ever said anything empowering to her before, and it resonated with her. Jack Bouvier was her champion, and that was something she'd never forget. Janet's father had no choice but to accept her decision.

After they were married on July 7, 1928, in East Hampton, Jack and Janet eventually moved into a spacious eleven-room suite at 740 Park Avenue, two blocks away from Central Park, built and owned by Janet's father. Not only had Jim reluctantly agreed to the marriage, he even gave the newlyweds a place to live—rent-free!

Janet was twenty-one when she gave birth to eight-pound Jacqueline Lee Bouvier, "Jackie," on July 28, 1929, in Southampton Hospital, Long Island. Three and a half years later, she gave birth to Caroline Lee, "Lee," named after her Bouvier great-grandmother, Caroline Maslin Ewing.

Janet explained that she gave both daughters her maiden name of Lee because she wanted them to always remember who they were, no matter whom they one day married. "I wished for them to be Lees as much as Bouviers," she said. Janet's only son, Jamie, also carries the middle name of "Lee."

In these early days, Jack Bouvier doted on his daughters. Even with money tight after the crash of '29, he still managed to make, lose, and then once again make a fortune. As the quarterly dividend checks kept coming his way, his girls were the pampered beneficiaries. They loved tooling about with their father in the back seats of his custom-built, maroon Stutz town car as they were chauffeured about town. On weekends, he would take them out in his Lincoln Zephyr and, according to his niece Kathleen Bouvier, bask in "the 'oohs' and 'aahs' from onlookers as they sped by and Jack's princesses alternated from one side to the other."

"Nothing could be more fun than to be Jack Bouvier's daughter," Kathleen recalled. "His love was so absolute, he went to any expense to please them. There was nothing he wouldn't do to make their lives interesting and special. Ignorant of the breadlines or the multitudes muttering, 'Brother, can you spare a dime?' Jackie and Lee spent indolent days bicycling, swimming, horseback riding, motoring, and playing with many friends and infinite cousins. Almost daily, there was somebody's birthday party or other little fête calling for a new pink taffeta dress or a new pair of glistening patent-leather Mary Janes. Meanwhile, Jack and Janet were the most handsome couple around town—East Hampton or New York. They were in demand at all social functions and talked about in society columns."

Of course, Jack loved Lee, but it was really Jackie who was the light of his life. "My God, how he idolized her," said John Davis in a letter in September 1998, "and Jackie thought the world of him, too. She loved that he always wanted to have the best of everything—the best clothes, the best cars, the best women. It's one of the reasons she'd feel that she, too, deserved the best life had to offer. 'Only the best for Jacks,' her father would say. He doted on her to the exclusion of everyone else, including his other daughter and his wife.

"Once he had Janet Lee for himself, though," John continued, "Jack let down his guard and revealed his true self. Whereas he'd hidden his drinking from her, he no longer cared what she thought of it, and he drank a lot. She'd believed he was motivated, someone who couldn't wait to roar into the day. However, she soon realized he was just plain lazy. Sometimes he made money, sometimes he didn't, and he was fine either way."

The biggest issue was Jack's infidelity. Janet thought he would be faithful. She couldn't have been more wrong. Unfortunately, the passion she had for him didn't dull despite his failings. She was hooked. Every time they separated, they ended up back together. However, any reunions they had, and there were many, would always be short-lived and end painfully for Janet. It would be years before she'd verbalize it, but in 1967, she'd admit, "I got lost in my marriage to Jackie's father."

For Jackie, not only did having an unfaithful father make her skittish about one day confronting her own cheating husbands, it also made her resolve to never be unfaithful herself. Throughout her life, she'd stick to that mandate except for a period of about a year and a half during her marriage to Aristotle Onassis, as we will see. For Lee, it was just the opposite: her father's behavior gave her license to do the same; she'd be unfaithful to both her husbands, and without a hint of remorse.

By the beginning of 1936, when Jackie was about seven, Janet had enough of Jack Bouvier and wanted out of the marriage. The separation became official late in the year. He ended up paying $1,000 a month in child support for his two daughters, a sizable amount—about $17,000 in today's money. Janet continued to live in her father's lavish Park Avenue duplex rent-free for a time before moving to a new home at 1 Gracie Square. Jack moved into a suite at the Westbury Hotel. Eventually, he could no longer afford it and ended up moving to a small apartment on 125 East Seventy-Fourth Street, which, at least, had a guest room for Jackie and Lee.

Jack's money problems continued as he spent more than he made, and poor investments and a gambling habit ate up his savings. Soon, he had to give up his cars and the chauffeur, too. It was as if he was losing everything as his life underwent seismic changes. "But all of it was at his own hands," said Kathleen Bouvier, "that he just couldn't seem to see it." After his beloved mother, Maude, died, Jack seemed to lose his spirit and enthusiasm for life.

Janet was still drawn to Jack, however, especially when he was at his most vulnerable following his mother's death. For the next three years, she'd continue to give herself to him. However, it was confusing for her, as it was for her daughters, to have him coming and going from their lives. It made Janet feel weak. Much to her consternation, it made her feel like her mother. Unlike Margaret, though, Janet would actually do something about her situation. By the end of 1939, her divorce from Jack Bouvier was final, and as she recalled years later, "Thank God I got out when I did."

GREAT MEN AND THEIR FLAWS

◇◇◇◇◇◇◇◇◇◇◇◇◇

By August 24, 1962, Jackie and Caroline had been in Italy for a little more than two weeks. Young John was with Janet at Hammersmith Farm being cared for by her and their nanny, Maud Shaw. On that morning, JFK telephoned to ask if he could also spend a few days in Newport. Janet welcomed him, of course, but was a little torn.

Janet continued to have a complex relationship with Jack Kennedy. Back in the 1950s after her daughter lost Arabella, she didn't want anything to do with him. However, when Jackie became pregnant with Caroline, she told her mother they needed to get past their anger. She reasoned that as long as Jack wasn't welcome in the Auchinclosses' home, Janet would never be able to see her grandchild whenever she wished. "If you're going to pit Kennedys against Auchinclosses," she warned her, "who do you think will win?" Janet knew she had no choice but to try to make peace with her son-in-law. Making things even more complicated, now he was president. Her son, Jamie, recalled, "The phone would ring and I'd pick it up, and it would be the White House switchboard saying, 'Is Mrs. Auchincloss available? The president's on the line,' I'd call out to my mother, 'The president's calling,' and then I'd wait for her to get on the line. I'd hear him say, 'Hello, Mummy,' and she'd just melt and coo, 'Oh my, *Mr. President.*' Maybe she wanted to be mad at him, but how could she?"

Hugh, too, was conflicted. He'd always wished he could sit down with Jack and talk, "man to man," about Jackie. He agreed, however, with Janet that marital discord was better left unaddressed by outsiders.

The president's few days at Hammersmith were happy, as was always the case when he visited. The Auchinclosses thoroughly enjoyed him. He conducted some official business—he signed two bills, one for the Peace Corps and another to approve a memorial for the USS *Arizona* at Pearl Harbor—played golf with Hugh, went sailing with the family on Narragansett Bay, and enjoyed time with them at Bailey's Beach. Before he departed, he presented Hugh with a gift: the president's flag that had flown at Hammersmith, along with the American flag during his first stay there as president in 1961. The flag would later be displayed in the entry way with the inscription: "The President's Flag Flown at Hammersmith Farm, Newport, Rhode Island, Presented to Hugh Dudley Auchincloss by John Fitzgerald Kennedy, President of the United States—1961."

Yusha and Jack had a bit of a sentimental moment. "Yusha tried to be close to JFK, but the knowledge of his life outside his marriage tormented him even more than everyone else because of his feelings for Jackie," said his friend Robert Westover. "One day, Yusha and Jack were standing in the Deck Room looking out at Narragansett Bay. Jack pointed and said, 'See, out there? That's where I trained on the PT-109. I remember being on the boat and seeing this grand house in the distance, and I thought, *Why, that's got to be the most beautiful place in the whole world.* So, to be standing here with you now is a real honor. Being a part of your family,' he said, 'has been the greatest honor of my life.' Yusha teared up. What a thing to say, considering this man was the leader of the free world. 'We've always been honored to have you,' Yusha said, 'Mr. President.'"

According to Jack Weston—son of Hugh's assistant at Auchincloss, Parker & Redpath, Clark Weston—a week after JFK's visit, his father and Hugh discussed the president over cigars and brandies. Hugh said Jack was the most gracious man he'd ever known. However, he was still perplexed by his personal life. In response, Clark offered Hugh a maxim from the French philosopher François de La Rochefoucauld: "None but great men are capable of having great flaws," to which Hugh offered one of his own from the same thinker: "If we had no faults, we should not take so much pleasure in noting those of others."

The next day, the president was back in Newport to greet Jackie and Caroline upon their return from Italy. Jackie seemed to glow, totally relaxed after her time away. "I missed you so much," she was overheard telling Jack. "Did you miss me?" He smiled and said, "I missed you so much, Jackie."

There was then an uncomfortable moment when Hugh happily strode up to Jack, slapped him on the back, and asked, "How are you, Jack? Welcome home." Surprised, Jackie turned to Hugh and said, "It's Mr. President, Uncle Hughdie." Hugh looked mortified.

Of course, Hugh knew that in public the family always referred to him as "Mr. President." Privately, it was "Jack." It had just been a slip of the tongue. For Jackie to bring it to his attention in front of everyone seemed unnecessary. Janet held her tongue, but later, at Hammersmith, she scolded her daughter, "You do not correct your uncle Hughdie in public," she said, "I don't care if you're the First Lady of the United States or the Queen of England." Jackie knew she was right. When she apologized to Hugh, he, of course, accepted it.

Now, the plan was for Jackie, Caroline, and John to stay at Hammersmith Farm into September and then through October, with Jack coming and going as his schedule permitted.

In mid-September, the America's Cup yacht races were held in Narragansett Bay. The oldest competition in international sports, the America's Cup—hosted in Newport from 1930 to 1983—is a series of contests between whichever yacht club won the previous year and a new challenger. In 1962, the New York Yacht Club was defending its title against Australia. On some days, the family would watch the competition while aboard the USS *Joseph P. Kennedy Jr.*—a destroyer named after Jack's deceased older brother. On other days, they'd find themselves on Jack's new yawl, *Manitou*. That season, JFK saw two races and part of a third; Jackie saw four.

There was also a great deal of activity at Hammersmith Farm relating to the races, including a reception for crew members and a black-tie dinner for the competitors on September 14. Jackie, along with Janet, Lee, and Janet Jr., hosted the second event. There was also a dinner at the Breakers hosted by Sir Howard Beale, the Australian ambassador, cohosted by Jackie and Janet.

On September 11, Jackie unveiled a model of the proposed $3 million National Cultural Center in Washington. She then formally announced that her mother was in charge of raising the $3 million, though Janet had already begun that fundraising. Janet would spend the next couple of years devoted to the center, which would eventually become the John F. Kennedy Center for the Performing Arts.

SISTERLY CONCERN

◇◇◇◇◇◇◇◇◇◇◇◇◇◇◇

One of Jackie's private concerns during late summer of 1962 had to do with the closeness that had developed between her half sister, Janet Jr.—who was nicknamed "Ja-Je" for Janet Jennings—and a young man named John Kerry, the same John Kerry who'd go on to become a district attorney, lieutenant governor, senator, presidential candidate, and secretary of state.

By September 1962, John Kerry was about to turn nineteen; Janet had recently turned seventeen. Kerry—whose father was a career diplomat stationed in Norway—attended St. Paul's School in Concord, New Hampshire. Interested in Democratic politics, he was also a volunteer for Ted Kennedy's senatorial campaign. Jamie Auchincloss, who also campaigned for Ted, thought John should meet his brother-in-law, the president. "I thought they'd hit it off," Jamie said, "Also, Kerry's initials being *JFK*—John Forbes Kerry—was a coincidence too good to pass up. I asked Jackie to invite him to the America's Cup races. When he arrived at Hammersmith, he signed the guest book: 'John F. Kerry, Washington, D.C. Guest of JLA [James Lee Auchincloss]. No further comment.'" Later that day, we were all out on the yacht together for the World Cup races. There are some great pictures of John Kerry, JFK, and Jackie together that day," said Jamie, "along with me and Janet Jr. and our parents."

"I sat in the cockpit, eating lunch with the president, soaking in the conversation about politics, issues and the world," John Kerry recalled in an email of his time out on the yacht with the Kennedys and Auchinclosses. "The President clearly reveled in the peacefulness of the moment. He lay in the sun, smoked a cigar and occasionally sat on the foredeck alone, thinking about God knows what. Later that day I enjoyed dinner with the family. Family was everything to the Auchinclosses, so meal time was lively with everyone telling stories and being very entertaining. Afterward, we sat in the drawing room with the stereo blasting. There was a lot of dancing, as always at Hammersmith, with Jamie and Janet [Jr.] showing the old folks how to do the Twist and the Loco-motion. Mrs. Auchincloss was a very good dancer, which always surprised people. She and Jackie had a little choreographed routine. It was a lot of fun watching them. They totally enjoyed each other."

At this time, while at St. Paul's, John also had a band called the Electras, in which he played bass. Andrew Gagarin, John's friend and the maraca player for the band, recalled, "The whole idea behind the band was to meet more babes. At that time, life wasn't worth living without a girlfriend, so we spent every waking moment of our lives looking for ways to meet girls." (The Electras' album is thought to be the first rock album ever recorded by a serious candidate for the Oval Office—Kerry ran against George W. Bush in 2004. It's available today on streaming services.)

Jackie thought Janet Jr. was too young to be involved in a serious relationship, and she seemed to be heading in that direction with John. She also wasn't thrilled with the idea of her becoming involved with a rock and roll musician, though Janet Jr. insisted John wasn't serious about the band. He was more interested in politics, she said. That didn't make Jackie feel any better. "Please don't get involved with a politician," she told her sister. "You'll live to regret it."

It was Janet Jr.'s idea that they sell copies of the Electras' album during the September 14 gala for the World Cup competitors at Hammersmith. She wanted to help the band make some money. Jackie told her it was out of the question. It wasn't a flea market, she told her. It was a dignified event at which the president and First Lady would be in attendance.

By this time, Janet Jr. had gotten used to the fact that having a famous sister often left her to her own devices. "When your sister is First Lady," she said at the time, "it's easy to get lost in the family."

She tried to distinguish herself, even in small ways. For instance, she often didn't call her mother "Mummy," like her siblings. For her, it was usually "Mother." Of her daughter, Janet recalled in her oral history, "Janet was unhappy; she lacked self-confidence at that time because she was a little bit overweight and self-conscious. I will always remember what the President said to her one day on the terrace outside of the house they had in Hyannis Port when we were having lunch. He said, 'You know, Janet, someday soon you're going to be one of the prettiest people there are.' He was always too kind to make comparisons. He never would have said, 'You'll be prettier than Jackie or Lee.' He was tactful; he never would compare."

There was also quite an age gap between Janet Jr. and her half sisters. In 1962, Jackie was thirty-three, Lee twenty-nine, and Janet Jr. seventeen. "That was a big age difference," said Jamie, who was two years younger than his sister, "but when we were kids, Jackie and Lee looked out for us. We had so many moments at Hammersmith and Merrywood as a family, more than I can ever remember—TV nights, Christmases, birthdays . . . the showing of home movies. They were our big sisters, and we were crazy about them."

JACKIE'S INTERVENTION

✧✧✧✧✧✧✧✧✧

Janet Jennings Auchincloss looked lovely on the occasion of the September 14 gala at Hammersmith for competitors of the World Cup. According to photographs taken on the day, she wore a cream-colored gown with white bugle beads and shoestring straps. She told the reporter for the Associated Press that Lee had sent the dress from Italy as a birthday gift.

On this night, Janet Jr. was distracted, her eyes filling up every time she noticed John Kerry dancing with someone else. Finally, she'd had enough and confronted him. It got loud. The president winced and shot Jackie a look. She made a beeline for her sister. Holding up her hand to silence her, she took her by the elbow into the main house, and then up to one of the third-floor guest rooms. A year later, Janet would recall to her Sarah Lawrence roommate Stella Brenton what happened next.

"Jackie said she didn't care what was going on, it was inappropriate for Janet to become emotional in front of company," said Stella. "She said, 'Get it out of your system right now.' With that, Janet dissolved into tears."

As Janet cried, Jackie didn't console her. Instead, she turned her back, went to the window, and gazed down at the partygoers. Meanwhile, Janet continued to sob. Perhaps Jackie wanted to give her sister the dignity of a somewhat private breakdown, or perhaps she just didn't know how to deal with her emotional reaction. After about five minutes and with her back still turned, she asked Janet, "Are you finished?" Composing herself, the teenager said she felt better, and only then did Jackie turn around.

After Jackie asked Janet to explain, Janet blurted out that she and John were having sex. In fact, they'd just been intimate the night before, therefore his dancing with someone else was hurtful. Jackie was surprised. She asked if their parents knew, and of course they didn't. Had John pressured her? No, she said. He lavished her with attention, she said, always sending cards and flowers and writing poems for her. "It's as if he's campaigning for me," she said.

"Typical politician," was Jackie's response. She told Janet she wanted her to stop immediately and wait until she was married.

However, Jackie herself had not waited. Back in 1951, when she was twenty-two and in France with Lee, she slept with twenty-six-year-old John P. Marquand Jr., the handsome son of the novelist John P. Marquand who would also go on to become a successful writer (*The Second Happiest Day*), using the name John Phillips.

It was a quick encounter in an elevator, which certainly said a great deal about Jackie's daring at the time. She didn't feel she should have to wait until she was married to have sex. It also said a lot about Lee that she couldn't wait to tell Mummy about it to win favor with her.

Jack Bouvier hadn't been convinced that Janet Sr. was a virgin when they were intimate prior to their marriage. She and Jack enjoyed a robust sex life even after they were divorced, which helps to explain what kept Janet hooked on him. But when she heard about Jackie's elevator encounter, she was disappointed. Quick sex in an elevator? She wanted something different for her daughters; she wanted it to mean something, It may have been a little hypocritical for Jackie to advise her half sister to wait for marriage, but she must have felt it was the soundest—and safest—advice she could give her. She just wanted her to be older and more experienced before she started having sex. "I want you to promise me you will wait," she insisted. Janet said she couldn't make that promise. The discussion couldn't continue, though, not with a party going on downstairs.

In this guest room, there was a writing table with pale blue stationery on it, as well as envelopes, postcards (with pictures of Hammersmith), pens, and even stamps. Jackie took one of the postcards, wrote on the back of it, and handed it to Janet. She said it was a direct line to her at the White House, which no one else in the family had, and she wanted to keep it that way. Janet promised to never give it out. "Call me and we can talk," Jackie suggested.

In about a year, Janet Jr. would give the postcard Jackie gave her that night to her friend Stella Brenton as a gift. She still has it today. The front of the card is a picture of the dock of Hammersmith at sunset. On the back is written in Jackie's hand: "EX3–33–07. I want you to call me! JBK PS—I also want you to WAIT."

◇◇◇◇◇◇◇◇◇◇◇◇◇◇◇◇◇◇◇◇

Jackie stayed on at Hammersmith Farm until October 9. That morning, she, John, and Caroline boarded a U.S. Air Force plane at Quonset Point, Rhode Island, to head back to Washington.

It was difficult for the Auchinclosses to say goodbye to Jackie after their six weeks together. "Thanks for a wonderful time, Mummy," Jackie told Janet before boarding the jet.

"Thank *you,* Jacqueline," Janet said, choked up. Then, leaning in, she added, "For what you did for your sister." Jackie looked at her, surprised. Did she know about their talk? Then, she remembered: *Mummy knows everything.*

Jackie returned to Washington on October 9. Unfortunately for her, Jack was back to his old tricks.

On October 8, the night before Jackie's return, according to White House visitor logs, JFK privately entertained a woman named Mary Meyer at the White House.

On October 10, the Kennedys hosted a dinner at the White House. Jackie invited a few friends; Jack did the same, including Miss Meyer.

The next morning, October 11, there was an appointment at the White House with National Symphony Orchestra director Howard Mitchell for a photo opportunity and also to receive the annual presentation of season tickets for the president and First Lady. As the Kennedys posed with Mitchell, Jackie gazed out at the small crowd, and there she was again, smiling at her husband—Mary Meyer.

"WHO'S SHE?"

◇◇◇◇◇◇◇◇◇◇◇◇◇◇

Mary Pinchot Meyer was the sister of Ben Bradlee's wife, Tony, and former wife of Cord Meyer of the CIA. She also happened to be an acquaintance of Jackie's; the two had gone to Vassar, though Mary five years earlier. They had also been neighbors in McLean in 1956, when Jackie endured the stillbirth of Arabella. Mary came from money, was highly educated and intelligent. She was also beautiful, a slim blonde who wore couture as if she were a model.

Jack, who'd known Mary for almost twenty years, often insisted she be invited to White House dinners. For instance, when Jackie hosted a black-tie state dinner in honor of Lee and Stas on March 15, 1961, Mary was present at his request. Since Jackie knew her, she didn't mind. Mary had been in the picture for so many years, she didn't think anything would ever happen between her and Jack. However, Lee said she'd noticed what she called "a current of something" between the two and didn't like it. For the rest of that evening, she said, "I kept my eye on her."

Mary attended several more dinners in 1961. According to Mary's later recollection, after a function on November 11, JFK propositioned her. She said she rebuffed his advances at that time.

Ten weeks later, on January 22, 1962, with Jackie and the children at Glen Ora, Janet substituted for the First Lady, hosting a breakfast for wives of the Securities and Exchange Commission. Afterward, she suggested that with Jackie gone, Jack might want to join her and Hugh for dinner either in the White House or maybe at O Street. Jack begged off, saying he had other plans. Suspicious, Janet decided to stick around the White House to maybe see what he was up to. She walked over to Evelyn Lincoln's office to chat her up and pass the time.

Evelyn told Janet that, the previous night, Caroline had a nightmare and had called out for her Secret Service agent Lynn Meredith, instead of Jackie. Jackie was upset about it, Evelyn said. "As well she should be," noted Janet. Evelyn also said Jackie went to James Raleigh, head of the Secret Service, and complained that the agents were getting a little too close to her children. "And she's right," noted Janet.

By 7:30, Janet hadn't learned much about Jack's activities and was ready to go home. As she was getting ready to leave, a pretty blonde walked into Evelyn's office and asked to see the president. After Evelyn announced her, she casually walked into the Oval Office as if it were the most normal thing in the world.

"Who's she?" Janet asked.

"A friend of Jack's," Evelyn answered.

"What kind of friend?" Janet asked.

"Her name is Mary Meyer," came back the answer.

The name sounded familiar. She hadn't seen her in almost twenty years, though, and couldn't place her.

According to what Mary later told her friend, the journalist James Truitt, it was on this very night that she and JFK made love for the first time.

For the rest of 1962, Mary would continue to be a fixture at almost all the dinners and dances hosted by Jack and Jackie at the White House, as well as smaller luncheon events. Also, while Jackie was away during the summer, Mary was logged in to the White House frequently, sometimes several times a week. For instance, on the night of August 6—two days after Marilyn's death and with Jackie at the Cape—Mary showed up at the White House at 7:32 p.m. At 11:28, the president called for a car to meet her at the South Gate to take her home. Other visits followed. She was at the White House with Jack for drinks on October 3. Then, as earlier stated, Mary was present at the October 10 White House dinner the night after Jackie returned from her vacation.

Also present at that October 10 dinner was James Truitt, at the time a reporter for *The Washington Post,* and his wife, the acclaimed artist Anne Truitt. Both were friends of Mary's who knew the full scope of her relationship with JFK. "I don't like to think about it," Anne, who divorced James in 1971, said in 2000. "I knew the president and Mary were having an affair.

I knew exactly what was going on. So, how dare I sit at Jackie Kennedy's table? It was wrong. I'm sorry it happened."

"It looked bad for all of us," said Secret Service agent Anthony Sherman. "It made us, the guys in the service, feel like we were complicit. There was also a concern that these women coming and going—not just Mary Meyer—might be carrying some sort of listening device or camera for purposes of blackmail. Your imagination couldn't help but run wild. While we loved the president and any one of us would've taken a bullet for him, we also felt bad for the wife. Why, we wondered, did she put up with it?"

"Why?" Jamie Auchincloss asked. "Because she was bred for it. Our mother put up with it with Black Jack, and Jackie had idolized him. He could do no wrong, and in some ways, she felt the same way about Jack Kennedy. They were two peas in a pod, the two Jacks—Bouvier and Kennedy."

DADDY

TEN YEARS EARLIER
AUTUMN 1952

You two have so much in common," Jackie enthused. "Tell Daddy about your work, Jack." Jackie leaned in to encourage Jack Kennedy to engage her father, Jack Bouvier. However, the two men sat at a small table in a restaurant in New York just staring at one another.

This was unusual. The one thing both men had in common was their ability to converse with anyone. Both were well-read and well-educated—Kennedy at Harvard and Bouvier at Columbia and Yale—both had been in the navy, and Bouvier had also been in the army. However, a major obstacle between them was that Bouvier hated Kennedy's father, Joseph Kennedy. Back when he was the first head of the Securities Commission in 1934, Kennedy had enacted laws that prevented investors from doubling their stock options, precisely what Kennedy himself had done to make his own fortune. "You can't indict Jack because of his father," Jackie told him. Jack Bouvier was also a staunch Republican, as was his whole family; they had that in common with the Auchinclosses.

Eventually, Jackie felt the only way the two men would engage would be if she forced the issue by just leaving them. "I need to call Mummy," she said as she rose. Kennedy looked at her, alarmed, his face suggesting the last thing he wanted was to be alone with her father. She smiled at him mischievously and excused herself.

She was gone for thirty minutes, and by the time she returned, her father and fiancé had hit it off and were trading stories about their military experiences. As the night went on, it became clear that they didn't really need her there. They'd had a couple of cocktails and had already become friends. "How's your Mummy?" Jack Bouvier asked her with a knowing smile. "Sends her regards," Jackie said. It was later revealed that Black Jack told Kennedy, only half-kidding, "If you have any trouble with Jackie, put her on a horse."

As he rose to leave, Jack Bouvier threw some cash on the table. Jack Kennedy protested. Bouvier told him, "You can get it next time." Jackie was happy as she left the restaurant; her two favorite men had really hit it off.

"They talked about sports, politics, and women," she later recalled, "what all red-blooded men like to talk about." Additionally, in an ironic Freudian moment considering what Jackie would contend with as JFK's wife, she added, "They were very much alike. They talked about all the things you would expect—business and . . . women."

It's an old saw that women marry their fathers, a generalization that usually doesn't hold up. In many ways, it would seem to have held true for Jackie.

HER WEDDING

∞∞∞∞∞∞∞∞∞∞

On the morning of September 12, 1953, Jackie Bouvier, in her rose-point-lace veil, sat in front of a vanity in a small room off St. Mary's Church. Her dark hair was closely cropped, her makeup meticulously applied. The dress she wore was a magnificent confection of white taffeta and tulle. She didn't like it, though. It was just too . . . much for her taste, but her mother and father-in-law approved of it, so it would have to do.

Jackie's stepfather, Hugh Auchincloss, stood behind her in his natty tuxedo, his hands resting on her slim shoulders. "I'll only do it if you want me to," he told her, according to Yusha's later memory, "but if you say no, then I'll tell Mummy no." He said the two of them could then sneak out the back door, get into his car, and race away so quickly that friends, family, and media wouldn't know what to make of it. Of course, she knew that was impossible and that he was just trying to lighten the moment. It was very much in character for Uncle Hughdie.

"I love you beyond measure," she told him, "and I admire you *so much.*" She said she'd be honored to have him walk her down the aisle.

Though many people in their circle would later claim that marrying into the Kennedy family was something the Auchinclosses thought of as a giant leap forward in the social stratum, that wasn't the case. The wealthy and very Republican Auchinclosses were already an established part of the Newport social scene and viewed the Kennedys as "new money." They weren't fond of Democrats and definitely weren't sold on the idea of the junior senator from Massachusetts, even though Hugh loved socializing with senators.

"Oh yes, Daddy loved public servants," said Jamie Auchincloss, "*Republican* public servants. Gore Vidal liked to say he was a 'senatorial groupie.' As a little boy, I remember him entertaining many Republican senators. I'd watch these old, white-haired, fat men in their three-piece suits, dressed wildly inappropriately for the Newport summer temperatures, come to Hammersmith Farm to drink the free alcohol provided by my father. Daddy used to say, 'Presidents come and go, but senators remain almost 'til death do they part.' Anyway, when Jack finally became a senator, he was not like ones we'd ever seen. He didn't wear a vest, first of all, like so many older senators did, with the pocket watch and all that. He dressed casually, which was often commented on by the other senators when he was in chambers. He wore baggy, unironed khaki pants and sport coats, very casual. Sort of a breath of fresh air as a congressman and, for sure, as a senator."

Janet had worked hard to get Jackie interested in Jack. However, just as had happened with John Husted, once Jackie was engaged to John Kennedy, Janet became unsure. One day, mother and daughter sat down to make a list of pros and cons about him. The cons mostly had to do with his age, reputation, and concerns about whether he'd be faithful. The pros were many. He came from wealth; Janet had heard his family was worth many millions. He was extremely ambitious and politically astute, he was a congressman, soon to be a senator, and had made his interest in the presidency quite clear to all. Janet told Jackie, "You could be First Lady one day, and I'm not sure you'd walk away from that." She added, "Who knows when someone else more suitable will come along?" Finally, she decided, "Get him a decent haircut, feed him a few good meals, put some meat on his bones, and he'll do just fine."

In November 1952, after Jack won his seat in the Senate, defeating Senator Henry Cabot Lodge by almost seventy thousand votes, Jackie began to take him more seriously. He was going places, and her practical side told her that she should go with him. On some level, she loved him, but she definitely loved the future she could have with him more. She was like her mother in a lot of ways, her sensible side especially, but unlike her mother, she'd never lose herself in passion the way Janet had over Black Jack. She liked sex, but she also liked to be in control. With Jack, she felt in charge, or at least she did at first. He wasn't really passionate for her, which didn't bother her as much as one might've imagined. "They were comfortable," said Jamie Auchincloss. "That was about it." Jackie later privately said, "Making love with him is kind of . . . *blah,*" confirming that they'd slept together before marriage even if it wasn't great for her.

"The day before the wedding, there was a lot of angst from Mrs. A. about keeping Jackie's father, Jack Bouvier, from walking Jackie down the aisle," recalled Adora Rule. Adora was eighteen at the time and had just begun working for Janet Auchincloss that very week to help with the wedding reception planning. She was sent to her by the Kelly Girl temporary agency and would end up staying with Janet for thirty-six years. "Mrs. A. was hell-bent that Mr. Auchincloss give his stepdaughter away. It added a lot of stress to what was already a stressful day."

Jamie Auchincloss, six at the time and the ring bearer, recalled, "After my mother married my father [Hugh], he provided Jackie with a first-class, expensive education, trips to Europe, and a stellar lifestyle. Therefore, my mother felt he deserved to walk Jackie down the aisle. Also, the wedding was in Newport, my father's hometown, where he was born. She wrote to Jack Bouvier and told him not to show up, that he wasn't welcome. It was cold and direct, but that was Mummy when she had her heart set on something."

There was another reason for Janet's decision, one that's always overlooked in the oft-told tale of Janet's deception. When Jackie was christened at the Church of St. Ignatius Loyola in New York, Janet's father, James T. Lee, was supposed to be her godfather. Janet was thrilled when he agreed to it since the two had such a stormy relationship. However, Lee was late for the service. Janet refused to give up waiting for him and insisted the baptism be delayed. Jack Bouvier had another idea. He pushed his nine-year-old nephew, Michel Bouvier (son of his younger brother, Bud) forward, and the priest dropped baby Jackie right into his arms. The next thing Janet knew, Jackie's cousin was her godfather. Janet was angry about it, but there was nothing she could do if her own father hadn't shown up. Now, more than twenty years later, Janet had yet another reason to want to cut Jack Bouvier out of Jackie's special day, and her obsession about it clouded the day.

"Jackie and I had struck up a rapport during the week," Adora said, "and she knew I had my own car. She said, 'I need you to get me out of here. Can you drive me somewhere?' I said, 'No. If your mother finds out, she'll fire me.' But she was emotional and wanted to go to a place called Stonor Lodge. We got in my car, and just as we were leaving, we heard a voice shout

out, 'Hey, wait for me!' It was Ethel Kennedy. Jackie said, 'Back up. I like that one. Let's take her with us.' Ethel got into the car and off we went."

As the three women drove off, Ethel asked Jackie if she was happy. Jackie said she was, "but it's all so noisy, isn't it? It's like a big play," she observed. The players were the bride, the groom, and the mother of the bride, "who sits in the front pew of the church and scowls at the bride as she walks down the aisle, critical of her posture." Meanwhile, she continued, "the bride is a bundle of nerves because the father on her arm should be holding her up but, instead, she's holding him up."

Adora recalled, "Ethel Kennedy glared at her like she was out of her mind. 'A simple no would suffice,' she said. 'You'd better not let Grandma Rose hear you talk like that.' Jackie stared at her and said, 'What Grandma Rose doesn't know won't hurt Grandma Rose, now will it?' She said she'd spent the whole week thinking about canceling the wedding. 'But why?' Ethel asked. Jackie didn't answer, she just stared straight ahead. 'You have cold feet, that's all it is,' Ethel told her. As Jackie continued to stare, her jaw set, I thought, *My gosh, is she going to even go back to Hammersmith?*"

They kept driving until Jackie pointed and said, "Over there." They then turned onto Bellevue Avenue and up to a large, colonial-style mansion owned by a wealthy family, friends of the Auchinclosses. They went inside. Jackie thanked Adora for the ride, and when Adora asked how she'd get back to Hammersmith, she said not to worry. She'd figure it out.

Adora and Ethel then drove back to Hammersmith. "I swear to God," Ethel declared, "if that girl leaves Bobby's brother at the altar, I'll kill her with my own two bare hands. She doesn't know how lucky she is to marry into this family." Adora decided not to venture an opinion; the two didn't say a word to each other for the rest of the drive.

Jackie did make it back to Hammersmith a couple of hours later. By the time she returned, Janet already had a plan of action. She sent Yusha and Lee's first husband, Michael Canfield, to go to the Viking Hotel and tell Jack Bouvier he wasn't invited to a party scheduled that night at the Clambake Club. After Yusha left, Michael helped Jack drink his sorrows away. By the next morning, Jack was too hungover to even get out of bed, and Janet's mission had been accomplished. "Your uncle Hughdie will give you away," she proudly announced to her daughter. Though Jackie was in tears, there was nothing she could do about it. "Daddy wasn't for it, either," said Jamie Auchincloss. "He saw a side of Mummy he didn't like and felt her sabotage of Jack Bouvier was terrible. He believed Jack should've had the chance to rise to the occasion and was very cross with Mummy for what she did to him."

More than three thousand people then converged on St. Mary's to catch a glimpse of the thirty-six-year-old groom and twenty-four-year-old bride. The church was full of admiring friends and family members. Despite all the behind-the-scenes drama, photographs taken at Hammersmith Farm of the wedding party at the reception would always stand as a testament to a day as full of promise as drama. Lee was the matron of honor; Bobby Kennedy best man; eight-year-old Janet Jr. was the flower girl; and six-year-old Jamie, in short black velvet trousers and jaboted white silk shirt, was the ring bearer and page, a role the impish little boy acted out with comical old-world courtesy.

That night, as Jackie Kennedy danced with her handsome new husband on one of the Hammersmith patios, she looked out at the crowd of well-wishers and locked eyes with Adora Rule. For a moment, she seemed sad, but then she smiled. Maybe the day hadn't worked out as she'd hoped, but she'd already decided to make the best of it and look to the future. She had no idea what was in store for her, though, how she'd find herself holding a position only thirty-four previous women had claimed, all former First Ladies. As President Kennedy's wife, Jackie would be at the center of some truly historical moments. One would prove particularly terrifying.

THE CUBAN MISSILE CRISIS

◇◇◇◇◇◇◇◇◇◇◇◇◇

On October 14, 1962, after a U-2 spy plane took hundreds of aerial photographs of military bases in Cuba, it became clear that nuclear missiles on launch pads had been brought to Cuba on Soviet ships. The Soviet leader, Nikita Khrushchev, was threatening the U.S. despite previous claims that he was only interested in weapons for defensive purposes. With Cuba only about a hundred miles off the coast of Florida, this was too close for comfort. "Khrushchev thinks Jack is weak and inexperienced," Hugh Auchincloss said. Historians later agreed.

On October 16, McGeorge Bundy, JFK's national security adviser, met with the president in his White House bedroom to alert him to the potential crisis. His advisers then tried to figure out how to respond while keeping the news from the public. Plans were put into place to protect the president, the First Lady, and their children, as well as principal players at the White House.

On October 17, Clint Hill was charged with briefing Jackie. "Jackie was scheduled to lunch with Ethel Kennedy that day," recalled Helen Thomas. "Ethel was to spend the night. The next morning, they were both to fly to New York to attend a reception at the Institute of Fine Arts of New York University."

"Oh, that's off," Jackie's personal secretary Nancy Tuckerman abruptly told Ethel without explanation.

"What's going on here?" Ethel then asked Jackie. "Everyone's running around like chickens with their heads cut off." Apparently, Bobby hadn't filled her in, and Jackie didn't know, either.

"It wasn't exactly, 'sit down, I have something to tell you,'" Jackie clarified in 1964 for her oral history when asked by Arthur Schlesinger about her conversation with the president about the crisis. "I remember one morning, there was a meeting in the Oval Room. I went into the Treaty Room to fiddle through some mail. I could hear them talking through the door. I went up and listened and eavesdropped. I guess this was a rather vital time because I could hear [Robert] McNamara saying something like, 'I think we should do this, that, this, that.' McNamara was summing up something and then [Roswell] Gilpatric was giving some summary, and then I thought, well, I mustn't listen. And I went away."

Jackie wanted to be supportive of Jack, but there was only so much she could do if he wasn't going to confide in her. Their relationship was on his terms. He was a traditional man of his time when it came to his marriage, and he didn't think Jackie needed to know more than just the broad strokes.

"That was really frustrating," said Jamie Auchincloss. "Their marriage was one of mixed messages. Sometimes, he cried with her as during the Bay of Pigs. Other times, he pushed her away as he did during the Cuban Missile Crisis. She was kept off balance. Making it harder, we weren't raised to be emotional people, and neither was Jack. So, you had two in a marriage with no clue as to how to be emotionally available or how to express themselves."

In Jack's defense, Jackie wasn't a feminist who expected to be treated with equality. Before her marriage, she'd proudly proclaimed, "I proved that I could support myself by holding down a newspaper job for a year and a half and by winning the Vogue Prix de Paris." After marriage, however, she became an adjunct to Jack, so much so that she couldn't imagine having an opinion that contradicted his.

Clint Hill gave Jackie more information than she'd gotten from her own husband. He also told her about the bomb shelter under the East Wing of the White House, known as "the bunker." If the worst happened, he said, he'd rush her, Caroline, and John to that location, where they'd be safe.

"My God," Jackie exclaimed, her eyes wide with fear. "Is this really happening?"

"Could be, Mrs. Kennedy."

"Then, we won't handle it like that, Mr. Hill," she decided. "If the end comes, I and my children will hold hands and stand on the South grounds like soldiers, and we'll face our fate just like every other American. We should be no different than any other. If they die, we die."

"I said to myself, 'Not on my watch,'" recalled Clint Hill. "I realized I was going to have to pick her up and drag her kicking and screaming to the bomb shelter. Tom Wells, one of the agents responsible for the children, would have to grab them, too." What Clint actually said to Jackie, though, was: "Let's just hope it doesn't come to that, Mrs. Kennedy."

The next few days were tense, with JFK and Bobby in constant meetings, feeling the weight of responsibility as they kept a close eye on the dangerous situation. Jackie still had no real idea of what was happening. "I remember she'd sort of be wandering the halls of the White House, looking for information," said Michael Vincent Forrestal, one of National Security Adviser McGeorge Bundy's aides. "She would come up to me and say, 'Mike, what's the news? What's going on?' and I would tell her what I knew. It was clear, though, that she wasn't getting much information, nobody was taking the trouble to tell her."

On Friday, October 19, Lee showed up at the White House with her children to attend a dinner on Tuesday the twenty-third for the maharaja of Jaipur and his wife. "I doubt that's happening now," Jackie told her. Of course, Lee had no idea there was even a problem. The world wasn't yet aware.

"The president felt it was best that Jackie and Lee go to Glen Ora for the weekend," remembered Helen Thomas. "Since he was scheduled to be in Cleveland and Chicago, why, he figured, should they stay behind at the White House? Jackie tried to argue that she should be with him. Maybe it felt to her as if he was pushing her away. An added problem was that John Jr. seemed to be coming down with something, and Jackie wanted him to stay in bed. JFK insisted, though. So, she packed her bags."

Jackie, Lee, John, and Caroline were driven to Glen Ora in the Chrysler previously used by Mamie Eisenhower. The press had started asking questions about Jackie's frequent use of government choppers to go from Washington to Middleburg, so now she was being driven. An army sergeant drove with Clint in the front passenger seat and Jackie and Lee in the back, chatting while smoking up a storm, with the kids crammed into the car. As soon as they got close to Glen Ora, they snuffed out their cigarettes; Jackie had always been successful keeping her habit from the American public. Hugh and his son Yusha met them at Glen Ora.

Meanwhile, Jack and Bobby discovered that the Soviets continued to ready fighter jets, bombers, and missile launchers. SS-5 missiles were also being readied, which had the capability of striking anywhere in the United States. Secretary of Defense Robert McNamara gave JFK three options: diplomacy with Khrushchev and Cuban leader Fidel Castro; a naval quarantine of Cuba; or an air attack to destroy the missile sites, which would most certainly trigger a Soviet counterattack. Jack said no to the air attack; he favored a quarantine to buy time to negotiate a missile withdrawal. He was careful to call it "a quarantine," because he knew a "blockade" would be considered an act of war. The stakes had suddenly become terrifying: survival or annihilation.

"This call came through from Jack," Jackie recalled, "and he said, 'I'm coming back to Washington [from Chicago] this afternoon. Why don't you come back?' There was something funny in his voice. I could tell something was wrong."

Happy to know he finally needed her, Jackie was anxious to get back to Washington. She and Lee quickly packed up the children and left. By this time, John had the flu and Jackie didn't want to spend any more time at Glen Ora, anyway; she wanted to get him to the White House and into his bed. Hugh and Yusha stayed behind to secure the house.

That same afternoon, Lee's husband, Stas, showed up at the White House. Lee had called him the night before to tell him what was happening. He was worried about her and the children, he said, and if the end was near, he wanted to be with them. Lee agreed he should come.

Jackie's parents, Janet and Jack Bouvier, had a complex and tortured relationship, but the one thing they had in common was their devotion to their daughter Jackie. Here they are with five-year-old Jackie at the Southampton horse show in August 1934. (WHITE HOUSE PHOTOGRAPHS / JOHN F. KENNEDY PRESIDENTIAL LIBRARY AND MUSEUM, BOSTON)

When Janet Bouvier married Hugh Auchincloss in 1942, Jackie became part of a blended family. From left to right in 1946, starting at the top: Jackie; Hugh (Yusha) Auchincloss III; Hugh's daughter, Nina; Jackie's sister, Lee; Janet, holding baby Janet Jr.; Hugh's son, Tommy (in the middle); and Hugh. Janet is pregnant with her only son, Jamie. (WHITE HOUSE PHOTOGRAPHS / JOHN F. KENNEDY PRESIDENTIAL LIBRARY AND MUSEUM, BOSTON)

Lee beat Jackie to the altar by five months when she married Michael Canfield in April 1953. Here she is on her wedding day with her mother, Janet, and grandfather (Janet's father) James T. Lee. (JAMIE AUCHINCLOSS COLLECTION)

Throughout her time in the White House (and even beyond), most people didn't know Jackie had two half siblings, her mother's children with Hugh Auchincloss—Janet Jennings and James (Jamie) Lee, born in 1945 and 1947, respectively. (JAMIE AUCHINCLOSS COLLECTION)

In this rare photo of Jackie's wedding to Senator John Fitzgerald Kennedy on September 12, 1953, we see her anxiety as she walks to the church with her stepfather, Hugh. Her mother, Janet (smiling in the background), successfully schemed to deprive Jackie's natural father, Jack Bouvier, of the honor. (ADORA RULE COLLECTION)

When Jackie's sister, Lee, married Prince Stanislaw Radziwill in 1959, she became a princess. By 1960, however, she was having an affair with the man who would become Jackie's second husband, Aristotle Onassis. (RETRO PHOTO)

Jackie in Paris during her official visit in May 1961. She's wearing a wool and silk dress designed by Oleg Cassini along with a pillbox she popularized, created by Halston.

President John F. Kennedy and First Lady Jaqueline Kennedy arrive at the National Guard armory for his inaugural ball, Washington, D.C., on January 20, 1961.

A year later, Jack and Jackie arrive for the first inaugural salute to the president at the National Guard armory. It's easy to see why Jackie was dubbed "First Lady of fashion" by the New York fashion press.

Jackie and John Carl Warnecke inspect Lafayette Square reconstruction plans, September 25, 1962. She's wearing the dress she'd later wear the day her husband was assassinated. After JFK's death, Jackie began a romance with Warnecke that turned into a lifelong friendship. (ROBERT KNUDSEN, WHITE HOUSE PHOTOGRAPHS / JOHN F. KENNEDY PRESIDENTIAL LIBRARY AND MUSEUM)

While photos were widely circulated of a grim LBJ taking the presidential oath on Air Force One after JFK's murder with Lady Bird John and Jackie Kennedy at his side, this rare shot shows the true emotional toll of the moment. (CECIL STOUGHTON, WHITE HOUSE PHOTOGRAPHS / JOHN F. KENNEDY PRESIDENTIAL LIBRARY AND MUSEUM)

Certainly, Jackie's courage was on full display on November 24, 1963, during the state funeral for President Kennedy, but little John Kennedy Jr. stole the hearts of all Americans when he saluted his father's casket. He would turn three the next day. (CECIL STOUGHTON, WHITE HOUSE PHOTOGRAPHS / JOHN F. KENNEDY PRESIDENTIAL LIBRARY AND MUSEUM)

Jackie's half sister, Janet Jennings Auchincloss, married Lewis Polk Rutherfurd on July
30, 1966. Janet then moved to Hong Kong
in part to escape her famous sister's shadow.
(ADORA RULE COLLECTION)

In 1967, when Jackie met Aristotle Onassis's sister
Artemis Garofalidis, her whole life changed. For
Jackie to solve her many problems, it was Artemis's
idea that Jackie marry her brother. The future
sisters-in-law came up with a plan . . . which worked!
(THEA ANDINO COLLECTION)

It could be said that Jackie got the better end
of the deal in marrying Aristotle Onassis—
financial security and protection without
intimacy, but he had Maria Callas on the side,
so it worked . . . for a while. Here they are on
their wedding day, October 20, 1968.
(RETRO PHOTO)

Jackie's half brother, Jamie, became a photojournalist and an in-demand presidential historian. "Nothing about my family is ever easy," he once said. "We're complicated, and we're messy." (JAMIE AUCHINCLOSS COLLECTION)

Jackie, sporting the "Jackie O" look associated with her at the time, leaves the Plaza Hotel in New York with her husband, Ari, and young son, John, on February 16, 1969. (PHOTO TIMES)

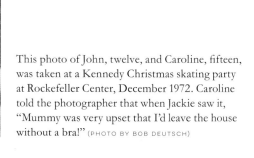

This photo of John, twelve, and Caroline, fifteen, was taken at a Kennedy Christmas skating party at Rockefeller Center, December 1972. Caroline told the photographer that when Jackie saw it, "Mummy was very upset that I'd leave the house without a bra!" (PHOTO BY BOB DEUTSCH)

Jackie, flanked by John and Caroline, at Aristotle Onassis's coffin, March 18, 1975. "I will help and protect you, always," he had told her. Whatever else happened, he'd kept that promise. (THEA ANDINO COLLECTION)

Jackie with her daughter, Caroline, and former brother-in-law Ted Kennedy at John's graduation from Phillips Academy, Andover, Massachusetts, June 7, 1979. (PHOTO BY BOB DEUTSCH)

After Onassis's death, Jackie had a secret romance with the acclaimed director Michael Cacoyannis. Their relationship ended when he asked her to choose between him and her new job at Viking Press. Here they are with actress Irene Papas and Caroline Kennedy at *The Bacchae* in New York City.

(PHOTO BY TOM WARGACKI / WIREIMAGE)

After Jackie's mother, Janet, was diagnosed with Alzheimer's, the two forged a new and deeper relationship. Here's Janet at her home on Hammersmith Farm. (JAMIE AUCHINCLOSS COLLECTION)

In 1975, Jackie joined the workforce when she was hired as a consulting editor at Viking Press. Here she is on her first day with Viking president Tom Guinzburg. Most people would believe she left the job over a dispute about a book when, actually, she left to focus on her mother's illness. (ALFRED EISENSTAEDT / BETTMAN-GETTY IMAGES)

Jackie eventually found contentment with Maurice Tempelsman. Here they are at a fundraiser for Senator Daniel Patrick Moynihan at the Helmsley Palace Hotel, New York City, October 20, 1988. (MARIETTE PATHY ALLEN / GETTY IMAGES)

GOD'S WILL

◇◇◇◇◇◇◇◇◇◇◇◇◇◇

On Monday, October 22, 1962, President Kennedy felt he had no choice but to alert the American public of the threat of nuclear war.

When she heard that a speech was imminent, Janet Auchincloss was concerned because, with Jamie away at school, Janet Jr. was at O Street with just the servants for company. When she called to check on her, she found her hysterical. John Kerry had told her that he'd heard a missile was headed straight to the White House. Of course, he had it all wrong. Janet didn't want to try to clarify things—she knew even less than Jackie—she just wanted her daughter to come to the White House to be with the family. Janet Jr. said she was too frightened to leave O Street. Therefore, Hugh went to be with her while Janet Sr. stayed with Jackie, Lee, and her grandchildren. This wasn't an easy decision; the Auchincrosses didn't want to be separated at such a frightening time, but they also didn't want Janet Jr. to be alone.

Janet, Jackie, and Lee walked out to the front portico just as a car pulled up to take Hugh on the short drive to O Street. Janet waved goodbye and then, with her daughters flanking her, slowly walked back into the White House. When they got to the private quarters, Jackie found the children's nanny, Maud Shaw, sitting in the kitchen reading a pamphlet, *Children and the Threat of Nuclear War.* She snatched it from her and asked where she'd gotten it.

Maud said Ethel had given it to her and told her she should read it if she were to be responsible for the president's children. Jackie snatched the brochure. "Panic is catching, Maud," she exclaimed. "I'll speak to Ethel about this."

That night, as the president prepared to go on the air to address the nation, everyone but Jackie waited in the Yellow Oval Room on the second floor. She still didn't have all the details; she just knew that she didn't want Jack to send her away again. She pulled him aside and reiterated what she'd earlier told Clint Hill. "I said, 'Please don't send me anywhere if anything happens,'" she later recalled. "'We're all going to stay right here with you. Even if there's not room in the bomb shelter at the White House—which I'd seen—then, I just want to be on the lawn when it happens. I just want to be with you. I want to die with you—and the children do, too—than live without you.' He said he wouldn't send me away, and he didn't really want to send me away."

In a dramatic eighteen-minute speech, President John Fitzgerald Kennedy appeared from the Oval Office to explain to Americans as much of the crisis as he felt comfortable sharing. "Each of these missiles in short is capable of striking Washington, D.C.," he said, "the Panama Canal, Cape Canaveral, Mexico City, or any other city in the southeastern part of the United States, in Central America, or the Caribbean area." He gave Khrushchev an ultimatum to back off or face the United States' military action. He also said the United States was enacting a naval quarantine of all weaponized ships and was requesting an emergency meeting of the National Security Council of the United States. The United States, he said, was prepared to use military force if necessary. With his face tensely set, it was clear the situation was dire and could end in catastrophe. A nuclear war was now a real possibility. He concluded, "The cost of freedom is always high, but Americans have always paid it."

Jack's speech to the nation was really the first time all the pieces of the puzzle were fitted together for Jackie. While it was frightening, at least she finally had a clear understanding, as did Janet, Lee, Ethel, and all the other women at the White House who'd been kept in the dark.

After his speech, Jack joined the others for dinner. At the table were David Ormsby-Gore, his British diplomat, along with his wife, Sylvia, known as Sissy; Benno and Nicole Graziani; Deborah Cavendish, the Duchess of Devonshire; Bobby and Ethel Kennedy; Janet; Yusha (who arrived from Glen Ora); Lee and Stas; Oleg Cassini and Dorothy Tubridy (a friend of the family's visiting from Ireland); Bill Walton and Mary Meyer.

By this time, Jackie was well aware of Jack's affair with Mary. Her mother had asked around, gotten the information, and clued Jackie in about it during her stay in Newport following her vacation in Ravello. Jackie had suspected it. Still, she couldn't believe Jack would be so cavalier about it by so often having Mary at the White House. Janet felt it was "beyond the pale," as she put it, and told Jackie she hoped she'd finally divorce Jack once the Kennedys finished their second term in office, provided they'd have one. This was the second time Janet had suggested divorce, the first being in 1956, when Jack didn't come to Jackie's side after the stillbirth of Arabella. But Jackie said she couldn't think that far in advance. For now, she'd just have to tolerate Mary Meyer.

Mary Meyer's name does not appear on the official White House visitor's log in the John F. Kennedy Presidential Library and Museum for October 22, 1962. Neither, however, do the names Lee and Stanislaw Radziwill or Janet and Yusha Auchincloss. These visitor logs didn't always reflect every visitor to the White House during the JFK administration. "There was an unofficial back door to the Oval Office that was supervised by Kenny O'Donnell," said Ron Whealan, the head librarian, "and we have no logs on any of those visits."

The meal served that night at the White House was sole Hortensia, *canard à l'orange,* wild rice, and *épinards aux croutons* with a 1959 Pouilly-Fumé. Jackie, the last to be seated, looked about the table, and there, sitting right next to Ethel, was Mary. If ever a woman should've been applauded indulging her husband, it would've been Jackie that night. Janet didn't see it that way, though. The idea that Mary was at the table on such an auspicious evening galled her, and as far as she was concerned, Jackie appeared, as she later put it, "hurt and hardened."

In a 1999 interview, Oleg Cassini recalled, "Jackie tried to be upbeat, but you could see the tension on her face. I asked her, 'Are you okay?' to which she responded, 'Are any of us, Oleg?'

"As we sat down, McGeorge Bundy [national security adviser] came to Jack and said he heard the Russians might back down. Jack inhaled his cigar, turned to me, and said, 'We still have twenty chances out of a hundred we'll be at war.' I whispered to him, 'My God, Mr. President, are you saying war is still possible?' and he said, 'Yes, it certainly is. We have to accept it, Oleg.' Then turning to the others, he said, 'We've done all we can do. There's nothing left.'"

"If this is the end of the world, then fine, it's God's will," Ethel declared. "We're in God's hands now."

"Hear, hear," said Oleg as he raised his glass.

"Hear, hear," said Bobby.

"God bless us all, everybody," Jackie said, also lifting her glass.

"Yes. May He bless us all," Mary Meyer repeated.

Everyone then clinked glasses around the table. However, when it came time to touch Mary's glass, Ethel—seated next to her—lowered hers and gave Jackie a look. She knew.

Late that night, Janet called Jackie and Lee into the kitchen. They said they were exhausted and just wished to go to bed. Jackie, in particular, didn't want to see her because she feared a conversation about Mary. She told Janet that, considering all that was going on, the presence of Mary Meyer at the White House should be the last thing on anyone's mind. However, Janet didn't want to press the issue; she had something else in mind. "Humor me," she told her daughter.

When the sisters sat down, Janet presented them with silver cups of her homemade butterscotch pudding, the same treat she used to prepare for them when they were little girls and she lost her temper with them. They were surprised. It made them smile.

Janet handed Lee a can of whipped cream, not Quip as in the old days but Reddi-wip. Lee sprayed her dessert, gave it to Jackie, who sprayed her own. Jackie then reached over and topped off her mother's, just as always.

Janet later said she was proud of Jackie for getting through a very difficult evening. She wanted to do something for her to relieve her tension, thus the impromptu and nostalgic treat. Enjoying it was a different experience, though, from when Jackie was younger. Now that she was a grown woman, things had changed for her, and not all for the better. "We sat staring down at our puddings and ate them very quietly," Janet recalled in 1976, "and we wondered, the three of us, how in the world we'd gotten there, and what the future might hold."

RESOLUTION

〰〰〰〰〰〰〰〰

For the next week, Americans remained on edge while bracing for the worst. Janet stayed at the White House with Jackie and Lee while Hugh remained at O Street with Janet Jr. Ethel and Joan and some of their children came to visit. "It seemed as if there was no waking or sleeping," Jackie recalled, "and I just don't know which day was which."

She recalled, "I can remember one night, Jack was lying on his bed in his room, and it was really late, and I came in in my nightgown. I thought he was talking on the phone. I'd been in and out of there all evening. And suddenly, I saw him waving me away—Get out. Get out. It was because Bundy was in the room. And poor puritan Bundy, to see a woman in her nightgown. He threw both hands over his eyes.

"As I say, there was no day or night. And, well, that's the time I was closest to him [Jack] . . . and when he came home, if I was asleep or napping, I would sleep with him. Sometimes, he would take me out for a walk around the lawn. You know, he didn't very often do that. It was just this vigil."

Meanwhile, Clint Hill sat in on meetings outlining once again how he and the other agents would get everyone out of the White House and who would be assigned which helicopter to get off the premises. Shockingly, a directive was given that if anyone tried to board a chopper he or she wasn't assigned to and insisted upon it, that person should be shot dead.

But a sense of normality was maintained. On Thursday, a camera crew from NBC showed up at the White House to film an interview with Jackie and Janet about the new National Cultural Center. It was the last thing mother and daughter wanted to do, but the network had a deadline and asked that it be kept.

On Friday, the twenty-sixth, things suddenly changed. Cooler heads began to prevail when Khrushchev agreed to keep his ships out of the quarantine zone for two days.

"That night, Jackie was scheduled to present the President's Cup at the Washington International Horse Show at the National Guard armory," recalled Helen Thomas. "Jack felt that for her to make any public appearances during the crisis would be poor politics and maybe not safe."

The president decided to send Janet. When Jackie asked her to stand in for her, Janet became emotional. She didn't want to leave and asked that they send someone else. No, Jackie said, the president wanted her to go. She said she'd send Clint Hill along to make sure she was safe and then get her back to the White House as quickly as possible.

Janet composed herself to rise to the occasion. She had no idea what she was in for, though; it turned out she'd have to stand on a stage before seven thousand people, give out a cash prize to the winner, as well as a replica of the vermeil Perpetual Challenge Cup. She later said she was "terrified" as she looked out at the crowd and wondered if there was a sniper or, worse, if a missile might strike the armory, killing them all. The name of the winning horse was Unusual, which Janet told the crowd was "something Jackie will find fitting given present world events." According to the AP report, as she was being rushed out, someone asked her about the national emergency. Janet said, "I can't comment. I must return to the White House to be with Jacqueline and my grandchildren."

The next morning, Jack felt Jackie and Lee should go back to Glen Ora for the weekend. Jackie asked Janet to accompany them. Meanwhile, because Lee's son, Tony, was coming down with something, she felt it best she and Stas stay behind at the White House with him. She sent Tina along with Jackie, Janet *mère*, Caroline, and John.

On Sunday, Jack called Jackie to tell her it appeared that the emergency was finally over. Khrushchev had agreed to dismantle the missiles in Cuba. The ships that had been carrying nuclear weapons would now be turned around. In exchange, Jack promised not to invade Cuba. (Later, it was learned that he'd also secretly agreed to remove U.S. missiles from Turkey.)

As is by now so well known, Khrushchev had sent two telegrams, one that was conciliatory and another that was threatening. Jack and Bobby decided to ignore the second one. Acting as if they'd never received it, they based their final negotiations on the good-faith nature of the first letter.

Jackie in her 1964 oral history: "I remember he [Jack] did tell me about this crazy telegram that came through from Khrushchev one night. Very warlike. He'd sent the nice one first where he looked like he would— Khrushchev had—where he might dismantle. Then, this crazy one came through in the middle of the night. I remember Jack being really upset about that and telling me they decided they would just answer the first."

In 2001, Lee said to Larry King: "It was the most memorable, extraordinary time of the White House years . . . and there was one moment nearing the end, when we—that's Jackie, the president, and myself—were in their private rooms upstairs, and the phone rang and it was McGeorge Bundy saying there was extreme trouble ahead. And then, when the president put down the phone, he said, 'In three minutes, we'll know if we're at all-out war or not.' And I can't tell you how long those three minutes seemed. I'm sure you can imagine, but you pictured missiles rising all over the world, submarines submerged. And then the phone rang, and the president had an extraordinarily tense expression on his face and hung up and said, 'The Russian ships turned back.' And there was such relief."

It's curious that Lee included Jackie in her anecdote when, in fact, Jackie was at Glen Ora. She must have felt it inappropriate to leave the First Lady out of the story.

When Jack arrived at Glen Ora, Jackie rushed into his arms, never happier to see him. He felt the same way. Following a horrifying, thirteen-day political and military standoff, President John Fitzgerald Kennedy had averted a crisis of epic proportions, a nuclear war. Jackie couldn't have been prouder or happier. Even given the presence of Mary Meyer during this dark time, she felt her marriage strengthened by the crisis. Their new closeness was obvious to the family, too. Maybe Janet put it best when she said, "It only took the threat of a nuclear war."

<hr />

After the Cuban Missile Crisis, Arthur Schlesinger began gathering eminent officials of the Kennedy government for discussions in what came to be called "the Hickory Hill Seminars," named for the venue of the first seminar at Bobby and Ethel's home. The format had it that an academic or historian would give a lecture and take questions.

In the winter of '63, Princeton professor and Lincoln historian David Herbert Donald spoke about the Civil War in the Yellow Oval Room of the White House. Jackie recalled, "I remember when the question period started, the President asked Donald, 'Do you think'—it was this one thing that was so on his mind—'would Lincoln have been as great a President if he'd lived? Would he be judged as great because he would have had this insoluble problem of the Reconstruction which, either way you did it, would have dissatisfied so many people?' That was his question.

"And Donald really by going round and round, finally agreed with him that Lincoln . . . you know, it was better for Lincoln that he died when he did.

"And then I remember Jack saying after the Cuban Missile Crisis, when it all turned out so fantastically, he said, 'Well, if anyone is ever going to shoot me, this would be the day they should do it.'"

◇◇◇◇◇◇◇◇◇◇◇◇◇◇◇◇◇◇◇◇◇◇

During the recent crisis, while she was at Glen Ora, Jackie was told the property's owner had decided against renewing the lease. At this same time, she heard of land near her friend Bunny Mellon's estate, called Rattlesnake Mountain. Isolated, it had plenty of room for her horses—forty acres—and she thought it would be ideal for her escapes from Washington. After she, Lee, and Jack toured it on November 4, the Kennedys agreed to the purchase. They began to build a house to Jackie's specifications, which they hoped to have finished by late summer of 1963. It was called Atoka, but Jackie would later rechristen it Wexford; the Kennedys had originally emigrated from county Wexford.

For the rest of the year, Jackie stayed busy with White House duties, especially the redesign of Lafayette Square, which she eagerly tackled with architect John Warnecke.

The Auchinclosses were also in the process of selling Merrywood, their estate in McLean, Virginia, which had become cost prohibitive. There was no way for them to maintain both it and Hammersmith Farm in Newport. After eighteen years together there, Janet and Hugh reluctantly decided to let go of Merrywood and keep Hammersmith.

After putting Merrywood on the market for $850,000, it eventually sold for $650,000, which is about $7 million in today's money. They used some of the proceeds to purchase the house at 3044 O Street in Georgetown, on the corner of O and Thirty-First. It was a towering four-story Queen Anne–style structure with impressive peaks and gables. Built in 1874, it was then and remains one of the largest residences in town with its nine bedrooms, seven baths, twelve fireplaces, and an attached three car-garage with apartments for the servants. Today, it's on the National Register of Historic Places.

On February 8, 1963, as testament to their new intimacy, Jackie happily told the family she and Jack were once again expecting. The baby was due in September, the first to be born to a serving United States president and his First Lady since the nineteenth century.

PATRICK

◇◇◇◇◇◇◇◇◇◇◇◇◇◇

On Wednesday, August 7, 1963, Janet Jr. and her parents had lunch with her new friend Stella Brenton at the Edwardian Room of the Plaza Hotel in New York. In a month, Janet Jr.—who graduated from Miss Porter's School in June—would begin classes at Sarah Lawrence, the prestigious all-girls liberal arts college.

Stella, who was eighteen in 1963—the same age as Janet Jr.—was descended from Governor William Brenton, a settler of Newport in the seventeenth century. He once owned a large farm that he, too, called Hammersmith. Of course, that name would survive in Newport as Hammersmith Farm. That shared bit of history bonded the two girls, both of whom were music history majors. They would be dorm roommates for the next three years.

During the meal, they talked about Janet Jr.'s upcoming debutante party at Hammersmith, which was scheduled for the thirteenth. There would be over a thousand guests, including seven foreign ambassadors, four United States senators, a retired Supreme Court judge, and dozens of affluent politicians. Stella recalled, "Mrs. Auchincloss was determined to get Jackie to the party so that it could be in the newspapers. 'But maybe she doesn't want her there because she's afraid she'll overshadow her,' Mr. Auchincloss said. Ja-Je said that wasn't true, but earlier, she'd told me that was exactly why she didn't want her there." In the end, Jackie would not attend.

"While we ate, a maître d' came to the table to tell Mr. Auchincloss he had an urgent call. 'Here?' he asked, surprised. 'Is it the president?' Then, as he rushed off, he looked at his watch and said, 'But he's supposed to be doing an interview with *The New York Times* about the Test Ban Treaty.'"

The Nuclear Test Ban Treaty, just signed two days earlier by the United States, the Soviet Union, and Great Britain, prohibited the testing of nuclear weapons in outer space, underwater, or in the atmosphere. It's considered perhaps the crowning achievement of the Kennedy administration.

Stella recalled, "I whispered to Ja-Je, 'How does your father know the president's schedule?' She rolled her eyes and said, 'Don't ask.'

"When he returned, Mr. Auchincloss said, 'Jackie's gone into premature labor. You have to get to Fort Hamilton immediately.' He said the president had arranged for Janet and Ja-Je to take a helicopter from Fort Hamilton to Otis Air Force Base hospital [in Falmouth, Massachusetts]. He—Mr. Auchincloss—had an appointment in the city and couldn't go with them. 'Oh my God, not the baby!' Mrs. Auchincloss exclaimed. They then threw some money on the table and dashed out, with me following.

"There was already a car waiting in front of the hotel. Ja-Je hugged me and, as she did, whispered in my ear, 'Jackie is five weeks early and has already lost three babies. Please say a prayer for my sister.'"

<hr />

That morning, Jackie was watching Caroline's horseback riding lesson at a farm near the Kennedys' home on Squaw Island when she suddenly felt unwell. By the time her Secret Service agent, Paul Landis, got her back to the house, Dr. Walsh was waiting for them. Though it was just a ten-minute chopper ride from Hyannis to Otis Air Force Base military hospital, by the time Jackie landed, she felt much worse. Once admitted, she'd undergo an emergency Caesarian and give birth to a baby boy who weighed just four pounds, ten ounces.

When the president arrived at Otis shortly before two o'clock, his son was already in an incubator. The infant was so small and weak it was decided to baptize him immediately; he was named Patrick Bouvier Kennedy, honoring Jack's grandfather and Jackie's father. One of the agents protecting the president, Larry Newman, had just gotten married, and, as Jack gazed at his son hooked up to all the machinery, he turned to him and asked, "How's married life, Larry?" He was obviously trying to distract himself. "Fine, sir," the agent said. They then stood side by side with their arms crossed while staring sadly at the struggling infant, not saying another word.

Sadly, after being transferred to Children's Hospital in Boston, Patrick died. His death was caused by a lung ailment common in premature babies, hyaline membrane disease. He'd lived just thirty-nine hours. In sharp contrast to his laissez-faire attitude toward his wife's previous pregnancies, most especially the death of Arabella, this time the president was wracked with grief.

The next morning, Jackie was informed of her baby's death by Dr. Walsh. "Jack walked in the morning about eight, in my room," Jackie recalled about a year later, "and just sobbed and put his arms around me. I told him, 'There's just one thing I couldn't stand—if I ever lost you.'" He nodded and, kissing her on the head, said, "I know, Jackie. I know."

By this time, Lee arrived at Otis. "Jacqueline's fine," Janet told her, "but we lost little Patrick." After they went into the room to be with Jackie, Janet closed the door for privacy.

Jamie, sixteen and about to start his senior year at Brooks School, was now an amateur photographer, and he wanted to document these difficult moments for the family's history. While at the Cape, he took a few pictures of the president on the patio, wearing white slacks and a polo shirt, with bare feet. Alarmed, Jack cautioned him. "No, Jamie, you can't do that," he said. "Put that camera away. It's the job of the White House photographer to take pictures of me, review them, and decide which are acceptable and which should be destroyed." Jamie stopped. Even in times of such great grief, he began to understand there were rules that had to be adhered to when it came to life with the president of the United States.

Jackie was so weak and sick, she wasn't able to attend Patrick's funeral, on Saturday, August 10, at Cardinal Richard Cushing's home on Commonwealth Avenue. Jamie recalled, "Jack broke down in the chapel with Patrick's coffin. That triggered us all to tears. Later, at the Holyhood Cemetery gravesite in Brookline, I told Daddy, 'It's so unfair. Why do these things have to happen?' This was my first experience with death. Daddy looked at me sadly and, with a choked voice, said, 'It's not our place to question God. It's our place to be there for your sister when she gets out of the hospital. That's our place.'"

TRYING TO GET ON WITH THINGS

◇◇◇◇◇◇◇◇◇◇◇◇◇

J ackie's grief continued long after she was released from the hospital on
  August 14. Once back at the Cape, she was inundated with letters and
cards of condolence.

"You give so much happiness—you deserve more," Lady Bird Johnson
wrote. She wrote that she and LBJ were praying for her and grieving with
her. She added that she wanted to say more, but then Jackie would have to
read it, "and I fear want to answer it—don't."

"I send you my prayers, dearest Jackie," Ethel Kennedy wrote. She
added that there was nothing greater in heartache than the loss of a child
and concluded that she and Bobby loved her.

Yusha wrote that he was sure to see her soon, "and until then, know
that my heart is with you."

A week after her release from the hospital, Jackie's mother and stepfather wanted her to come to Hammersmith. Jack Weston, son of Hugh's
assistant Clark Weston, recalled, "Jackie's personal secretary Mary Gallagher called Mr. A. to tell him Jackie didn't wish to come to Hammersmith
or go anywhere else. She said she couldn't even get her to come out of the
bedroom. Fine, Mr. A. said. He hung up and told my father to start packing
suitcases. He and Mrs. A. were going to the Cape to be with Jackie. Someone then called Mrs. Gallagher to give her the news. Minutes later, a very
upset Mrs. Gallagher called to say, 'Absolutely not. The First Lady cannot
receive you. I will let you know when she's available.'

"When my father told the Auchinclosses, they both became upset. My
old man said, 'This is crushing them.' He then went into the den, closed the

door, and called the White House. It was the first time and, I'm pretty sure, the only time he ever called the president. I don't think he got through, but he did talk to Evelyn Lincoln."

An hour later, Rose Kennedy called Janet. She said Evelyn had called her upset about something having to do with Jackie. She wanted to know if she could help. When Janet explained that she and Hugh were being prevented from seeing her, Rose was surprised. She told Janet she'd just talked to Jackie, who'd told her, "This grief is unbearable. I don't know how to do this." She asked, "Why haven't Mummy and Uncle Hughdie come?" That was all Janet needed to hear. Now she was furious. When Rose asked who was stopping her from seeing her daughter, Janet said Mary Gallagher was the culprit.

"Who does she think she is?" Janet exclaimed.

"You leave that one to me," said Rose.

An hour later, the Auchinclosses got word that the White House was sending a helicopter to pick them up and bring them to Hyannis Port. Soon after, a green-and-white government chopper landed on the Hammersmith beach near the pier. Jack Weston stood on the sand and watched as Hugh and Janet walked slowly, arm in arm, toward it, the wind from its rotors kicking up sand and blowing Janet's skirt. A maid followed dutifully with two suitcases.

They were about to board when Janet turned to Hugh, smiled at him, and threw her arms around him. She then waved goodbye to young Weston.

Meanwhile, back at Squaw Island, Jackie pulled herself out of bed, showered, dressed, and put on some makeup. She called Jack, who was in Washington in meetings to discuss proposed economic assistance programs for Laos, to tell him how happy she was her parents were coming to visit.

After about thirty minutes, Clint Hill drove Jackie and the children the one mile to Rose and Joe's home. From the porch of the Big House, Jackie and Rose watched the chopper land. Then, as Janet walked down the helicopter's metal stairs, Jackie went to her. She embraced her and then Uncle Hughdie. Arm in arm, the three then walked up to the Kennedys' Big House, Caroline and John behind them, trying to keep up.

LEE'S BAD IDEA

∞∞∞∞∞∞∞∞

Back in 1953, after Lee Radziwill was told by her mother that Jack Kennedy would be off-limits to her as a suitor, she needed to figure out a way forward. In what seemed like a race to get to the altar before her sister, she quickly became serious about someone else. She ended up marrying the sexually ambiguous Michael Canfield, young and handsome scion of a wealthy publishing family, in April of '53. That was just five months before Jackie walked down the aisle.

Lee's marriage to Michael failed when she became romantically involved with Prince Stanislaw Radziwill. She divorced Michael and married Stas in 1959 and had two children, Tina and Tony.

Now, in 1963, Lee was cheating on Stas with Greek tycoon Aristotle Onassis and had been for at least two years. Onassis was fed up with her, though. She couldn't seem to choose between him and Stas, and if he couldn't be number one in her life, he didn't want to be in it at all. While he was still involved with his longtime mistress Maria Callas, he also didn't want to share Lee. Lee said she wanted to divorce Stas and be with Ari, but it wasn't that easy. There was no way Stas would let her go, and her mother wouldn't allow it, either. She had a plan, though. What if she could get Jackie to support her? She then decided that the three of them should go on a cruise together.

Obviously, Lee's goal was for Jackie to get to know and like Onassis and then approve their relationship. People respected Jackie. Her opinion mattered, not only within the family but publicly. If Lee could get her on her side, maybe it would help her cause with Stas. Maybe he'd actually grant her a divorce if Jackie asked him. Lee had to know, though, how Jackie felt about extramarital affairs and would never cooperate.

Playing on the president's sympathies, Lee proposed the cruise to him, saying it might help Jackie get over Patrick's death. Jack gave his permission. "He sent me to Greece," Jackie said in her oral history, "which was, you know, for a sad reason, but he thought I was getting depressed after losing Patrick."

On October 1, Jackie, Provi, and Secret Service agents Clint Hill and Paul Landis took off from New York City on a TWA flight headed to Rome and then to Athens. They arrived the morning of October 2 and two days later set sail on Onassis's yacht, the *Christina,* with about a dozen other passengers.

Aristotle Onassis was on the deck ready to greet the Bouvier sisters. After he kissed Lee, Jackie approached. "Welcome aboard," he told her. When he then kissed her on the cheek, Clint Hill cringed. Two years earlier, the president had told him to make sure he kept Onassis away from his wife. Now here he was kissing her and running his hands down her arms.

What happened on this cruise has been documented many times in the past. Jackie was flirtatious with Ari, holding his hand and speaking with him to the exclusion of everyone else. Onassis was intrigued by her. "Sometimes unhappiness in a woman can be sexy," he said. He talked to her about Patrick, saying he had a son of his own and that he was sympathetic to her loss. They had some sort of chemistry, no doubt about it, and Lee's plan had definitely gone off the rails. However, in fairness, Jackie wasn't aware of Lee's strategy. If she had been, it might have changed the way she behaved with Onassis. As it was, Lee was very concerned because she knew Ari well. "For him, life was a chess game," she said. "Once he had made his winning move, the game was over."

As the *Christina* sailed back to shore, Ari found Lee on the deck, gazing out at the sea, deep in thought. Ari approached her from behind and wrapped his arms around her. When she turned to face him, he kissed her on the forehead. After burying herself in his chest, she kissed him fully on the lips. It was a bold move considering that Jackie was less than twenty feet away, sunning herself on a chaise. With Lee still in his arms, Ari looked over at Jackie. They locked eyes.

Later that day, as Jackie read a book on the deck, she heard squeals and splashing sounds. When she rose to investigate, she found a nude Lee frol-

icking in the ocean with Ari, who had on swim trunks. It seemed inappropriate to Jackie or, as she later put it, "beyond the pale," especially since Lee
had chosen a spot where she knew Jackie would notice them. The *Christina*
was such a mammoth yacht, she could've just as easily jumped off a side farther away from her sister. She obviously wanted Jackie to see. Later, Jackie
told one intimate, "That was such a bitchy thing for Lee to do."

On the way home in the plane, the Bouvier sisters were chatty and con-
vivial as they shared sparkling white wine and talked about their vacation.
Lee was always good at covering up her feelings, and even though she was
concerned about her sister's rapport with Ari, she didn't show it. Jackie was
adept at camouflaging her feelings, too. It's one of the things they had in
common, the ability to hide their real feelings from each other. As they
spoke about their host, Jackie compared him to Odysseus from Homer's
poem *The Odyssey*. "He's shrewd and generous and noble," she said of Onassis. When it came to sheer sex appeal, however, there was only man who
could possibly compare, and they both knew who that was. "Daddy," Lee
said with a resigned smile.

"Exactly," agreed Jackie.

BLACK JACK'S DECLINE

✧✧✧✧✧✧✧✧✧✧✧✧

Jackie Bouvier analyzed her father as she sat next to him in one of two stiff, uncomfortable chairs in front of the black-and-white television. As he watched it, she watched him. She began to speak. "Quiet, Jackie," Jack Bouvier scolded her. "*Gunsmoke*'s on."

When her father's long-term caregiver, a woman named Esther Lindstrom, called Jackie to tell her Jack wasn't well, Jackie knew she needed to go to East Hampton to see him. She showed up on a Friday night, planning to spend the weekend and leave first thing Monday morning.

As soon as Jack opened the door, Jackie was alarmed. It had only been a couple of months since she last saw him, but he barely looked like that same man. He was just sixty-six but seemed much older to her. He was pale, his hair once so jet-black and full, now gray and thinning. His skin was blotchy, his hands and arms blighted with unsightly red sores.

Letting her eyes roam about the small, cramped living room, Jackie found herself lost in family history, which was assiduously documented by photographs in silver and gold frames. There she was at the age of four with her mother at a horse show; at the age of seven with her father in one of his custom-made cars; at the age of eighteen in her debutante gown. While one or two pictures of her sister, Lee, were also on display, most of the photographs in this room were of her at different stages of her life, from her infancy in 1929 to her wedding to John Kennedy in 1953. There she was, over and over, that same face, sometimes brooding, sometimes smiling, staring from every tabletop.

Beset with money problems, Jack had recently been forced to sell his seat on the exchange for about $90,000. That was a disappointment. He felt it should have gone for much more, but that was a decent amount, almost $1 million in today's money. Finances weren't an issue for him. Apathy was his biggest problem. Without a seat to trade from on Wall Street, he fell into a deep depression and now saw no reason to even leave the house. His only brother, Bud, had died of alcoholism a few years back, and his three sisters, Edith and twins Maude and Michelle, had their own problems. Edith, for instance, was living in a run-down mansion in East Hampton called Grey Gardens with her daughter, nicknamed "Little Edie," and the two were recluses whose home had been overrun by stray cats. When Jackie asked how they were, he just grunted. He had no idea.

As she became older and more experienced, Jackie began to see her father in a different light. She had idolized him when she was younger and felt he could do no wrong. She'd even joked with him about the other women in his life, not taking his womanizing seriously. However, by the summer of 1957, she was in an unhappy marriage of her own. Now, she found herself more conflicted about him. With maturity came judgment, and she identified strongly with what her mother had gone through. Still, he was her father; she loved him with all her heart and tried not to hold his earlier poor decisions against him. "All men are rats," he used to tell her, and as a young girl, Jackie wondered if that was true. As a grown woman, she knew exactly what he meant.

On Saturday, Jack seemed drunk from the moment he woke up until that night when he began a fitful sleep under the influence of tranquilizers. Sunday was the same. When Jackie left on Monday morning, she felt anxious about his condition. She must have been desperate because as soon as she got back to Washington, she called her mother and asked for a favor. Would she please go with her to see her father? He needed help.

Janet responded, "I'd sooner have all my teeth pulled." She hadn't spoken to her ex-husband since she betrayed him at Jackie's wedding. Now, four years later, Jackie was appealing to her to help a man who, had it not been for Janet's behavior that day, might never have fallen off the wagon. But if anyone could reach him, Jackie knew her mother could.

As angry as Janet still was at him for the way he'd treated her during their marriage, there was still room for affection. Her life had worked out. She was now happily married and living in two lavish estates—Hammersmith Farm and Merrywood—whereas Jack was stuck in a small, dingy apartment, an alcoholic with limited prospects. He was still a link to her past, the father of two of her children. Moreover, it had been because of his influence on her that she had the courage to leave her father's home and become her own woman. Jack had been the only one to support her when she needed it, and she couldn't forget it.

Jackie really wanted to straighten out any misunderstanding about her wedding. She had written to her father from her honeymoon to forgive him for what had happened, but she knew it wasn't his fault, it was her mother's. She hated the fact that her mother's little plot had stained the day for her, and she wanted to somehow make it right before her father was gone. She insisted that Janet go with her to see Jack. She wouldn't take no for an answer. Janet finally agreed, and a visit was arranged for the last week in July of 1957. Before the first rays of sun shimmered over bucolic Merrywood, mother and daughter were on their way to the airport in Washington for the one-hour trip to New York.

When Jackie and Janet walked into Jack's living room, Jack Bouvier was sitting in his chair doing what he did all day—watching television. He was so completely immersed in his program he didn't even hear them enter the room. When he looked up and saw his ex-wife standing before him, his first instinct was to crack a joke: "Well, well, well, Janet Lee! As I live and drink." But then his eyes misted over. It happened whenever he was in her presence. She was older now at fifty but, as far as he was concerned, she was still the same young girl he'd met thirty years earlier at the Maidstone Club. She was just as fresh and just as beguiling. He wanted to hate her, but how could he?

Janet demanded that he get out of his chair and give her a hug. As he struggled to stand, she caught her breath in surprise. Like Jackie, she couldn't believe how much he had changed. He was bent over and brittle. How could a man so vital and handsome in his prime turn into such an old, sick person?

Though Janet was dismayed by Jack's appearance, she did precisely what Jackie hoped she'd do: she gave him hell, saying she knew he was better than what he'd become in recent years. "You need to pull yourself together and live your life," she told him, according to Kathleen Bouvier, Jack's niece. "'You're still a young man, but look how you're living,' she said. 'This isn't the Jack Bouvier I knew.'"

When Janet asked Jackie to leave so that she could have a private moment with her father, Jackie went into the kitchen with Jack's caregiver,

Esther. In the kitchen, framed on the wall next to the refrigerator, was a photograph of Jackie and Lee posing with their father at the Central Park Zoo. Every time Jackie saw it, she couldn't take her eyes off it because it held such a strong memory for her.

NEW YORK CITY, 1937

"Your father will be here in fifteen minutes," Janet was telling her daughters. "Now, take off those new Mary Janes."

It was 1937. Jackie was eight, Lee, four. Jack Bouvier was coming to take them to the zoo, and they couldn't have been more excited about it. They took off their shoes and handed them to their mother. Lee's Mary Janes were black, Jackie's were white. Janet took a red pen and wrote her phone number on the inside of each one: "Rhinelander 4–6167." Just as she was doing so, Jack Bouvier showed up at the front door, tan and good-looking as ever in his three-piece suit and jaunty hat. "Why, Janet?" he asked as he watched her write inside the shoes.

"You know why," she said. "Bruno Hauptmann!"

Jack shot back, "Not that Lindbergh baby, again."

Janet was deathly afraid of her daughters being kidnapped and murdered the same way as aviator Charles Lindbergh's twenty-month-old son had been five years earlier. The media called it the "Crime of the Century," and it made an indelible impression on Janet as it did parents across the country. It didn't matter if a mother was famous or not, the idea that her child could be kidnapped struck fear in the hearts of many American women, including Janet, who, when she became nervous about the girls' safety, would repeatedly exclaim, "Bruno Hauptmann! Bruno Hauptmann!" Whenever the girls got new shoes, Janet would write their telephone number on the inside soles.

Jack took it as a personal affront, as if she didn't trust him to watch over his own daughters. She handed the shoes back to the girls. They put them on quickly and were out the door with their father.

When Jack returned them to his ex-wife at the end of the day, they had on new shoes, red Mary Janes. "What happened to their other shoes?" Janet asked.

"I got rid of them," he said.

Janet sent the girls to their bedroom.

The sisters then listened with their ears to the door as accusations flew back and forth. When he was gone, Janet went to them and let them have it. Why would they give their brand-new shoes to their father?

"Because he asked us to," Jackie said, "and bought us new ones, Mummy. And they're red!"

"You do not give your shoes to your father. Do you hear me?" Janet screamed. She then smacked Jackie across the face. As Jackie squealed, Janet stormed from the room and slammed the door hard.

EAST HAMPTON, JULY 1957

As Jackie stared at the picture on the refrigerator, Janet called her back into the parlor. She leaned down and hugged Jack and whispered something in his ear. He smiled and nodded. Janet turned from him and told Jackie she'd be in the hallway: "Say goodbye to your father."

Jack and Janet had finally had a long-overdue heart-to-heart about Jackie's wedding. If Janet truly didn't want him to give away their daughter, he told her, all she had to do was ask him to beg off and explain why. He wanted to know why she felt she had to go through all the trouble of getting him drunk and embarrassing him in front of everyone.

Jack's question really made Janet think. She was sorry she'd handled it as she had, she said, but she did it for Jackie. Her parents had cleared the air as Jackie had hoped they would. It would still sometimes be hard for her to look at her wedding photos, but knowing she'd been able to reconcile things between her parents meant a lot to her.

After Jackie arranged her parents' reconciliation, she continued to monitor her father's health. It never improved, and he continued drinking.

Jackie spent her twenty-eighth birthday, July 29, with the Auchinclosses at Hammersmith. Jack Kennedy wasn't with her; he was at Hyannis Port with his parents because the Auchinclosses were still unwilling to welcome him in their home. Jackie didn't fight it. She spent her birthday week helping her mother pack for a cruise she, Hugh, Jamie, and Janet Jr. had planned. They left on August 1.

On August 3, Jackie got word that her father had collapsed and had been taken to Lenox Hill Hospital. It was kidney cancer. He'd secretly been battling it for some time. When he slipped into a coma, Jackie made plans to be at his side.

Unfortunately, Jackie and Jack Kennedy arrived at Lenox Hill just moments after Jack Bouvier passed. Jackie stayed with him, kneeling at his side while crying and praying until a nurse told her it was time for her to go. After Jack helped her up, she walked away from the father who meant the world to her but who was also disappointing in so many ways—but not before turning to take one last look.

The funeral was on August 6, 1957, at St. Patrick's Cathedral in New York. Jackie was able to get in touch with her mother on the cruise to tell her the news, but it was impossible for Janet to return for the services.

About two weeks after the funeral, Esther called Jackie to say she and Lee might want to go through their father's things and take any precious heirlooms or mementos before his siblings rummaged through them. The Bouvier sisters made plans to go to East Hampton together.

Once in their father's bedroom, Jackie and Lee were overwhelmed. There was just so much to go through: his expensive suits, jewelry, scrapbooks of photographs, framed pictures. Jackie and Lee just sat on his bed, gazed around, and wondered how they'd ever be able to make any decisions about what to keep. As they were sitting on the bed, something came over Lee—she would say it felt like "an intuition"—and she was compelled to reach under the bed. When she did so, her hand touched a box. She pulled it out. It had Jackie's name on it. The sisters looked at one another, and Jackie reached under and pulled out a similar box with Lee's name on it. They traded boxes, then opened them.

Carefully nesting in white tissue paper was a pair of shoes in each box. "My God," Jackie said as she held up a white Mary Jane.

On the sole, in red pen, was written: "Rhinelander 4–6167."

EVERY GODDAMN SECOND

◇◇◇◇◇◇◇◇◇◇◇◇◇

Hugh Auchincloss didn't think the president should go to Texas. It was October 25, 1963, and he was reading a *Washington Post* story about Adlai Stevenson, the U.S. ambassador to the United Nations, getting booed, spat on, and struck with placards by protestors outside the Dallas Memorial Auditorium. Hugh found it disgraceful.

He was sitting in his study at O Street with Clark Weston; Clark's son, Jack; and Margaret Kearny, who worked for him in the Washington bureau of his brokerage firm. Hugh sat on one side of a chess board, Margaret on the other. As they made their moves, he barely concentrated while also reading the newspaper.

Hugh opined that the quickest way for Americans to lose their right of free speech would be to permit mob rule and its attacks on government officials. Whether someone liked Adlai or not, Hugh said, he deserved respect. "This kind of nonsense after a speech about peace gives the Soviets and everyone else a terrible impression of America," he said.

In a column next to the article, a writer editorialized, "The President of the United States will be here in November. We trust he will be welcomed and accorded the respect and dignity that go with the office he represents."

"Jack shouldn't go," Hugh said. "Too much hate and extremism." He said JFK had no friends in Texas. When Margaret asked if Jackie was going, Hugh doubted it since she never went on domestic political trips with the president. However, since she and Jack were much closer these days, anything was possible. "I'll find out," he said.

As Hugh picked up the phone and dialed, everyone smiled. They knew he got a kick out of showing off that he could get the president on the line. "NA 8–1414," he said aloud as he dialed the number by memory. (The NA stood for "National," and this had been the phone number for the Executive Office of the President for many years.) After a moment: "Evelyn Lincoln, please." Then, a moment later: "Mrs. Lincoln, this is Hugh D. Auchincloss. Is Jack in the Oval Office?" After a pause, he said, "No. It's not important, Mrs. Lincoln. Just had a question." He hung up and turned to the others and said the president was at a luncheon for Radio Free Europe. He added that he and Janet would be joining Jack and Jackie at their new summer home, Wexford, over the upcoming weekend, and he'd bring up Texas then.

The next day, Hugh called Jackie to tell her he was worried about Jack going to Dallas. That's when she told him that she was, too. Now he was really worried.

Jackie shared her stepfather's apprehension. She and Jack recently had dinner with Franklin and Suzanne Roosevelt, both of whom felt it wasn't safe to go to Texas. (That dinner took place on October 25, the day after the Adlai Stevenson incident in Texas.) However, the conservative governor John Connally and the liberal senator Ralph Yarborough were feuding at the time, and Jack was worried it could threaten the Democratic Party in Texas. He thought Jackie might be a breath of fresh air.

"Jack's poll numbers are down in the South," Jackie said, "because of Civil Rights. Whites in the South think he's moving too fast and Negros think he's not moving fast enough. He can't win."

Earlier in the year, JFK hosted a reception at the White House for Black leaders, with Sammy Davis Jr. as a special guest. At the time, Sammy was married to a white woman, the Swedish actress May Britt. Jack was reluctant to have the couple photographed together because he worried about the political blowback. He had an aide ask Jackie to come down from the private quarters and take May aside so that she wouldn't be photographed with her husband. Jackie refused. Eventually, Jack coaxed her downstairs, but she wouldn't do as he asked. Strongly supportive of civil rights, Jackie always made sure African Americans were invited to the White House, and often as special guests. Sammy and May had been banned from the inauguration three years earlier. Had things not changed at all? Jackie wanted to now help Jack raise his numbers in the South, where racism ran rampant. "And we all want Jack to be reelected, don't we?" she asked Hugh.

Hugh couldn't argue with her. The JFK–Johnson ticket had carried Texas by only about forty-five thousand votes in 1960, so there was certainly work to be done there. Jackie said she'd talk to the Secret Service about making sure security for her and Jack was adequate.

"I'm very proud of you for going," Hugh told her, "but I fear you'll really hate it down there." She laughed.

"Oh, Uncle Hughdie," she said, "I'm sure I'll hate every goddamn second of it."

JFK'S NEW LEAF

◇◇◇◇◇◇◇◇◇◇◇◇

By this time, the fall of '63, Vietnam had become a real worry for President Kennedy. Following the overthrow of his government by South Vietnamese military forces on November 2, President Ngo Dinh Diem and his younger brother Ngo Dinh Nhu were captured and executed. At the time, the United States denied having any knowledge of the coup that had overthrown Diem. Although Jack was aware of and the U.S. had had communication with the generals who'd organized the plot and had encouraged them, no one expected it to end as it had. Arthur Schlesinger said the president was "somber and shaken. I had not seen him so depressed since the Bay of Pigs."

Jack felt the matter had been handled badly and that he should've given Robert McNamara and Maxwell Taylor more time to weigh in on the risks. In a short time, America would become more heavily involved in Vietnam to stabilize the South Vietnamese government.

The day of the murders, Jack was supposed to go to Chicago for the army–air force football game. He decided not to go; instead, he made a big change in his personal life. He and Jackie had gotten much closer in recent months, which may explain why he sent for Mary Meyer on November 2. When she showed up at the White House, he ended their affair. Some intimates heard that Jackie had insisted upon it. Others felt that taking such a stand wasn't in her character and speculated that Jack had made the decision for the sake of their marriage. When asked about Mary, all Jackie said was, "We're not social with her any longer."

(Mary Pinchot Meyer would meet a tragic death in October 1964. She was murdered while on her daily walk along the Chesapeake and Ohio Canal towpath in Georgetown. The crime was never solved.)

The next weekend, Jack and Jackie welcomed Janet and Hugh to their new home, Wexford. It was the third time the Kennedys had been there for the weekend. Ben and Tony Bradlee were also present.

While the women toured the new house, Jack talked to Hugh and Ben about his tax reduction bill, the biggest in history. He complained about it being hopelessly stuck in the House Ways and Means Committee. The Civil Rights Bill was also tied up in the House. He was frustrated by the way government worked, or as he put it, "doesn't work." However, he still believed in the process of legislation and felt sure he'd sign both bills into law by the summer of '64.

Soon they were talking about Texas. Jack told Hugh not to worry about Jackie. He said he'd never allow anything to happen to her in Texas or anywhere else. He then revealed that he and Jackie had just finalized a lease on an estate next to Hammersmith in Newport, called Annandale Farm. "Mummy's going to be so delighted," Hugh said. "Having you two as neighbors? You sure you want us that close?" The men laughed. Things were so much better, all around. Jackie's marriage was intact, and Hugh—who had once barred JFK from entering his home—was now comfortable having him live next door.

Less than a week later, the announcement was made by Pierre Salinger: the president and First Lady would be going to Texas on November 21. It was to be a quick, two-day, five-city tour—San Antonio, Houston, Fort Worth, Dallas, and Austin—in preparation for Jack's 1964 presidential campaign. On that same day, Nelson Rockefeller was the first to officially announce his candidacy, attacking JFK's "failures at home and abroad."

There was a lot of surprise about Jackie's decision to go to Texas since it would be the first domestic trip she'd ever taken with Jack as president. When Jackie's press secretary, Pam Turnure, asked how she might explain it to the press, Jackie was clear: "Say I am going out with my husband on this trip, and that it will be the first of many that I hope to make with him. Say yes that I plan to campaign with him, and that I will do anything to help my husband be elected president again."

"Will we see you at Thanksgiving?" Rose Kennedy asked Jackie. "Maybe you can teach me to do that Twist dance?" Jackie was packing for the trip to Dallas when her mother-in-law called. Rose had just gotten home from Mass and felt a strong intuition to talk to her daughter-in-law before golfing her usual nine holes. Jackie said she'd be at the Cape for the holiday, and if Rose was game, Jackie would love to teach her the Twist.

The weather had been mild, Rose told Jackie, so the garden flowers were still in bloom—the black-eyed Susans, geraniums, catmint, wild morning glories, and Russian sage, all hearty, alive, and bursting with color just as Jackie liked. Jackie said she couldn't wait to get there. Texas would be behind her. Rose said she was proud of Jackie for wanting to be at her son's side. When she asked her to take care of him, Jackie chuckled. "The president doesn't need taking care of," she said. "It's the First Lady who's likely to be a mess."

Rose laughed. "Oh, you'll be just fine, my dear," she said. "God has blessed you, Jackie. God has always blessed you."

BOOK II

The Tragic Heroine

FRIDAY, NOVEMBER 22, 1963

∞∞∞∞∞∞∞∞∞∞

DEALEY PLAZA

My God, what are they doing? My God, they've killed Jack, they've killed my husband, Jack, Jack.

As the Lincoln convertible picked up speed, Jackie suddenly began to climb out onto the trunk while reaching out. It wasn't clear at first, but soon the horror of the moment registered: she was trying to retrieve a piece of her husband's skull. Clint Hill, who'd been running behind the car, heroically jumped up onto the trunk, grabbed her, and pushed her back into the automobile. Jack slumped into her lap.

Covered in his blood, Jackie cradled him.

THE VIGIL

◇◇◇◇◇◇◇◇◇◇◇

Within hours, Jackie was at the Bethesda Naval Hospital in Maryland. The president was dead, and she and her brother-in-law Bobby had brought his body to Bethesda for an autopsy. It had all happened so fast, and so horribly.

When the elevator doors opened, Jackie walked out, dazed and confused. Immediately, she was surrounded by people who didn't know how to act around her. All they could do was stare and cry. She looked haunted, her eyes vacant, her dress and stockings splattered with blood and brains. Searching the crowd, she found her mother. When their eyes met, she could see the shock on Janet's face. Earlier, when asked if she wanted to change, Jackie had been firm; her answer later became part of history. "No. Let them see what they've done."

Ignoring the blood, Janet walked quickly to her daughter. "Oh, Jacqueline," she exclaimed as she took her into her arms. "I'm so sorry, but if this had to happen, thank God Jack wasn't maimed."

Jackie looked at Janet with confusion, as did everyone who heard the comment. But then, she understood, because she knew something the others didn't, something only she and her mother shared.

When Jackie's father suffered his stroke and was paralyzed, Jack Kennedy had told her that if anything like that ever happened to him, he wouldn't want to live. He'd said, "I can't be an invalid. Don't allow it." Years later, he'd bear witness to his own father's suffering after his own stroke. As he and Jackie watched Joseph try to communicate with Hugh Auchincloss at the Cape, he said to her, "Don't let that be me."

"And I hope you will never live anyplace but in this country because Jack would want that," Janet quickly added.

This, too, seemed odd, but it was actually a fear that had haunted Janet for years. She always worried that Jackie, who'd wanted to move to Paris after she won the Prix de Paris as a younger woman, would one day actually do it and want to stay. Janet had made her turn down the prize back then. But now, all these years later, with Jack gone, her imagination ran wild, and she worried that Jackie might leave and take the children. Jackie looked at her mother with dismay. "But of course, I'm going to live in Georgetown," she said, "where Jack and I were."

Hugh then took Jackie in his arms. "For this thing to happen to you and Jack breaks my heart into a million pieces," he told her. As he held her in his arms, Bobby walked over, and Jackie asked about his mother.

Bobby explained that Rose Kennedy had been lying down for a nap when she heard her niece Ann Gargan's radio blaring down the hall. She rose and asked her to turn it down. Ann told her she'd heard on the news that someone had shot the president. Bobby called soon after to confirm it. Rose then decided not to tell Joe until Ted and Eunice could get to the Cape from Washington. The staff unplugged all the television sets in the house to prevent Joe from watching the news.

Bobby then pulled Jackie aside and whispered in her ear. When she returned to the Auchinclosses', she told them someone had been arrested for Jack's murder. "Jack didn't even have the satisfaction of being killed for something that matters, like civil rights," she said. "It had to be some silly little Communist." Hugh's mouth dropped open.

Jackie turned to her mother and asked, "Will you both stay with me tonight at the White House?"

Janet said yes, of course they would.

But what about the children? Janet told Jackie they were at O Street.

"But why?" Jackie asked.

Janet explained that Maud Shaw had called to say she received a message that Jackie wanted them out of the White House. "It's okay," Janet said, "they're with Jamie." Jackie became upset.

"But I never said that," she insisted. In fact, she wanted them in their own bedrooms at the White House, where things could be as normal for them as possible. In fact, Secret Service agents Clint Hill and Bob Foster had told Maud that Jackie wanted Caroline and John taken to their grandmother's home without first checking with Jackie.

Hugh turned to a police officer. "You heard Mrs. Kennedy," he said. "Use your talking machine [walkie-talkie] to tell someone to fetch the children at our house and bring them to the White House."

Janet then asked Jackie how she wanted the children to be told about their father. Jackie said Maud should do it. The Auchinclosses looked at each other with surprise. *Maud should do it?*

Soon, the suite was filled with people, including Mary Gallagher, Evelyn Lincoln, Dave Powers, Robert McNamara, Pam Turnure, and Charles and Martha Bartlett. "I looked around and realized that these people were the same ones who'd gathered when Patrick died just three months earlier," said Mary Gallagher, "and as that thought hit me, I felt a wave of nausea and had to sit down. It was such a small space and so packed with people, very hot and very loud."

Janet talked about being with Joan Kennedy that same morning, helping her plan a party to celebrate her and Ted's fifth wedding anniversary. Afterward, she dropped her off at Elizabeth Arden to get her hair done. "I guess that's all for nothing now," she said, absently. Joan was home in bed, Bobby said, after having taken a strong sedative.

When Ethel Kennedy arrived, Jackie fell into her arms. "Don't worry. Jack went straight to heaven," she assured Jackie. Jackie wished she had Ethel's faith. "Bobby's been so wonderful," she told her.

"He'll always help you," Ethel said.

In the tradition of an Irish wake, it began to feel almost festive. Bobby became obsessed with finding a record player. Sandwiches and cold drinks were served. Jackie sat in the kitchenette at a small table, still in her blood-soaked clothing, telling anyone who'd listen every detail of what happened in Dallas. "Nothing was repulsive to me," she said. She talked about Jack's body on the gurney at the Parkland hospital and the moment doctors told her he was gone. "I know," she'd whispered. She talked about kissing his lips, how his foot, so deathly white, stuck out from under the sheet and how she kissed it, too. She talked about how he was given the last rites while she held his cold hand, how she put her wedding ring on his finger, how she kissed his fingers.

"Talking it all out over and over became a kind of purgation for her," is how Robert McNamara later put it.

She also talked about the flight from Dallas, how Lyndon Johnson insisted she stand at his and Lady Bird's side as he took the oath of office.

Jackie also spoke about Jack's impending funeral and how she wanted it designed, as much like President Abraham Lincoln's as possible. "She had me look into all of the details of that," White House curator James Ketchum recalled. "We got out our history books and really did a lot of research into how to make this as historically accurate as possible." There was also discussion about where Jack should be buried; the Kennedys wanted him at Brookline, but Jackie felt he should be interred at Arlington National Cemetery. They also talked about Governor John Connally, who'd been shot in the same car as Jack, and how relieved they were that he was recovering at Parkland. When Jackie noticed Ben Bradlee in the crowd, she snapped at him, "None of this is for *Newsweek,* Benny."

Kenny O'Donnell, Jack's chief of staff, was determined to get Jackie's wedding ring back to her. Feeling she'd one day regret not having it, he went to the morgue and asked for it. Rear Admiral Dr. George Burkley took it from Jack's finger but then decided he wanted to be the one to return it to Jackie. He brushed by a seething O'Donnell and raced up to the seventeenth floor.

On and on the vigil went, with people coming and going, for eight long, punishing hours. Yusha arrived late; he took a flight from New York after just having returned from Beirut. When Jackie saw him, she fell into his arms. Janet kept asking Jackie to change her clothing until, finally, Ethel snapped at her, "How many times must she say no?" Offended, Janet stormed off. Jackie then explained to Ethel that she wanted to keep wearing the dress not only because of what it represented but also because of the smell of Jack's blood. "It's all I have left of him," she said.

After a few hours, Hugh thought Jackie looked exhausted. By this time, Lee Harvey Oswald had been formally charged; everyone knew it from the television blaring in the bedroom. Hugh felt Jackie should get back to the White House. He was also concerned about her mother, who, by now, was also wilting. Hugh, in his gentlest voice, told Jackie, "It's time for Mummy and me to go. Won't you come with us?"

Jackie grabbed Janet by the shoulders. She asked where she and the children would now live. "It can't be the White House, Mummy. So, where? I have no home." Janet, taken by surprise, didn't know how to respond. "Then, you must stay here," Jackie begged, "so we can figure this out, Mummy."

It was then that it occurred to Hugh that Jackie didn't want the day to end. It made sense. After all, it was the last day Jack had been alive. Tomorrow would be the first day he'd be truly gone. "Please, Jackie," he pleaded, "we should go. This day has to be over."

No, Jackie said, not yet. The autopsy wasn't finished. She wanted to stay with Bobby until it was done so that they could then bring the casket back to the White House. What was taking so much time was the reconstruction of Jack's head in case of a public viewing. Jackie had said no to the idea, it would be too "morbid." Bobby insisted on an open casket, though, so Jack's body had to be ready just in case.

As the Auchinclosses began to leave the hospitality suite, Jackie again asked if they'd stay at the White House. She now had an additional request: Would they sleep in Jack's bed? Again, Janet and Hugh were taken aback. Yes, Hugh said, they'd stay at the White House and would sleep anywhere Jackie wished.

SATURDAY, NOVEMBER 23, 1963

◇◇◇◇◇◇◇◇◇◇◇◇◇◇

By about 3:00 a.m. on Saturday, work was finally finished on President Kennedy's body, and it was ready to be released. Bobby viewed it and decided Jackie was right. The casket would be closed. Within an hour, it would rest in the East Room of the White House on the same assembly used for President Abraham Lincoln in 1865. Soon various officials and heads of state would view the flag-draped coffin.

Once back at the White House, Bobby Kennedy and his sister Jean retired to the Queen's Bedroom on the northeast corner of the second floor, down the hall from Jackie's suite—Jean in the actual bedroom and Bobby on a convertible couch in the sitting room. Meanwhile, Janet and Hugh waited in the living room for Jackie. "Do the children know?" Jackie asked when she found them. Janet said she'd told Maud to tell them, just as Jackie had insisted.

Poor Maud. It was she who had to tell Caroline about the death of her brother Patrick three months earlier. Now this? "Permission to overstep?" Maud asked Janet, who nodded her consent. "I can't take a child's last happiness from her," Maud said. "I don't have the heart to do it." Janet was too exhausted to argue about it. This was Jackie's wish, and Maud needed to do it without question.

After Jackie thanked Janet for handling Maud, she turned to Hugh. "Uncle Hughdie," Jackie said, "I want you to sleep in Jack's four-poster bed tonight. I don't want it empty." Surprised, Hugh didn't answer until Janet nudged him. Yes, he said, he'd sleep in Jack's bed.

In the southwest corner of the White House residence was Jackie's bedroom and sitting room. Janet went with her to help her change out of her clothes.

The bedroom was massive, with an enormous crystal chandelier hanging at its center. The drapes were a pale blue, the furniture French antiques. There was a double bed with a turquoise corona suspended at the head of it, with draperies extending down to the front corners. Jackie's personal assistant, Provi, was sitting on the edge of that bed when Jackie and Janet walked in. When she laid eyes on Jackie, she nearly fainted at the sight of blood now dried to a brownish color.

Janet and Provi waited while Jackie bathed, and then put her to bed. Dr. Walsh came into the room to give her an injection of Amytal, after which Janet and Provi turned off the lights and left. Meanwhile, Hugh sat in the parlor thinking about sleeping in Jack's bed. Though he was uncomfortable about it, he couldn't help but think of it as an honor. He wasn't sure why Jackie had been so adamant, but if she'd asked anyone else, he would've been offended. While it maybe wasn't something he wanted to do, it was something he knew he needed to do. As Hugh sat and stared at the blaze in the fireplace, Janet returned. He took her hand, and they walked to Jack's bedroom, in front of which was a rack with his luggage already returned from the trip. They walked into the room, JFK's inner sanctum, which Hugh had never before seen.

In the president's bedroom, the curtains were a blue print, the carpet pure white. There was a comfortable ivory-colored easy chair in one corner, a pale blue settee in another. A television in a wooden cabinet sat in another corner with a clutter of books and magazines on top. On an end table was a silver mug of pens and a tablet with the presidential seal. A stack of messages was clipped together next to the telephone. There were prescription bottles on a nightstand. A red tie was flung over a settee. The room was anything but pretentious.

After the Auchinclosses changed into their pajamas, they got into Jack's bed, turned off the lights, and stared at the ceiling. The mattress was made of horsehair. There was a stiff board beneath it. It was the most uncomfortable bed in which they'd ever slept, and they couldn't imagine how Jack—especially given his bad back—ever managed it. Hugh noticed that someone had rolled a cot into the room—maybe Jackie had arranged it?— and decided Janet would be more comfortable there. She got up and lay down and was asleep in minutes. Meanwhile, he stayed in the bed, knowing there was no way he'd sleep. His mind raced. How, he wondered, had he even found himself in such a strange situation?

When he was about forty, five years before he married Janet, Hugh Auchincloss became practically obsessed with a book called *Think and Grow Rich* by Napoleon Hill. One of the first self-help books ever published, it became a guide to success for him. He said it helped him understand that "you have to be open to life because you just never know. You just never know!"

"It's strange but true," Napoleon Hill wrote, "that the most important turning points of life often come at the most unexpected times, and in the most unexpected ways." It was another line Hugh often parroted. Tonight, as he tossed and turned in the bed of the United States president at the insistence of his First Lady on the night of his assassination, those words couldn't have resonated more with Hugh D. Auchincloss.

UNCLE HUGHDIE'S SAFE PLACE

Jackie Bouvier, fourteen, stood in her favorite spot in the Deck Room of Hammersmith, a place where the sweeping view of the dock and of Jamestown in the distance was its most vivid and majestic. Before her was her easel, and on it a watercolor rendering of all she surveyed. She'd been working on her art for two weeks. As she stood staring at it, her stepfather, Hugh, walked into the room and stood behind her. Jackie asked him what he thought. "What do you think?" he asked.

Jackie said her mother didn't like it, felt it was too basic, she said, and didn't capture the subtle nuances of the way the water glistened. "It's not just blue," Janet said of the bay water, "it has greens in it, and browns and all sorts of colors." She didn't like it at all. "Junk it and start over," she said.

"I didn't ask what Mummy thinks of it. What do you think?" Hugh said.

Jackie said she was so affected by her mother's critique, she didn't know what to think. That was a real problem, Hugh told her. She couldn't improve the painting or even discard it unless she had a real belief about it.

Again, she pushed for his opinion.

He took it in. "I agree with Mummy," he said candidly. "It's not your best work. But don't give up on something meaningful. Keep an open mind and make it better. You never know how things will turn out until you follow through."

She smiled and agreed, and then went back to her work.

Whereas her mother was inevitably critical and her father always flattering, Jackie's stepfather provided balance in Jackie's life. He believed in her.

"One of the many reasons Daddy was a success," his son Jamie said, "was because he embraced possibility. Anything was possible if you worked at it. That's how we were raised by him."

In 1939, when his sister Esther introduced him to her friend Janet Bouvier, Hugh could tell that she was at the end of her rope. After her divorce from Jack Bouvier, Janet lived chronically beyond her means, just as her daughters would. No matter that her income was diminished, she still required a maid, a cook, and a governess as well as all the latest fashions. Her Park Avenue apartment had to be filled with exquisite furnishings. At one point, when Jack Bouvier stopped giving her money, she got a job at Macy's as a model to bring in extra income. She hated the work and found the modeling of cocktail dresses for fussy women demeaning, but she did it.

One might've thought Hugh, a man so conscious of finances, would've been dismayed by Janet's spending, but he wasn't. He saw that she wanted to have a big life and was going to act as if she had one until she actually did have one. Meanwhile, she was willing to work if she had to, and he admired it. He wanted to help her. He wanted to give her the life she wanted for herself and her daughters. As he got to know them all better, he became more determined to do just that.

Hugh Auchincloss was born at Hammersmith Farm as Hugh Dudley Auchincloss—or Hughdie (as in Hugh D.)—in 1897 to Hugh Sr. and Emma Brewster Jennings of Fairfield, Connecticut. His father was descended from a distinguished Scottish family, his mother the daughter of Oliver B. Jennings, brother-in-law of William Rockefeller and business partner of John D. Rockefeller. Jennings was a chief investor in Rockefeller's Standard Oil, which had put millions in the family's coffers and which is why Hugh Jr. was so wealthy.

Hugh graduated from Yale in 1920 and went to Russia two years later as a New York representative of the Student's Friendship Fund. He then served as a sailor in World War I. He became a lawyer in 1924 and then a special agent in aeronautics for the Department of Commerce. In 1927, he was appointed an aviation expert in the State Department. He married his first wife, Maya de Chrapovitsky, in 1925. Their son, Hugh Dudley Auchincloss III—Yusha (Russian for "Hugh")—was born in 1927.

Yusha was about a year old when Hugh started his own investment firm with Chauncey Parker and Albert Redpath in Washington, and later New York, called Auchincloss, Parker & Redpath. The Auchinclosses lived in a penthouse in New York until Hugh bought Merrywood, a Georgian-style brick mansion on forty acres of woods along the Potomac, which became their primary home. He would later also inherit Hammersmith Farm as a summer home.

In 1935, Hugh divorced Maya and married Nina Gore Vidal, who had one son from a previous marriage, ten-year-old Gore Vidal, who would grow up to be the famous novelist and playwright. The three of them were soon joined by two more when Nina had Nina—nicknamed Nini—in 1937 and Thomas—Tommy—in 1939. Hugh and Nina divorced in 1941.

Hugh was a sincere man, full of heart. When he married Janet on June 21, 1942, he eagerly welcomed her and her girls into Merrywood and Hammersmith. The girls were conflicted about it, because no one could ever replace their father. They'd loved spending their summers in East Hampton, and all of that changed when their mother remarried and they ended up summering at Merrywood or Hammersmith.

For the next thirty years plus, Hugh Auchincloss would be the father Jackie never had in Jack Bouvier. "Jackie, Lee, Janet, and my father and I soon discarded any reference to 'step,'" recalled Yusha of the youngsters' bonds. "My father financed the sisters' childhood and teen years, paid for their trips to Europe, their debutante parties, and all of the other milestone events. He gave them the kind of life their own father never could've given them."

Jackie would be greatly influenced by her two fathers, Jack Bouvier and Hugh Auchincloss, but in different ways.

From Bouvier, Jackie was taught to expect and accept only the best.

From Auchincloss, Jackie got a different message. He taught Jackie to at least try to understand the value of a dollar. He was wealthy partly because he didn't blow all his money, and he tried to teach his stepdaughters to also be smart about finances. A stockbroker, attorney, and money manager, he understood the importance of fiscal responsibility.

"From the beginning, Daddy reached out to Jackie and made a connection with her," said his son Jamie. "He tried to do the same with Lee, but she was so closed off, it was impossible. Daddy wasn't a psychiatrist. He was just a man, and he had his own problems with intimacy. He couldn't go the extra mile with a person like Lee. But with someone like Jackie, who'd meet him halfway, he could have a real influence. She felt safe with him because he always told her the truth. She trusted him."

N ow, a little more than twenty years after Janet brought her daughters, Jackie and Lee, to live with him at Merrywood, Hugh Auchincloss found himself sleeping in a president's bed in the White House. Whoever could've predicted such a thing?

As he grappled with the bedsheets, trying to get comfortable, he heard a light tap on the door. He rose to answer it. It was Jackie, in her nightgown. She looked pale and troubled. "I can't sleep," she said. She seemed afraid. Perhaps she'd had a nightmare about Dallas. He took her hand. "Come in, Jackie," he said.

They walked to the bed. She lay down. He pulled the blanket up to her neck and tucked in the side. He kissed her on the forehead and told her everything would be okay. He then walked around and got into the other side of the bed.

In moments, Jackie was asleep.

THE ARRIVAL OF A PRINCESS

〰〰〰〰〰〰〰

I t was early Saturday morning when a woman walked down the Center Hall of the White House's second-floor Executive Residence. She wore a smart, cream-colored skirt with leather boots and a tan lynx fur coat. The coat was unbuttoned, revealing a cream-colored turtleneck with a tangle of gold necklaces.

Princess Lee Radziwill was trailed by a uniformed valet who seemed weighed down by luggage. Behind him was Hugh Auchincloss and Jack Weston, the son of Hugh's employee, Clark Weston.

Lee turned to face the valet. "Now, the Queen's Bedroom is just past this landing and to the left, opposite the East Sitting Hall," she said. Of course, the valet knew exactly where the Queen's Bedroom was.

Jackie had asked Hugh to meet Lee's plane at Dulles and then drive her to the White House. However, because of bad weather and his own poor eyesight, Hugh asked the young Jack Weston to do the driving. Jack now followed Hugh, carrying two more suitcases.

Just a tad earlier, at 7:30, the door to the president's bedroom burst open, and young Caroline Kennedy surprised her grandmother by dashing into the room. By this time, Jackie had awakened and was already gone.

"She came in and she had her big giraffe with her, which I think her father had given her," Janet recalled. "She knew we had slept in there; Miss Shaw had told her. She walked over to the bed after she had pushed the giraffe ahead of her, which was sort of to ease her entrance, and John came in pulling some toy. She came over to the bed and pointed to the picture of her father, which covered the front page of the newspaper, and said, 'Who is that?' I said, 'Oh, Caroline, you know that's your daddy.' And she said to me, 'He's dead, isn't he? A man shot him, didn't he?'"

After Janet comforted the children, Maud came to fetch them. Once they were gone, Janet leaned up against the bedroom door to compose herself. That's when she heard Lee arrive. She walked quickly toward the trio in the hallway. "Quiet, Lee," she scolded. "This is the White House. Not the Waldorf."

After Janet had a reunion with her daughter, she told her she wouldn't be sleeping in the Queen's Bedroom, after all. Jean and Bobby were in there. Janet asked Lee if she'd checked with Nancy Tuckerman, Jackie's personal secretary, in advance as to her accommodations. Lee hadn't. Janet then suggested they find Nancy and sort it all out. A Catholic Mass was scheduled in the East Room at ten o'clock, she told her. It would be best to get her settled before then.

Lee slipped off her wet coat and handed it to Jack Weston without looking at him. "Thank you, dah-ling," she told him. As they walked off, Jack heard Janet say, "That was beneath you, Lee." Then, she glanced at her daughter's outfit and asked, "This is what you wear when a president dies?"

Mother and daughter took the elevator downstairs. "It turned out Jackie wanted Lee to stay with her in her bedroom," Nancy Tuckerman recalled. "So, I had her bags taken to the First Lady's room."

After a few words with Nancy, Janet and Lee walked down the long Center Hallway on the first floor, past the Press Corps Offices and Briefing Room. They continued to walk, passing the Cabinet Room before arriving in the alcove just outside the Oval Office. Janet noticed the door to the Oval Office open. As she peeked in, she couldn't hide her surprise. All of Jack's possessions were boxed and being moved out. Later, when she told Jackie about it, Jackie understood. "There can be no gap," she said. "Democracy can have no interruptions. It's what Jack would want. President Johnson is doing the right thing."

Janet and Lee then walked down the West Colonnade, halfway through the Center Hall until they got to the Map Room.

The Map Room was a large sitting room decorated in the Chippendale style with Queen Anne furniture. A rare 1755 French version of a map charted by colonial surveyors hung on a wall next to a case of world maps presented to Jack by the National Geographic Society.

Looking at a map of Washington, Bobby was explaining to Jackie the details of the funeral procession from the Capitol to the White House to St. Matthew's.

The sisters had a tearful reunion during which Jackie wondered about Stas. Lee said he was arriving tomorrow. Jackie then told their mother she wanted Jamie to walk behind the caisson with Bobby, Ted, and Sarge. "Oh, my," Janet said, almost moved to tears.

After Bobby again reviewed the funeral plan, Lee wondered if it was safe, considering the buildings on each side of the road. After all, Jack had just been killed by a sniper. "It's what I want," Jackie insisted. "It's what Jack would want. It's what people will remember." Then, turning to Lee, she said, "It was awful." She wanted to tell her sister about everything. "And I want to hear it, Jacks," Lee said, holding her hand.

EAST ROOM MASS

◇◇◇◇◇◇◇◇◇◇◇◇◇◇

The solemn morning Mass for family and close friends was to be held in the newly restored Family Dining Room. There had been some talk of having it in the East Room, but the idea of asking Jackie to attend a service next to Jack's coffin seemed wrong. Therefore, they set up a portable altar with folding chairs in the Dining Room. Though the room was lovely with its soft yellow walls and matching silk curtains, the makeshift altar looked primitive and not fitting.

Hugh, Janet, Jamie, Janet Jr., and Lee took their seats behind the Kennedys—Bobby and Ethel, Ted and Joan, Sarge and Eunice, Jean and Stephen, and Pat Kennedy Lawford (not Peter, who hadn't arrived yet from Los Angeles). Rose was also present.

After everyone was seated, Jackie, dressed in all black, walked in slowly holding Caroline with one hand, John with the other. Earlier, Father John Cavanaugh, who'd perform the Mass, had heard Jackie's confession. She was contentious with him. "What is it I'm supposed to say?" she asked. "That I ate meat on a Friday three months ago? It's preposterous." If the priest had all the answers, she said, "then tell me why God took Jack so horribly. Tell me that, and maybe I'll tell you my terrible sins."

As she sat down, Jackie looked around disapprovingly. "Why are we doing this in here?" When someone explained, she disagreed and asked that everything be moved into the East Room.

Prior to the service, there had been some controversy about who would be entitled to accept Holy Communion because only Catholics were allowed to receive at the Mass. The Auchinclosses were Episcopalian. Jackie and Lee were Catholic, like their father. "Jamie had just been confirmed in the Episcopal Church that spring," his mother recalled. "Yet, he rose and walked up to the priest to accept his wafer."

The sixteen-year-old then stood waiting patiently at the railing for wine, like Episcopalians. People smiled, including Jackie. Finally, someone tapped him on the shoulder and asked him to move along. Afterward, he and Jackie had a giggle about it.

Following lunch, Jackie wanted to go to the Oval Office to see the new furnishings she had installed just before Texas. By the time she got there with chief usher J. B. West and agent Clint Hill, most of Jack's possessions and furniture had been removed for Lyndon Johnson. She stood in the middle of the new crimson carpet. "This would've been so nice for Jack," she said wistfully. "I wanted him to have the Oval Office he deserved." She gazed around. "This'll be the last time I'll ever be in this room, Mr. Hill," she said.

Clint choked back tears. "Let's go, Mrs. Kennedy," he told her.

She took one last look and walked out.

A SURPRISE GUEST

◇◇◇◇◇◇◇◇◇◇◇◇◇

Jackie spent the rest of Saturday in her private quarters on the second floor, conferring with Bobby and Sargent on details about the funeral. When the telephone rang in her bedroom, she almost didn't answer it. Everyone she wanted to talk to was already at the White House. Reluctantly, she ran in to pick it up. Much to her surprise, it was Aristotle Onassis.

"Are you on the *Christina*?" Jackie asked. No, he said he was in Washington to extend his condolences. When she asked where he was staying, he said the Willard Hotel. "Oh, it's awful there," she told him.

"She said he should come to the White House," recalled Agnetta Castallanos, who was a vice president of Onassis's Olympic Airways. "He said he wouldn't think of imposing on her. However, she said he'd come all the way from Greece for Jack, the least she could do was find a place for him. According to what he told me, he said, 'I also came for you, Jackie.'"

Aristotle had been in Hamburg, Germany, at a cocktail party celebrating the launch of a new tanker when he got the news about the president. He called Lee to express his sympathy and said he wanted to go to Washington to personally give condolences to Jackie. Lee said it was a bad idea. She didn't want the complications she knew his visit would present, but Onassis was insistent.

Lee said she'd get back to Onassis with permission from the White House. He then just packed up and flew to the States. Later, he'd claim he received a formal invitation from Angier Biddle Duke, chief of protocol, which was untrue. He would not have gotten an official invite given Bobby's dislike for him.

No sooner had Jackie hung up with Ari than Lee knocked on her door. Reportedly, they then had a heated conversation about Onassis. Lee was surprised to know he was in Washington and asked where he was staying. Jackie told her she'd invited him to stay at the White House. "Why would you do such a thing?" Lee asked.

"What choice did I have?" Jackie countered. She said nearly every room in the White House was occupied; there hadn't been that many people staying there since Jack's inauguration. Onassis, it would turn out, would be one of only six people in residence who weren't family members. Still, she managed to find a place on the third floor. It wasn't even a bedroom, just a small sitting room on the third floor across the hall from the Utility Room. It had no bathroom; he'd have to use one down the hall. Lee cringed at the thought. "Oh, please, it's not so bad," Jackie said, "Luella is right next door," meaning Luella Hennessey, the nurse tasked with treating Kennedy women after their pregnancies. Considering the extravagant way he'd treated them on the *Christina,* Lee couldn't understand why Jackie wouldn't find better accommodations for Ari. If this was the best she could do, why had she even invited him to the White House?

Jamie Auchincloss believes Onassis misunderstood Jackie's intentions while they were in Greece. "She sent him signals on a fantasy vacation that were tantalizing but not necessarily accurate," he speculated. "He thought she was interested. She wasn't. Eventually, reality always catches up to fantasy."

Later that evening, Onassis arrived at the White House, which, he later said, was "the center of the world that week, so I should have been there."

Jackie had left instructions for him to be taken straight to his room and brought a menu and then a meal of his choice. She didn't see him. When Lee finally screwed up the courage to visit him, it was as bad as she'd feared. "He's being kept like a prisoner of war," she exclaimed with typical theatrical flair.

"Imagine it," recalled Ari and Lee's mutual friend, the noted writer Taki Theodoracopulos. "There he sat, this Greek titan, one of the wealthiest men in the world, accustomed to all of the extravagances of the rich and powerful, in a sitting room that didn't even have a bed, just a small couch, which, comically enough, fit him when he stretched out on it. There was a black-and-white television, shelves teeming with volumes about American history, and, unfortunately, no window."

Ever the showman, Ari greeted Lee as if welcoming her into a grand suite at the Hotel de Paris in Monte Carlo. A silver tray with french bread and cheese and crackers was on an end table. He offered her red wine. He didn't mind the meager accommodation, he told her, because it reminded him of when he was down to his last $2 million in 1940s New York after escaping the war. Onassis never acted as one might expect him to. Lee was thrown. Taki added, "Knowing her, there had to be a part of Lee that thought, *Okay, if this is how Jackie treats him, perhaps I overreacted when I feared she was making a play for him on the cruise.* Typical of their relationship, Lee was put off balance by Jackie, and now she didn't know which end was up."

Making things all the more complex, Ari had a special request: he wanted to take part in tomorrow's funeral.

When Lee asked Jackie, "What should I tell him?" she answered, "Tell him to stay in his room and watch it on television like the rest of America. We should be back by two." She said that even Joseph Kennedy would be watching the funeral on TV. In fact, Kennedy's doctor had told him he was well enough to attend in person, but he decided to stay home with his friend Father John Cavanaugh and watch it on TV. Rose would attend the funeral without him.

That night, a dinner was scheduled in the President's Dining Room for twelve, including Bobby and Ethel, Ted and Joan, Steve and Jean, and Lee and Stas. Typical of the way feelings of great grief are sometimes associated with inappropriate levity, Bobby snatched Ethel's wig and passed it down the table so that some of the guests could try it on. The laughter must have offered relief for those present. At the completion of the rowdy meal, they all went down to the East Room to kneel by the catafalque and pray for Jack's soul.

Jackie didn't attend the dinner. Instead, she stayed in her bedroom. When the White House's maître d'hôtel, Charles Ficklin, offered her sandwiches, she waved him off. She'd have only a cup of broth while reviewing plans for the funeral cortège, which would leave the White House at noon the next day. There had been a great many last-minute details, which she'd worked on with the help of Bobby and Sargent. Later, she wrote a long letter to Jack, page after page of ruined hopes and dreams for their future together, which she wanted to be put into his coffin.

AN ICONIC DRESS

⬥⬥⬥⬥⬥⬥⬥⬥⬥⬥⬥⬥

On Saturday evening, as the Auchinclosses prepared to leave the White House and go back to O Street to spend the night with Jamie and Janet Jr., Provi walked quickly to Janet and handed her a white box. "What's this?" Janet asked. Provi couldn't answer; she just shook her head sadly and walked away.

Janet took the box to a corner and opened it. Her throat tightened. She quickly closed it.

When Janet and Hugh got back to O Street, she took the elevator, recently installed because of Hugh's emphysema, to the third floor. In her hands was the box Provi had given her. She then climbed the stairs to the attic. Turning on the light, she walked to the back of the attic. There on a top shelf was stored Jackie's wedding trousseau. On top of the box was written: "September 12, 1953."

There was a small desk under a window. Janet put down the box she'd been carrying. With a red pen, she wrote on top of it: "November 22, 1963." She then gently placed the box containing the clothing from the worst day in her daughter's life next to the one from what she thought of as the best day.

Jackie's carefully folded, bloodstained dress, along with her blouse, her handbag, shoes, and stockings, all with blood still on them, was never cleaned. It's now kept in an acid-free container in the National Archives and Records complex in Maryland (where the Constitution and Bill of Rights are stored) along with an unsigned note on "Janet Auchincloss" letterhead stationery: "Jackie's suit and bag worn Nov. 22, 1963." The handwriting appears to be Janet's.

The temperature in the vault is kept between sixty-five and sixty-eight degrees, the humidity at 40 percent. The outfit will not be seen by the public until at least 2103, 140 years after the assassination, in accordance with the wishes of Caroline Kennedy.

Jackie's hat is missing. One of Janet's family members says Mary Gallagher retrieved the hat at Parkland Memorial Hospital. She gave it to Janet a week after JFK's funeral; Janet decided to keep it for herself. It's not known what happened to it.

JACKIE'S VISITOR

◇◇◇◇◇◇◇◇◇◇◇◇◇◇

Back at the White House, late that night, Aristotle Onassis decided to take a stroll. In the hallway, he ran into one of maître d'hôtel Ficklin's six butlers, who asked if he needed help; he said no, he was fine. He then ambled down to the South Lawn, lit a cigar, and gazed about, enjoying the frigid night air. He glanced up to the Truman Balcony off the Yellow Oval Room of the private quarters, and there, according to what he later recalled, he saw Lee staring down at him. Their eyes met. She turned and walked away.

Lee then went to Jackie's room where Jean Kennedy Smith and Pat Kennedy Lawford, JFK's sisters, were there tending to her. Dr. Walsh also showed up to give Jackie a half-gram injection of Amytal. After about twenty minutes, they all left and walked back to the Family Dining Room for coffee and dessert.

About a half hour later, Lee wished to go to bed. She was in the Center Hall, headed to Jackie's room, where she planned to spend the night, when she spotted Ari. He didn't see her. She ducked behind a large column.

According to what Lee later remembered, Onassis stepped into the stately alcove that led to Jackie's bedroom. There was an end table on either side of the double-wide mahogany door. Chinese porcelain vases sat on both of them. An oil painting hung above each table, all of it framing the entrance to the former First Lady's private boudoir.

He knocked on Jackie's door. It opened. He walked into the room.

The door closed.

SUNDAY, NOVEMBER 24, 1963

We don't know what happened in Jackie's bedroom between her and Onassis since neither ever spoke of it. Probably nothing more than conversation. Jackie had just been treated by her doctor; she had to be sleepy. Moreover, she was so racked with grief—Bobby, the next day, was quoted as saying, "Jackie's had another bad night." She was probably polite but firm in asking Onassis to leave.

That Onassis had the temerity to go to Jackie's bedroom the night before her husband's funeral demonstrates his relentless pursuit of her. When one of his associates once asked him what happened in Jackie's room, he blew up and said, "Do I look like an idiot? I'm not telling you."

"Ari had a plan," observed Taki Theodoracopulos. "He'd had Lee and had now made up his mind to go after the real prize—her newly widowed sister. There was no other reason he would have put up with such poor hospitality at the White House."

Lee could have gone down the hallway and let herself into Jackie's room—especially since Jackie was expecting her to sleep there. She didn't. Instead, she composed herself, returned to the Family Dining Room with the others, and waited. An hour later, when she finally did knock on Jackie's door, there was no answer. She let herself in, found her sister asleep, and then also retired for the night.

On Sunday, there was another Mass for friends and family members in the East Room at the White House. After the service, Jackie had Caroline write a note about how much she loved her daddy. She also had John scribble something. She put each note in its own envelope, along with the letter she'd written to Jack the previous night. She also had a set of gold cuff links she'd given Jack before they married, which she wanted buried with him, along with a scrimshaw bearing the presidential seal, which she'd given him last Christmas. She and Bobby then prepared to go down to the East Room.

Jackie was dressed in a black knee-length skirt with a black veil when Clint Hill met her and Bobby to take them down. Bobby could tell she hadn't eaten or slept. They went down to the East Room at a little after 12:30. When the casket was opened for them, they both knelt before it.

This would be the first time Jackie had seen Jack since her final moments with him in the trauma room at Parkland. "It's not Jack," she kept telling herself. "It's not Jack." After she put her gifts in the casket, she asked Clint to see if he could fetch a pair of scissors from the usher's office. When he returned with it, Jackie cut a few locks of Jack's hair. After roughly ten minutes, they left the East Room.

∞∞∞∞∞∞∞∞∞∞∞∞∞∞

The forty-minute convoy that took President John Fitzgerald Kennedy's body from the White House to the Capitol is what many people would always remember—the drummers, the horse-drawn carriage bearing the coffin, the riderless horse, a military cortège followed by automobiles with Kennedys, Auchinclosses, and the rest of the family. The new president, Lyndon Johnson, with the new First Lady, Lady Bird, were in the lead limousine with Jackie and Bobby. They all gazed out at the mournful thousands who'd come to pay their respects.

As the Auchinclosses slowly proceeded up Pennsylvania Avenue, Jamie noticed that many people in the crowd seemed agitated. He feared that perhaps they'd heard a gunshot. "My God," Janet exclaimed. "What if something has happened to Jackie or the new president?" Hugh theorized that maybe the commotion was because people had learned that Jackie and Bobby decided to walk the rest of the way, "because they couldn't be in the same car with the Johnsons." No, Jamie decided, "something terrible happened." He asked the driver to turn on the car radio, and that's when they all learned that Jack Ruby had killed Lee Harvey Oswald.

Jackie and Bobby had gone into the East Room to view the slain president at 12:34 p.m., Washington time. Just thirteen minutes earlier, at 12:21, all of America watched as Oswald left a Dallas jail and was shot dead by Ruby. As Jackie and Bobby knelt before Kennedy and put their gifts in his coffin, Oswald lay on a gurney in Parkland's Trauma Room 2, where Governor Connally had been treated after being shot. When Jackie and Bobby began the procession to the Capitol, they'd had no idea the murder had occurred.

In the Auchincloss limousine, the news of Oswald's death prompted a sense of finality. First, the president had been murdered, and now his assassin was also dead. Hugh said, "I hope we can close the book on this terrible story now," and Janet agreed. They had no idea the story had only just begun. How Ruby got so close to Oswald was a mystery and became fodder for the many conspiracy theories about the Kennedy assassination. It wasn't until about half past two, when the service at the Rotunda was finished, that Jackie heard about Oswald's murder. "Just one more awful thing," she said.

The fourteen-minute service in the Rotunda was as emotionally draining as one might imagine, especially at its conclusion, when a tearful Jackie walked Caroline to the casket to, as she told her, "say goodbye to Daddy . . . and tell Daddy how much we love him and how much we'll always miss him." Seeing mother and daughter at the coffin brushing their lips against it was another wrenching moment. By this time, John had been taken from the Rotunda because he'd been too fidgety. He spent the time in the Speaker's Office, where he played with two agents from the kiddie detail.

As the Auchinclosses left the Rotunda, they tried to compose themselves. "I was standing next to Lee and my [half] brother, Yusha. Lyndon and Lady Bird Johnson were behind us, and Mummy and Daddy alongside them," Jamie recalled. "Jackie, Bobby, Ted, and some of the other Kennedys were in front of us. Walking down those many steps, I kept my head down partly because I was so sad, but also, God forbid, I should stumble and fall right into Jackie when the eyes of the whole world were on her. For a sixteen-year-old, that was a terrifying thought."

After the Auchinclosses and Kennedys left the Capitol, more than a quarter of a million people filed past JFK's flag-draped coffin, the line stretching for forty blocks, eight abreast. Meanwhile, Jackie and her family, friends, and members of Jack's cabinet went back to the White House.

It's not known if Jackie realized it, but Ari was still in his sitting room after having watched the funeral on television. Whatever conversation he had with her in her bedroom the previous night hadn't resolved his predicament; he still had no place at the ceremony. He couldn't even make calls from his room. He'd tried to do so, but the White House operator didn't pick up. It was as if the entire White House was closed for business, and the only people left in it were butlers, maids . . . and Aristotle Onassis, hidden away in a sitting room.

It probably hadn't occurred to Ari that Lee's husband, Stas, wasn't in residence yet. In fact, Stas arrived while everyone was at the Rotunda. He would later tell William Manchester that Washington was like "Versailles after the king had died." Stas asked Jackie if he might see Jack's lying in state at the Rotunda but avoid the crowd. Jackie summoned Clint Hill, who accompanied him. As the prince knelt by the side of his friend's casket, he broke down in racking sobs.

ONASSIS GETS A REPRIEVE

◇◇◇◇◇◇◇◇◇◇◇◇

On Sunday night, the Kennedy contingent in residence at 1600 Pennsylvania Avenue split up for dinners. Rose wanted to eat with Stas. Jackie and Lee dined with Bobby. The other Kennedys planned a family dinner in the President's Dining Room.

During their meal with Bobby, Jackie and Lee finally told him about Onassis. Bobby had no idea he was in the White House. "He was angry," recalled one source, "which wasn't a surprise. 'The president would never want that man here,' he said. 'Jack's not even in his grave yet.' Jackie was firm with him. 'Stop it, Bobby,' she told him. 'Ari is my friend.' Bobby's response? 'Since when, Jackie? Since when is Ari your friend?'"

Jackie said she'd given it some thought and now felt perhaps they should be more hospitable to Onassis. "Do we really want him going all over the world saying what bad hosts the Kennedys were after the death of the president?" she asked. Bobby said he didn't care what Onassis thought about anything. Ignoring him, Jackie picked up the phone and summoned Dave Powers, who had been JFK's special assistant. When he arrived, she asked him to invite Onassis to the family dinner in the President's Dining Room.

As well as Dave Powers, eating in the President's Dining Room that night were Ted and Joan Kennedy; Ethel Kennedy; Sarge and Eunice Kennedy Shriver; Pat Kennedy; Robert McNamara, JFK's secretary of defense; and Phyllis Chess Ellsworth Dillon, wife of Clarence Douglas Dillon, JFK's secretary of the treasury. All were seated and about to eat in the large, elaborately decorated room with its heavy gold curtains and antique furniture. A fire burned in the marble fireplace, casting everyone in a warm glow.

The door opened, and in walked Aristotle Onassis, escorted by one of the butlers. People were shocked. Ted bolted up and demanded to know what he was doing there. Dave Powers said, "I invited him, at Jackie's request." According to what Eunice Shriver remembered years later, Ethel was very direct with Powers. This was a sacred place, she told him, the president's table. How dare he invite Onassis to sit with them? Dave reiterated that it wasn't his idea, it was Jackie's. "But she's out of her mind with grief," Ethel exclaimed. "Don't you dare blame this on Jackie."

Onassis then took a seat and made himself at home. Everyone at the table was cordial to Onassis with the exception of Ethel, who wouldn't even look at him. They asked him questions about his yacht and his life in Greece and seemed genuinely intrigued by the idea of having a man of such notoriety at their table.

At around ten, Bobby joined them for dessert. According to several accounts, Bobby insulted Onassis, saying that he fancied himself as some kind of "selfish royal with your big yacht and private island." Ari protested and claimed to be very charitable, which, from most accounts, wasn't true. He did support over fifty relatives, though, and employed more than ten thousand fellow Greeks.

After they'd all had too much to drink, one thing led to another until Onassis scribbled on a napkin a promise to give half his wealth to America's poor. He signed it and gave it to Bobby, who crinkled it up and tossed it over his shoulder. Later, William Manchester would describe a lighthearted scene—"comic relief of sorts," he called it in *Death of a President*. In fact, that same night, Onassis called his business partner Costas Gratsos and said, "Bobby did everything he could to humiliate me tonight, but I didn't take the bait. The more I smiled, the madder he got."

Stanley Levin, who, along with his brother-in-law attorney Thomas Lincoln, helped manage the Onassis empire from its New York office, recalled, "About two hours later, Bobby, Ted, Dave Powers, and Stas Radziwill retired to the Treaty Room for scotch whiskeys and cigars. As they spoke, Onassis popped his head in and asked to join them. In retrospect, the idea that he was free to roam the White House and wonder what the Kennedys were up to in the Treaty Room seems a little incomprehensible, but it was true. Ari told me that as soon as Stas saw him, he jumped out of his seat and exclaimed, 'What the fuck?' He then bolted out of that room like a ball shot from a cannon. He went up to the president's bedroom to retire, as per Jackie's request that he sleep there. Then, Ari made himself at home in the Treaty Room. Bobby poured him a drink. 'I'm not as bad as you fellas think,' he said, to which Ted Kennedy responded, 'Yeah, you're a lot worse.'"

Not much else is known about this brief private time the Kennedy brothers and Onassis shared. Stanley Levin said, "Apparently, Lee's relationship with Onassis came up, as inevitably it would have. Bobby said something about how much Stas loved Lee and that they'd been married for four years. Ari said, 'My goodness. Four whole years. A lifetime of happiness.' Ted told him, 'We don't give a shit what you think.'"

Levin added, "Onassis told me it ended with Bobby reminding him that Jackie and Lee were as close to him as his own sisters. He said their mother and stepfather were dear friends of the family's, and he added—and this is according to what Ari told me—'If you hurt them, I'm coming after you. Do you understand me? I'm coming after you, Mr. Onassis.' Ari said he just sat there and smiled at him like a Cheshire cat. He was riled, though. You just didn't talk to him like that."

Eventually, Ari rose. "Gentlemen, I want to thank you for your hospitality," he told Bobby and Ted. "My deepest condolences for the loss of your brother."

He then turned and walked out of the Treaty Room.

MONDAY, NOVEMBER 25, 1963

◇◇◇◇◇◇◇◇◇◇◇◇

At about seven in the morning, Lee Radziwill opened the double doors to Jackie's bedroom and rushed in. Jackie was at her vanity, putting on her makeup, as Provi and Janet stood at her side. "He's gone," Lee exclaimed, according to what Janet would remember in 1976. Jackie glanced at her, then went back to her reflection.

Today was President Kennedy's state funeral. Jackie could barely even drag herself out of bed, she was so depleted. There had been a thousand logistical details to consider. There was nothing more she could do. Though she hated to admit it, she couldn't wait for the whole thing to be over. History has painted her as being strong and courageous throughout this time. In front of the world, yes, that was certainly true, but privately, she was plagued by doubt and insecurity. "I just want this to all be wonderful," she had told Ethel Kennedy, "and I'm so scared that I'm going to do just one thing wrong and everyone will know it."

Adding to Jackie's sadness was the fact that today was John's third birthday. Four days earlier, he'd cried while she and his father boarded Marine One to leave the White House en route to Texas. She promised him that his birthday would be special and full of surprises. How could she ever live up to that promise now?

With all of this on her mind, the last thing Jackie needed was her sister standing behind her agitating about Aristotle Onassis. Something must have happened at the family dinner, Lee speculated, because when she went to his sitting room to greet him this morning, he was gone. She was told he'd left the White House in the middle of the night. She said she didn't know how she'd be able to repair things with him. Janet locked eyes with her and gave her a look that stopped Lee dead in her tracks. Changing course, she put her hand on her sister's shoulder and told her that if she needed anything, she'd be there for her. She then turned and walked out of the room.

According to Janet's later memory, she stood behind Jackie, gazing at her in the mirror. "Later," she began, "I'm going to talk to Bobby about your future and that of your children," she said.

Jackie gazed at her mother and said in a level voice, "You should know, Mummy, the Kennedys don't respond to threats or intimidation. If you want them to give me money, be kind."

"GRIEF THAT DOES NOT SPEAK"

◇◇◇◇◇◇◇◇◇◇◇◇◇◇◇◇

The rest of Monday would go down in American history, every moment unforgettable for anyone who witnessed it, even on television.

The difficult day began with a procession up Pennsylvania Avenue from the Rotunda back to the White House with President Kennedy's flag-draped casket. There was a crowd of thousands of onlookers as far as the eye could see.

Then came the long walk behind the caisson—the military escort, band, and the symbolic riderless horse with boots reversed in the stirrups, carrying the body of the fallen president from the White House to St. Matthew's Cathedral.

Jamie Auchincloss is the only surviving member of the immediate families who took part in the walking procession.

The night before, the Auchinclosses received a delivery of envelopes at O Street by White House messenger, each individually addressed with specific instructions for the next day. Jamie's said: "Mr. James Auchincloss is cordially invited to join the procession on foot from the White House to St. Matthew's Church." Janet and Hugh couldn't have been prouder.

Jamie was filled with overwhelming grief. That night, he told the others about his last Fourth of July with Jack at the Cape. They admired a large model sailboat given to Jack by the president of Italy for little John. "Think it floats?" Jack asked.

Jamie said, "Let's see."

Float it did, too far out. Jamie and Jack jumped into a dinghy to retrieve it. But the water was so rough, the dinghy kept capsizing. Because of his bad back, Jack kept having trouble getting into the dinghy. The more Jamie pulled him up, the more he slipped back into the water. At one point, Jamie said, he feared the potential headline: TEENAGE BROTHER-IN-LAW KILLS PRESIDENT OF THE UNITED STATES ON FOURTH OF JULY. While struggling, they kept going out farther and farther and at one point passed the *Marlin,* the Kennedy boat, with Bobby Kennedy and his father, Joseph, gazing at them with confusion. Finally, Jamie recalled that he and Jack managed to get the dinghy back to land, but just barely. Once on the shore, they both collapsed with laughter. Now, less than six months later, Jack was gone and Jamie was taking part in his funeral.

Jackie had decided Jamie would walk directly behind her, Ted, and Bobby, next to Sargent Shriver. Jamie recalled, "Bobby was in front of me, LBJ and Lady Bird behind me, and then, behind them, heads of state, cabinet members, and Kennedy staffers. I was taller than Bobby but shorter than Lyndon. Clint Hill was next to me, but it crossed my mind as we were walking that if any shots rang out, he'd jump to protect Jackie in front of me. I would've been the uncoordinated, slow obstacle between them. Another agent [Paul Landis] was on the other side of Sargent, and he'd go for Bobby or Teddy. LBJ, behind me, had his own security team. So, basically, I was just a sitting duck. I also knew what my duty was, no matter the risk. In my family, you answered the call to duty.

"I remember the silence," he recalled of the procession, "and the weeping. The haunting bagpipes. The clip-clop sounds of horses. From the sublime to the ridiculous, I was afraid that, since we were so close together, my big shoes would snag the back of Bobby's, and one of his shoes would then be pulled off. I imagined Bobby Kennedy, walking with one shoe. That was the kind of thing going through my sixteen-year-old head. In most of the pictures, I'm looking down because I was trying to predict Bobby's next step. Then, I had this random, odd thought: *I wonder where Rose Kennedy is right now.*"

Rose didn't take part in the procession. Not that she couldn't have done it, even at seventy-three. She later explained that she felt "queasy and quite unwell that morning."

The requiem Mass at St. Matthew's followed, Jackie sitting with John on one side and Caroline on the other, her face tranquil, her composure intact as always, despite whatever sharp pangs of grief she felt. "She held on," is how Ted Kennedy later put it, "and in doing so, the country hung on. We were together in it not only as a family but as a nation, and that was the only way we could've gotten through it."

Afterward, Jackie and the children slowly led the mourners from the cathedral. As they stood on the steps, the casket was then placed on the caisson. When it was finally secured, the military saluted it. Then, as the world watched, Jackie leaned down and whispered something in little John's ear. In response, he stiffened his back, stood as tall as any three-year-old boy had ever stood, and gave his father one last, crisp salute. Anyone who saw it would never forget it.

Jackie then sent her children back to the White House. Janet, who joined them there for about a half hour before returning to the ceremonies, told her grandchildren they might not remember a lot about these sad days—and, she added, in some ways she hoped they wouldn't—"but you must never forget how remarkable your mother was today, for all of us and for your entire country."

Janet returned to the funeral in time to see Jackie riding behind the caisson to Arlington National Cemetery. There was then a twenty-one-gun salute, the idea of which had made her and everyone who loved Jackie nervous, considering Dallas. Somehow, she got through it, though. She was then handed a lighted torch. Bending forward, she ignited the flame—the Eternal Flame. She passed the torch to Bobby, who then passed it to Ted, as they both symbolically also lit the flame.

The United States flag was folded and given to Jackie.

The bugler played taps.

Jackie thanked the military commander, got into her waiting limousine, and was driven back to the White House.

The public mourning was over.

There was then a small reception in the Yellow Oval Room, followed by a larger one for foreign dignitaries in the Red Room. At both, Jackie was surrounded by Kennedys. When the matriarch took Jackie in her arms, it seemed as if she'd never let go. "Jack would want courage in this moment," Rose told her, "and he would be so proud of you." She also told her she was going back to Hyannis Port that evening to be with Joe. Jackie asked her to give him a kiss and promised that she'd see him soon. Rose wanted to know if she'd still be coming for Thanksgiving. Jackie said she couldn't know how she'd feel by Thursday, but she'd certainly try.

The Auchinclosses approached Jackie in the Red Room. "My favorite person," Hugh whispered as he hugged Jackie. "You were braver than I ever knew a person could be," he added. She'd come into his home a twelve-year-old who loved to paint, read, and learn languages, a beautiful girl full of dreams with wanderlust. Now, barely twenty years later, here she stood, a former First Lady who'd been so strong for a nation of broken hearts. Her life had turned out in ways neither ever could've imagined.

When Hugh stepped back from Jackie, Janet took his place. She stared at her daughter, her lips parted to speak, but she had no words. She wanted to acknowledge the moment in some meaningful way, but she struggled. Hugh put his arm around her and—typical of a man with a quote for every occasion—offered Henry Wadsworth Longfellow: "There's no grief, like the grief that doesn't speak." Janet shook her head in agreement, stepped forth, and wrapped her arms around her daughter.

CAMELOT POSTSCRIPT

ooooooooooooo

Jackie and the children arrived at the Cape on Wednesday, November 27, 1963, for Thanksgiving, just as Rose had hoped. While the Auchin-closses had invited her to a scaled-down holiday meal at O Street, Jackie felt she needed to be with Jack's family. "Jack is gone," she told Joseph Kennedy, "and things will never be the same, Grandpa. Never." She told him the whole story, every painful detail. She then left in his bedroom the flag that had been draped over Jack's casket.

"Something so incredible about them is their gallantry," Jackie said of the Kennedys. "You can be sitting down to dinner with them and so many sad things have happened to each, and—God—maybe even some sad thing happened that day, and you can see that each one is aware of the other's suffering. And they sit down at the table in a rather sad frame of mind. Each one will start to make a conscious effort to be gay or funny or to lift each other's spirits; and it's infectious that everybody's doing it. No one sits and wallows in self-pity. It's just so gallant, it makes you proud. And you think, look at these people and the effort they're making. It's a lesson you want to take with you."

The night before she left for the Cape, Jackie sat down and wrote a six-page, heartfelt letter to President Johnson. "Thank you for walking yesterday behind Jack," she wrote. He didn't have to, she noted, and she was certain he'd been advised against it. She'd long thought Lady Bird should be First Lady, she added, "but I don't need to tell you here what I think of her qualities—her extraordinary grace of character—her willingness to assume every burden." She loved her "very much." She then thanked the new president for all his kindnesses to her and Jack over the years, "and now, as President." The relationship between the president and vice president was always, historically, strained, she added, "but you were Jack's right arm." She noted that JFK had become a senator—"just another little freshman"— when LBJ was the majority leader. Jack had looked up to him and taken orders from him, she noted, so she admired LBJ's willingness to then serve as VP under him. "But more than that," she wrote, "we were friends, all four of us."

Jackie also wrote about the Oval Office and noted that LBJ would be the first president to sit in it as it now appeared. She had purchased a crimson rug for Jack, she wrote, and had curtains designed to match. But Jack never had a chance to see the new décor. She had instructed movers to remove all of JFK's marine paintings from the walls, she noted, because "I remembered all the fun Jack had those first days hanging pictures of things he loved." She thought he—LBJ—would now want to put "things from Texas" on those same walls. "I pictured some gleaming long horns, and I hope you put them somewhere," she wrote. She signed it "Thank you, Mr. President, Respectfully Jackie."

Three nights later, on the stormy night of Friday, November 29, Jackie walked with purpose into the parlor of Rose and Joe's Hyannis Port home to greet a visitor. She looked wan in her black capris and gray knit sweater, her hair combed back behind her ears. This was the night she called upon the services of Pulitzer Prize–winning writer Theodore H. White to help frame the Kennedy years for history. He came to the Cape to interview her for a story in *Life* magazine, one that would forevermore define the way the administration would be viewed by generations to come—as "Camelot."

"One thing kept going through my head, the line from a musical comedy," she said. "At night, before going to bed . . . we had an old Victrola. He'd play a couple of records. I'd get out of bed at night and play it for him. . . . It was a song he loved most at the end. Camelot. 'Don't let it be forgot, that for one brief shining moment, there was Camelot. There'll never be Camelot again.'"

At first blush, Camelot is a fable about how idealism and right can endure despite human frailty and envy. It's also about King Arthur's flawed wife, Guinevere, who betrays him with his best friend, Lancelot, thereby triggering the kingdom's downfall. It's not exactly romantic or triumphant. But that was overthinking it, and Jackie knew it. She was always whimsical about Jack and his family, though. She often drafted poems that cast JFK in a romantic, heroic light, such as one that ends:

> He would find love
> He would never find peace
> For he must go seeking The Golden Fleece
> All the things he was going to be
> All of the things of the wind and sea.

That was Jackie, romantic and idealistic where Jack was concerned. The poem is dated October 1953, ten years before his death.

BOOK III

Rebirth

THE PASSING OF A YEAR

<><><><><><><><><>

A black Mercury convertible sped along Interstate 195 on a crisp November day in 1964. The driver, a handsome, middle-aged man sporting a golf cap, took a deep breath of cool air as it gusted in from the bay. Turning to his right, he beamed at his passenger, a gorgeous woman wearing large sunglasses, her dark hair tumbling behind her in the breeze. He put his hand on hers and smiled. Not a care in the world, either of them.

At a respectable distance, a black sedan followed. The woman turned around to spot it and then, in a whispery voice so unmistakable, told the driver, "Go faster, Jack. I'll bet we can lose them."

He pressed the gas pedal. The car roared as it raced down the stretch of highway. She laughed, a silvery peal. "That's more like it," she said.

"You're loving this, aren't you?" he asked.

It was true. She did love it. These kinds of carefree moments had become rare for Jackie Kennedy. It was good to see her happy.

One year ago, to the month, her husband was murdered.

<><><><><><><><><><><><><>

So much had happened in Jackie's life this last year, not the least of which had been the surprising emergence of a new love interest, the noted architect John Carl Warnecke, known to all, ironically enough, as "Jack."

The rest of 1963 had, not surprisingly, been difficult. Jackie couldn't wait for December to come around because that was the month—on the sixth, to be precise—she was to leave the White House. With its memories of Camelot being replaced by a new administration, she knew she had no place there even though the Johnsons said she could stay as long as she liked.

Looking back, Jackie would say she should've moved out the day after Jack's murder, like Eleanor Roosevelt had when her husband died. "But I had no place to go," she said. Hugh kept reminding her that this wasn't really the case. O Street had nine bedrooms. "Why don't you and the children move in, even if just temporarily?" he asked.

"Only if Mummy moves out, even if just temporarily," Jackie answered. It was a joke—or was it?

Though she spent the holidays with the Kennedys and Auchinclosses, these special days just weren't the same. If not for the children, she wouldn't have bothered. Jack had been the beating heart of the family, and without him sitting at the head of the table, it all felt useless no matter how hard relatives tried to lift her spirits. She was so depressed, she felt she had no future. "There is one thing that you must know," she wrote to her friends Ben and Tony Bradlee. "I consider that my life is over," she wrote, and she added that she intended to spend the rest of her life "waiting for it really to be over."

Janet and Rose tried to talk to Jackie about her grief, but it was of no use. Both matriarchs felt the best way to get past it was to fill the days with activity, just get on with things, "don't wallow," as Rose put it. Jackie didn't want to debate her mother-in-law; she had lost a precious son. If only Janet would have let up, though. Within months of Jack's death, she was impatient with Jackie. "I'm sorry, but I have feelings, Mummy," she would say. "And they're in the way!" Janet would counter.

"As well as losing her husband, Jackie lost her identity," said Jamie Auchincloss. "Being the First Lady wasn't just her job. It's who she was. Every moment had been filled with important things that mattered. People deferred to her. She'd gotten used to a certain way of life. Without it, she didn't know who she was. Mummy felt that loss, too. We all did. We'd had a certain station, and suddenly, it was ripped from us. None of us was in a position to help the other, let alone help Jackie."

When she returned to Washington after the '63 holidays, Jackie moved into temporary quarters in Georgetown offered by Janet's friend Marie Harriman, wife of Averell Harriman, JFK's undersecretary of state for political affairs. Jackie only stayed in that house until the end of January, when she bought a three-story house across the street at 3017 N Street, an eighteenth-century colonial, for about $190,000. Joan Kennedy had recommended it after she and Ted considered buying it.

For a short time, Lee and her children moved in with Jackie and hers; Lee thought she might be able to help Jackie through the terrible time. It was more than she'd bargained for. Jackie started drinking heavily and taking pills within weeks of the assassination. She was also temperamental. The sisters fought periodically, and Jackie would sometimes slap her just like their mother had, two smacks with the same hand.

Her friends were of no help. Because they reminded her of Jack, she started cutting them from her life. "I would call," Joan Braden remembered, "and she wouldn't call back. I knew I reminded her of better days."

One night in the summer of '64, Yusha went to visit Jackie and found her drinking vodka and crying over a scrapbook of photos. She told him she believed "a group of right wingers" had something to do with Jack's death. Yusha knew Janet felt LBJ had something to do with the murder. She didn't know how or why, but she was sure of it. Jackie didn't think LBJ was the culprit, but she, like Ethel, feared that Bobby's dogged investigation of the mob had something to do with it. Jackie and Ethel both agreed that there had to have been more than one assassin—"Let them see what they've done," Jackie had famously said.

Yusha believed Jackie was obsessing over Jack's murder and needed to get away from Washington and all the memories it held. When he suggested it, she was amenable. She said Bobby had told her the same thing. She hated the house, anyway, and its lack of privacy with its steep stairs leading right to the front door. She'd peek out the window, see the surging crowd, and cringe. Tour buses would stop, people leaning out its windows taking pictures, no surprise since the sale of the house was headline news in the local press with the address for all to see, and even the price.

There were also complications presented by President Johnson, who wouldn't stop bothering Jackie to come back to the White House for a visit, imagining the political mileage he'd gain if she returned for even an hour. Worried about whether Bobby planned to run for president in '64, Johnson would've done anything to take advantage of his relationship with Jackie. He was known to summon people, including reporters he was trying to impress, into the Oval Office and dial Jackie's number. He'd flatter her— "You know how strong you are?"—be inappropriate—"I'll spank you if you don't come to visit"—be flirtatious—"Come over and put your arm around me"—and say whatever he thought it would take to get her to return. In one conversation, he called her "darling," and told her he'd like to be her children's "daddy." Finally, Jackie said she would not visit him. "I've really gotten hold of myself," she told him. "I'll do anything for you. I'll talk to you on the phone. I'm just scared I'll start to cry again."

LBJ had even told Pierre Salinger he wanted to appoint Jackie ambassador to Mexico, replacing JFK appointee Thomas C. Mann, set to retire in March of 1964. "I talked to her a while ago and she just *oohed* and *aahed* over the phone," he said. "She was always nicer to me than anybody in the Kennedy family. She made me feel like I was a human being. God, it would electrify the Western Hemisphere," he enthused. "She can just walk out on that balcony and look down at them and they'll just pee all over themselves every day."

Jackie turned down the offer. Afterward, Bobby called Pierre and said of LBJ, "He's using Jackie. Tell him we know it, and we want him to fucking stop it." But Jackie wasn't offended. She viewed Lyndon as harmless. When Ethel told her he was exploiting her, she agreed that was probably true. "I'm not stupid, Ethel," she said. He'd also been kind to her, though, as had Lady Bird. She had shared some terrible moments with them. As far as she was concerned, they could do no wrong, especially Lady Bird, to whom she was so grateful for promising to continue her work at the White House. It's just that she could not go back to, what she called in her LBJ Library oral history, "that place. Even driving around Washington," she said, "I'd try to drive a way where I wouldn't see the White House."

"Maybe I will be remembered as the one who started restoring the White House, but you will be remembered as the one who PRESERVED IT," Jackie wrote to Lady Bird on December 1, nine days after the assassination. "That was the moment I was always scared of—Would the next President's wife scrap the whole thing as she was sick to death of hearing about Jacqueline Kennedy—or would she forget about me and insure [*sic*] that the White House will always be cared for? Well, you have done that—and I thank you."

"You have been magnificent and have won a warm place in the heart of history," LBJ wrote to Jackie on that same day, December 1. "I only wish things could be different—that I didn't have to be here. But the Almighty has wished differently."

JACK WARNECKE

∞∞∞∞∞∞∞∞∞

t was in the middle of May 1964, when Jack Warnecke, the architect Jackie hired to design President Kennedy's memorial at Arlington National Cemetery, called to ask her out. "On a date?" she asked. "Because I don't date, Jack, and I never will again," she said emphatically. No, Jack told her, it wasn't a date. It was just dinner. She said she was unsure, but she didn't say no. She'd get back to him. That night, he showed up at her door with flowers. "But, Jack, I didn't say yes," she told him, annoyed.

"But you didn't say no," he said with a smile.

Jackie let him inside and prepared a simple meal for them. "That's when it started between us," Jack Warnecke recalled in a 2007 interview. "She cried. She told me the whole Dallas story. The fact that I also knew Jack comforted her, and she let her guard down."

As he was about to leave, Jack tried to kiss Jackie lightly on the lips. When she turned quickly, he ended up in her hair. "I thought, *Okay, that was too pushy,*" he recalled. "We stood on the other side of the door out on the top of the landing, and I asked, 'Will I see you again?' She shook her head no. I asked, 'Why?' and she got snappy with me. 'Look down there,' she said. I did, and there were all these people staring back up at us with Secret Service agents keeping them at bay. 'Do I look like a woman these people will ever let date?' she asked."

In some ways, it started for Jackie with the second "Jack" before she was robbed of the first one. She would always remember the night of October 10, 1962, as the beginning of her attraction to John Carl Warnecke. It was the night after Jackie returned to Washington following her summer in Italy and in Newport. There had been a dinner at the White House and dance at the British embassy, which marked the beginning of his and Jackie's work to save and restore Lafayette Square in Washington, mostly nineteenth-century brownstones that the Eisenhower administration had no use for and had decided to authorize their demolition. Jackie loved the quaint neighborhood and felt it should be preserved. "Back then, no one cared about historic buildings in Washington," Jack Warnecke said. "They were old and should be replaced, end of story. Jackie was the first to campaign hard for preservation."

Jack Warnecke was so tall and handsome that night in his black tuxedo that when he asked Jackie to dance, she had to say yes.

The day after the dinner party, Warnecke was scheduled to present his plan for Lafayette Square to the Fine Arts Commission. The commision had already opposed the idea but had been persuaded by Jackie to change its mind. Therefore, it was to be a tough crowd. "Nervous?" Jackie asked him as they danced.

"I don't get nervous," was his response.

Jackie smiled and whispered, "I'm nervous all the time."

John Carl Warnecke was an accomplished architect whose work had long been appreciated by President Kennedy. The two had been friends since 1956, when Kennedy's Stanford frat brother Paul "Red" Fay introduced them. Prior to that, Kennedy had admired Warnecke from afar. In 1940, Kennedy spent time in California taking writing courses at Stanford while Warnecke played left tackle on that college's undefeated football team, which later went to the Rose Bowl. Once they met and became pals, Kennedy started calling Warnecke "Rose Bowl." As often happened when JFK befriended someone, Warnecke ended up being privy to his private life outside his marriage. "I was a beard for him," Jack admitted, "and helped him get girls back when he was a senator and, yes, married to Jackie."

A handsome divorcée, forty-three in 1962, Jack, too, was a ladies' man. Six foot three, 215 pounds, with blue eyes and chiseled features, he was a Harvard man. Wealthy and successful, he took pride in the fact that women viewed him as quite the catch. Not only did he have homes in California, Washington, and Hawaii, he had a ranch on the Russian River.

"What can one say about Mr. Warnecke?" asked Robin Duke, wife of Kennedy's chief of protocol. "He was bigger than life, a matinee idol, sophisticated, knew how to dress, fit well in high society, good looking. The word 'dashing' comes to mind, a certain breeding, too. Someone like Jackie would look twice at such a man. It's not surprising there was a spark."

Jack Warnecke seemed to know Jackie without her having to explain herself. He knew she was struggling in her marriage, for instance. It was unspoken, but because of his experiences with her husband, he imagined her pain. He wanted to make her laugh that night at the embassy, and he did. He had a great sense of humor, didn't take himself seriously; he told her he looked like a "giant penguin" in his tux and "my enormous feet make it hard to dance."

When Jackie was in his arms, the spark was difficult for her to ignore. "It was a lovely attraction," Jack recalled. "Besides the physical, we were simpatico. She liked my passion for my work, my creativity. She was drawn to creative types. I told her about my design of the U.C. campus at Berkeley, for instance, and she was intrigued. She told me she spent as much time away from the White House as possible and it was nice knowing someone who genuinely enjoyed his work. My father had also been an architect, so I was running a successful family business. She liked that, too. I had a little money, a little power."

Of course, Jackie was married to the president, and she'd never have an affair. JFK's paramour Mary Meyer was at the same dinner dance that night in October, and Jackie had wondered about her presence and, later, would learn much more about her relationship with Jack Kennedy. But even if she'd known the details back then, she never would have retaliated with Jack Warnecke. All she could do was tuck away any feelings she may have had for him and chalk it up to a fun flirtation, nothing more.

Jack had his own complications. Two years earlier, he divorced his wife, Grace, the mother of his four children. He'd loved her deeply; they'd been married for fifteen years. He rebounded with another woman. When she moved to Europe, he intended to join her there. But the president approached him with the idea of helping Jackie with her crusade to save Lafayette Square. He couldn't very well turn down that offer, so his relationship ended. Afterward, he ended up with another woman and—"with Washington being a small town and Jack Kennedy being a big dog"—it turned out she was seeing him and the president at the same time. Therefore, he felt it best to keep his distance from Jackie.

At the meeting about Lafayette Park the day after the White House dance, Jack kept his professional distance from Jackie. She wore the same outfit she'd later wear in Dallas, but without the pillbox hat. Other than further discussions and meetings about the square, and photo opportunities relating to it, he tried to stay clear of her.

After the president was assassinated, Jackie hired Jack to design his grave site at Arlington. "She wanted me to design a permanent memorial grave," he recalled. "She and her friend Bunny Mellon [a noted landscape gardener] felt that the Eternal Flame, already there, had to be the focus, and that everything around it should be simple and dignified. No statues of saints or anything like that, just slate tablets with passages from JFK's inaugural speech."

Jackie told herself Jack deserved the job because he was the best at what he did. Her friends had to wonder, though. They saw the way she looked at him, the admiration in her eyes. Bobby Kennedy wondered, too. He felt anger every time he laid eyes on Jack. He believed Jack was moving in on Jackie too quickly. "Nothing about this Warnecke guy is right," he said. Therefore, the two men disagreed on every element of the JFK memorial.

"It's too soon, Jackie," Bobby told her.

"For what?" she asked.

"For this," he exclaimed.

She was thoughtful as she digested those two, simple words: "For this." She then leveled with him: "This is none of your business, Bobby." A smile and a kiss on the cheek lessened the sting.

◇◇◇◇◇◇◇◇◇◇◇◇◇◇◇◇◇◇◇◇◇◇

Two days after Jack showed up on Jackie's doorstep unannounced, he telephoned her. She seemed in a better mood, talking about the furnishings in her new home and some new pieces she and Rose Kennedy had just acquired at auction. She agreed to have dinner with him again, and then a few more times after that.

By the end of May 1964, Jackie and Jack had seen each other six times. When she said she wanted him to meet her mother and stepfather, he was a little hesitant. He knew this was a big step, though, so he agreed to dinner with the Auchinclosses at O Street. "Family dinners are so vitally important to Mummy and Uncle Hughdie," Jackie warned him. "It's always a major ritual with the maids and the butlers serving this and serving that . . . and all the talk, talk, talk . . . so you must be ready. I suggest you read some newspapers and maybe a couple of *Time* magazines," she joked. Though it sounded intimidating, Jack said he was definitely game.

It went well. Hugh liked him, thought he was respectable, easy to know, full of interesting stories. He liked his positive attitude and said it was no wonder he was a success in life. Janet took a moment to consider before concluding, "I would say he's . . . plausible."

In July of 1964, Jackie decided to move to New York City and start her life anew away from Washington in a fourteen-room penthouse across from Central Park at 1040 Fifth Avenue. She told Jack she was going to spend September 15 to October 1 living at the Carlyle while the apartment was remodeled and her furniture moved into it.

In November, it was time to vote in the 1964 presidential election, with LBJ running against Senator Barry Goldwater. Jackie couldn't bring herself to do it, though, as much as she liked President Johnson.

"I heard that he was hurt that I didn't vote," she said in her oral history for the LBJ Library, many years later on January 11, 1974. "People in my own family told me I should vote, I said, 'I'm not going to vote.' This is very emotional but maybe you can understand. You see, I'd never voted until I was married to Jack. I guess my first vote was probably for him for senator. And I thought, I'm not going to vote for any other person because this vote would have been his. Of course, I would have voted for President Johnson. It wasn't that at all. It was some emotional thing. They were all rather cross with me. . . . They said, 'Now, please, why don't you?' It will just make trouble.' Bobby said I should vote, and I said, 'I don't care what you say, I'm not going to vote. It was just really emotional . . . something a widow would do. It doesn't make any sense, but that's what it was.'"

"TIME QUALIFIES THE SPARK"

◇◇◇◇◇◇◇◇◇◇◇◇◇

As Jack and Jackie sped along Interstate 195 in his convertible on that beautiful November day in 1964, it felt to them that, other than Bobby Kennedy, there were no obstacles to their romance. Even Jackie's mother seemed to approve; she now freely called him "Jack," no more "Mr. Warnecke." She was relieved that he was watching out for her daughter, as was Hugh. They were both excited when Jack and Jackie announced plans to be in Newport. Hopefully, the visit would allow them to get to know him better.

Jack showed up at Hammersmith a day before Jackie. He signed a page of the guest book alongside of recent guests Mohammad Ayub Khan, president of Pakistan; Jawaharlal Nehru and Indira Gandhi; and John Kenneth Galbraith: "John Carl Warnecke—USA."

Time alone with the Auchinclosses hadn't been the plan. Jackie had a problem with the plumbing at her home on the Cape and, with everyone gone for the winter, had to schedule a plumber and wait for him. While she was nervous about Jack being alone with the Auchinclosses, there was simply no way around it.

Janet insisted Jack sleep in the president's bedroom on the third floor. She opened the door with a flourish, and they walked into the small room. On a nightstand was a blue breakfast menu in case Jack wanted it served in bed. In the fireplace, a fresh fire blazed behind a pleated fan. The third-floor maid's name was Maria, Janet told him, and she'd be more than happy to draw him a bath. In a corner was a small writing desk with a bronze plaque listing the various bills the president had signed into law there. Jack looked around knowing his friend had slept there. It felt as if he were stepping into his shoes, as though any man could ever fill them. "You must dress for supper," she said. "It's formal and we have a lot of very interesting guests this evening." As she ducked out, she said, "So, we'll see you at seven sharp and don't be a second late."

There were at least twenty people for dinner that night, all wealthy and dressed to the nines. After they took their seats, Janet smiled at her guests. "Shall we?" she asked as she rang a bell. A parade of servants then appeared with food. After dinner, everyone went to the patio for drinks. That's when Hugh pulled Jack aside and asked, "How are things, son?"

Jack said his and Jackie's work on the Arlington site was going well, and so was the renovation on Lafayette Square. They were also planning the John F. Kennedy Presidential Library and Museum at Harvard. It would eventually be moved to another site in Massachusetts. The primary reason he and Jackie were in Newport, he explained, was to choose the stone for the Arlington memorial from the John Stevens Shop. They also intended to meet carver John Everett Benson, who'd made a number of samples from which they could choose.

Hugh told Jack he couldn't believe it had been a year since the assassination and remarked that it had been the worst year of their lives. He said Jackie had regrets about some aspects of the funeral service, often second-guessing herself and wondering if she'd properly honored the president. She actually agonized over it, he said, as if it hadn't been the most impressive, historic funeral of all time. All he and Janet wanted, he said, was "for time to do its promised thing" so that Jackie could finally get on with her life. However, they also wanted her to take it slow, he added. He raised his glass. "Love is begun by time, and time qualifies the spark and fire of it," he intoned.

Jack looked confused.

"*Hamlet*," Hugh explained.

It wasn't a toast as much as it was advice.

Jack clinked his glass.

"NOTHING ABOUT JACKIE IS EASY"

⬦⬦⬦⬦⬦⬦⬦⬦⬦⬦

The next day, Jackie drove down to Newport from Hyannis in her black Mercury, with Clint Hill and another agent following. She and Jack had lunch and then went to meet the stonecutter. Jackie loved his work and hired him for the job. However, she was deeply affected by the meeting. "Every time I have to think about this thing, it takes me right back to Dallas," she told Jack, crying.

That night, the Auchinclosses entertained again, another dozen people, no repeats from the previous evening, and, again, everyone dressed formally. Over daiquiris made by Yusha, as usual, Jackie told the story of how, when she was a little girl during wartime and Hammersmith was the last working farm in Newport supplying vegetables, eggs, and chickens, she and Yusha had the chore of feeding over two thousand chickens every morning. He'd always sleep late, she said. Yusha smiled because he knew where this story was headed. One morning, as he slept, Jackie put hydrogen peroxide on a rag and wiped it all over his face and hair to teach him a lesson. It smelled terrible, which was the point. "'Get up,' she told me," Yusha recalled, laughing. "'We have work to do.'" They then collected eggs, mowed the lawn, tilled the soil, and milked cows.

"You milked cows?" Jack asked incredulously.

"She did," Yusha said, "and she liked it."

After dinner, there were more cocktails in the Deck Room as, with humor, Jackie tried to teach poor Hugh how to do the Twist. As everyone danced, Janet turned the music up. She and Jackie then took to the middle of the floor to perform their little routine, which always brought the house down.

Jackie was in good spirits, at least at first. Soon, though, she began to look uncomfortable. After all, how many nights had she and Jack Kennedy spent in this same space? It had only been a little more than a year since they'd celebrated their tenth anniversary in this very room.

The rest of the night was tense. Eventually, people started filing out. Finally, when everyone was gone, the Auchinclosses retired for the evening.

Once Jack and Jackie were alone before the fireplace, the tears came. Jackie apologized, saying that being at Hammersmith always made her feel melancholy. "Tell you what," Jack said as he produced a handkerchief, "what if we blow this popcorn stand tomorrow?" Jackie dabbed at her tears and suggested they drive to her house on Squaw Island. He agreed. She said she needed some alone time in front of the fire. He brushed his lips quickly across hers, covered her with a blanket, left the Deck Room, and walked outside to one of the many patios.

Looking out at the distant city lights of Jamestown trickling up to the stars, Jack took a cigar from his vest, clipped off the end, and lit it. After puffing for a few moments, he felt a presence next to him. "I'm Jamie," said the young man as he extended his hand.

By this time, Jamie Auchincloss was a good-looking seventeen-year-old. He was home from boarding school for the holiday and had been "hiding" in his room rather than joining them for dinner. Jack began to introduce himself, but Jamie said, "I already know who you are, John Carl Warnecke. What I want to know is, what are your intentions toward my sister?" Jack said he had no "intentions." He just liked Jackie and certainly hoped she felt the same, but that was about it. "I just want to take it easy with her," he said. "Easy does it, right, kid?"

"I wish you luck, then," Jamie said, "because, believe me, nothing about Jackie is easy."

"How's that?" Jack asked.

"Let me tell you a story," Jamie said.

Four months before the assassination, Jamie—sixteen then—was at the White House with President Kennedy. The president asked if he planned to join his parents at Hammersmith for the weekend. He said yes, he intended to take the train to Newport, a nine-hour trip each way from Washington. "That's crazy," Jack said. "Why not hitch a ride with me on Air Force One?"

Who could say no to that? Jamie agreed, excited. A half hour later, as he was walking back to O Street, he could hear the phone ringing incessantly from one of the open windows. He raced into the house and up the stairs to answer it. It was Jackie, pregnant at the time with Patrick, calling from the Cape. "How dare you?" she asked in an indignant tone. "Air Force One, Jamie? That is not appropriate. The government should not have to pay for you to go back and forth to Hammersmith. Who do you think you are?"

Jamie told her it had been the president's idea, not his own. However, she believed he'd somehow coerced the president, and, besides, she didn't care whose idea it was, it just wasn't happening. When she was done with him, she slammed down the phone.

"Welcome to my world," Jamie told Jack, "where your sister is the First Lady who gives you a lot of shit because the president suggested you take Air Force One home instead of the train."

Jack looked at him with an amused expression, but Jamie wasn't joking. "I know you think Jackie's easy," he said, "but she's not. None of us are, Mr. Warnecke. We're complicated. We're messy. If you want to pick up the pieces of my sister's broken life you'd better be serious because it's not going to be easy."

With that, Jamie turned and walked back into the house.

Jack had to smile as he puffed on his cigar.

TOO SOON?

∞∞∞∞∞∞∞∞∞∞

The next morning, Jack and Jackie awakened early, as planned, and had a quick breakfast. Jackie seemed in much better spirits as they got into her Mercury convertible and started off for Hyannis with the Secret Service following.

As guards waved Jack and Jackie through the entrance of the Kennedy compound, it became clear that no one was around. The houses all appeared shuttered for the season. There were no children playing on the expansive green yards, no one frolicking on the beach. No football games, no boats sailing. Jack had heard a lot about this hallowed place and always imagined it bustling with activity, certainly not being this quiet. It was also freezing, the air from the port becoming chillier with the passing of the morning.

"We drove about ten minutes down Hawthorn to her home on Squaw Island," he recalled. "It was lovely. Two stories, gray shingles, nice lawn, patio. Modest, I thought. Not a mansion, just a nice family home." Because there was no help, Jackie prepared a light lunch, and they ate out on the slate patio. Afterward, they bundled up and walked down to the pier. "We had an enjoyable time," he recalled. "When we got back, she showed me her watercolors. We had dinner—clam chowder—and talked and talked until the sun went down, and then talked beyond that. Lafayette Square, the Arlington memorial, the Kennedy Library . . . it was as if we'd never run out of things to say to each other. Then, one thing led to another."

Jackie took him by the hand and walked him upstairs to her bedroom, the same one she'd once shared with Jack Kennedy. Much to Jack's surprise, she wanted to make love . . . and so they did.

The last time Jackie made love to a man, it had been to her husband. It was the night before he was assassinated. She had gone to bed but couldn't sleep. Something felt off to her. She didn't feel safe. So, she slipped into Jack's room at about two in the morning and woke him. They made love and fell asleep in each other's arms. The next morning, he was dead.

After his time with Jackie, Jack Warnecke confessed that he'd been in love with her ever since their first dance at the British embassy. "I love you, too, Jack," she said before closing her eyes and turning away from him.

The next morning, Jack awakened to find Jackie gone. He dressed and walked out onto the patio, where he found her staring out at the beach. He tried to talk about what had happened the night before, but she didn't want to. Instead, she asked him to leave. It was like a knife to his heart. Their lovemaking had meant so much to him, but now he realized it had been too soon for her. He wanted to acknowledge it, let her know they agreed about it. It didn't need to ruin everything. "Mr. Hill will take you to the airport," she said, barely able to look at him.

ROSE'S ADVICE

After Jack Warnecke left the Cape, Jackie spent a few days alone at Squaw Island, not wanting to see anyone. She then flew down to Palm Beach for Thanksgiving with her children and the Kennedys.

It was also the first anniversary of President Kennedy's death.

"Time goes by too swiftly, my dear Jackie," LBJ wrote to Jackie. He added that not a day went by "without some tremor of a memory or some edge of a feeling" that reminded him of all that they went through together. He asked that she let his "young friends," Caroline and John, know they were loved by the Johnsons.

Ethel Kennedy wrote that she kept thinking of Jackie's courage "and how proud we all were, and are."

Joan Kennedy wrote that she and Ted were "with you on this anniversary, just as always."

To commemorate the anniversary, Jackie wrote a tribute to Jack that appeared in *Look*'s November issue. "I don't think there is any consolation," she wrote. "What was lost cannot be replaced. I should have guessed that it could not last. . . . I should have known that it was asking too much to dream that I might have grown old with him and see our children grow up together. So, now, he is a legend when he would have preferred to be a man. . . . I must believe that he does not share our suffering now. I think for him—at least he will never know whatever sadness might have lain ahead . . . not age, not stagnation, nor despair, nor crippling illness, nor loss of any more people he loved."

As always, being with the Kennedys felt comforting. Rose hovered over her as she usually did. Bobby had told his mother about his disdain for Jack Warnecke, but she said nothing for the moment. They had many pleasant walks on the chilly beach while gossiping about family matters.

"Are you still sad?" Rose asked Jackie at one point as they walked along, according to one recollection. Jackie said she was sad and feared it would always be the case. "Fear not," Rose told her. "God has a way of taking care of these things. You'll see." Coming from a woman who'd lost a son and a daughter in plane crashes and then another son to an assassin's bullet, Rose's advice was significant for Jackie. "Take your time," Rose told her. "Don't rush into things."

Was she talking about Jack Warnecke? Had she somehow heard about the rendezvous at the Cape? Jackie found the idea mortifying.

On December 8, Jack received a letter from Jackie with news that she'd decided *not* to use him to design the Kennedy Library. She was, instead, giving the job to the Chinese American architect I. M. Pei.

JACKIE KENNEDY ON A BUDGET?

✕✕✕✕✕✕✕✕✕✕✕

M oney, or the lack of it, had been a chief concern of Jackie's until she
married Jack Kennedy. Even if she did one day divorce him—which,
at times, seemed likely—she'd be set for life. No one counted on things
working out the way they did.

Any money Jackie got from her father's estate was long gone. She'd
accepted she wasn't going to be getting anything from Hugh. What about
Janet's rich father, James T. Lee—Grampy Lee—who was elderly and not
in good health? Janet told both Jackie and Lee not to count on him for an
inheritance, either. "Misers usually make great ancestors," she said, "but not
this one." Jackie was dismayed. "Why is it all these men have money, yet we
have none?" she complained.

On the day of Jack's funeral, Janet had told Jackie she was going to talk
to Bobby Kennedy about her future. Jackie had warned her to "be kind."
About a month later, Hugh hired a team of lawyers to work with the Kennedys' Park Avenue office and Stephen Smith—Jean Kennedy's husband,
who ran the family's business affairs—on exactly how much Jackie could
count on. Jack's will provided for $150,000 a year for Jackie from a trust in
her name. Besides that, the government would give her an appropriation of
$50,000 a year. Could she live on $200,000 a year? In today's money, that
would be about $1.7 million a year, plenty for most people, but not enough
for Jackie.

The Kennedys' fortune at this time was estimated at over $100 million.
Rose Kennedy was said to be getting $500,000 a year. She was incredibly
thrifty, though, as everyone knew. Hugh still couldn't get over the fact that

every year Rose put a ten-dollar bill along with five dollars in a birthday card for each of her grandchildren. "That seems insulting to me," he said. Once, when the Auchinclosses were at the Cape for a lobster dinner, he overheard Rose tell the cook not to serve baked potatoes because it took too much electricity to cook them in the oven.

Hugh's attorneys felt Jackie should get at least as much as Rose, which was probably overstating Jackie's value. As an attorney himself, Hugh was used to fighting for what he wanted. Still, he didn't want to appeal to Bobby. If anyone should do it, it should be Janet. She was the one who had a good relationship with him.

In February of 1964, Janet went to see RFK at Hickory Hill. She reminded Bobby of how much Jackie had contributed to Jack's administration, how she'd suffered because of his murder and that now she had his children to support. She wouldn't be able to do it on $200,000 a year.

Bobby said all financial matters needed to go through Stephen Smith. He also pointed out that he'd loaned Jackie the money to buy her house in Georgetown and that when she sold it, she didn't return his investment. Since Janet didn't know about this arrangement, it put her in a weak bargaining position. Moreover, as she spoke to him, she began to realize he wasn't the same man. He was thin, gaunt, and looked terrible. She continued to push, but with less heart because she now felt at such a disadvantage. In the end, she got nowhere.

When Janet told Jackie about the meeting, Jackie was concerned not only by its result but by Janet's feeling that Bobby was in such emotional turmoil. She and Bobby had seen a great deal of each other after the assassination, but she'd been so consumed in her own grief she hadn't fully recognized his own. Bobby's aide John Seigenthaler recalled that his emotional torment was so deep he'd taken on the look of a man in physical pain, "almost as if he were on the rack or that he had a toothache or that he had a heart attack." Pierre Salinger put it this way: "He was virtually nonfunctioning."

JACKIE, BOBBY, AND ETHEL

◇◇◇◇◇◇◇◇◇◇◇◇◇◇

About two months later, Jack's widow and his brother took a vacation together to Antigua with Lee and Stas. They stayed at Bunny Mellon's twenty-seven-acre estate on Half Moon Bay. Bunny had donated about a half million to the Lafayette Square project. She'd also styled state dinners at the White House and did all the work on the East Garden, which, later, would be called the Jacqueline Kennedy Garden. She was presently working with Jack Warnecke on the Arlington memorial.

Jack's old college friend Charles Spaulding was present, as was Clint Hill. Because LBJ had decided Jackie and the children should keep their security detail for the near future, Clint was still protecting Jackie.

"On this trip, we were surrounded by a lot of opulence, but we all felt like survivors of a disaster—namely, Jack's murder," recalled Charles Spaulding. "No one was in his right mind. Jackie and Bobby were remarkably close, reading Greek literature and taking long walks, holding hands on the beach. While he was a destroyed person, he still had a little life in him. This vacation was the first I'd heard of him thinking about running for the senate in New York. Jackie said, 'Yes, Bobby, you should do it. Just never be president. You must promise me you'll never run for president. I can't bear to lose you, too.' Bobby promised, but then he turned to me and winked."

While Bobby was with Jackie in Antigua, Ethel was in Stowe, Vermont, skiing with their children. She was also pregnant with their ninth child. Bobby just wanted to be with Jackie, though. He felt only she could understand his pain. Whereas Ethel tended to utter platitudes—"Jack's in heaven and looking down on each of us"—Jackie could just be there with him, which somehow felt comforting to both of them. They spent a lot of time together, so much, in fact, that many people began to think they were having an affair. They weren't, but whispers about it persisted to the point where Ethel became worried. There was always a little tension between the two women.

"You don't like me very much, do you, Jackie?" Ethel asked Jackie in 1964. She had just offered Jackie temporary accommodations at Hickory Hill after the White House. Jackie declined. Ethel pointed out that if they hadn't married brothers, they were so different they'd probably never have anything to do with each other.

Another incident in 1968 would be more explosive, with Ethel calling her "the same old selfish Jackie Kennedy" and saying JFK was "spinning in his grave." Jackie became so upset, she told Ethel she was no longer a part of her life. That promise held for a couple of months. Another episode occurred that same year, one that would later become infamous among Kennedy aficionados. When LBJ announced he wasn't running for reelection, which cleared the way for Bobby's candidacy, Jackie exclaimed, "Won't it be wonderful when we get back in the White House?" to which Ethel snapped, "What do you mean *we*?"

"Their dynamic was predictable," the singer Andy Williams, who was close to Ethel, once explained. "When Ethel wanted closeness, Jackie pushed her away. When Jackie wanted closeness, Ethel did the same. Today [2002], we'd say they were afraid of intimacy. We didn't talk like that in the 1960s, though."

As far as the rumor about an affair between Jackie and Bobby, Joan Braden once said she and Ethel were at a party when Ethel saw Jackie across the room. Their eyes met, and Jackie smiled at her. In that moment, according to Joan, Ethel was sure the stories weren't true. Jackie would never hurt her in that way. Later, Ethel was direct with Jackie about it. "She said, 'Look, people are whispering about you and Bobby,'" said Jamie Auchincloss. "Jackie was mortified and said she would never do something like that, and that was the end of it. Ethel believed her."

While they were in Antigua, Jackie appealed to Bobby about her finances. How could he resist her? He decided to add another $50,000 a year for her.

JACKIE'S LEDGER

◇◇◇◇◇◇◇◇◇◇◇◇

Even with the extra money from Bobby, Jackie spent the rest of 1964 and then 1965 fretting about her finances. It had become a real obsession. She kept reviewing expenditures, wondering where she could cut back and lamenting the fact that she'd bought the New York apartment, for which she'd paid $200,000. She sold the country home she shared with Jack; it needed to go, anyway, because of the memories. Of course, the plans to rent next to Janet and Hugh in Newport had also been canceled. Once, when a carpenter finished work for her at 1040 Fifth Avenue, she stood before him with a pen in one hand and a checkbook and photograph of herself in the other. "Now, I can pay you with a check," she said, "or . . . I can offer you a lovely, signed photograph, which would be worth much more money. You choose." He chose the check.

"She kept a ledger," Mary Gallagher recalled, "and it was handwritten with every dime she spent, no matter how much or how little. Five dollars for milk and bread? Deducted. Ten dollars for a hat for Caroline? Deducted. Ten thousand dollars for a new gown? Deducted. Everything down to the last penny, as if she was on the edge of financial ruin—and she was. But that didn't stop her from spending like crazy. I kept telling her she needed to slow down, but she wouldn't. I thought maybe it was tied to her grief. So much of her life was out of control."

Jackie eventually decided she couldn't afford to keep Mary Gallagher and decided to let her go. Provi was also on her way out because her son, Gustavo, lived in Washington, D.C., while attending private school—which Jackie paid for—and she wanted to be with him. A young woman from Ireland, Kathy McKeon, would replace her.

Jackie's former White House press secretary Pam Turnure would stay on and help staff an office in New York for Jackie, handling her mail and arranging her schedule. Nancy Tuckerman stayed on, too. Jackie still had responsibilities relating to Arlington and Lafayette Square and other projects she wanted to undertake, such as fundraisers for the Kennedy Library. However, she was determined to do it all on a budget.

It was at this time that the attorney André Meyer, who'd worked for the Kennedys for a number of years and was a senior partner of Lazard Freres & Co., came into prominence in Jackie's life. She had known him since 1961; he had a suite directly below hers and Jack's at the Carlyle. André was thirty years her senior, and everyone knew he had a bit of a crush on Jackie. She felt perhaps he could straighten out her finances, or at least put her on a budget, even though she quipped, "Jackie Kennedy on a budget. Now, that's rich."

Mona Latham, a close friend of André's who worked for him as a securities analyst, recalled, "Jackie said, 'No one around here makes more than seventy-five dollars a week.' While that seems like not much, in today's money, it's about six hundred seventy-five dollars a week. Her total annual household budget, including food, liquor, wine, and salaries came to about five thousand a month, about forty-five thousand dollars in today's money. So, where was all her money going? When she showed us her books, we realized it was going to couture designs, first-class travel and accommodations, and elaborate household furnishings.

"As we spoke, she saw I was staring at a life-size marble statue of a headless woman behind her. 'May I ask what you paid for that?' I said to her. She started thumbing through her ledger until she found the entry. 'One hundred thousand dollars,' she told me. 'Jackie, you've got to be kidding me,' André exclaimed. 'That's almost half your annual income.'"

ROSWELL GILPATRIC

◇◇◇◇◇◇◇◇◇◇◇◇◇

One evening in the spring of 1965, a terrified Jackie Kennedy was forced to hide in her bedroom with her children, seven-year-old Caroline and four-year-old John. Someone had phoned in a bomb threat. Jackie's Secret Service agent John Walsh—who'd recently replaced Clint Hill—had ordered a police search of the entire building. The other tenants had to stay in their apartments; the whole place was roped off.

Jackie tried to keep it light with the children by having them recite the names of the states of the union while Caroline spelled them out. John couldn't think of many but was fine with just jumping up and down on the bed with his black-and-white cocker spaniel, Shannon—given to JFK when he visited Ireland—and Shannon's puppy, Whiskey.

At one point, Jackie left the children in her bedroom and went into another room to call Bobby Kennedy. By this time, Bobby had won a Senate seat in New York, and Ted Kennedy was Senate-seated in Massachusetts. "Bobby said Jackie was crying on the phone and afraid for herself and her children," Kenny O'Donnell recalled. "She felt like a prisoner in the new home, just as she'd been in Georgetown, trapped, she said, like a caged animal. Bobby was there in a few hours. By the time he arrived, though, the scare was over, no bomb was found."

The next morning, Bobby called Roswell Gilpatric, who had been JFK's deputy secretary of defense, and asked him to stop by and see Jackie.

Gilpatric, who was fifty-nine in 1965, had played a pivotal role in the resolution of the Cuban Missile Crisis. Kennedy had brought him into the administration to work under Secretary of Defense Robert McNamara because he worried the latter was inexperienced in the political machinations of Washington. Historians have said that if not for those two men, things might have turned out differently in 1962. Gilpatric and McNamara had argued vociferously against escalating the conflict by bombing Cuba, which was the route National Security Adviser McGeorge Bundy wanted to take. He and McNamara proposed the blockade as a strong response solution, which turned out to be the right decision.

Jackie had always liked Roswell—whom she called "Ros"—a thoughtful, smart, and handsome man. During the White House years, there were whisperings of the two having a romantic involvement, a tantalizing rumor some wanted to believe was retribution for JFK's infidelities. Besides the fact that Jackie would never be unfaithful to Jack, Gilpatric—married at the time to his third wife, Madelin—was too enamored of the president to ever betray him. After the assassination, Gilpatric told the writer Joe Alsop, "You know, Joe, when the president died, I suddenly realized that I felt about him as I've never felt about another man in my life." Yet there was definitely a flirtation between him and Jackie. She could often be coquettish and flirty.

Back in the summer of 1963, Jackie wanted to go to Camp David to take a look at some of its furnishings, with the idea that she might want to move some of them to her and Jack's new country home. She'd spent little time at Camp David, and Jack didn't want her to go alone. He had to be in California for a demonstration of naval weaponry and then was off to Hawaii for a presidential visit there. As it happened, Roswell Gilpatric needed to go to Camp David to close out some business there. He was preparing to leave the administration at that time for private practice in New York. Jack suggested he and Jackie go together. The two then spent one day and one night at Camp David, which served to underscore the rumors about them. But then again . . . When one considers a letter Jackie wrote to him, it's clear she was at least enamored of him. A week after their return, she wrote to him how much she enjoyed their time together and added, "I know the spell will carry over until tomorrow."

Regarding Gilpatric's leaving the administration, Jackie wrote, "I always push unpleasant things out of my head on the theory that if you don't think about them they won't happen—but I guess your departure—which I would never let myself realize until tonight—is true." She felt sorry for whoever would succeed him, she wrote, and she said she'd never warm to that person, he would always live in Roswell's shadow. "But I feel much sorrier for us—In this strange city where everyone comes and goes so quickly you get used to its rather fickle transiency—So when anyone's departure leaves a real void—you should be really proud of that . . . Please know Dear Ros that I will wish you well always—Thank you—Jackie."

Gilpatric didn't help dispel rumors about himself and Jackie when he was quoted in 1996—the year he died—in a biography of Jackie as saying the two had been "romantically involved" when she was First Lady. "We loved each other," he remarked to the author Christopher Andersen. "She had certain needs, and I am afraid Jack was capable of giving only so much. I suppose I filled a void in her life . . ."

Two years before that book, Gilpatric wrote in an email that "the President was closed off and not always able to give Jackie the emotional support she needed when she needed it. However, Mrs. Onassis and I had never had any sort of affair, not during the White House years." He obviously left the door open for the possibility of a "sort of affair" *after* the White House years.

In 1965, after Bobby phoned Roswell about Jackie, he called to check on her. She told him about the bomb threat, how frightened she was, and asked if he would come to see her. He had never before been to her new home. He recalled that Jackie greeted him wearing a black turtleneck sweater and cream-colored slacks, her hair much longer than he'd remembered it during their White House days. They had a warm reunion before she took him on a tour of her home. When they walked into the guest room, Roswell couldn't help but notice an enormous, framed photograph of JFK hanging on one wall. "I stood there transfixed by it," he recalled, "and she became a little nervous and said, 'I hung that there but I'm not sure how I feel about it. When people see it they do what you're doing right now, which is nearly faint.' We had a little chuckle and moved on."

For the next week, Roswell spent a lot of time at 1040 Fifth Avenue, coming by daily to make sure Jackie was faring well and even spending some nights, and according to staff members, in Jackie's bedroom. "They were very comfortable with each other," said one person who worked at 1040 at the time, "and we just figured they were a couple."

Roswell would recall being surprised by her lifestyle. He never understood how pampered she was until that week when he had a chance to see it for himself. "I watched as servants scampered about doing her . . . bidding, I guess, you might say, though that sounds pejorative."

It's true that Jackie had certain standards. For instance, her bedsheets were changed every day, freshly ironed, including pillowcases. Her white tiled bathroom floor had to be shined three times a day. Nightgowns were worn just once, washed and ironed, and then put into rotation. A menu appeared every day for all three meals. Her leather gloves were cleaned after every use with a toxic fluid, and then spread out on a crisp, white towel and massaged with baby powder for softness. She had at least two hundred pairs of high heels and boots, and every time she wore a pair, it was quickly polished for the next time. Whenever she got a new pair of pumps—size ten—someone had to carve a deep X into the leather sole with a knife so that she didn't slip on marble floors. (There was a quarter-inch lift on one of every pair of shoes because one of Jackie's legs was shorter than the other—who knew?) All her clothes were meticulously arranged by color . . . breakfast in bed every morning promptly at eight, along with her newspapers, magazines, and tabloids.

STILL SUFFERING?

✧✧✧✧✧✧✧✧✧✧✧

In 1965, Jackie visited her mother and stepfather at Hammersmith, spending a few weeks with them in August, accompanied by Jack Warnecke.

After what had happened between Jackie and Warnecke at the Kennedy compound in November of 1964, Jackie had pulled away. However, by spring of 1965, the two had reconnected and, again, were romantically involved. The summer trip to Newport was a step forward in that direction.

As usual, Jack slept in the president's bedroom. Apart from the bed, there were few furnishings. Near the door was a crude wooden chest, which Jackie said had belonged to Jack Kennedy when he was a young boy. She opened it. It was filled with neatly folded clothing. She took from the top of the pile a flannel robe. It had been Jack Kennedy's, she said, and he'd worn it in the hospital back in the 1950s. She gazed at it lovingly, held it up to her face, and took in a deep breath. Smiling sadly, she then put it back in the chest and left the room. It was such an overwhelmingly sad gesture, it took Jack a moment to recover. He knew she still missed her husband desperately and had to wonder if there'd ever be room in her heart for him.

After Jack returned to Washington, André Meyer, Jackie's business manager, came to Newport for a few days. Jackie had wanted him to meet Hugh since they were peers who both worked in finance; Hugh was sixty-eight, André was sixty-seven.

One morning, Jackie was in the Deck Room painting when the two men walked in with a question. "Do we know exactly how much money John Warnecke makes?" André asked. They said they'd asked around about Jack and could find no one with knowledge of any major portfolio held by him. If he had money, he was hiding it well.

Jackie said Jack seemed to be doing well, he owned a number of homes, had his own successful business. "I thought you liked him," she said to Hugh. Hugh did like Jack very much, he said. However, he was a little concerned about Jackie possibly considering marriage to someone with such a murky financial picture. André's biggest worry wasn't how much wealth Jack possessed but how much debt. If he and Jackie married, he noted, she could end up being responsible for it.

Jackie said she wasn't sure there was anything she could do to get more information about Jack's finances without appearing invasive. Besides, she wasn't considering marriage to him. She didn't think she could ever marry again.

Later in the fall of 1965, Jackie took a few more steps into the light after two years of darkness, when she and Jack Warnecke attended an art exhibit at the Asia Society on Park Avenue. It was followed by a black-tie dinner at the Sign of the Dove restaurant near the United Nations in honor of John Kenneth Galbraith, who'd served as ambassador to India under the Kennedy administration. Jackie looked stunning in a ribbed, white ermine coat lined in black satin, her hair styled in a typical-Jackie bouffant. Galbraith said he didn't know until his arrival that she'd booked the entire restaurant for the night.

That night, Jack Warnecke felt certain Jackie was feeling better about things because she'd invited many of the friends she'd cut out of her life after Dallas to the party, including Joan Braden and Tony Bradlee, Ben's wife. Lee was also present and introduced Jack to Andy Warhol. Andy and Jackie had, apparently, met previously.

During the festivities, Jack saw a side of Jackie he'd never seen—the girlish, carefree side—as she did the Twist, the Frug, and many other dances popular at the time. They left at about two in the morning in a cab. However, much to his embarrassment, he'd lost his wallet or gotten pickpocketed. He had no money for the fare. That's when he learned Jackie never carried cash, just two quarters in case she needed to make a call. No worries, though. He also found out that the doorman at 1040 always paid for her cabs.

Jack spent the night, not in Jackie's room but in the guest room that featured the enormous photograph of President Kennedy, which, he had to admit, he found off-putting.

While it was a fun night for Jackie, it came with a price. She woke up in a bad mood with a terrible hangover. Jack watched as she sat at the kitchen table rubbing her temples while John and Caroline went on and on about new friends at their schools. He tried to get Jackie to eat breakfast, but she wasn't hungry. When she said she needed a smoke, Kathy McKeon lit an L&M for her, which Jackie smoked from a silver cigarette holder to keep her fingers from staining.

That same morning, Lee showed up with Bridget, her children's Gaelic governess. Jackie had no idea why they were there, and she had them wait in the library so long, an annoyed Lee just got up and left.

Meanwhile, Jack had a meeting in Washington and had to leave for the train station. She barely smiled at him on his way out and didn't even look at him when he said goodbye. He kissed her on the cheek and walked out thinking, as he later put it, "I'm not sure who that woman was, but she was definitely not a morning person."

Jackie's mood that morning was the start of a pattern that began to emerge over the next couple of years, hot and cold, happy and depressed. It was as if she didn't feel she had a right to have fun, not after Dallas. Today, it might be called survivor's guilt. Back then, people just thought she missed JFK. It was an emotional seesaw, up one moment, down the next. Every time she thought she felt better, she soon realized she didn't. "It's all performance art," she later told Jack Warnecke. "Every time I think I'm having fun, I look down on myself from above and can see that it's all performance art and, still, I'm suffering."

JANET JR.'S CHOICE

◇◇◇◇◇◇◇◇◇◇◇◇◇

Someone just needs to show that boy how to be rich," Jackie said as she took a long drag from a cigarette in its silver holder.

"People say money can't buy happiness, Jackie," Janet Jr. told her.

"Only people who don't know where to shop," Jackie quipped. As the sisters cracked up, Jack Warnecke was happy to see Jackie laughing again.

It was November 1965, and Jackie was back at Hammersmith for Thanksgiving with the Auchinclosses, and with Jack along for the visit. This time, she suggested his children join them, including his son Roger, who was in college in Massachusetts, and daughter, Margo, who was in school in New York. They were joined by their younger brother, Fred. Jack's eldest son, John, stayed behind with his mother in California.

Jackie's children celebrated their birthdays at Hammersmith, John now five and Caroline eight. "Your telegrams were so touching," Jackie wrote to Lady Bird Johnson. She wrote that she wished Lady Bird could have seen the children opening them. "They felt so grown up," because they'd never been sent telegrams before. She asked her to thank the president and added that she hoped he wouldn't become too exhausted by the stress of his presidency.

Janet Jr. had just turned twenty in June and was now out of Sarah Lawrence and working at Parke-Bernet Galleries auction house. Not surprisingly, she hadn't waited until marriage to continue having sex, as Jackie had asked of her years earlier. The sisters did stay in touch about it, though, and there are many private letters between them to attest to their continued closeness. On this autumn day, Jackie presented Janet Jr. with her favorite

French perfume, Joy, which, she said, took three hundred roses and ten thousand jasmine flowers to make just one ounce. She also gave her a copy of a scrapbook she and Lee had made for their mother back in 1945 when Janet Jr. was born. Called *The Red Shoes of Janet Jennings,* it was based on the story of *The Wizard of Oz.* Janet hadn't seen it in years and was excited to have it.

Over lunch with Jackie and John, Janet said she was now torn between two men, John Kerry and his former roommate Lewis Polk Rutherfurd. Lately, she said, she found herself drawn to Lewis. She needed to make a choice since both had asked for her hand in marriage. Jackie wasn't fond of John Kerry. Not only didn't she like that he'd gone to bed with her sister, he was a politician, a big strike against him. Jackie said Yusha agreed with her. "He's no fan of John Kerry's, either," she said, "and he's smarter about men than I am."

When Jackie asked for more information about Lewis Rutherfurd, Janet said he was Republican but not interested in politics. His family was wealthy. "Mummy will love that," Jackie remarked.

Lewis was the son of Winthrop Rutherfurd II, whose father, Winthrop, was famous for his marriage to Lucy Mercer, President Franklin D. Roosevelt's mistress. He was a senior at Princeton, studying for a bachelor's degree in East Asia studies. Despite his family's affluence, he wasn't extravagant. "He's so cheap," Janet said, "he won't even take me to a restaurant with cloth napkins."

That was when Jackie made the crack about how to be rich. Though amusing, it bothered Jack. Any time Jackie made an equivalency between money and power, it worried him.

If every man has his secrets, Jack Warnecke's was that his company was strapped for cash. André Meyer and Hugh Auchincloss had been right. He really was in over his head and not as well-heeled as Jackie assumed. To hear him tell it years later, a lot of his money had gone toward financing their upscale lives together. "I didn't know how to tell her," he said, "and I just kept putting it off, a sword of Damocles hanging over my head. It was inevitably going to fall, I just didn't know when."

THE GRAND GESTURE

◇◇◇◇◇◇◇◇◇◇◇◇

By the summer of 1966, Jackie had been with Jack Warnecke on and off for two years. However, just as he had his secret about money, she had hers—a lifestyle that was always financed by someone else. She, too, was living beyond her means. Somehow, she'd even managed to convince André Meyer to allow her to rent a retreat in Far Hills, New Jersey, where she'd be able to ride her horses. It was located near the Essex Fox Hounds, an expensive, private fox-hunting club. "André thought she was out of her mind," recalled Mona Latham. "Even as a rental, it was a big investment, especially considering the care of her horses. He told me, 'She can barely afford her kids. Why must she have horses?' Money was going out so quickly, he was concerned about her future. He told Hugh she could survive maybe another year before she'd have to sell 1040."

Despite any financial concerns, Jackie spent the first few months of 1966 traveling the world—skiing in Gstaad with John Kenneth Galbraith, solemn moments in Rome with the pope, fun with the kids for Easter in Argentina, and bullfights in Spain. Every stop cost thousands. While she worried about finances, she was still determined to enjoy her life. Of course, everywhere she went, chaos followed.

"She was as popular as ever," said Jamie Auchincloss, who was in England from September of 1965 until June 1966, "and for no reason other than because she was who she was—the former First Lady who had electrified the world during the Camelot years. All over Europe, next to Elizabeth Taylor, she was massively famous. Jackie didn't really have to work for it, either, whereas Elizabeth had to work like a dog making movies since she was about twelve. Any man would've loved to have been able to say he was Jackie's but, as we in the family knew, only one had that distinction, and it was still Jack Warnecke."

While Jackie was abroad, Jack began construction on the new Executive Office Building and the Court of Federal Claims building in Washington, a major project for him, which he desperately needed for the income. He couldn't help but read about Jackie's exploits while she was gone, though, and be concerned. This was definitely a new Jackie, a woman who loved to dance, drink, party, and have fun in full view of everyone. The American press couldn't help but take note of this change in scathing newspaper editorials expressing disappointment she was no longer the buttoned-up First Lady they'd known and loved during the Camelot era.

Jack was happy for her, but he wasn't sure who the "new Jackie" was. It felt to him as if he was losing her. He knew what he had to do—a grand gesture, something that would impress her and make her feel special . . . make her his. "I decided I wanted to ask her to marry me," he recalled, "but I needed just the right spot to do it."

In the spring of 1966, Jack took Jackie to Hawaii. He'd just won a major commission to design the Capitol Building, a good excuse for a vacation. They arrived on June 5. For the next month, they'd enjoy the tropical island while staying in a leased home. Jack and five-year-old John Jr. bonded, the two of them swimming together, walking on the beach, and just talking. John Jr. called him "Mr. Jack." Jackie loved the idea of her son having such a strong male influence. It's what she'd always wanted for him ever since his father was killed.

It all went so well, Jackie wanted to extend the trip another month. Since the lease was up, Jack suggested she and the children move into the home he owned on the island. She declined the invitation, however, and said she'd find other accommodations. To Jack, this felt like a bad omen.

The main reason Jack had brought Jackie to Hawaii was because he wanted to propose. That didn't happen. They simply began talking about marriage as if it were a fait accompli, but it bothered Jack that no formal plans were being made, yet. Still, their intimacy didn't suffer. Warnecke said they had sex not only in the privacy of their bedroom but also in cars and on beaches "and as often as possible. She was sexual . . . alive . . . exciting to be with."

Despite the sexual fireworks, Jackie returned from the vacation unsure about things. Something was off in her relationship with Jack Warnecke, she said, and she didn't know quite what that was.

∞∞∞∞∞∞∞∞∞∞∞∞∞∞∞

Jackie spent her thirty-seventh birthday, July 28, 1966, with her family at Hammersmith Farm.

Two days later, Janet Jr., now twenty-one, married Lewis Rutherfurd at St. Mary's Church in Newport. She'd ultimately chosen him over John Kerry.

Just before the wedding, Janet had told the family she and Lewis were moving to Hong Kong. Lewis would work for an investment firm there, and Janet would teach. It was to be a new life for them, and Jackie approved even though she knew part of Janet's decision was based on her desire to escape the shadow of her famous sister. When their mother asked Jackie to try to change Janet Jr.'s mind about Hong Kong, Jackie said no, she felt it was the right decision. "If I could leave and start over in a place where nobody would know me," she said, "I'd be the first one on that plane."

TRUST ISSUES

⬦⬦⬦⬦⬦⬦⬦⬦⬦⬦

By the end of 1966, Jackie and Jack seemed to grow further apart. They hadn't been the same since Hawaii. When they dined with Lee Radziwill, Truman Capote, and others in New York, everyone was taken aback by the tension. As they ate, Jackie tried to make a point about something, but Jack cut her off, saying, "I think what she means to say is—" Jackie gave him a sharp look. "Excuse me, but I can speak for myself," she said. He tried to apologize. "I hate it when you do that," she told him. They kept at it until, finally, Jackie held up both hands and said, "I am not having this conversation with you now." Everyone was surprised, but especially Lee. Jackie never would have stood up to Jack Kennedy that way. After all, this was the same woman who told Lee in Italy that JFK was always right.

For the rest of the evening, Jackie was quiet and seemed depressed. When she went to the ladies' room, Lee cracked, "How can a woman who takes so many uppers be such a downer?"

At around this same time, Jackie got into a public disagreement with the writer William Manchester, whom she'd authorized to write a book about Jack's death called *The Death of a President*. While it wasn't yet published, Manchester sold an excerpt to *Look* for $650,000, the biggest deal of its nature in publishing history, worth about $5.5 million today. Jackie was angry about it. In her mind, Manchester was profiting in a mammoth way off her husband's grisly death, and she found it unconscionable. Plus, after several trusted friends such as historians Arthur Schlesinger and Theodore Sorensen, and even Ethel Kennedy, read his manuscript, they objected to much of it. However, Manchester refused to make any changes and, worse, some of the unacceptable text was even set to appear in the excerpts. Complicating things, Bobby Kennedy had approved of it. Jackie didn't care, she wanted it canceled, all of it—the book *and* its serial.

No doubt adding to Jackie's stress, several Kennedy associates had begun to write books about the family, including, much to her greatest dismay, Maud Shaw.

Earlier, Jackie and Maud had taken the children to England for the unveiling ceremony of the John F. Kennedy Memorial at Runnymede. While there, Jackie told Maud it was time to part ways after seven and a half years. Jackie must have always intended for Maud not to return to the States because she had at the ready an expensive leather valise already inscribed: "Maud Shaw. November 27, 1958–May 12, 1965. With our deepest love. You brought such happiness to all our lives and especially to President Kennedy because you made his children what they are. With love, Jacqueline Kennedy."

Heartbroken, Maud remained in England while Jackie and her crying children ("We want Miss Shaw") returned to the States. Jackie told them Maud would only be gone for the summer, but, of course, she never returned. For years to come, they'd miss her terribly. "But it's time for all of us to move on," Jackie told them.

The fact that Maud would now write a book called *White House Nanny* felt like a huge betrayal. Maud sent Jackie the manuscript as a courtesy. Jackie hurled it against the wall, and, with no rubber band around it, the pages fluttered all about the drawing room.

Jackie continued to pay Maud's pension, but she wasn't happy about it. "She will live up to the promises made to you even if you have broken the trust she and President Kennedy had put in you," Nancy Tuckerman wrote to Maud. Six months later, though, the checks from Jackie stopped.

A few months after she sent Jackie the manuscript, Maud called to say she'd be in New York for the book's publication and would love to see the children. Jackie said, "I think not," and had Nancy write her to say it wouldn't be possible. Afterward, in a newspaper interview about the book, a chagrined Maud claimed Janet told her, "One thing you must learn. Once Jackie sticks the knife in, she never takes it out." Offended, Janet shot off a note to Maud. "Never would I disparage my daughter to you," she wrote on February 1, 1966. "While we sometimes had our differences, I always liked you, Miss Shaw, and do not understand why you would attribute to me something so unkind." She added that Jackie "didn't believe for a second" she would've ever said such a thing to a "servant."

Suffice it to say, Jackie was sensitive at this time about books she viewed as invasive, like William Manchester's. After summoning Mike Cowles, chairman of the board of *Look,* to Hyannis Port to hash it out, Jackie offered a million dollars to the magazine to cancel the deal. Anyone privy to the reality of her finances would've been hard-pressed to figure out where she was going to get that much money. It didn't matter, though; Cowles rejected the offer.

Jackie wasn't used to being told no; that hadn't happened in a long time. At least since 1960, she'd been treated with deference. Jamie Auchincloss said, "The last time someone told my sister no was when she was in the crib and Mummy wouldn't give her a rattle, and even then, she cried until she got one." She was already edgy, and now, with Cowles rejecting her offer, Jackie became downright unhinged. She called him a "son of a bitch and a bastard" and asked, "How dare you do this?" When he apologized to her, her response was, *"How dare you apologize to me?"*

Jackie had bared her soul to William Manchester when he interviewed her in 1964, just as she had to Theodore White in 1963. The difference was that White didn't publish any of Jackie's detailed account of Jack's murder and its aftermath. He didn't want to offend or displease her. (However, he did later, in his 1978 memoir, *In Search of History.*) She assumed Manchester would extend her the same courtesy. "I should know by now that you can't trust journalists," she said. "In fact, these days, I am loath to trust anyone." As for losing her temper, she was fine with that. "It felt good to lose control," she told one intimate many years after the fact. "I'm sorry, but it did. Sometimes, you just have to let slip the dogs of war."

Jackie felt William Manchester had lied to her. Therefore, Jack Warnecke picked the worst possible time to share his secret. He called to tell her he was $1 million in debt, the equivalent of more than $8 million in today's money. After a long silence, her response was a vacant: "Oh?"

While confiding the truth to Jackie was difficult, Jack said he hoped it wouldn't totally ruin things for them. Before he hung up, he told her he loved her. She didn't respond. While she didn't actually come out and tell Jack they were over, as far as she was concerned, that was the case. She stopped returning his calls.

Telling her mother and stepfather the truth about Jack was the last thing

Jackie wanted to do. Janet's reaction was predictable. For her, Jack became history the moment the words "in debt" rolled off Jackie's tongue. She felt deceived. She'd thought him "plausible" for Jackie, "but," she said, "it turns out, he's *fathoms* beneath you. Why did you ever think to be with him?"

Yusha had to agree. His friend Robert Westover said, "Yusha told me Jackie always had great taste, except in men. Of course, his view was likely colored by his own deep feeling for her."

When Jackie told Hugh that Jack had only recently learned of his indebtedness, Hugh didn't believe it. He said a man doesn't suddenly find himself bankrupt. When he called to get the whole story, Jack gave him the details as if commiserating, one businessman to another. "From my understanding, Mr. Auchincloss completely understood," said Jack's business partner Harold Adams. "'These things happen,' he told him. He felt sure Jack would get back on his feet. He was just too smart and too focused and too positive about his life to fail. However, he was equally sure Jackie wouldn't wait around for that to happen."

Jackie couldn't help but correlate Jack Warnecke's duplicity to that of William Manchester's. As far as she was concerned, both had deceived her and caused her to doubt her instincts. "I should've known better," she told her mother, to which Janet responded, "Obviously."

"Is Mr. Jack coming over today?" little John asked his mother one afternoon at Hammersmith.

"No, honey," she said, scooping him up in her arms. "We won't be seeing Mr. Jack again."

◇◇◇◇◇◇◇◇◇◇◇◇◇◇◇◇◇◇◇◇

So, what to do about William Manchester?

Lee's first husband, Michael Canfield, was the son of Cass Canfield, president and chairman of Harper & Row. Jackie decided to meet with Cass personally and dispense with the legal middlemen. She hoped Cass would remember that he owed her a favor. Back in 1955, Jackie had been instrumental in helping Cass Canfield win one of his biggest books. During JFK's recovery from back surgery, he wrote *Profiles in Courage,* and when the manuscript was finished, Jackie called Lee to ask if her husband might show it to his father. Cass loved it. He met with Hugh, Jackie, and Jack at Merrywood to hash out a deal so that Harper could publish it, which it did in 1956. *Profiles in Courage* then went on to win a Pulitzer Prize. Jackie now hoped Cass might be on her side.

Unfortunately, when Jackie met with Cass Canfield and Manchester's editor Evan Thomas, it didn't go well. Cass said his hands were tied, the book would have to go forward; he wouldn't stop it. Jackie still managed to embrace him on her way out for old times' sake, but as she did so, she looked over his shoulder and said to Evan Thomas, "I hope you know I'm going to ruin you."

After Jackie met with him, Cass Canfield had the temerity to write to LBJ and ask if he could use some of the letters the president had written to Jackie in the book. LBJ would not give his permission. Instead, he forwarded the letter to Jackie. She was furious. She truly felt as if she were being ignored.

A week before Christmas, Jackie filed a lawsuit against William Manchester, *Look,* and Harper & Row to stop the publication of *The Death of a President.* Bobby had asked her not to do so; "prior restraint" felt like censorship to him. Jackie risked looking spoiled and imperious. She appeared not only to be challenging the First Amendment's right of freedom of the press, it also looked as if she were trying to whitewash important American history. "It was my recommendation that Bobby not join her in that suit," said Frank Mankiewicz, his press secretary. "He didn't have the same concerns about the book as she did."

"Bobby felt Jackie was really tumbling from her pedestal by this time," noted Jamie Auchincloss, "a pedestal which still had value to the Kennedys because, I think he feared, if she fell off hers, he was next to fall off his."

Bobby was right. The press he and Jackie received after the legal filing was terrible. The poor response from the media served to make her even more distrusting of it. There were many factors that played in her decision to sue, not the least of which was the publication of some critical thoughts about LBJ.

LBJ wrote to Jackie on December 16 and told her not to worry about any of it; he wasn't offended. "One never becomes inured to slander," he wrote, "but we have learned to live with it. In any event, your tranquility is important to both of us and we would not want you to endure any unpleasantness on our account."

She responded immediately that she was "sick" about the whole affair. "Not to sue would have been to let them print everything and take such cruel and unfair advantage," she wrote. She added that Manchester and *Look* "broke their word and I finally understood that was what they intended to keep doing—play cat and mouse with me until I was exhausted."

She felt even suing "seems a hollow victory," since much of what she wished to litigate was ending up in the press anyway. "I am so dazed now I feel I will never be able to feel anything again," she wrote.

Later while on vacation in Antigua, Jackie saw a magazine report alleging that she'd told Manchester she hated it whenever LBJ called her "honey." She immediately sat down and wrote LBJ another letter. "All the rage that I have been trying to suppress and forget down here boiled up again," she wrote. "It's a trivial thing but so typical of the way that man has twisted everything." She added that she'd never be offended by his use of that term of endearment, and she hoped he would "not become embittered by all this and by all life, really." She added that she was sure to have second thoughts about this letter and probably regret sending it, but she just wanted him to know how she felt "and how I will always feel for you—no matter what happens and no matter how your feelings might change toward me. Once I decide I care about someone—nothing can ever make me change—so I just wanted to tell you that as we begin the new year."

She wasn't the only one affected by it. William Manchester ended up having a nervous breakdown over the fracas and was sent off to a Swiss sanitarium. "Do you think you've suffered more than Jackie and me?" Bobby asked him when Manchester talked about it.

Hugh was perplexed to learn that Jackie hadn't even finished the manuscript in question. Why would she stop a book from coming out she hadn't completely read? She said she'd started reading, but it was too painful for her. While he understood, he advised her to read it in its entirety before making any more decisions about it. He was fairly certain that she'd lose her lawsuit based on the First Amendment and that the publicity would be very negative. The former JFK pollster Lou Harris had recently conducted a poll that showed that a third of all Americans now thought less of her. A two-to-one margin said the public had a right to know about JFK's assassination and that Jackie was wrong to try to stop the book.

Jackie finally read the manuscript. Later, in her 1974 oral history for the LBJ Library, she said she never read it, but she was likely referring to the finished book and not the manuscript.

In the end, she asked for 1,600 words to be cut. She then dropped her lawsuit. The excerpts came out, as did the book, in late April of 1967, about a month before Jackie and LBJ christened the aircraft carrier USS *John F. Kennedy* (May 27). Ironically, *The Death of a President* remains the definitive publication about the Kennedy assassination.

In 1974, Jackie, in her oral history, said what was excised were "private things which were mostly expressions of grief of mine and Caroline that I wanted to take out of the book. Now," she admitted, "it doesn't seem to matter so much but then I had such a feeling."

A year later, in 1975, a colleague at Viking Press, where Jackie would work as an editor, asked her what she'd learned from the Manchester litigation. The company was getting ready to litigate against one of its authors, and the coworker wondered if Jackie had any wisdom to share. She pondered the question and suggested they be very sure before they litigate because, "truly, it can take everything out of you."

ARTEMIS

<small>◇◇◇◇◇◇◇◇◇◇◇◇◇◇</small>

By about the summer of 1967, one woman would become instrumental in Jackie Kennedy's future, someone who'd be key in her life for almost the next ten years. She was someone who, like Jackie's mother, was a formidable presence in her own family, the Onassises. Her name was Artemis Garoufalidis, Aristotle's older sister and the matriarch of his family. Like Janet, Artemis's relatives feared her as much as they loved her. She could be punitive when crossed, and her loved ones knew better than to contradict her or stand in her way if her heart was set on something. She could also be endearing and loving, someone with great and intuitive understanding, always available for advice and guidance.

Artemis was a slight woman, not even a hundred pounds, with a short, ink-black coif. Her complexion was dark, and she loved wearing heavy lashes and mascara to highlight her best feature, her lively brown, almost black, eyes. Her lips were usually slashed with bright red color, sometimes hot pink. A stylish woman, she could wear anything and make it look special. She was born in 1902, so she was five years older than Jackie's mother. She was married to her second husband, Professor Theodore Garoufalidis, and from all accounts, they were happy. However, her primary interest and focus wasn't on her marriage. It was on her beloved brother, Aristotle.

"In Greek culture, the son is most prized in the family, often leaving the daughters to feel less loved, less admired," observed Ari's private secretary Kiki Feroudi Moutsatsos, who began working for him and Olympia Airways in 1966, when she was just seventeen. She knew Artemis for twenty years. She referred to Aristotle as "Aristo," as did many of his intimates. "Aristo had three sisters—Artemis, Merope Konialidis, and Kalliroi Patronikiolas," she recalled, "but she was the only one with whom he shared a mother and father. Because they died when Ari was six and Artemis ten, the siblings had a deep bond.

"After his divorce from his first wife, Tina, Aristotle moved next door to Artemis in Glyfada, and so his two children, Alexander and Christina, were practically raised by her. Aristo would seek to please her and make her happy with his decisions. But, still, she had to be cautious when venturing an opinion. He could be cruel. She was scared of him. If he took out his fury on her, she wouldn't recover for days. Their relationship could be combustible, frightening. She very much wanted a wife for him, and when she met Jackie, she knew she was the one."

As soon as Jackie Kennedy moved to New York in 1964, Aristotle Onassis began campaigning for a place in her life. Though one might've imagined he'd been insulted by her treatment of him at the White House during her husband's funeral, he was actually intrigued and even emboldened by it. He sent her roses every so often with a card that would simply say, "Aristotle." He'd occasionally show up in person without notice with an expensive trinket, a diamond bracelet or brooch.

Onassis was now sixty-one, with a net worth estimated to be about $500 million, about $4 billion in today's money. Not only was he still involved with Jackie's sister Lee Radziwill, the famous opera star Maria Callas had been his mistress since 1959. It was because of her that his marriage to Tina Niarchos, mother of his two children, had ended. Famously obsessed with each other, the press chronicled every dysfunctional, abusive Onassis-Callas moment. Maria and Lee continued to volley for first place in Ari's life, a competition that had made them detest each other. Jackie had been hearing about it for years and didn't take it seriously. So, when Onassis invited her to Greece for a break in June of '67, Jackie didn't give Lee a second thought.

While she was in Greece, Ari introduced Jackie to Artemis. Jackie sensed she was like Janet, but without the critical edge, more like Rose Kennedy. Jackie felt free to express herself without fear of reprisal or recrimination. Jackie also appreciated that Artemis spoke only French and Greek, no English. Jackie loved speaking French and was never more engaged than she was when speaking the language. It quickly became a big part of their bond.

For a little more than a week, Jackie had an enjoyable and restful time with Ari and Artemis on their home turf. Artemis was the consummate hostess. A dinner at her ancient estate in Glyfada prepared by her loyal staff was always a unique experience—only the best Greek foods and the best Greek company, whether government officials or her brother's business associates; celebrities such as Elizabeth Taylor and Richard Burton, Bette Davis, or Greta Garbo; or just family. Five servants, three drivers, and one gardener, who lived in separate attached quarters, could attest to her strict, taskmaster ways; she wasn't an easy woman, known to become irate at staff in front of guests. Jackie was impressed with Artemis, and the feeling was mutual.

It was also on this trip that Jackie and Aristotle were first intimate. According to what he told others, they made love "many times" that week. Costas Gratsos, his longtime friend, reported in 1975, "Ari said she seduced him. I think that may have been true because for him to admit a woman held any power over him was unusual. Of course, who knew if that was true, or not? The only thing I knew for certain was that he was enchanted by her. 'She's quite the woman,' he told me. 'She's smart, sexy, fun . . . famous.' All of it was there, for Ari."

Four months later, in December 1967, Jackie returned to Greece for another visit and, this time, was able to spend more time alone with Artemis. "What's your life like, my dear?" Artemis asked her one day at lunch when they were joined by her sister Merope Konialidis.

Thea Andino, Merope's secretary, recalled, "Mrs. Konialidis told me the three of them clustered together at the end of a long, antique wooden table. It was intimate and cozy even considering the length of the table, which I knew seated a dozen. Before them, on a handmade silk tablecloth, was a feast of Greek delicacies including Artemis's special meatballs with chili along with Italian cheeses and French breads and Merope's baklava and galaktoboureko [crème caramel] for dessert. It was served by two nervous handmaids and a butler named Panagiotis, who lorded over the whole thing while seeing to their every need, even if that meant just topping off their Greek coffee. They were smoking, all three of them, like chimneys. Typical lunch at Artemis's."

"You seem so sad to me," Artemis said to Jackie. "Are you unhappy? Or am I misunderstanding?" Their conversation was in French, of course.

It was a good question. Ordinarily, Jackie would just say all was well. She wasn't a woman given to confiding in people she barely knew. However, something about these two made her want to unburden herself. She told them about a truly embarrassing encounter she'd recently had with an old friend, the British diplomat David Ormsby-Gore.

Son of the conservative politician William Ormsby-Gore, Fourth Baron Harlech, forty-nine-year-old David was British ambassador to the United States during the Kennedy administration. His first cousin the Marquess of Hartington was married to JFK's sister Kathleen, who'd died in an airplane crash in 1948. He'd played a significant role in the Cuban Missile Crisis and, along with Prime Minister Harold Macmillan, had helped JFK secure the Test Ban Treaty in 1963. When his father died in 1964, he took his seat in the House of Lords as Lord Harlech. His wife, Sylvia—known as "Sissy"— had just died in a car crash in Wales in May. Jackie was close to her years before and had even planned to name her godmother to baby Patrick.

Jackie said she had an idea to visit the twelfth-century temples of Angkor Wat in Cambodia. Even though the United States had severed relations with Cambodia because of the Vietnam War, Robert McNamara was able to pull some strings and get Cambodia's chief of state, Prince Norodom Sihanouk, to agree to the visit. Jackie then asked Lord Harlech to accompany in case she needed to call upon his diplomatic skills.

Once there, she confided to Artemis and Merope, she and David made love. Afterward, Jackie said she regretted it and felt it had been a terrible mistake. When she told him she was on the rebound—probably from Jack Warnecke—he was upset. The next day, they began to argue about her obligations to Prince Sihanouk and her insistence that she do only so much publicity, which wasn't much. David accused her of being "childish and spoiled," which hurt her feelings. She knew his anger stemmed from her rejection of him, and now, she said, she felt stuck in Cambodia with him. What was she to do? To make things worse, in the middle of this conflict, completely out of the blue, David asked her to marry him.

Jackie said she was stunned. She had no feelings for David other than friendship. Two days later, CBS reported she would shortly announce her engagement to him. Even Lady Bird sent word of congratulations, which was humiliating. Jackie assumed David had planted the story in advance, thinking she'd accept his proposal. She found it all deeply disturbing.

Artemis told Jackie she needed someone in her life with whom she shared a spark, someone like her brother. Changing the subject, Jackie said she had complications in her life far more pressing than who she should date.

"I'm known for my lifestyle," Jackie said, "you can understand that." Of course, the Onassis women could relate; few had bigger lifestyles than they did. Jackie wasn't specific about her financial issues, but the Onassis women came to understand that she wasn't swimming in money. "Artemis told her, 'A woman like you with such problems, it's unbelievable,'" recalled Thea Andino. "She said, 'You must remember that money means nothing,' and told her she'd hate for her to have even a second's worry about something so meaningless. She also said, 'I have a feeling money will be there for you soon.'"

GRAMPY LEE'S DEATH

◇◇◇◇◇◇◇◇◇◇◇◇

A significant event in Jackie's life occurred that would contribute greatly to decisions she'd later make regarding Aristotle Onassis, and that was the death of her grandfather, James T. Lee—Grampy Lee—on January 3, 1968.

Jackie had few memories of her grandfather, and not good ones. She'd often recall a time when she was thirteen and he came to visit Merrywood. One night, before going to bed, he wanted warm Ovaltine, a popular milk-flavoring product that many people drank for a restful sleep. When Jackie offered to prepare it, he said he'd rather a servant do it. Jackie protested, saying it was a simple task, just adding powder to milk. "I said, I want a servant to do it," he told her angrily. "Now, walk away, Jacqueline. Just walk away." She never forgot that moment and would often use the phrase, "Just walk away," when remembering him.

Years later, James T. Lee told Joseph P. Kennedy, who was an acquaintance, that he was planning to buy the Chicago Merchandise Mart as a good investment. Joseph took the tip and bought it out from under him. "Grampy Lee hated Joe Kennedy after that and, by extension, also his son," said Jamie Auchincloss. "He did not approve of Jackie's marriage to him, at all.

"Jackie visited him in 1964 right after she moved to New York," Jamie continued, "and according to what she told our mother, Grampy Lee was sitting behind his desk, and she was seated in a chair before him. There was a framed photograph facing him. He turned it to face her. It was a signed, black-and-white photograph of President Herbert Hoover: 'To my good friend, James T. Lee.' As she stared at it, he said, 'So, are you still married to that son of a bitch John F. Kennedy?'

"Jackie exclaimed, 'Grampy, he was assassinated in Dallas. You know that.' 'Oh, yes,' he said, glaring at her, and then he sneered, 'Pity, that.' She got up and fled his apartment, never to return."

James T. Lee was worth almost $12 million, about $80 million in today's money. However, after the estate was settled, only $3.2 million was left for his heirs, about $25 million today. Janet and her surviving sister, Winifred, got about $1.6 million, $12 million today. (Her other sister, Marian, died in 1947.) About $500,000 went to James Lee's nieces and grandchildren. Also, the James T. Lee Foundation Inc. was established with an initial funding of $1.5 million; it still functions today, subsidizing charities that focus on arts and health care. Jim also set up trusts for "the children of Janet Lee Auchincloss," but specifically named only Jamie and Janet Jr.—not Jackie and Lee.

Janet had warned Jackie and Lee not to expect any money from Grampy Lee. They wouldn't be as lucky as they'd been when their eighty-three-year-old paternal grandfather, Grampy Jack, died (on January 14, 1948) and each got $3,000, about $35,000 in today's money, from his $800,000 estate. Of course, Janet certainly could've given her daughters a portion of the $1.6 million from her father, but she opted not to do so.

Neither Jackie nor Lee would attend the funeral. Jamie, who was named after his grandfather and who was a sophomore at Columbia at the time, did attend. Today, he continues to benefit from the James T. Lee Trust. He also inherited classic pieces of Grampy Lee's furniture.

GREEK MAGIC

I n May 1968, Aristotle Onassis extended another invitation to Jackie to cruise with him and friends around the Virgin Islands on the *Christina*. Jackie joined him on May 25. It was during this trip that Artemis pulled her aside to talk about money. She wanted to know if Jackie had told Aristotle about her finances. Of course she hadn't. "Tell him," Artemis urged her. "He can help you. I'm sure of it."

Apparently, Jackie did as Artemis suggested. "She confided in Aristo about her finances," said Kiki Feroudi Moutsatsos. "She said she felt vulnerable and anxious because she was running out of money. Aristo couldn't believe it. It was so surprising to him considering she'd been a First Lady and had suffered so. It seemed a poor reflection not only on the United States but also the Kennedys. He felt she should go to the press with her plight. It would cause such an outrage, the Kennedys would have no choice but to care for her."

Jackie knew better. It was her lifestyle that was doing her in, not the Kennedys. She realized the public would see it that way, too. The damage she'd suffered to her image because of the Manchester affair was significant. She didn't want to do anything to make things worse.

Later that night, Artemis and Jackie had another conversation. She told Jackie that her only daughter, Popi, had died at the age of eighteen from the rare inflammatory disease polymyositis. She could barely get the words out without racking sobs. Jackie's heart went out to her. "Artemis said she now thought of Jackie as a daughter and that she wanted to help her," recalled Thea Andino. "In fact, she suggested, maybe they could help each other."

Artemis said her brother had been in a bad relationship for many years with the wrong woman, the tall, dark-haired beauty Maria Callas, of course. "She's of peasant stock and has no class," she said. She also thought Maria was too fat, not smart, and also not very nice . . . to her. Quite simply, she wasn't good enough for Aristotle.

"Artemis had heard from her sister Merope that Aristo was thinking of marrying Maria in November," said Thea. "She wasn't sure she believed it. She knew Ari wasn't big on marriage. He didn't think it was necessary. He believed Greek men should give a woman everything she wanted, but just short of wedlock. 'He just needs to love her,' he used to say, 'with all his heart and all his money.'"

Artemis suspected that Maria had somehow forced Ari's hand. She couldn't allow that to happen, and now the clock was ticking. She wanted to get the opera star out of the picture so that she wouldn't continue to pose a threat to her family. Ari needed to move on from her, and Artemis believed Jackie was the way forward.

"You are much more suitable for my brother than Maria Callas," Artemis told Jackie. "Talk to him, Jackie. Talk to him, *pedimou* [my child]."

Everyone knew Artemis was the puppet master in the family, always pulling the strings of relatives to have her way with them. "But actually," noted Thea, "in this case, it was difficult to know who was pulling whose strings."

A couple of days later, Jackie approached Onassis on the *Christina* with the idea of a future together. While she didn't ask him to marry her, she said she was just "curious." It turned out, he was "curious," too, and eager to discuss. "But we can't go any farther with it until I talk to Bobby," Jackie said. While Ari was annoyed that she had to run anything at all by Bobby Kennedy, he said he understood.

In the days after the cruise, Jackie sent Ari a note: "I will die for Bobby if that will ever help—but until then—I want to stay in the *etat d'aire* [state of play] I found on the *Christina*—it was *imprevu* [unexpected] and a surprise—and it made me so happy. All your cares Dear Ari—to make it so carefree for me—How can I thank you for that? I can't. Thank you dear Ari—for those lovely days—I hope you don't miss your ship as much as I do." She signed it just "Jackie."

Meanwhile, Artemis continued her matchmaking campaign. According to sources very close to the Onassis family, she brought to her brother's attention the possibility that if Bobby Kennedy ever became president, "he'll put the horns on you," meaning he would be out to get him. This had already occurred to him. As president, Bobby would come after Onassis with every tool of the United States government that was available to him, and it would likely result in indictments. But if he was Jackie's husband? Bobby would probably back off in deference to her. Also, Artemis knew that her brother had an idea of building a superport in New Hampshire. It had been on his mind for some time. With his bad reputation in the States, there was no way that could ever happen. But as Jackie's husband? Maybe.

"She just kept pecking away, like a little bird," is how Kiki Feroudi Moutsatsos put it. "She felt she knew what was best for her brother and what was best for Jackie, and she was determined to see it through. I'm not sure any of it ever would've happened had she not continued to work on them both, little by little, with her Greek magic."

ARTEMIS'S ADVICE

Y ou must make him miss you," Artemis told Jackie.

Artemis Garoufalidis was in New York on business relating to Olympia Airways and had come to visit Jackie at 1040 Fifth Avenue. "You're too available," she told her, according to her later memory.

How ironic. It was the same advice Janet had given her back in 1952 about John Kennedy. Then, it had been the catalyst for Jackie to go to Europe, and JFK began to miss her, and the rest is history. Now, Artemis was suggesting that Jackie should stop cruising with Onassis, stop communicating with him so often, and maybe even go out with other men. When Jackie asked if she thought a marriage could actually happen, Artemis came back with a question of her own: "Do you really want it to?" The answer was yes. "Then, we make it happen," she said.

She had one more word of advice. Jackie should not ask him to marry her. She told her, "a real Greek man" has to ask for a woman's hand in matrimony. Apparently, Maria Callas had asked him to marry her in the past, which was one of the reasons, according to Artemis, they never wed.

In the weeks to come, Jackie did as Artemis suggested and became less accessible to Ari. She decided to accept Roswell Gilpatric's invitation to go to Mexico to see the Mayan ruins. "I had this trip planned and told her about it over lunch. She said she'd love to tag along," he recalled. "My marriage was about over by that time, and I saw no harm in it."

Once Jackie and Roswell got to Mexico, she leveled with him about Onassis. "I realized then there was no hope for me," he said. "She was leaning toward becoming serious with one of the wealthiest men in the world, which was the death of anything I could've hoped to have with her.

She said she felt she could count on Onassis to be there for her and her children, that he was protective of her and could afford to take care of her. I understood. We then had a good time in the Yucatan. She wanted to hold hands in public, and there were a few kisses, too. I enjoyed every second of it. She was obviously using me to make him jealous, which was fine with me. I loved it."

Roswell Gilpatric wasn't explicit about it, but it did not appear that he and Jackie were intimate while on vacation, unlike the week with her at 1040 three years earlier. "He pined for her and he really wanted her," said a close friend of his, "because that one week was pure heaven for him. But then, he spent years chasing that high. She just wasn't interested, and he was never able to create the atmosphere where it could happen again. 'That's just not us,' she kept telling him. 'Don't be silly, Ros.' He told me, 'I wished to God I'd never made love to her, because it kept me hooked long after I didn't want to be hooked.' Being with her while not able to really be with her was torturous for him."

As expected, Aristotle Onassis wasn't happy to see the news reports of Jackie with another man in Mexico. The ruse had its desired effect: it made him jealous. It also, apparently, upped the ante when it came to expensive baubles, because the next time he saw her, he gave her a diamond brooch that exceeded in value anything he'd given her up until this time. The couple began talking more about the future, not matrimony specifically, but about just "spending more time together." Artemis was pleased, but others in Jackie's circle were less enthusiastic.

"What do you think of Aristotle Onassis?" Jackie asked André Meyer when she returned from Mexico.

"Horrible man," André said.

"Based on what?" she asked.

André said his opinion was based on the common perception of Onassis as a criminal and lothario. He knew Jackie had been spending time with him, and he didn't like it. "You are America's First Lady, and you can't be seen with this man," he told her.

"I am not America's First Lady," she said. She knew, however, that André's critical opinion would be shared by most people.

"Have you thought of Bobby?" he asked her. As much as Jackie wanted to move forward with Onassis, she knew André was right in this respect. She had still not said anything to Bobby Kennedy, especially important now that he was running for president. He'd announced his campaign on March 16.

Bobby's announcement set off a dizzying couple of weeks of American history. Being blamed for the Vietnam War combined with his not wanting to run against Bobby, LBJ announced at the end of the month that he wouldn't seek reelection. Four days later, Martin Luther King was murdered in Memphis, causing the country to erupt in race riots. It seemed to many Americans that only Bobby could unite the country. Jackie now felt she had no choice but to level with him about Onassis.

Bobby couldn't believe his ears when Jackie talked about having Aristotle Onassis in her life. When did she become so serious about him? He called the Greek tycoon "a family weakness," alluding to Lee's relationship with him. Besides the fact that he thought Onassis was terrible for her and her children, he said her association with him could hurt his candidacy, just as she'd anticipated. If she was determined to see it through, he asked her to wait until after the election. She agreed. She also said she'd have Onassis contribute to his campaign, which probably felt disingenuous to Bobby but was a nice gesture just the same.

When Bobby told Ethel of Jackie's plans, Ethel asked to see her at 1040 for lunch. She brought with her a copy of the Jacqueline Susann novel *Valley of the Dolls*. "You've got to read this," she told Jackie. "It's such a scandal, I couldn't put it down."

At lunch, Ethel asked Jackie to slow down with Onassis. According to Jackie's Greek chef, Nicolas Knoaledius, who served the sisters-in-law Greek cuisine, Ethel said, "For heaven's sake, don't marry him. Don't do this to Bobby. Or to me." Jackie said she'd agreed to Bobby's request to wait until after the election before moving forward, and she was going to honor that promise. "Of all the men in this world, I cannot believe you've chosen this criminal," Ethel said. Jackie was clear in her response: "You don't get to tell me how to live my life."

Jackie didn't talk to Janet about Onassis—not yet, anyway. Instead, she confided in Hugh, who she knew would be on her side. She was right. Hugh thought marriage to Onassis was an interesting prospect. While they'd never met, he certainly knew of his reputation and, of course, had discussed him in 1961 with the Kennedy brothers in relation to Lee. He knew Jackie had to find some way to secure her future. He'd been telling her for years she needed to think about it. It made sense to him that she would marry for money. Many people he knew had done the same thing, his wife—Jackie's mother—included. "Is this what you want?" he asked Jackie. She said she was leaning toward it. She just had one favor to ask: "Please don't tell Mummy."

TURNING POINT

◇◇◇◇◇◇◇◇◇◇◇◇◇

The catastrophic event that forced Jackie's hand where Aristotle Onassis was concerned was Bobby Kennedy's murder on June 6, 1968, in Los Angeles. She was at home, at 1040, when she learned about it from Stas. She was distraught and crying, and Roswell Gilpatric immediately escorted her to the airport for her trip to LA to be with the Kennedys at Bobby's bedside. Bobby had been such a source of comfort for her after Jack's death, and now it fell upon her to sign papers and direct doctors to have him taken off life support; Ethel, pregnant with their eleventh child, simply couldn't do it.

Bobby's untimely death at just forty-two was a nightmare for the Kennedy and Auchincloss families. With him now gone, Jackie felt adrift. Not only was she frightened, she was also re-traumatized by horrible memories of Dallas. It all felt hopeless. "She told me, 'We would welcome death if not for the children,'" said Frank Mankiewicz, RFK's press secretary from 1965 until his death. "She feared for herself and her kids and wanted to get the heck out of a country she now saw as cruel."

In one of their earlier conversations, Ari had told Jackie he had his own private security force on Skorpios, seventy-five heavily armed men. He'd said his homes in Paris and in Athens were also guarded. Wherever he went around the world, his security team followed. These were the kinds of defenses Jackie said she needed against the outside world, and that was before Bobby was murdered. Now, she needed all of it more than ever.

"I will protect you, always," Ari told her after Bobby was killed, and she believed him. According to members of the Onassis family, Jackie ended up breaking Artemis's principal rule. "Marry me, Ari?" she asked.

She didn't have to ask twice.

MEETING THE KENNEDYS

⋄⋄⋄⋄⋄⋄⋄⋄⋄⋄⋄⋄⋄⋄

B efore she could confidently move forward with Aristotle Onassis,
Jackie wanted him to meet her families, the Kennedys and the Auchinclosses. It was more a show of respect than anything else, because even if
there was disapproval, her mind was made up. She and Roswell Gilpatric
planned to be with the Kennedys for her thirty-ninth birthday on July 28.
She decided to bring Ari with her.

Aristotle Onassis walking the hallowed grounds of the Kennedy compound in Hyannis Port? Where Jackie once spent so many idyllic moments
with Jack, Bobby, Rose, and her other relatives? This wasn't an easy scenario
to imagine. Jack and Bobby had always had such strong animus for Onassis,
and it had been less than two months since Bobby's death. Maybe it was too
soon? "My taking Aristo there is loaded with symbolism," was how Jackie
put it to Roswell Gilpatric. "I'm not sure how I'll react to it, it's so emotional
for me. It's facing the future. It's letting go of the past."

Complicating things even more, Jackie had been a little dismayed by
Rose's stoic religiosity in the face of Bobby's death. "We cannot always understand the ways of Almighty God," Rose said on a television broadcast
"The crosses which He sends us, the sacrifices which He demands of us. It
is not easy. But we know His great goodness and His love and we go on our
way with no regrets from the past, not looking backwards to the past, but
we shall carry on with courage and we are at peace."

Jackie had reservations about Rose's proclamations of faith. "What
kind of God would do this to Jack and Bobby?" she asked at the time. "No
God of mine." She had turned away from her religion at the same time

her mother-in-law clung even more tightly to it. However, she would never discuss it with Rose. She held her in too much regard to voice an opposing view about something so personal and valued so deeply by her.

In the midst of this emotional upheaval, Jackie now wanted Rose to meet Aristotle Onassis. The timing felt bad, but would it ever be good? Jackie couldn't bring herself to call Rose to ask if she'd consent. She asked Roswell to do it for her. When he picked up the phone to make the call, Jackie left the library, saying she couldn't bear to hear his side of the conversation. Ten minutes later, he called out to her: "Okay, Jackie, it's safe."

Jackie peeked into the room. "I spoke to Rose," Roswell said, "and she was upset." Jackie cringed. "I told you she'd be cross," she said. "No," he said, smiling. "She's upset because she couldn't understand why I was calling instead of you. Yes, she wants you to invite Ari to the Cape for your birthday," he said, handing her the phone. "Now, call your mother-in-law."

Barbara Gibson, Rose's secretary, recalled, "Picture it. All of us on Rose's wraparound porch, the entire staff . . . the many Kennedys—Ted and Joan, Sarge and Eunice, Stephen and Jean, Pat, Rose, and Joe, now disabled and in a wheelchair. John and Caroline were there, too. They'd arrived a couple days earlier. Ethel was absent; she'd fibbed and said she had a cold. Loyal to Bobby, she wanted nothing to do with Onassis.

"We all watched as a black sedan pulled up," Gibson continued. "A driver got out and opened the front passenger door. Jackie slid out, looking gorgeous in green slacks and a white turtleneck sweater. I remember thinking, *Look how long and luxurious her hair is.* Then, from the back seat, another man came out, tall and good-looking. I thought, *Okay, Onassis isn't so bad, after all.* That turned out to be Roswell Gilpatric. Then, there appeared this squat, little man with sunglasses and I thought . . . *Oh my.*

"Jackie walked up onto the porch and went to Joseph, leaned down, and kissed him. The Kennedys surrounded her, hugging and kissing her, happy to see her. Her children ran to her, excited. Rose walked up to Onassis, extended her hand, and said, 'Welcome to our home. It's lovely to see you again.' He took her hand and kissed it. Afterward, I whispered to Mrs. Kennedy, 'Again?' She said, 'Yes. We know each other from Monte Carlo before Jack's election.'"

Much to everyone's surprise, Rose approved of Onassis. She was concerned because he wasn't Catholic—he was Greek Orthodox—and she would rather Jackie marry within their own faith. She was also worried about the age difference. "His figure is short and stocky and his trousers always look voluminous," she wrote in her diary. However, she decided not to stand in Jackie's way.

"The fact that he was so different from Jack is what cinched the deal for Rose," said George Smathers, who was also present at the Cape that weekend with his wife, Rosemary. "If he'd been anything like Jack, she might not have approved. It would've been easier to compare. Anyone who knew Rose also understood that also playing into her decision was how much money the Kennedys would save if Jackie married well. She wouldn't need their measly two hundred thousand dollars, anymore, and I'm sure that didn't escape Rose. The diamond bracelet Onassis gave Rose toward the end of the visit didn't hurt."

"Jackie deserved a full life, a happy future," Rose would later write. "Jack had been gone five years, thus she had plenty of time to think things over. She was not a person who would jump rashly. I decided to put my doubts aside and give her all the emotional support I could in what I realized was bound to be a time of stress for her in the weeks and months ahead. I told her to make her plans as she chose to do, and to go ahead with them with my loving good wishes." Rose also wrote that she felt Lord Harlech might have been better for Jackie. "David Harlech seemed to be an almost ideal choice," she wrote, "due to the fact that he was close to the family and compatible intellectually and we all knew him as a man of integrity and charm." However, she realized it wasn't her place to interfere.

Jackie appreciated Rose's support. "I think it's sick when you hear those mother-in-law jokes," she later said when speaking of her affection for Rose Kennedy. "They used to make me sad even before I had a mother-in-law because I'd think, are people really like that? And then this woman, my mother-in-law, she just bent over backwards not to interfere. I think it's doubly extraordinary coming from that strong family where all the ties were so centripetal. She was just the most extraordinary mother-in-law. Belle-Mère [French for mother-in-law]."

Rose later wrote that she was gracious in accepting Ari's diamond bracelet, but also a little leery, "because I had seen copies of these bracelets before." Privately, she went to Jackie to ask if it was a fake. Jackie said there was no way Onassis would ever give her costume jewelry. Still suspicious, Rose later had the bauble appraised. "To my astonishment, it was worth about $1500," she wrote. She also had a similar appraisement made of a goblet Ari had given Joe. He didn't fare as well; it was worth fifteen dollars.

That afternoon, George Smathers revealed to Ted that he wasn't going to run for Senate again at the end of the year; he'd been the senator from Florida since 1951. He and the Kennedys had been friendly for years, and, for Ted, he was a strong link to Jack. He had been a groomsman at Jack's wedding and even spoke at the rehearsal dinner. "Things are changing," Ted said as they enjoyed the view from Rose's porch. Watching Jackie and Ari talk to family members was surreal. George said he was certain they were going to marry. Why else would she bring him to the Cape? It felt sad. As long as she was single, Ted observed, she was theirs, but as soon as she married Onassis, she'd be his, "and we just have to accept it," he concluded.

The next night, there was a small party at Rose's home with Nellie, the cook, bringing out a birthday cake. Everyone sang "Happy Birthday," while Joan Kennedy played the piano. Jackie blew out the candles to whoops and hollers. "There was this great relief that we could have a moment of happiness after what had happened to Bobby less than two months earlier," recalled Rosemary Smathers in 1999. "I found Onassis charming. He regaled us with stories of his upbringing, his life, which was quite exotic. He invited Mrs. [Rose] Kennedy on his yacht and was flirtatious with her, as she was with him, all in fun. It was lovely."

"Well, look at you," Jackie exclaimed as Ethel walked out of the kitchen. "Over your cold?" Ethel went to Jackie and embraced her. How could she be angry at her? The night Bobby died, Jackie had left her a note. "My Ethel," she wrote, "No one in the world could have ever been like you were yesterday—except maybe Bobby." She wrote that she stayed up the night before thinking and praying for her now and for the months ahead. "I love you so much." She signed it, "With my deepest, deepest love, Jackie." Certainly, no one could relate to Ethel's pain and grief like Jackie, both now forever bound by similar tragedies.

The moment Jackie reintroduced Onassis to the widow of one of his great nemeses seemed loaded with meaning. Who knew how she'd react? She was still grieving deeply and also exhausted, pregnant with her and Bobby's eleventh child. She didn't have the energy to be contentious. She barely had it in her to make the appearance. "Holding in all that grief the way Kennedys hold in grief is worse than just letting it out," Jackie once said.

Jackie took Ethel aside and spoke quietly to her. After a few moments, Ethel kissed her on the cheek. She then told the others she had to go; she said she'd just wanted to wish Jackie a happy birthday. "I am here for you, if you need me, Ethel," Jackie told her as she walked her to the front door. "I will always be here for you."

"Once Jackie and Ethel were out of the living room and on the porch," Roswell Gilpatric recalled, "Rose turned to me and said, 'There's been too much tragedy in this family. We must now support Jackie's courage in trying to have a better life.' Since she knew we had gone to Mexico together, it was a pointed message to me that I should now move on. Of course, I had already decided to do that. We all just wanted the best for Jackie."

MEETING THE AUCHINCLOSSES

After the visit to the Kennedys less than two months earlier, Jackie hoped for a similarly good reaction to Aristotle Onassis from a tougher audience: her own family. By this time, Janet had met Ari, in London and in New York, and wasn't exactly a fan. Jackie could only hope that five days together might change her mind. It was September 23, 1968, when she and Ari, as well as his daughter, Christina, and sister Artemis Garoufalidis arrived at Hammersmith Farm in Newport.

On that fated morning, a black Rolls pulled up to Hammersmith's wide porte cochere entrance, where, along with Janet, Hugh, and Jamie, stood a line of uniformed servants, the women in crisp white skirts, men in black jackets with white bow ties.

Onassis was behind the wheel. He got out of the car and opened the front passenger door, from which Jackie exited. She walked up to her mother and kissed her, then embraced her stepfather just as Onassis opened the car's back door. Artemis slipped out, followed by Christina.

The big moment came as Ari stepped to Jackie's side. "Aristo, say hello to Mummy," Jackie said with a smile.

He took Janet's hand and kissed it. "Have you been well?" he asked.

"Quite well," she responded. Jackie then introduced him to Hugh. They shook hands. They all then walked into the house, followed by housemen with baggage from the trunk of the car.

Considering Ari's outsize personality and reputation, Hugh was surprised by his height, a mere five foot five. Hugh towered over him with his lumbering six-foot-four frame. As they walked into the mansion, he clapped Ari on the back while whispering in his ear.

The biggest surprise of the week was how well the two men got along despite their background differences. Hugh was Yale educated and a voracious reader, whereas Ari had just a rudimentary education. Hugh's backstory was pure upper-crust Americana, while Ari's was mythical with its Greek influence and hardscrabble origins.

Onassis explained that he was born to wealth in Smyrna (Turkey) in 1906, but his family lost it all during the war when they became refugees fleeing to Greece. His mother, Penelope, died when he was six. He arrived in Buenos Aires, Argentina, at the age of seventeen in 1923, his first job as a telephone operator. He went into business for himself, became a tobacco trader, and was a millionaire by his midtwenties. Investing in the cargo shipping business in New York during the Depression, he made a fortune on sheer smarts and instinct and, also, by flouting international law and being unconcerned about the consequences. He was generally able to buy his way out of any legal jam.

Puffed up with bravado as he told his own story, Ari talked about how he moved in on Monaco in 1953 and practically took over the principality until having a falling-out with its prince, Rainier Grimaldi. "We had different visions," he told Hugh. He was presently working on what he called "a gift from the gods"—the launch of Project Omega, a $400 million investment scheme that would build oil refineries in Greece, funded by the First National City Bank in America, as well as an aluminum plant, a shipyard, and an underground air terminal in Athens. There would also be tourist resorts and hotels spread along the Aegean and Ionian. It was to be the largest economic undertaking in Greek history, and, adding to the controversy, it would be in partnership with the dictatorial regime of the Geórgios Papadopoulos.

"Being rich is fucking great, isn't it?" he asked Hugh with a hearty laugh. That comment made Jackie cringe. She wanted Hugh's approval and feared Ari was coming on a little strong. But Hugh took Ari's boasting with good nature and had to agree, there *was* something "fucking great" about being rich. "It's not a crime to succeed," Ari told Jackie when he got a whiff of her apprehension. Hugh had to agree with that, as well. Later, Ari told him he discouraged Jackie from learning Greek because he wanted to be able to say whatever was on his mind without her understanding it. She knew "maybe five words, if she's lucky," he said, and that was plenty. Hugh said there were times he wished he knew a language Janet didn't know, "just so I could jolly well talk back to her once in a blue moon," he said, chuckling.

In the end, Hugh Auchincloss was impressed with Onassis, and Onassis liked him, as well.

Ari didn't have as much luck with Janet. When she was able to steal him away, she made it clear she wouldn't sit back and watch him trade in one daughter for the other. She called the triangle "very unpleasant on the tongue." She also talked about the "reputational disaster" that would befall Jackie if she married him.

"Jackie's a big girl," Onassis said. "She can take care of herself." She reminded him that Jackie was still not over Jack's murder. "I agree that your daughter is broken," Ari said, "but only I can fix her." They came to no consensus.

"I'm suspicious of anyone with that much self-confidence," Janet later said. The fact that Hugh told her Ari reminded him of Jack Bouvier didn't help matters.

Artemis was a different story. Janet wanted to dislike her but couldn't, because they were so much alike and had so much in common. "I understand they had an instant rapport as soon as Artemis gifted her with a colorful Greek crocheted bedspread," said Thea Andino, secretary to Ari's sister Merope Konialidis. "Of course, it had a story behind it. It was hand-made by an old nun who'd been blinded by a gypsy's curse . . . or something like that," Thea quipped, "and Mrs. Auchincloss said she loved it."

As Artemis spoke only Greek and French, which Janet also understood, the two could talk in French for hours. Artemis was also such a stylish woman, Janet was impressed with her flair. Every outfit was couture and worthy of acclamation. Artemis's greatest passion, though, was her family, and Janet could understand and appreciate that, as well. The one thing Janet didn't approve of was how much Artemis smoked. Janet, too, had been a smoker, but quit because of Hugh's emphysema. She felt that, given Hugh's problems, Artemis shouldn't smoke in her home, but she never asked her not to. Where they disagreed, of course, was on any future her brother would have with Janet's daughter.

"Artemis was surprised to learn that Lee was even part of the equation for her mother," said Kiki Feroudi Moutsatsos. "As far as Artemis was concerned, Ari had never been serious about Lee. She felt any true romance with him was strictly in Lee's head. Jackie had only one real rival for her brother's affection, and that was Maria Callas, certainly not Lee Radziwill." Still, Artemis was sensitive enough to not discount Janet's concerns, especially on her home turf. "My brother is a good man," Artemis told her. "He would be good to your daughter and grandchildren. I will make certain of it."

After dinner one night, Artemis entertained everyone by reading coffee grounds in their cups, an old Turkish tradition. In her own home, Artemis always had a "gifted" old woman named Letta, whom she and Ari had known since they were children, do the honors. Just for laughs, she now undertook the task herself. Studying the remnants on the bottom of Jackie's cup, Artemis told her, "Decisions you make in the coming months will bear fruit in ways unimaginable."

Jackie was delighted. "You see that, Mummy," she exclaimed.

"Very nice," Janet said. "I never knew Maxwell House was so perceptive."

Jackie wanted her mother to approve of Ari, but it didn't seem likely. She complained about everything from his clothes to his cologne, which she claimed was a cheap fragrance used by Jamie's friends called Hai Karate. (It wasn't.)

Janet also wasn't convinced Jackie wanted to leave the country because she was afraid. She thought she was just using Bobby's death as an excuse. In Janet's mind, Jackie had wanted to live abroad since she was a young girl, and Janet had refused to allow her to accept the Prix de Paris award. Yusha later tended to agree with his stepmother on that count. Many years later, he told his friend Robert Westover, "I didn't feel that fleeing to Greece was much protection. The world's a big place, and if someone was after her, they could find her in Greece. But I decided not to offer that opinion to Jackie."

On the last day of the visit, Hugh watched as Jackie and Ari sat on the dock, their bare feet dangling over the edge as they fished for mackerel. With them was the standard poodle Jackie had bought for her mother, named after the Polish freedom fighter Count Casimir Pulaski. Every now and then, Jackie nuzzled the Count, but not so much the tycoon. While they seemed friendly, she and Ari were far from amorous. However, Hugh wasn't exactly a romantic, either. But he and Janet always had a rapport, and he sensed the same between Jackie and Ari. Later, he asked her, "Do you want this bad enough to go to war over it with your mother?" Jackie said yes. In fact, she didn't just want it, she needed it. He kissed her on the forehead and told her he understood.

Later that day, Jackie brought her mother into her room and handed her a small box. When Janet opened it, her eyes went wide. It was an engagement ring, a forty-carat marquise-cut Lesotho III from Harry Winston. Janet had never seen anything so spectacular. Jackie put it on Janet's finger. Their eyes met. It had finally happened: Janet was speechless. But not for long. She slipped the ring off, put it in Jackie's hand, and folded her fingers over it. "Keep the ring," she said, "but not the bearer." (The ring was so priceless, Jackie would only wear it a handful of times, keeping it in a bank vault in New York. After her death, it would be auctioned for $2.59 million.)

"I need your approval, Mummy," Jackie told her, according to family history.

Janet rose from her chair, looked down at her daughter. "I'm sorry," she said, "but you do not have it."

THE DEAL

◇◇◇◇◇◇◇◇◇◇◇◇◇◇

After Jackie brought Aristotle Onassis to meet both families—the Kennedys and the Auchinclosses—Ted Kennedy helped her negotiate a marital agreement. He managed to get just $1.5 million in a lump sum from Onassis if Jackie agreed to sign a document saying she wouldn't go after more money at his death. At first, Jackie was happy about it. After talking to Hugh, however, she wanted more. "I think we can do better," she said.

In the end, André Meyer was able to work with Onassis to get the settlement up to $2 million (which would be about $150 million in today's money). In the past, it was always thought to be $3 million, but documents surfaced in 2020 to clarify that it was $2 million.

André further negotiated $30,000 a month after taxes for Jackie's expenses for the duration of the marriage. That's about $200,000 in today's money. Moreover, John and Caroline would receive $1 million each in saving accounts, and the interest on that amount would be given to Jackie annually. Upon Onassis's death, Jackie would get $150,000 annually. It sounds like a lot, but considering his tremendous wealth, it really wasn't.

Things were moving forward quickly, but then Jackie had a change of heart. Between the time she first became interested in Onassis and the time she committed to marrying him, she realized she had no sexual compatibility with him. According to what she told one intimate whom she trusted implicitly, "We tried it once. It didn't work. I simply don't want to go there with him again. I don't think of him in that way."

It happens. People often date and in the course of doing so realize that the attraction just isn't there. At that point, they often go their separate ways. However, when there's $2 million on the table and you're Jackie Bouvier Kennedy raised by a mother who always told her, "The secret to happily-ever-after is money and power," it's not that easy to just walk away. Jackie's financial situation had not changed. She still needed Onassis's help, and she was so close to getting it.

It's never been revealed before because her friends have always been so understandably protective of her privacy, but people in Jackie's life say she asked Onassis if there was a world in which they could still marry, but not have sex. There was a lot they could share, she told him, they didn't need physical intimacy.

Agnetta Castallanos, who was a vice president of Onassis's Olympic Airways, recalled, "The way I heard it, they made a deal. She could be his wife, but he would still have his own life, which meant he could still have Maria Callas. It was obvious what Jackie got out of the deal. Money. But what did he get? He got to say he was married to the most famous woman in the world. She was his. Period. That's what he got, an ego boost, which, if you knew Ari, meant a lot."

A big part of the deal Jackie and Ari made was to never reveal their arrangement to outsiders. "It was embarrassing," one intimate of Jackie's said. "No one needed to know. She loved him, just wasn't in love with him. She said he was her good friend. She would never hurt him by humiliating him, and he felt the same way. They were adults, and this was the arrangement they made. End of story."

"She was Jackie Kennedy, the most famous woman in the world," noted Stanley Levin, "and that was worth all the money in the world to a man like Aristotle Onassis. He felt she'd legitimize him in the eyes of the world. I also believe that, deep down, he loved her in his own way and wanted to help her. His heart went out to her. She had that effect on people. He had Maria Callas on the side. Jackie accepted it. She knew the terms of their arrangement from the very beginning."

In years to come, there would be many published accounts about the Onassises' sex life, which was always reported as being very robust. Onassis often bragged about their lovemaking, but it was all for show to boost his image. Some of his employees from that time now admit he actually paid them to spread these sorts of rumors in the tabloids.

In 2022, Alexios Diakos, who worked for Onassis on Skorpios for ten years helping to maintain the *Christina,* said, "Many of the guys on the crew supplemented their income for years by spreading stories about having stumbled on Onassis and Jackie making love in their stateroom on the *Christina,* or on the deck or other public places. None of it was ever true.

"The boss was getting sex from Maria Callas, and everyone knew it. But he couldn't very well advertise it, so he'd come up to you, slip some money in your pocket, and tell you a reporter would be on the island. We knew what that meant. There was no way Onassis would invite a reporter onto the island if he didn't have an agenda. We'd put our imaginations to work then see our handiwork in print and laugh about it. It was a harmless way to make money."

Jackie never concerned herself with any of the stories. Many years later, in the 1980s, she confided in one close friend that the arrangement she had with her second husband was "private, between me and Ari. It worked for both of us."

THE KENNEDYS SEND THEIR REGRETS

∞∞∞∞∞∞∞∞∞∞

t was Wednesday, October 16, 1968.

"I don't know that I can do this if you're not there with me," Jackie was saying. She was on the telephone with Rose Kennedy from her bedroom at 1040 Fifth Avenue while Kathy McKeon packed her suitcases.

Barbara Gibson, Rose Kennedy's secretary at the time, recalled, "Jackie explained to Rose that a Boston newspaper was preparing an exposé on her and Ari, confirming their wedding plans. She said they needed to marry immediately because the global attention generated by the article would make it impossible for them to have a small, quiet wedding, as if such a thing could ever happen. The ceremony was now set for Sunday on Skorpios. She desperately wanted Rose there."

Jackie already called Janet to tell her to pack her bags and be in Greece by the weekend. It was too soon to get anyone else from the family to Greece. Jamie was away at school, Yusha was out of town, and Janet Jr. was in Hong Kong.

Lee was in Tunisia on vacation. Ari felt it best that he break the news to her. He'd called and told her he still loved her but had waited long enough and was now going in "a different direction," as if in a business deal. Lee said she couldn't bear to witness the wedding, "but he begged me to come," she later said. She knew she'd lost the battle, not that she ever really fought for him. "I loved him too long to say goodbye," she said, "but I had no choice."

Now, Jackie was asking her mother-in-law to pack up and be in Greece by Sunday. Barbara Gibson: "Rose's answer was quick and decisive: 'No.'"

As much as Jackie wanted Janet and Hugh at the wedding, having Rose there was even more important. She was Jack's mother, after all, and having her present would be validation of his widow's decision to remarry. It would most certainly calm angry naysayers for whom she'd fallen off her pedestal when she announced her intention to marry Onassis. Also, Jackie loved her and wanted her to share in the day. "But I can't leave Joe," Rose explained. "I'm sorry."

"Later, Rose would admit to me that she couldn't bear to see Jackie marry another man," said Barbara Gibson. "Her heart was breaking over it. 'It was better that I not be there, lest my true feelings emerge,' she told me."

Ted didn't want to go, either. He had already upset certain political operatives by negotiating Jackie's deal with Aristotle Onassis, thereby appearing to approve of her decision. He told Jackie he had Senate business. Joan felt if Ted wasn't present, she shouldn't be, either.

Ethel also begged off. Eunice and Sargent were also a firm no because Sargent, who'd been LBJ's ambassador to France since March, had his own political aspirations to consider.

In the end, the only Kennedys at the ceremony would be the two with no political agendas at all, Pat (now divorced from Peter Lawford) and Jean (married to Stephen Smith).

ONE STEP FORWARD

◇◇◇◇◇◇◇◇◇◇◇◇

Jackie Kennedy was having a bit of a breakdown. "This goddamn thing is awful," she said as she struggled out of a sleeveless, ivory satin sheath. She said she hated it because it made her look like a bride. She was almost forty, she said, and she'd been married before. She had two children. "I am anything but a blushing bride," she said.

"But I think it looks—"

"It looks awful," Jackie said, cutting off the woman standing behind her. She wondered why she'd even packed it.

"But I didn't—"

"Oh, never mind," she said.

Once the gown was at her feet, Jackie kicked it into a corner like a cheap rag. Adora Rule went to pick it up. Jackie commanded her to leave it and then pointed to the closet. "The Valentino," she said.

It was 4:00 p.m. in Greece. In a little more than an hour, Jackie would become Mrs. Aristotle Onassis. She and Adora were tucked away in a small room off a chapel known as Panayitas, or the Little Virgin.

Adora wasn't even Jackie's assistant; she was her mother's. While Jackie had plenty of help in New York, her trip to Greece had been arranged so hastily she didn't have time to organize everyone's schedule. She just brought her children's nanny, Kathy McKeon, to watch over them. Once the family was together in Greece, Janet told Adora to stay with Jackie because, as she put it, "all hands on deck for the sinking of the *Titanic*."

Adora went to a garment bag hanging in a small closet, unzipped it, and pulled from it a cream-color, chiffon-and-lace knee-length dress with long bishop sleeves. She handed it to Jackie. "This one?" she asked. Jackie snatched it without answering. As she stepped into the dress and pulled it up, there was a knock on the door. It opened, and a young woman walked into the room. Jackie whirled around to face her. "Kathy, when one knocks on a door," she said, "one waits until the person on the other side says, 'Come in, please.' One doesn't just barge in like a wild horse into a barn."

Kathy cringed and gave her an apologetic smile.

"Fine, fine, fine," Jackie said as she pulled the dress up to her shoulders. She then began to adjust it, all the while gazing into a full-length mirror. "Cigarette," she said, glancing at Kathy.

Kathy walked to Jackie's large purse on a card table, took a Salem from a pack, and nervously inserted it into a silver cigarette holder. She lit it, took a quick puff, and handed it to Jackie. As Jackie took a drag, she asked about the children. Kathy said they were fine and waiting outside the church for her. After sharing a look with Adora, Kathy bowed out of the room and closed the door behind her.

Jackie put the cigarette down on an ashtray and began to adjust the bishop sleeves on the dress. "What do you think?" she asked Adora.

"I think it looks good," she said.

She leaned in to check her makeup, fluffed up her mane of dark hair, and then adjusted the large, ivory-colored satin ribbon that hung from it. She asked if the bow was "too much." Adora said she liked it. "Fine," Jackie said, "the bow stays." Adora then said Janet wanted to come back and see her. "Oh, God, no," Jackie said as she took another deep drag. "Keep her out of here. I'm nervous enough." She asked about Lee.

The night before, she saw Lee on the deck of the *Christina*. They had a brief conversation that ended with Lee agreeing that Jackie should be the sister who ended up with Onassis. Later, Lee explained fear had influenced her decision. What if something happened to Jackie or to her niece or nephew because she'd denied them Onassis's protection? How could she live with herself?

"I tried to get her," Adora told Jackie, "but she said no. She said she'd see you in the chapel."

There was another knock on the door. It was Hugh. "I'm so glad you're here," Jackie said as she embraced him.

"Where else would I be?" he asked. He took her in and complimented her appearance. "You're sure about this?" Hugh asked her.

She said she was and added, "It's time for me to do something to make my life work." While it wasn't the most romantic reason to take a husband, Hugh understood. "Thank you for giving me away," she told him as she fixed his tie.

"I give you away at all of your weddings," he said with a smile. "You're still my favorite person," he told her, repeating his old saying about her. He then slipped a red velvet box from his vest. He said Ari had given it to him earlier. Opening it, he revealed a key ring with a gold chain and gold medal. "Saint Gorgonia," he said, "patron saint of Greek marriages."

Jackie touched it. "For good luck," she said.

"Yes," he said. "Good luck." He kissed her on the cheek. While doing so, Ari's sister Artemis Garoufalidis joined them. Hugh excused himself so the two women could talk.

"Just let me look at you," Artemis said as she stood back and took her in and then gave her customary kisses on both cheeks. "Never have I seen a bride more beautiful," she said, holding both her hands. "We made it happen, you and I, didn't we? Are you happy now?"

"I have an awful headache," Jackie told her as she rubbed her temples. "And such pain in my shoulder."

"From what?"

"Nerve damage," Jackie said. "From Dallas."

Jackie then explained, "When the back of Jack's head was shot, I held on to his skull so hard to keep his brains in, doctors say I damaged my shoulder. There's nothing they can do about it. I just have to live with it."

Artemis couldn't hide her shock. Ari had warned her that if Jackie was to be in the family, they'd have to get used to shocking details about Dallas. "You mustn't think about any of that now," Artemis told her as she patted her on the shoulder. "You can't go backward, dear. Take just one small step forward." When Jackie asked about Onassis's children, Alexander and Christina, Artemis was frank with her and told her she had to work hard to persuade them both to attend the ceremony. Jackie was happy about it, saying, "Aristo needs them there."

As Artemis left, Hugh walked back into the anteroom and took Jackie by the arm. They then walked around to the front of the small chapel. It was raining, and not a romantic drizzle but a steady, pummeling one as if a bad omen. In Greek lore, rain is supposed to foreshadow a successful marriage, but if Greek mythology was to be considered, maybe a thunderclap or an earthquake or even an eclipse of the moon might've been more appropriate.

The small group formed a processional line, Jackie's children—seven-year-old John and ten-year-old Caroline—in front, holding candles, then Lee, her matron of honor, then Janet, followed by the bride and her stepfather. Janet didn't approve of the lineup. She said she wanted to walk behind Jackie, not in front of her. But if so, Jackie argued, the last person people would see coming into the chapel would be the mother, not the bride. "And that would be wrong because . . . ?" Janet asked. Fine, Jackie decided. Letting her have her way was just easier.

Ari appeared in his blue suit and white tie and said a few words to Jackie. She nodded as he kissed her on the cheek. He then walked proudly down the center of the chapel and took his place next to the priest.

Hugh stood beside Jackie and said, "I'm sorry your father can't be here."

"He is," she told him with a smile.

"Are you ready?" he asked.

She looked at him with hesitation and bit her lip. Later, he would remember that, for a moment, he thought she would change her mind. He leaned into her. "The beginning," he said, "is the most important part of the work." It was a quote from the Greek philosopher Plato. She nodded her understanding and took his arm.

She then took one small step forward.

BOOK IV

Decisions and Consequences

MRS. ONASSIS

◇◇◇◇◇◇◇◇◇◇◇◇◇◇◇

To Ari and Jackie," Lee Radziwill said as she raised a glass of champagne. A year had passed. It was now October 1969, and the Onassises were celebrating their one-year anniversary on the *Christina*.

"Life doesn't give us what we expect," Lee said. "It gives us what we deserve."

Everyone clinked glasses.

"How lovely," Jackie said, giving Lee a look.

Many dozens of books have been written about Jacqueline Onassis's second marriage, and thousands of magazine and newspaper articles have been devoted to it. It's been picked apart, analyzed, and dissected in countless different ways from countless different viewpoints, but never completely accurately. It's interesting, looking back on it all these years later, that the one statement Onassis made about the marriage really said it all:

"Jackie is a little bird that needs its freedom as well as its security, and she gets them both from me," he said. "She can do exactly as she pleases—visit international fashion shows and travel and go out with friends to the theater or anyplace. And I, of course, will do exactly as I please. I never question her and she never questions me." It's as if nothing else ever needed to be written—he said it all, outlining for anyone who cared to really think about his words, precisely the terms of their marriage.

Ari eagerly picked up with Maria Callas immediately after marrying Jackie, rendezvousing with her as often as possible in her apartment in Paris. "Jackie and Aristo had a lot going for them," said Kiki Feroudi Moutsatsos, "but there was obviously a deficiency in their marriage. Maria filled a role for

Aristo Jackie couldn't fill. He never brought her into his world the way he did Maria. Maria was the flip side of Aristo, two sides of the same coin. It was much more than sex between them. He needed her to discuss his problems, his innermost thoughts and feelings, things he would never discuss with Jackie. He wouldn't allow her to assume that role, and I think perhaps she didn't want it either because she didn't push for it, ever. He and Maria were a perfect match, and he was with her as often as possible. I know this because I was the one who arranged his trips to Paris to see her in her home at 36 Avenue Georges Mandel. It seemed to me that their love grew even stronger after he married Jackie."

There have been decades of reporting that Jackie was humiliated by Ari's relationship with Maria, saddened by it, devastated by it, even. All of it untrue. "Maria was part of the deal," said Agnetta Castallanos. "Jackie knew what she was getting into. It's always bothered me that Onassis was painted as treating Jackie so badly where Maria was concerned. That's not how it was."

Another fascinating aspect of Ari's relationship with Maria is that he didn't want Jackie to meet her. Some in his life have speculated that he didn't share with Maria his bargain with Jackie and was afraid it might come out if they knew each other. "He did have his pride, after all, and it made more sense to him that Maria thought he was cheating on his wife with her," said one source. "He thought it made her feel special, I guess. He didn't want them to meet, and Jackie tried many times. He just wouldn't allow it." In a 1974 interview with Barbara Walters, Maria Callas confirmed that she never met Jackie.

"You'll never guess the name of Maria's older sister," Artemis told Jackie one day over breakfast. Jackie waited. "It's Jackie!" Artemis exclaimed, delighted. "Isn't fate funny?"

"How strange," Jackie said. "How does Maria treat her?" she asked.

"Oh, she hates her," Artemis said. She said she resented her sister because their mother always preferred her. "She'd shoot her in the head if she could," she added, laughing.

Jackie didn't think it was very funny.

Did Artemis know about her arrangement with Ari? Artemis seemed unaware of it and often tried to comfort Jackie about Maria. She'd also remind Jackie that her brother loved her with all his heart. So, it's very possible she didn't know about their arrangement.

Where Jackie's immediate family is concerned, the marriage did a lot of damage.

In October 1969, Lee returned from another visit to "the nervous hospital" in Switzerland, having once again been treated for anorexia, which became an even bigger problem after the marriage. This time, Jackie, not Stas, paid for it.

Lee was supposed to stay at the clinic for six weeks. After three, however, she left the facility. Jackie thought she was still in Switzerland when Lee called from London, said she'd had "enough treatment" and was fine. Though Jackie was upset and tried to convince her to return, Lee refused.

Once out of the clinic, Lee had to face the reality of her sister's marriage. When someone asked how she was doing regarding the Onassises, Lee said sadly, "I keep waiting for something good to happen to me. Meanwhile, I feel nothing."

Trouble erupted with Jackie's mother as soon as Jackie got back from her honeymoon. They got into a fierce argument when Janet accused Jackie of marrying Onassis only for his money—as if that was so unusual in the family. It ended with Janet slapping her. It didn't matter that her daughter was the most famous woman in the world, she had ignored her warnings about Onassis. Jackie decided she'd never again ask Janet to cruise with her and Ari on the *Christina*. There was no way Jackie would allow her to enjoy Onassis's generous hospitality since she seemed to disapprove so strongly of the marriage. Hugh was welcome, but not Janet—and Hugh would never be well enough to go.

They also fought over Jackie's care of the children. She seemed distant and preoccupied, and Janet didn't like it. She felt her grandchildren were being neglected. Maud Shaw had once felt the same way. "You used to complain that your parents were always too busy to be with you," Maud recalled telling Jackie. "Don't let your children suffer in the same way."

At this same time, Janet joined a theater group in Washington called La Marotte, primarily to keep up with her French. There, she met a young girl named Marta Sgubin, who worked for a member of the French embassy. Janet took a liking to her and suggested she leave her job and work for Jackie. After Jackie agreed to hire her, Caroline and John met Marta in September 1969 while staying with their grandmother at Hammersmith.

During her first week of employment, Marta showed she had backbone.

Lee's two children, Tony and Tina, were also in Newport with their grandmother. Every morning, the four cousins would sit in the hallway and, one by one, be summoned into Janet's bedroom for the day's planning, a long tradition of Janet's going back to her own children. Marta actually had the nerve to tell Janet, "They're your grandchildren, Mrs. Auchincloss, not your royal subjects." Although Janet didn't like when she called Jackie in Greece to tell her about it, Jackie's response was, "She's not wrong, Mummy." One morning soon after, Marta noticed Janet talking about the day's plans with the children as they sat around the breakfast table. Clearly, Marta had already made an impact on the way things worked in the household.

Marta would stay with Jackie and the children for more than twenty-five years and eventually become their chef. She would then go on to work for Caroline and her own family.

As all of this was happening, Hugh's health continued to decline. "With his chronic emphysema worsening and his weak lungs, the last-minute trip to Skorpios had taken a real toll," recalled Garrett Johnson, who worked at Auchincloss, Parker & Redpath. "His doctors wanted him to be treated at St. Barnabas Medical Center in Livingston, New Jersey, which specialized in lung disorders, with the largest hyperbaric chamber in the country. After Jackie and Ari flew to the States to examine the facility, they approved and agreed to pay for it. Hugh began treatment there.

"Upon his release, he had no choice but to reorganize our New York office. Even though it had cut costs, the brokerage still suffered due to the recession. We had to merge with Thomson and McKinnon to survive, and then we operated under the name of Thomson & McKinnon, Auchincloss."

RUTH AND NAOMI

◇◇◇◇◇◇◇◇◇◇◇◇◇◇

After she became Mrs. Onassis, Jackie filled the maternal void in her life left by the mostly absent Janet with an even closer relationship to Rose Kennedy. She continued to be inspired by her. "God will not give us a cross heavier than we can bear," Rose said in a cover story feature in *Life* at this time, in anticipation of her eightieth birthday. "Either you survive or you succumb. If you survive, you profit by the experience. You understand the tragedies of other people's lives. You're more sympathetic and you're a broader person."

Understanding Jackie's trauma, Rose not only embraced her new marriage, she'd often enjoy cruising on the *Christina,* beginning with a New Year's visit six weeks after the death of her own husband, Joseph, in 1969.

"Jackie was always so happy when she'd have to ask me to arrange for Mrs. Kennedy's travel," said Kiki Feroudi Moutsatsos. The only uncomfortable moment on that particular cruise occurred after Rose became seasick. While she was sound asleep, Onassis slipped into her stateroom to check on her. When he later mentioned it, she was alarmed and told Jackie she found it off-putting "to know I was sleeping and he was standing over me." Jackie told her to just make sure her door was locked in the future.

After that trip, in a February 1970 diary entry, Rose noted that Jackie sent her an album of photographs of her time in Greece. "Along with the album she sent a letter which quite overwhelmed me," Rose wrote, "with her really heartwarming expressions of the pleasure all of them shared in my last visit at New Year's, and how utterly unexpected was life's chain of events—that she and I, after all our other experiences together, should now start to share new experiences in an extremely different environment and atmosphere." She wrote that she was happy things were turning out as they were, because it meant she would always be in contact with Caroline and John. She felt that New Year's was much better for them, and more familiar, because their grandmother was at their side. She wrote that she was certain there were very few mothers-in-law who had ever received as beautiful a letter from a daughter-in-law as the one Jackie sent her, "and in any poll I am sure we would top any daughter-mother-in-law team. Even Ruth and Naomi."

Jackie, too, compared herself and Rose to the Bible characters Ruth and Naomi, a daughter-in-law and mother-in-law who remained loyal to each other after their husbands died. "Whither thou goest I will go," Jackie signed letters to Rose, quoting Ruth's devotion.

Sometimes, though, there was testiness. Once, in Palm Beach, Jackie was hot and annoyed and wanted to go back to the docked *Christina* after a shopping expedition. She was accompanied by a man named James Connor, a Palm Beach police officer who sometimes worked for the Kennedys. "I want to leave," Jackie said petulantly. She was told that they needed to wait for Rose. "But I'm hot and I'm faint and I want to leave now," she exclaimed. No, she was told, not until Mrs. Kennedy arrived. "Fine," she said. "You know what? You're fired! How do you like that?" Rose approached just in time to hear the altercation. "You can't fire him, Jackie," she said. "He works for me, not you." Then she turned to the guard and sweetly said, "We can go now."

"Rose could be a real character, but when she was on the *Christina* or on Skorpios, and sometimes even in Paris, Ari also got along well with her," said her secretary Barbara Gibson. "He found her well-known thriftiness— which Jackie called her 'New England puritanism'—amusing. Once, in Paris, Rose insisted she and Jackie get into a cab with a perfect stranger just so they could split the fare. She never tipped cabbies, either. Instead, she'd hand out a small, signed card with JFK's picture and a passage from his inaugural speech. 'Keep this,' she'd say, 'it'll be worth money one day.' Sometimes, to make it more special, she would write the cabbie's name on top of the card. Onassis got a kick out of that."

During another trip, Ari presented Rose with a gold bracelet with a serpent's head covered with diamonds. Afterward, he wrote to her: "You are one of the good Lord's most blessed children, because in the process of making an exemplary grandmother, he preceded it by making you an outstanding symbol of a man's most loyal companion and his children's mother."

Once, over dinner, Jackie, her eyes welling with tears, said to Rose, "I wish my mother and I had the relationship you and I have."

"Oh, dear," Rose said, touching her hand. "I'm sure she loves you very much. Do you know the problem mothers have?" she asked with a smile. Then, after a beat, "Daughters," she said with a wink. It was a good joke, and it did make Jackie laugh. But then, just as quickly, Jackie seemed overwhelmed with emotion. "Excuse me," she said as she put her hand to her mouth. "I'm sorry," she added as she left the table.

PETER BEARD

◇◇◇◇◇◇◇◇◇◇◇◇◇◇

During the summer of 1970, Jackie reacquainted herself with a young man she'd met in passing about three years earlier, a photographer named Peter Beard. She found him fascinating and was definitely attracted to him but, at the time, was grappling with her relationship to Jack Warnecke. Plus, Peter was twenty-nine to Jackie's thirty-eight, and she thought him too young. Still, she toyed with the idea of him.

Peter was a Yale graduate who, after college, moved to Kenya, where he began working at Tsavo National Park and taking photographs of wildlife. He published a book in 1965 called *The End of the Game,* featuring his work. A wildlife conservationist, he loved Africa and purchased a property there, Hog Ranch, outside of Nairobi. By 1967, he was dividing his time between Africa and New York City and supporting himself as a freelance photographer. Someone once dubbed him "half Tarzan, half Bryon."

Peter's great-grandfather James Jerome Hill had founded the Great Northern Railway and would leave about $50 million at his death. His family was well off, and Peter was raised affluently in New York. His father, also a Yale graduate, was a successful stockbroker. Peter, however, was estranged from his parents. A trust fund—which he described as "like being on welfare, it's so small"—helped to keep him going.

In 1970, after seeing him at a party in Paris, Jackie decided to invite him to Skorpios. She later said she invited him to photograph Caroline and John and to teach them how to paint. Anyone seeing the blond, gorgeous, and muscular Peter Beard would've been hard-pressed to believe Jackie wanted him on a tropical island just so he could teach her kids to watercolor.

However, since she had always been so adamantly opposed to extramarital affairs, most people took her at her word. She said she'd never sleep with Peter, and people believed her. But after Peter's death in 2020, his friends (and some of Jackie's) have been franker.

"Oh, please, of course Jackie and Peter were intimate," said one of his friends. "Why else was he there? He was crazy about her and she was about him, but it was just sex and intelligent talk. There was no emotional involvement to spoil things. Still, he told me he was afraid Ari would be upset with him and break his legs or something . . . but Jackie kept saying, 'Don't worry about that. Ari's fine. He has his life, I have mine.'"

"I can't say much about Peter Beard," said Kiki Feroudi Moutsatsos. "He had been around Maria Callas, too, so Aristo knew him from then. When he showed up at Skorpios, he wasn't happy about it, but he let it go. He figured he had his other life, so . . ."

A year later—in July of '71—Jackie again wanted Peter on Skorpios. Caroline flew over with Marta Sgubin, but John had the flu and ended up being cared for at her mother's estate in Newport. When he recovered sufficiently, Jackie asked Peter to go to Hammersmith, get John, and bring him to Greece.

A week after Jackie was reunited with her son on Skorpios, Lee and Stas showed up. "Lee had just recovered from a hysterectomy, which was why Jackie invited her," her biographer Diana DuBois once said. "Stas knew Peter and considered him a friend; they had taken safaris together. That didn't stop Peter from scoring with Lee, or maybe it was the other way around, depending on which one was later to tell the story."

There were three houses on the property: the Pink House, which was mostly for guests; the Hill House, which was where Jackie, Ari, and close family members stayed; and the house in between the two, which had no name but which was where the children stayed with Marta. Soon, Lee was staying in the Pink House rather than the Hill House, and Peter was seen going into her quarters late at night and then slipping out in the morning.

At the end of July, Aristotle Onassis's twenty-year-old daughter, Christina, eloped in the States with forty-eight-year-old real estate agent Joseph Bolker. "Ari went on a rampage," said Kiki Feroudi Moutsatsos. "It was the first time I saw him and Jackie argue, as they celebrated her forty-second birthday party."

David Frost and Diahann Carroll were guests of Onassis's at the time.

Carroll's television series *Julia* had just been canceled, and she was depressed, which is why she was on holiday. Everyone was drinking champagne, and Jackie was a little tipsy as Ari roared his disapproval of Christina's elopement.

"Jackie thought Mr. Bolker reminded Christina of her father and could provide her with the stability she needed," said Kiki. "Artemis was genuinely delighted that her niece had found a man who was making her happy. She always believed a woman should marry a man at least ten years older."

Ari disagreed with both of them and threatened to hire someone to beat Bolker up and break his legs. "You'll do no such thing," Jackie exclaimed. The two got into a heated argument, and when Onassis said something insulting to her, Jackie tried to slap him. He grabbed her hand before she could make contact. "Don't even fucking try it," he said. At that, Diahann Carroll bolted up and shrieked, "Enough! This is supposed to be my vacation!" With that, she stormed out, with David Frost meekly following.

"SOME THINGS YOU JUST DON'T TALK ABOUT"

◇◇◇◇◇◇◇◇◇◇◇◇◇

I n the fall of 1971, Jackie was in Manhattan to get Caroline and John settled for the new school year when, one morning, lobby security called to tell her she had a visitor. It was her mother. When the elevator doors opened into her apartment, there stood Janet, suitcase in hand. "I've left your uncle Hughdie," she announced.

Of course, Jackie was surprised and, after she got her mother settled, wanted more information. Janet was very emotional, however, and said she didn't want to discuss it. A few days went by until, finally, she opened up.

Apparently, three years earlier when Janet and Hugh were making last-minute arrangements to go to Greece for Jackie's wedding, Janet couldn't find her passport. She and her maids rummaged through both houses, Hammersmith and O Street, searching for it, but to no avail. As Janet looked through Hugh's office, she went to a bottom drawer in his desk and, much to her surprise, found four magazines hidden there called *Eros*. She thumbed through them and was shocked. To her eyes, it looked like pornography. She took the magazines.

Eros—named after the Greek god of love—was a high-priced, lavishly produced magazine of erotica that published just four editions in the 1960s. Its focus was the burgeoning sexual revolution. It was erotic, not pornographic. However, to a woman of Janet's time and place, it's not surprising that she would find them indecent.

After telling Jackie about them, Janet went to her room and, much to Jackie's surprise, returned with the magazines. Also perhaps to her surprise, one of them had Marilyn Monroe on the cover. It's not known if Jackie was aware, but Bobby Kennedy had filed a lawsuit against the magazine's publisher, Ralph Ginzburg, claiming he'd violated federal anti-obscenity laws by publishing the seductive pictures of Marilyn, taken by Bert Stern. They were far from pornographic, though; Marilyn was just topless.

Hugh Auchincloss had been known to have had a collection of pornography when he was much younger. More than thirty years earlier, his second wife, Nina Gore, left him because he was chronically impotent. His mother had told her she'd paid for years of psychiatric treatment to get to the bottom of it only to be told it was the result of excessive masturbation. That actually made sense to Nina. Jamie Auchincloss explained, "When she married Daddy, she'd found a huge collection of magazines she insisted be disposed of in the Potomac, lest they get into the hands of her young son from her previous marriage, Gore Vidal. Gore later said Daddy held back a few of the magazines, which he found under his bed. It's all part of the family history, and who knows if it's true or not. It's not like we ever confronted Daddy about it. But it is generally agreed that Daddy was impotent for his entire marriage to Mummy."

Janet was forced to make a life-altering decision when she married Hugh in 1942 because, at the time, she and her ex-husband, Jack Bouvier, were still enjoying a robust sex life. Was she willing to give that up for financial security for her and her daughters? The answer was yes, but it had been a genuine sacrifice. She and Hugh then ended up having two children together, Janet Jr. and Jamie.

It's understandable that finding Hugh's magazines all these many years later was upsetting to Janet. She'd always assumed he just wasn't a sexual person, but finding these publications made her wonder if he just was never attracted to her. As much as she didn't want to care about that, she did, and it hurt.

"Why did you keep these all this time?" Jackie wanted to know.

Janet was at a loss to explain. After she took them from Hugh's office, she didn't know how or when to return them. He never mentioned that they were missing, of course, and the years just flew by. It had been nagging at her for all this time until, finally, she and Hugh had a fight about something totally unrelated and she just decided to pack her bags and leave and bring the magazines with her.

Jackie's heart went out to her mother. Janet would be sixty-four in December and still wanted to feel attractive to her husband even if they were never intimate. Jackie was overwhelmed that she had taken her into her confidence.

According to family members, when Janet asked if she should confront Hugh, Jackie advised her not to. "People should be allowed to have secrets. We all have them," she said. Jackie was also not the type to be forthright about sexual matters. "We were much too discreet and private in my family to talk about those things," said Jamie Auchincloss. Jamie is gay but never had a conversation with Jackie or his parents or any of his relatives about it. "I assume they knew," he said, "but, no, we didn't have long talks about it. That would never have happened in our family. We knew where to draw the line. 'There are some things you just don't talk about,' Mummy used to say."

Janet went back to O Street after a week with her daughter, the matter settled. Upon Hugh's death, his son Yusha would discover the magazines. He gave them to Jamie, who still has them today.

<hr />

About six months later, in autumn 1972, Jackie had her own little scandal relating to private pictures taken of her on Skorpios. They were taken while she was using an outdoor shower on the beach of Skorpios and published in an Italian magazine called *Playmen* (and, then, a couple of years later in *Penthouse*).

Jackie had never been shy when it came to public nudity; there are many stories of her sunbathing in the nude; she had been caught doing so by friends, relatives, and lovers, such as Jack Warnecke. However, she had never been photographed naked, not to anyone's knowledge, anyway. As expected, the publication of such pictures caused an international sensation.

When the pictures were first published, Jackie was, of course, embarrassed. Ari was furious—at her for being so careless. Onassis became determined to get to the bottom of how the photographs had been taken; meanwhile, he told her, "Do me a favor and keep your panties on in public."

When Ari tried to investigate, the magazine's publishers refused to co-operate and said he'd have to go to court if he wanted answers.

Artemis Garoufalidis felt terrible about the pictures and said that who-ever was responsible should be punished. Jackie wasn't really that upset. "I don't treat it as a reality," she told *Newsweek*. "It doesn't touch my real life, which is with my children and my husband. That's the world that's real to me."

Some have speculated that Onassis was behind the photos. He arranged for them to be taken, or so it's been reported, to embarrass her because of their marital problems.

"It was Artemis who figured out the truth," recalled Thea Andino. "'Who most hates Jackie?' Artemis asked her sister Merope. Only two people came to mind: Christina and Alexander.

"When they were young, Christina and Alexander were incredibly close; they used to have a secret knocking system on the wall that divided their bedrooms, allowing them to communicate with each other all night long," said Thea. "As teenagers, they became competitive, mostly for their father's affection and, also, their rightful places in his empire. But now, with Jackie as a common enemy, they were again close and in league against her.

"Christina would pepper Kiki Feroudi Moutsatsos with questions about Jackie's schedule just so she wouldn't inadvertently run into her. If she did see her and Jackie was sweet, Christina felt she was being fake and called her a hypocrite. Both she and Alexander were so rude, Jackie always found herself complaining to Ari about them. He didn't seem to care, or maybe there was nothing he could do about it. 'You worry about your bratty children,' he'd tell her, 'and I'll worry about mine.'"

When Artemis confronted Christina, she hotly denied any involvement, and Artemis believed her. When she then spoke to Alexander, he, too, claimed innocence. However, Artemis had known him all his life and was more a mother to him than his own mother, Tina. All she had to do was give him that *look,* and he cracked and confessed.

Alexander explained that the pictures had been taken two years earlier by a paparazzo named Settimio Garritano. Garritano had stored them in a Swiss bank while he tried to figure out what to do with them. Then, in the spring of '72, Garritano snapped topless photos on a beach of Alexander's fiancée, Baroness Fiona Campbell von Thyssen. To prevent their publication, Alexander made a deal with the photographer to, instead, photograph Fiona in an exclusive setting. During that negotiation, the two got along so well, Garritano mentioned he had naked pictures of Jackie locked away. He was afraid of publishing them, he said, because he feared the wrath of Alexander's father. The Onassis scion was as delighted as he was shocked; naked photos of his wicked stepmother? Of course, they should be published immediately! He told Garritano his dad would "love it and think of it as a great joke," which of course was far from the truth. Alexander, obviously hoping to humiliate both his father and stepmother, was then instrumental in brokering the deal for Garritano with *Playmen*.

"As disappointed as she was furious, Artemis asked Alexander why he'd do such a thing," said Thea. "He then went on and on about how much he hated Jackie for marrying his father. He'd always wanted his parents to get back together and blamed Jackie for standing in the way of that happening. 'Fine. Three things happen now,' Artemis told him. 'First, you grow up.' And with that, she slapped him hard right across the face. 'Second, you tell your father what you did. Third, you go to church and you tell Him,' she said, pointing above."

Alexander was terrified to tell his father what he'd done. He put it off for so long that finally Artemis decided to do it herself. At first, Aristotle refused to believe his son would do such a thing. When Onassis confronted him, Alexander denied it. When he eventually revealed the truth, Ari was devastated. He couldn't believe the son he loved so much would do such a thing. He couldn't even look at him, which caused Alexander to burst into tears. "No Greek tragedy is worse than when a Greek son lets down his Greek father," Artemis said.

After Ari told Jackie that Alexander was the culprit, she was shocked not only by what he'd done but that he hated her enough to do it. She knew she'd get no sympathy from her mother but did talk to Hugh and Yusha about it. "I can't believe this family I married into," she told them. "Who would do a terrible thing like this?" While Hugh thought she should press legal action against Alexander, Yusha felt it would just make things worse. He felt she should at least try to make things right with him. To that end, Jackie had a long talk with Alexander and tried to smooth things over with him. She thought she'd made some headway, but she was wrong, as evidenced by a conversation Thea Andino overheard him having with Christina. Bragging about humiliating Jackie, he said, "Madam got exactly what she deserved. They both did, she and Father."*

---

* Demonstrating that she wasn't ashamed of it, Jackie later gave a print of one of the nudes to Andy Warhol and signed it: "For Andy, with enduring affection, Jackie Montauk," referencing their holiday home on Montauk. It was discovered after Warhol's death among his possessions.

JACKIE'S THERAPIST

◇◇◇◇◇◇◇◇◇◇◇◇◇

In the early 1970s, the burgeoning feminist movement influenced women all over the country to live their lives on their own terms. Jackie felt she'd always done just that, even though most people felt she lost herself in her marriage to JFK.

"Why do people always try to see me through the different names I have had at different times?" she asked the reporter Maryam Kharazmi. Kharazmi managed to score a very rare interview with Jackie for *Kayhan International* when the Onassises were in Iran. It was in May of 1972, and they were there at the invitation of the National Iranian Oil Company, which was interested in purchasing oil tankers from Ari. "People often forget that I was Jacqueline Bouvier before being Mrs. Kennedy or Mrs. Onassis. Throughout my life I have always tried to remain true to myself. This I will continue to do as long as I live. I am a woman above everything else."

At this time, Jackie and Ari disagreed on just about everything. As far as she was concerned, they might as well be officially separated. Determined now to chart her own course independent of him, she was living primarily in New York while he was in Greece. Meanwhile, Lee's marriage to Stas was all but over, so she, too, was living in New York.

To Jackie, being true to herself came with a price. Whatever deal she had in place with Ari had worked for her, and now without it, she began to feel lost, as if the underpinnings of her life were once again cracking. She complained to intimates about a frightening incident that had occurred three years earlier and kept coming back to her in recurring dreams:

She had just attended the funeral of Lord Harlech's wife, Sylvia, in

England and decided to spend six weeks in Ireland. While there, she liked to slip off and drive to a cove where she could swim in private across the channel. One afternoon, she decided to ditch the Secret Service and go for a swim in her special spot. The water that day was unusually rough, so much so that even Jackie, expert swimmer that she was, had trouble. As it got worse, the high tide kept pulling her farther from the shore, and she began to panic. Midway across the channel, she realized she'd never be able to get back to shore. She struggled. But then . . . she stopped fighting and just let herself go. As she did so, she began feeling a release from all her problems, her pain and sadness . . . and it wasn't so bad. In fact, it felt good. Then, as she later recalled it, "a great porpoise" appeared at her side and rescued her. The "porpoise" was actually one of her Secret Service agents. In her recurring dream, though, she wasn't rescued. She just drifted off into a dark abyss. She'd wake up disturbed and anxious. This dream and her ongoing PTSD over the assassination became the catalyst for Jackie to begin therapy with Dr. Marianne Kris, a noted Austrian physician and psychoanalyst who had trained under Sigmund Freud.

Jackie first met the seventy-one-year-old Kris at a cocktail party at Andy Warhol's in January of 1971. The two women struck up a friendship, and Jackie offered her a ride home. After the driver pulled up to Kris's Fifth Avenue apartment, she handed Jackie a business card and told her to stay in touch. Jackie looked at the card and realized Marianne was a psychiatrist. According to what the doctor later recalled, Jackie froze. "It's just my day job," Marianne told her with a smile, "no need to fear."

At this same time, President Richard Nixon and First Lady Pat Nixon invited Jackie to a long-overdue unveiling of her and President Kennedy's official portraits by the painter Aaron Shikler. Jackie had already said she couldn't do it. Pat Nixon, however, was very persuasive and able to wear Jackie down a little. Unsure how to proceed, Jackie reached for the business card and called Dr. Kris and told her she hadn't been back to the White House since leaving in 1963. In fact, whenever she went to Washington, she instructed her driver to detour around it because she couldn't even bear to see it. She explained it was because of Dallas. However, Dr. Kris felt there was another reason: Jack's infidelity while he and Jackie lived there. She felt it was time for Jackie to face those memories and at least try to find some peace around them. She urged her to go back and take her children with her so that they might see the only place they'd ever known their father.

Jackie agreed. She wanted to make some progress in her healing and so, as difficult as it would be, she'd return to the White House. As long as the visit could be conducted with the utmost secrecy with no reporters and no photographers, Jackie told the Nixons she'd come for an unveiling. A few weeks later, on February 3, 1971, the Nixons sent a military jet to fly her, Caroline, and John to Washington.

Much to Jackie's surprise, her return to the White House was cathartic. As well as the portraits, she and the children also saw the Jackie Kennedy Garden, which had been dedicated in her honor during the Johnson administration with Janet standing in for her. After dinner with the Nixons in the private residence, Nixon escorted them to the Oval Office, which Caroline remembered very well, though vaguely. It's a shame there are no photographs of such an important day, but that was Jackie's wish.

Of course, there were a few moments of sadness, but even those she later described to intimates as more like melancholic. It had been almost ten years since Jack's death. While she was certainly not over the tragedy itself, she'd at least come to terms with their marriage. Regardless of its deficiencies, she really had loved being in it and she missed it. She missed her husband.

The next day, Jackie wrote to Pat Nixon, "Can you imagine the gift you gave me? To return to the White House privately with my little ones while they are still young enough to rediscover their childhood—with you both as guides?" She wrote that she could only hope Caroline would turn out as well as the Nixon daughters, Julie and Tricia. She also added that the visit had allowed her to explain more to John about his childhood with his father. "Your kindness made real memories of his shadowy ones," she wrote. "Thank you with all my heart," she concluded. "A day I dreaded turned out to be one of the most precious ones I have spent with my children." It would be Jackie's one and only return to her former home.

"I'm not going to hang on to bitterness or sadness any longer," she told Janet and Hugh after the visit. Hugh said they'd come too far and had been through too much to be angry about any of it. "We got through it as a family," he said, and he, too, just wanted to now honor Jack and let go of the past. Janet agreed.

Dr. Kris's suggestion had been good advice and would turn out to be the catalyst for Jackie's decision to go into treatment with her. A New York patient of Kris's recalled walking into her home office at 135 Central Park

West one morning to find Jackie sitting in the waiting room, perusing a magazine, "dressed in a long, peasant skirt with strappy sandals, her hair pulled into a colorful scarf—very Valerie Harper in *Rhoda*—and wearing her trademark Jackie O. sunglasses. I was taken aback. 'Is the doctor in?' I asked. She nicely said, 'She's with another patient. I'm early,' and went back to her magazine.

"At this same time, Norman Mailer was either getting ready to release or had already released a biography of Marilyn. Everyone in New York was talking about it. I looked at the cover of the magazine Jackie was reading, and, sure enough, it was an article about the Mailer book with photos of Marilyn. I couldn't help but stare for a moment. She noticed and looked up from the magazine and said, 'So iconic.' Just those two words. Then, she went back to her reading. It really struck me. I knew I'd never forget it.

"Later, I had to ask Dr. Kris about it. She said she wouldn't discuss Jackie, but she also said, 'Don't believe everything you read about President Kennedy and Marilyn Monroe,' which somehow seemed significant.

"After that, I'd see Jackie in her office quite often. Once, she smiled at me and said, 'We really must stop meeting this way.' She wasn't the least bit uncomfortable. What struck me was that everyone in town was talking about Marilyn, and here Jackie was before me, flesh and blood, looking like any other New Yorker, so accessible there was no reason I couldn't have just asked her some god-awful question. I had to wonder how many others did just that, and I thought, my God, how brave she is to put herself out there and not care."

"Dr. Kris would never discuss Mrs. Onassis, citing doctor-patient confidentiality," said Patricia Atwood, Kris's secretary from 1972 to 1974, in an email. "They addressed Mrs. Onassis's ongoing PTSD over the assassination, as well as certain nagging issues about their marriage. He went out in a blaze of glory, Mrs. Onassis said, according to one of the [Kris's] notes I read. The way he died had completely robbed her of the right to hate him, she said. Next to that entry, Dr. Kris wrote that her grief was anything but, as she put it, 'tidy.'"

In the spring of 1971, Jackie invited Marianne to spend the weekend with her and the Auchinclosses at Hammersmith Farm. Some in Jackie's life are, still today, puzzled by this decision. The truth, though, was that Jackie was concerned about her mother's recent episodes of confusion and forgetfulness. Some were small moments, but alarming just the same. For instance, Janet would say she'd just talked to Jackie on the telephone when she hadn't. One, in particular, was more upsetting. Mother and daughter planned to meet at the Russian Tea Room for lunch and Jackie waited an hour. Worried, she called Hammersmith from a pay phone to ask Hugh if Janet had left, and Janet picked up. She said the two had no such plans. Then, a couple weeks later, Janet's version of the story was that *she* was the one who had waited for Jackie at the restaurant, not the other way around. Because of more odd moments like that one, Jackie wanted Dr. Kris to surreptitiously observe Janet to see whether she thought something was wrong. But Janet was in fine form the weekend of Marianne's visit, taking her on a tour of home, pointing out where JFK had signed certain bills and reminiscing about the Camelot years. The doctor came to the conclusion that, likely, any lapses in memory had to do with old age. She suggested they just keep an eye on her.

When Janet learned that Jackie and Marianne hadn't known each other long, she became suspicious. Jackie certainly wasn't the type to bring strangers home. She rarely warmed up to people quickly and would usually want to make sure she could completely trust a person before welcoming him or her into her private world. Not only that, Marianne looked to be a peer of Janet's; they seemed as if they were the same age. (Actually, Marianne was seven years her senior!) Janet was used to Jackie having older friends—for instance, Ari's sister, Artemis, was five years older than Janet—but, still, something didn't seem right. According to the family history, while Jackie and Marianne were on the dock talking, Janet went through Marianne's purse and found something (it's not known what, exactly; some say it was a business card, others suggest a prescription bottle) that revealed her true profession. Naturally, Janet was upset. Marianne had asked many personal questions of her, and now Janet felt she'd been tricked. After an embarrassing confrontation, Janet demanded that Jackie and Marianne leave Hammersmith immediately. They both felt terrible about it.

The consequences of Marianne's unfortunate visit might've ended there had it not been for Yusha's recognition of her name. At first, he couldn't pinpoint it, but after making a few telephone calls he remembered that Marianne Kris had once been Marilyn Monroe's psychiatrist. In fact, she was the doctor who had institutionalized Marilyn at the Payne Whitney Psychiatric Clinic in February 1961. It had been in all the papers that Marilyn's estranged husband, Joe DiMaggio, ultimately had her released against the vehement objections of Dr. Kris. Marilyn then fired Marianne and began even more intensive therapy with another psychiatrist, Dr. Ralph Greenson. His arguably unsuccessful treatment of Marilyn would go on to become historically controversial.

Jackie was hurt and angry when Yusha told her about Marianne's past. How could she have kept such vital information from her? "Everyone on the planet knows what I went through with Jack and Marilyn," she reportedly said.

When Jackie confronted her, Dr. Kris said she felt no responsibility to inform her about any former patients in the same way she'd never reveal that she'd ever treated Jackie. We don't know a lot about their discussion only that Marianne asked, "How is this relevant?" to which Jackie responded, "How is it *not* relevant?" According to Dawn Morris, a student of Dr. Kris's who assisted her in researching her paper, "The Psychoanalytic Study of the Family," for the New York Psychoanalytic Society & Institute in 1972, the doctor defended her actions by saying that had Marilyn completed her treatment at the sanitarium, she might've still been alive. "Dr. Kris wouldn't apologize for having taken what she believed was the best care of her patient," says Dawn Morris. "People don't know she was also the one who recommended Dr. Greenson as her replacement. She believed in him at the time, though she later felt her trust had been misguided. Somehow, Dr. Kris and Jackie worked out these issues, though I don't know the details. Jackie did decide to continue as a patient."

Apparently, Jackie even told Marianne about the phone call she'd gotten in 1962 from a woman who said she was Marilyn. Arguably, violating her earlier stated code of ethics, Dr. Kris told Jackie she felt fairly certain the call *had* been from Marilyn because she'd once told her she'd placed a call to Jackie but didn't speak to her. This revelation surprised Jackie. All these years later, to have it reliably confirmed that the caller had actually been Marilyn Monroe was a little staggering.

Dawn Morris recalled, "Dr. Kris was fascinated by the fact that, ten years after, Jackie was still so moved by that call, even disturbed by it. But she told me Marilyn had that effect on people. 'If you'd ever been touched by her or had any interaction with her no matter how distant, it somehow never left you,' she said."

MONTAUK

⬦⬦⬦⬦⬦⬦⬦⬦⬦⬦⬦

When not in the city, the Bouvier sisters spent a great deal of time in Montauk, New York, at the twenty-acre estate of Andy Warhol. The famous photographer, illustrator, and filmmaker was now a close friend of Lee's and becoming closer to Jackie. The estate was a compound of five small homes and a large five-bedroom lodge, and then four more houses on the edge of a cliff. Because there were always guests such as Mick and Bianca Jagger, the property was usually bustling with people. Peter Beard was always present, taking photographs of celebrities. On some days, Jackie appeared to be with him, as Lee glared at them. On other days, Lee was with him, as Jackie looked on with disapproval.

James "Jay" Mellon, heir to the Andrew Mellon fortune and a good friend of Lee's and Peter's, didn't think Jackie had any real attachment to Peter. "I thought it was Peter and Lee who were intimate," he said, "not Peter and Jackie. But how could anyone be sure?"

Mellon said, "Lee was femme fatale. Jackie was saucy sophisticate. They were different, but both sensuous women. Their values, though, were questionable. Money. All about money. Jackie had it and flaunted it. Lee didn't have it and coveted it, which made her seem desperate. Jackie never helped. Lee said she paid her phone bill once and she never heard the end of it.

"Get them out of the city, however, and away from the complexities of their lives and they were different . . . laid-back and genuine. Trying to figure them out was difficult. They lived in their own rarified world, one in which all things were possible and all men were available to them."

Peter Beard later put it this way when talking about them: "Lots of loyalty. Lots of bad things."

"Peter, Peter, *Peter*," said Jamie Auchincloss with a chuckle, "that's all we heard about for about a year there. Very charismatic. Good-looking. Naughty. Played fast and loose with rules of engagement. Dangerous. He had an incredibly intense focus on his art, yet still found time to challenge the women in his life to do things they weren't willing to do. Always running off with the next best thing, too. That was Peter."

"I wish she would be more of a Greek wife," Ari's sister Artemis told their sister Merope when she learned Jackie was spending so much time in New York. "Jackie is not doing so well to leave Aristo and go to New York for weeks at a time." Though Jackie and Artemis still had a good relationship, Artemis was at a loss to understand why Jackie was so unhappy. She really wasn't, though. She'd got what she wanted from Ari. Money and protection. Onassis was the unhappy one. By the end of 1972, he'd begun to feel taken advantage of. He now felt Jackie had gotten the better part of their deal. Now she was on her own in New York and seen dancing at clubs with Peter Beard. It was one thing for him to be with Maria, but another for Jackie to be with Peter.

"Onassis would fly in from time to time that summer and autumn [1972] and stay at his suite at the Pierre," recalled Stanley Levin, who helped manage the Onassis empire. "He'd call Jackie and ask to see her. Whereas early in their marriage, she'd have him stay at 1040, now she didn't want him around, which would enrage him. 'I'm Aristotle fucking Onassis,' he'd roar. I'd say, 'Yeah, well, she's Jackie fucking Kennedy, and she's not going to kiss your ass, Ari. She already got what she wanted out of you.' He said he wanted to see the kids if he couldn't see her. She'd allow it with John only; she wanted him to have a relationship with the boy, not so much Caroline."

"Aristo definitely felt Jackie got the better end of the bargain," said Kiki Feroudi Moutsatsos. "She got money and protection, which is what she wanted. In return, all he got was the honor of saying his wife was Jackie Kennedy. That did little to nothing for him. It didn't bring in new business. I saw the negative results of the marriage. His relations with American businessmen and government officials didn't improve and, in fact, got much worse because he'd taken their precious First Lady. He never asked her to accompany him to meetings because business was something he shared exclusively with Maria, not with her. If anything, the marriage maybe made him look a little foolish to outsiders because they knew the only reason he ended up with Jackie was because of his money."

"How best to describe this time in our lives?" asked Janet's assistant Adora Rule rhetorically. "Everything up in the air, is how I'd describe it. No one was happy, everyone was acting. The sisters were in Montauk with the kids. Mrs. A. was upset seeing Jackie and Lee on TV leaving nightclubs late at night. Jackie would send the kids to Hammersmith for weekends, and we all wondered what she was up to when they were gone."

While it had taken a couple of years, by the end of 1972, Prince Stanislaw Radziwill came to terms with Lee's romance with Peter Beard by also becoming involved with someone else. He would file for divorce early in 1973, and it would be finalized the following year.

At this same time, Jackie decided she no longer wanted Peter in her life. He was handsome and sexy and, as a photographer, very talented, but she had nothing in common with him other than the fact that she was sharing him with Lee.

It would overstate it to say that Peter became a problem between the Bouvier sisters. For that to have happened, they would've had to address the complication. They didn't. They rarely had in-depth, heart-to-heart talks about important matters. If they had, maybe Jackie wouldn't have ended up with Onassis!

In 2015, one of Jackie's close friends recalled, "What happened was that Jackie was at a party at Truman Capote's. Lee and Peter were talking, and Jackie overheard Peter say something very precious to her like, 'It's impossible not to love you.' That really affected Jackie. When was the last time anyone had ever said anything like that to Lee? Probably never. That week, Jackie and her therapist came to the conclusion that she had to get out of the way. She had taken Onassis from Lee, did she really want to take Peter, too? So, she phased him out, and Lee took him in. Jackie and Peter stayed good friends, however."

"Lee was crazy about Peter once he was hers for good," said Truman Capote. "My God, he was all she talked about. Peter this and Peter that."

Also at this time, and with Truman's help, Lee was writing a memoir about her childhood in East Hampton. People in her life hoped these positive changes would maybe facilitate a healing of her sisterhood with Jackie. They did not; the wounds were just too deep.

Life went on. It didn't stop because of Jackie's broken relationship with Lee. Not only were there children involved—cousins who loved one another—there were friends and relatives whose lives satellited around those of the Bouvier sisters. Therefore, there would still be vacations at the Cape and in Newport and cruises on the *Christina* and fun times spent on Skorpios.

"MUTUAL WAIVER & RELEASE"

◇◇◇◇◇◇◇◇◇◇◇◇◇◇

n November of 1972, Jackie got word that Hugh Auchincloss wanted
to meet her at his office. Despite his health challenges, he'd still been
coming into New York three days a week. On the agreed-upon date, she
arrived at ten in the morning, and he got right to the point. "Hammersmith
is going under," he told her. The property taxes alone were $32,000 a year
(about $190,000 today). "Plus," recalled Jamie Auchincloss, "the chickens
had come home to roost where my father's previous two marriages were
concerned. He'd been paying huge amounts of alimony for years. His business was bad, the economy was bad, and there was no way to sustain Hammersmith."

Earlier, Janet had asked Jackie to talk to Ari about bailing them out
with $200,000—about $1.3 million today. While Jackie really did want to
find a way to save Hammersmith because it meant a lot to her, especially
given that she and JFK were married there, she was reluctant to ask Onassis for anything. She said she'd think about it. A few months passed. Now,
Hugh sat before her asking, "Have you talked to Ari?"

"For Jackie, putting Janet off was easy, but doing the same to Hugh
was tougher," said Garrett Johnson, who worked at Thomson & McKinnon, Auchincloss. "However, Hugh also had a relationship with Ari. He
and Jackie had been at Hammersmith several times since their marriage.
The last time, Ari shared a bottle of his favorite Black Label scotch with
Hugh and stayed up all night as Onassis smoked Cuban cigars and gave him
business advice. Hugh, of course, didn't smoke because of his emphysema,
and Onassis should never have smoked in his presence. Anyway, Jackie said

it would make more sense if he talked to Onassis himself. Hugh had too much pride, so she told him, yes, she'd do it."

Jackie had gotten a lump sum of $2 million when she married Onassis, which, over the last few years, had grown with interest. But she wasn't going to spend any of it to bail out Hammersmith. Instead, she decided to appeal to Ari. On November 25, which happened to be John's twelfth birthday, she took the elevator up to Ari's suite at the Pierre. Ten minutes later, she found herself sitting across a desk from him and asking for $200,000.

"Ari didn't flinch; that amount was peanuts to him," said Stanley Levin. "However, by this time, Ari had more than a few issues with Jackie, not the least of which was his ongoing frustration about the inequity of their marriage. As she sat across him, he asked her directly: 'What did I get out of the deal?' He mocked her by imitating her breathless voice: '*I'm so afraid. Death all around me. Only Aristo can save me.*'"

It also bothered him that Jackie kept a very large, framed photograph of President John Fitzgerald Kennedy hanging on one of the walls in a guest room. Every time he walked by the room, he'd slam its door closed. Even Kiki Feroudi Moutsatsos was put off by the picture when Jackie installed her in that guest room during a visit. "It was a lovely photograph, very noble and distinguished, but it was huge and I couldn't lie in bed and stare at it," she recalled. "I went to Jackie's room and explained to her that it felt like President Kennedy's spirit was in that room and I couldn't sleep there. She got tears in her eyes and said she understood and moved me to another room. But I know Aristo wouldn't have been pleased about that enormous picture. It linked Jackie to a past where I think he felt maybe she was happier."

"I was a fool to let her talk me into this marriage," Onassis had begun to say to people in his inner circle.

As Jackie sat before him, Onassis opened his desk drawer, pulled a document from it, and slid it over to her. It was entitled "Mutual Waiver & Release." Jackie took a moment to review it. This was a document she was supposed to sign when they married. Its purpose was to substitute the lump sum of $2 million for the 12.5 percent of Onassis's estate she would've been entitled to as per Greek law upon his death. It wasn't a great deal, but she had agreed to it. She'd never signed it, but he'd still given her the $2 million.

Apparently, Onassis badgered Jackie into finally signing it, a decision she would soon regret.

GIVING UP A FORTUNE

∞∞∞∞∞∞∞∞∞∞∞

Ari got me to sign this," Jacqueline Onassis was saying to André Meyer and Mona Lathan about six weeks after her meeting with Onassis at the Pierre Hotel. It was a winter day in January 1973 when she showed them a fully executed copy of the waiver, which Onassis's office had sent to her home.

André looked at it with surprise. "I thought you signed this five years ago," he exclaimed. She said no, she just did so the other day. "But why would you do that?" he asked, getting upset. "You just gave up a fortune, Jackie." She explained that since she'd already received the $2 million guaranteed by the waiver, she thought she should sign it. "André was really upset," said Mona. "He thought she'd been a fool for signing. She'd just given up something like sixty million. 'That bastard knew what he was doing,' he said. 'He tricked you. Why would you even go to see him without me?'"

Jackie explained that Hugh Auchincloss had asked her to appeal to Ari for money to save Hammersmith Farm. One thing led to another, and instead of getting $200,000 for Hugh, she ended up forfeiting $60 million for herself. When the gravity of it all hit her, she broke down and began to cry. "I'm so stupid," she said. "What's wrong with me? Why am I so stupid?"

THE BEGINNING OF THE END

◇◇◇◇◇◇◇◇◇◇◇◇◇◇

On some level, Jackie probably hated Aristotle Onassis after she signed that waiver. But she softened when on January 22, 1973, his son, Alexander, was in a serious plane crash.

"Alexandros had a difficult life in many respects," said Kiki Feroudi Moutsatsos, who was so close to him she named her son after him, "but he was just coming into his own when this horrible thing happened. It devastated us, even Jackie who held out hope that there would be a way forward for them. No words can express how ruined we were by this tragedy."

Also President Lyndon Johnson had died on the same day of a massive heart attack at just sixty-four. His daughter Luci called Jackie with the news. Immediately, she telephoned Lady Bird. "You were so kind to telephone me at a time I know your own heart was so full," Lady Bird later wrote to her. She added that Lyndon had lived his sixty-four years to the fullest and that no one could really ask for more.

Alexander was just beginning his life at twenty-four. "Aristo and Jackie immediately caught an Olympia airline flight from New York to Athens," said Kiki. "When they got to the hospital, Alexander was brain-dead, only machinery keeping him alive. 'You must let him go,' Jackie told Aristo. Once the machines were turned off, Alexandros was dead and things would never be the same for any of us."

"That's when Ari's personality changed dramatically," said Letitia Baldrige. "Greeks are fate oriented, and he felt it was a curse that Alexander had died and that he was somehow responsible. He suffered a nervous breakdown and unfairly blamed Jackie. It became inevitable for that marriage to not work."

During the dark, terrible months after Alexander's death, Jackie realized that somewhere deep down, buried beneath other feelings she may have had for her husband, there was love and compassion. "I was with her and Ari in Acapulco after Alexander was killed," said the noted fashion publicist Eleanor Lambert, "and when it was midnight and fireworks began, Ari started to sob. Jackie put her arms around him, just like Pietà, and held him. She let him cling to her for what seemed like ten minutes. It was so touching because he was not kind to her. But she stuck by him in this awful time when he was mourning so terribly."

Jackie wanted to be there for Ari because she understood the grief and pain of losing a child. She felt closer to him than ever before and wanted to help him. She felt that if he could spend time with his friend Hugh Auchincloss, it might do him some good.

"Mrs. Auchincloss was very annoyed with Jackie at around this time because she found out Jackie had given money to her aunt Edith Bouvier Beale [Black Jack's sister] and her daughter, Edie, to help renovate their dilapidated estate, Grey Gardens," recalled Garrett Johnston. "Janet wanted to know why, if she'd bail out Grey Gardens, she wouldn't do the same for Hammersmith?"

Janet didn't know that Jackie had, in fact, asked Ari for money to save Hammersmith, but he hadn't given her any. Also, she hadn't asked him to help her aunt with Grey Gardens; he'd volunteered. So, there were definitely some unaddressed issues between Jackie and her mother when in July of 1973, she, Artemis, and Ari showed up at Hammersmith.

Upon his arrival, Ari signed the guest book, "Aristotellis Onasis"—Greek for his name. Jackie signed, "Jacqueline B. Onassis."

Hugh was startled by Ari's appearance and demeanor. No longer was he the boisterous, entertaining pirate he'd been when first they met four years earlier, his arrogant manner now replaced by a deflated air. His son's death had been bad enough, but making things even worse was an Arab oil embargo causing one of the largest depressions in the history of the tanker shipping business. Ari was being hit hard by it. He'd already lost $20 million. Within the next year, he'd see his assets cut in half. He was also trying to sell Olympic Airways, which was hemorrhaging money. The government was willing to take control, but he wouldn't agree to an assessment of its worth at almost $70 million and felt like he was being cheated. He was a mere shadow of the man who'd last been to Hammersmith. Even Janet expressed concern. "It's as if he's just waiting to join his son," she said.

Jackie, Ari, and Artemis stayed in the so-called Castle that week, while the children slept in the main house. The Castle was the oldest building on the Hammersmith property and was actually a large farmhouse built around 1720 for the British admiral Jahleel Brenton. Its name came from an oft-told fable about two married servants, a maid and a butler, who'd once lived on the property. When children would go to visit the maid, she'd greet them by saying, "Welcome to my castle." Adjacent to it was a garage, over which was a three-bedroom apartment, which, oddly enough, was called the Palace. Janet Jr. and her husband, Lewis, were also in town from Hong Kong with their children for five weeks. They stayed in the Windmill, the structure that had been rebuilt by Jack Warnecke.

It was good for Aristotle to have someone like Hugh in his life at this time. They played golf and chess and drove in Hugh's cobalt-blue Bentley to the clubhouse at Bailey's Beach, the playground for Astors and Vanderbilts. Relaxation in the Auchinclosses' Cabana #73 seemed far away from his personal tragedy and business setbacks. So much of it he found completely enchanting, such as the custom of flying the Bailey's Beach flag at half-staff upon the death of any member. Hugh, Ari, and Yusha would talk late into the night.

About a month earlier, Janet had bought a jet-black, Jaguar coupe 2+2 (meaning four seats). On one of the rear doors were her hand-painted initials, *JLA*. At breakfast one morning, Ari said he wanted to take a drive and get some fresh air. Everyone looked at Janet with expectation. "Fine, Mr. Onassis, as you wish," she said as she rose. "I'll get my keys." She and Ari then walked outside, got into the car, and off they went. "My God. She's probably taking him to the airport," Jackie joked.

When they returned, Ari was laughing. "Your mother drives like a crazy New Yorker," he told Jackie. He also said that when they spotted a disheveled hitchhiker, Janet pulled over for him. He jumped into the car, and they drove him to a grocery store. On their way, he and Janet glanced at each other, barely able to suppress their giggles. Ari said, "I thought to myself, my God, now I know where Jackie gets her daring." It was good to see him laugh.

That week, there were a number of extravagant dinners with Newport socialites, as usual. "Bring along one of your pretty girlfriends for Ari," Jackie suggested to Yusha. "So, I did," he recalled, "but I did it for Jackie, because she was desperately trying to keep him going." There was good food, the people were interesting, the conversations fascinating, as usual at the Auchincloss table. Ari always said he heard the most fascinating stories while at dinner with the family.

One night, Jackie told the story of Janet Jr.'s birth in 1945 in Washington, D.C., when their mother, by arrangement of Grampy Lee, had around-the-clock nurse's care. After a few days, Janet Sr. no longer needed such care. When another patient became ill with an intestinal infection, she was asked if she'd mind giving up her nurse for that patient. Of course, Janet agreed to it. "And you will never guess who that other patient was," Jackie teased. "*Lady Bird Johnson.*" The elder Janet added that when Jackie first introduced them, Lady Bird said, "You don't know me, Mrs. Auchincloss, but you saved my life."

Ari was taken aback. "What an incredibly bizarre coincidence," he said as everyone laughed. "I wish I'd met you people twenty years ago," he added as he glanced about the table with admiration. It was a sad comment, though, as if he hadn't met many decent people in recent memory. "You have a beautiful family," he told Jackie. "You should be proud."

During his week in Newport, Ari's spirits lifted considerably. By the time he, Jackie, and Artemis were ready to leave, there was a marked improvement in his mood. He had done so well in Newport, Jackie thought she'd take him to the Cape to see his friend Rose Kennedy.

At first, Rose was happy about the possibility of a visit but then called Jackie to tell her she'd changed her mind. It was too much for her, she said. She was eighty-three now and found it difficult to rally for the day. "I'm not as I once was," she wrote to Ari about two months later. She noted that they both well understood the challenges of aging, and she hoped that the next time he was in the States she would be able to "welcome you with open arms, dear Ari. All my love and sympathy, Rose Kennedy."

A HOLLYWOOD KISS

◇◇◇◇◇◇◇◇◇◇◇◇◇

Hammersmith Farm got another financial reprieve when Truman Capote told Jackie the exciting news that he was writing a script based on F. Scott Fitzgerald's *The Great Gatsby,* which was to be made by Paramount starring Robert Redford. Capote thought it would be interesting to shoot the movie at Hammersmith. After he made the connection between the studio and the Auchinclosses, a deal was struck. Though Janet and Hugh didn't go to the movies and weren't even quite sure who Robert Redford was, they were relieved that the new income would buy them more time. But then, Truman's script was rejected by Redford and the movie's director, Jack Clayton. Francis Ford Coppola was brought in for a rewrite. Hammersmith remained as one of the locales for the shoot.

That summer, Robert Redford and his family moved into the Castle, and the British director Jack Clayton and his family moved into the Windmill. According to Janet's guest book, shooting of the film began at Hammersmith on June 11, 1973, but, according to Janet's notations, there was also another location, a Tudor home in Newport called Rosecliff, which was managed by the Preservation Society of Newport County.

"I was about ten years old at the time," recalled Redford's son James in 2010. "It turned out, the Auchincloss kid and I had the same name—Jamie. I remember everyone as being very la-de-da rich," he said. "I later heard from my father that the Auchinclosses were having money problems, but you sure would never know it.

"The parents [Janet and Hugh] hosted a picnic for the cast and crew, which, as well as my father, included Mia Farrow, pregnant at the time,

Bruce Dern, and Sam Waterston. Jackie Onassis and her sister [Lee] were there, which was a thrill even for a ten-year-old because everyone on the planet knew who she was. Even little kids knew Jackie O. We were on the dock, and she came walking by, big sunglasses, lots of black hair blowing, and I exclaimed to my dad, 'Wow. Look, Pop! It's Jackie O.' He shushed me and said, 'Of course it's Jackie O. She lives here. Now be quiet about it and don't embarrass me.' The filming went well. It was fun being at Hammersmith."

In the Hammersmith guest book, James Redford wrote, on July 14, 1973: "I love the Castle. So many strange things happened here but it's the best house I've ever stayed in." His father, Robert, gifted the Auchinclosses with a green, leather-bound copy of *The Great Gatsby* script and inscribed it: "To the pleasure of your kindness and hospitality of spirit—Robert Redford, September 1973." Janet then carefully signed his name again in parenthesis in case future generations couldn't read the signature.

One humorous sidebar to the filming of *The Great Gatsby* is Jackie's flirtation with Robert Redford. During filming, she appeared one day, much to everyone's surprise, and watched the movie being shot. During a break, she and Robert Redford were seen slipping off together. No one knew where they went. They returned a half hour later. It would be more than ten years before Jackie would confess to a good friend that she and Redford had gone to the Castle together. "I made out with Robert Redford," she said, giggling.

Jackie said Robert told her he'd always wanted to ask certain questions about the Cuban Missile Crisis and that was his chance to do so. She humored him. They then started talking about Nixon and Watergate—which, she said, he was "totally obsessed with." Before she knew it, she recalled, "he leaned in and kissed me. What was I to do? He's Robert Redford for Christ's sake, and he's drop dead gorgeous."

A kiss was all that happened, she said. His wife was somewhere nearby and, besides, she didn't even know him. "He told me he just wanted to be able to say he made out with Jackie O.," she said, "so, now I get to say I made out with Robert Redford, and we're even."

"WILL WE EVER GET OVER IT?"

◊◊◊◊◊◊◊◊◊◊◊◊◊◊

November 1973 would mark ten years since the assassination of President Kennedy. As Jackie continued therapy with Dr. Marianne Kris, she worked on trying to put what happened to her and Jack in Dallas into some perspective. "Dr. Kris still felt she was suffering terribly from PTSD and that this was maybe why she'd been such an absentee mother of late," wrote Patricia Atwood, Dr. Kris's secretary, in an email. "She felt they wouldn't get anywhere until they really faced it head-on. She liked to say the measure of a woman wasn't what she'd been through, it was how well she coped and how honest she was with herself going forward. Mrs. Onassis said she'd been raised to push through problems, not analyze them. So, I think, at first, she looked at therapy as being too self-indulgent. In time, though, she got a lot out of it."

The many tributes on television and in newspapers and magazines for the tenth anniversary of JFK's murder just served to bring it all back to Jackie. For her, pain, heartache, and grief were always right under the surface, but she tried to be optimistic, at least publicly. In writing about Jack in an essay for the JFK Library, which was then widely published, she noted, "One must not let oneself be numbed by sadness. He would not have wished that. I don't know how he would have coped with the problems that lay there like sleeping beasts, but I know how he would have approached them. The problems are so huge now. Man seems so tiny in this technological age. Resignation is tempting. But then I think of Jack—the bright light of his days. He would be older now and wiser, and he would still maintain his deep belief that problems can be solved by men. And so they must be."

To commemorate the anniversary, Ethel Kennedy hosted a memorial Mass at her home at Hickory Hill, which Jackie attended with her children. The entire Kennedy family also showed up, including Rose.

As soon as Jackie walked in, she saw a *Ladies' Home Journal* on the kitchen counter with a winsome picture of Caroline and the headline, "Caroline Kennedy Turns Sixteen by Her Former Nanny, Maud Shaw." She stiffened as she picked it up. Also touted on the cover was an interview with Eunice Murray, who'd been Marilyn Monroe's nurse, and the serialization of the rerelease of Jim Bishop's book *The Day Kennedy Was Shot.* "Why, Ethel?" Jackie asked, dismayed. "Why?" Ethel grabbed the magazine and said, "Oh, Jackie, you can't take that stuff seriously." But then, just as suddenly, she burst into tears, her moods clearly all over the place. "Just look at us," she said as Jackie took her into her arms. "It's so unfair. First Jack, then Bobby. Will we ever get over it?"

Noelle Bombardier, Ethel's personal assistant, stood watching the sisters-in-law. "Oh God," Jackie exclaimed, now also crying. "I thought, *These poor women,*" Noelle recalled. "How was this even possible, both married to brothers they witnessed being murdered in the same way?

"Later that day, Jackie said to me, 'I try to hold it together all year long, but then this anniversary comes and I fall to pieces with all of these terrible magazine stories. It just takes such a toll.'" She then asked Noelle, "Do you think Mrs. Kennedy will ever get over what happened to Bobby?" Noelle said she just didn't know. "The reason I ask," Jackie explained, "is because I keep thinking maybe if Ethel does, so will I."

"How's it going with Ari?" Ethel asked Jackie.

"Don't ask," Jackie answered.

Through the rest of 1973 and into 1974, Jackie's concerns about Ari would grow. "He'd not reconciled Alexander's death, was drinking heavily, not sleeping," recalled Stelios Papadimitriou, his personal lawyer. "He looked terrible. Meanwhile, he was suffering severe career reversals because of his lack of concentration. The Arabs declared an oil embargo, which ruined the world tanker market and affected all of our businesses, including Olympic Airways. It would have to be sold. The walls were closing in on him."

At the end of 1973, Ari visited Stelios in his office at Olympic Airways to tell him he'd written his will with new provisions for Jackie. He produced a document, in his own handwriting. It said he was still willing to give her

$200,000 a year for the rest of her life and $25,000 a year to both her children until they reached twenty-one. At his death, Jackie would also get a 25 percent share in Skorpios and the same amount in any sale of the *Christina*. It could be argued that Onassis's latest offering was still a pittance considering his $500 million fortune, his fleet of ships, his real estate holdings, including the Olympic Towers on Fifth Avenue, as well as homes in Athens, Monte Carlo, and Paris and hundreds of millions held in stocks and bonds. But everything was tied up in the complication of his business reversals of the last year, so it was difficult to know just how much he was still worth.

Ari also asked Stelios to, upon his death, refrain from saying anything critical about Jackie. "She's been good to me, and I love her family," he said. "I don't want to embarrass her, her sister, her mother, or stepfather. You must promise me." Stelios agreed.

Ari then asked Stelios to draw up formal divorce papers. He wanted out of the marriage. He just hadn't told Jackie yet.

MARITAL TENSIONS

◇◇◇◇◇◇◇◇◇◇◇◇◇

Perhaps what happened next was inevitable. It seemed as if Onassis had been slowly dying ever since his son was killed. All that remained was to hear the final death knell. It came in 1974 in the form of a devastating autoimmune disease called myasthenia gravis. It's so rare an illness, when Ari received the diagnosis, he viewed it as punishment from the gods for his hubris, boastfulness, and extravagant lifestyle. "How can I lose?" he'd often asked when he was in good health. "The rules don't even apply to me." Now, he felt he was paying the price for his massive success by losing everything—his son, his money, even his health. Soon, he wouldn't be able to keep his eyes open, the neuromuscular disorder weakening his face so much. It seemed like a cruel, horrible way to go out. "I may as well be dead now," he told Jackie. "I can't live like this."

The cortisone prescribed to Ari—which JFK had also taken for his Addison's disease—had its own debilitating effects. The drug swelled him up and gave him terrible headaches and excruciating back pains. "It's as if he'd brought all of it onto himself overnight," said Kiki Feroudi Moutsatsos. "He sometimes quoted an old Roman proverb: 'The way we die is sadder than death itself.' This illness came on so swiftly and so painfully, it took our breaths away."

"The disease made him meaner," said Peter Beard. "The shouting at Jackie, which I witnessed many times, was hard to take. He'd constantly compare her to Maria Callas, saying Maria was a real artist whereas Jackie was just a big nothing. You wondered if it was the disease, the medication, or maybe just cruelty."

One night on Skorpios, Jackie was so sick of hearing about Maria Callas, she screamed at Ari to shut up before storming out of the house and slamming the door behind her. After about a half hour, Artemis became worried and sent servants out to look for her on the nearby beach. Louis Georgakis, director of Olympic Airways, was present and chastised Ari, begging him, "Stop throwing Maria in your wife's face. You have what you want. Why must you flaunt it?" Ari's response: "Fuck her. She has her life. I have mine. I should be with Maria anyway, a woman who actually loves me." The chief maid, Georgia Betta, recalled, "It was Mrs. Garoufalidis who finally found Jackie an hour later, alone under a tree in the garden, crying. She persuaded her to come back into the house. As she walked back into the living room, Jackie said, 'I'm so sick of this goddamn woman, and I've never even met her.'"

Jackie had heard so much about this mysterious woman with whom Ari was so obsessed, she decided she wanted to know her. What did she have that had so transfixed Ari for all these years? Though she understood their marital agreement in principle, she couldn't help but be jealous.

Jackie went to Paris with the idea of knocking on Maria's door, introducing herself, and using the excuse of Ari's illness to maybe have a conversation with her.

"She told Merope she went to Maria's home and sat across the street on Avenue Georges Mandel—which was very near where her and Ari's apartment was at 88 Avenue Foch," said Thea Andino, Merope Konialidis's secretary. "She did everything she could think of to get up enough nerve to go inside the building, but she couldn't do it. She said, 'I saw her walking out of her building, this lonely-looking woman in a drab raincoat wearing a babushka and big sunglasses, and I thought, *My God, look at her. She's so small, fragile and sad, how can I intrude on her privacy?* I realized she was probably just like me. Who knew of her suffering? Who knew what she was going through?' She said she decided to leave the poor woman alone just as she would want to be left alone."

PRENEZ BIEN SOIN

◇◇◇◇◇◇◇◇◇◇◇◇◇◇

In the summer of 1974, Jackie and Ari hosted a group of friends on the *Christina* in a cruise from Palm Beach to the Bahamas, including Lee and her children. Lee was very distressed the entire time after having just discovered Peter Beard in bed with a model named Barbara Allen de Kwiatkowski. Truman Capote said it "really shook her to the rafters" and that it was "the beginning of this period of hers of feeling totally undone." Jackie extended herself to Lee during the trip and tried to reach some accord with her. By the time they docked back in Palm Beach, it did appear to some observers that they were a bit closer. They actually seemed playful with one another and even made plans to visit their mother together in September.

After the cruise, Jackie brought Ari back to Newport for a week with the Auchinclosses. As usual, Artemis accompanied them and, this time, Marta, too.

Janet and Hugh had asked Jackie to put the visit off until the fall because they'd been able to rent Hammersmith Farm out for the summer to the W. J. Strawbridge Syndicate, the firm who'd designed the yacht *Intrepid,* which had been the winner of 1967's and 1970's America's Cup. Its executives, spouses, and race crew leased Hammersmith from June to September, generating more much-needed income to keep the estate going. During that time, the Auchinclosses would be staying in the Castle. They suggested Jackie, Ari, and Artemis wait until September to visit so that they would have full access to all of Hammersmith. However, Jackie felt it imperative that they come immediately. Ari wanted to see Hugh, and she wasn't sure how much longer he'd be able to travel. She suggested they'd all stay in the Castle.

Once she got Ari to Newport, Jackie knew the trip had been a bad idea. He was just too sick. "He spent the entire week in his bedroom," Adora Rule recalled. "Jackie said doctors told her the disease weakened the heart, and she was afraid he'd have an attack. It was terrible, this once vital man suffering so from this awful disease. Mr. A. was devastated, and Mrs. A. was also quite upset. Even she had empathy for him. One day, I brought a bowl of Marta's special mango ice cream to Mr. Onassis's bedroom. Much to my surprise, he and Mrs. A. were chatting. She was sitting on a chair next to him."

According to Adora, Ari told Janet, "I'm ashamed of my faulty judgment of you, Mrs. Auchincloss. Once my boy died, I understood you better." He said he regretted disregarding her concern for her daughters six years earlier when he said they were old enough to take care of themselves. "You're a good mother," he told her. "You never failed your children as I failed mine."

His words touched Janet. "That means so much to me," she told him. By the time the two finished their conversation, Janet agreed to sail with him and Jackie on the *Christina* at Christmas. Hugh would likely not be well enough, she said, but she would go without him for a couple of days, especially if Artemis was on board. She then took his bowl and went down to the kitchen to get him more ice cream.

Artemis, now in her early seventies, was visibly worn down by her brother's decline. She and Janet spent a lot of time together, walking on the property and chatting in French. After a few days, both were also worried about Hugh. He looked terrible; Ari's illness had taken a toll. Jackie, too, seemed like a wreck. She was nervous, chain-smoking more than ever, and her eyes always seemed reddened from crying. Artemis felt they should all just go. She then quickly arranged for their return to Greece.

As they prepared to leave, Ari was so unsteady on his feet he could barely walk. With the disease making it impossible for him to keep his eyes open, Jackie taped them open with Band-Aids. She then put dark sunglasses on him so he wouldn't be ashamed. As they waited for their car in front of the Castle, a line of uniformed servants stood by, as always, to bid them farewell. When the driver pulled up, Hugh shook Ari's hand and said he wished him well. "I left something for you in my room," Ari told him. He and Artemis were about to get into the car when Janet came rushing out, asking them to wait.

For all the years he'd been her son-in-law, Janet insisted on being formal with him, calling him "Mr. Onassis." Out of adversity, perhaps, something meaningful had begun to grow between them. "Ari. I have something for you," she said as she approached. She handed him a string of amber beads and explained it was a rosary that had been blessed by the pope. She wanted him to have it. Ari glanced at it and said, "God no longer exists for me, Mrs. Auchincloss."

"No, Aristo," Jackie said. "God is with you, always. Take it."

Janet folded Ari's fingers over the rosary. "Take care of yourself," she said. "I'll see you at Christmas on the *Christina*." She then embraced Artemis. "*Prenez bien soin,*" Janet told her—"Take good care."

Taking a few jerky steps, Aristotle managed to get into the car. Jackie hugged her mother and stepfather and then slipped in next to him, after which Artemis also got into the car. As they drove away, Hugh and Janet waved goodbye.

When Hugh went to Ari's room, he found a bottle of ouzo and a note. "I wanted to share this with you," Ari wrote in his own shaky hand. "Maybe next time."

There would be no next time. That would be the last time Hugh and Janet would ever see Ari or Artemis.

OUTSIDE OF HERSELF

◇◇◇◇◇◇◇◇◇◇◇◇◇◇

I n 1975, as Jackie continued with her therapy, she became more self-aware and self-critical, not in ways that would erode her self-esteem but, rather, deepen her self-perception. One of her chief dissatisfactions about herself at this time was that she felt so completely self-absorbed. "I think she'd begun to find that much of her life was petty and dull, or as she would say, 'dreary,'" wrote Joan Kennedy in 2005. "She needed a sort of pick me up or something to do of value. She missed her White House days, back when she was doing so many things that interested her, the renovations and revitalizations that gave her life."

In early February, Jackie had the opportunity to dedicate herself to a pursuit that nourished that part of her hungry for purpose. She read in *The New York Times* that the designation of Grand Central Station as a national landmark had been legally voided in order for a building to be built atop it.

For Jackie, as for many New Yorkers, Grand Central was symbolic of the old Manhattan to which she had a strong emotional connection because of the work of her grandfather James T. Lee—Grampy Lee. He'd built some important city landmarks, including 740 Park Avenue.

"Grand Central meant something to us," Lee Radziwill recalled, "and Jackie decided to join with the Municipal Art Society in its fight to save the terminal. Ten years earlier, the Society had unsuccessfully fought the tearing down of the original Pennsylvania Station. It was replaced with a building New Yorkers found hideous, a gigantic black structure that's now Madison Square Garden. People here [in New York] feared the same thing would happen with Grand Central because what was being proposed looked rather like a shoebox tilted on its side. It was dreadful."

On February 24, 1975, Jackie wrote an eloquent letter to New York mayor Abraham Beame, who, at the time, was facing one of the city's worst economic crunches since the Depression. He'd recently complained he didn't have the funds to fight the railroad's development plans. "Is it not cruel to let our city die by degrees, stripped of all her proud moments, until there is nothing left of her history and beauty to inspire our children?" Jackie asked. A week later, Beame agreed to join in the fight. "Grand Central Station was designated a landmark because it is a landmark in every sense of the word," he wrote. "It is a symbol of life in the City of New York."

Just as she'd been instrumental in the redesigning of Lafayette Park and the White House, Jackie committed herself to saving Grand Central Station, even making a rare appearance at a press conference in its Oyster Bar. "If we don't care about our past we can't have very much hope for our future," she told the media. "We've all heard it's too late, or that it has to happen, that it's inevitable, but I don't think that's true," she said. "I think if there's a great effort, even in the eleventh hour, you can succeed. I know that's what we'll do."

On the same day as that press conference, Jackie got a troubling call from Artemis that Ari was in a Paris hospital. He'd had the flu, gotten past it, and then got into some heated exchanges with Greek officials and shareholders relating to the government's wanting to take over Olympic Airways. The next thing they all knew, he relapsed and was now in serious condition. She felt Jackie should be with him. However, Jackie had firm commitments with the Municipal Art Society, including important dinners with donors. "This is what I signed up for," she told Artemis, who felt she should drop everything.

"What's more important?" Artemis asked. "What you're doing there for some ancient building or what you should be doing here for your husband, my brother?"

Jackie had every intention of being with Ari. She was in the process of rearranging her schedule, she explained, so she could leave in three days. She'd talked to the doctors herself, and they told her he wasn't near death. However, Artemis wouldn't accept no for an answer. The two ended up in an argument, the first they'd ever had, about Jackie's ego, which Artemis felt was out of control.

In the past, Artemis had often speculated that Jackie's self-esteem was one of the reasons she'd been able to endure Jack's assassination. She refused to be destroyed by it, Artemis claimed, because she loved herself too much. It wasn't a criticism, even if it sounded like one. It was more like an observation. But now, Artemis told Jackie her self-involvement was ruining things. So concerned was she with in her own needs, she didn't even care about her dying husband. Not only that, Artemis claimed during this argument, the reason Jackie never bonded with Christina and Alexander was because she was just too selfish to bother trying.

Though Artemis's words were hurtful, Jackie chalked it all up to her anxiety over her brother's illness. She hung up on her before things got more out of hand.

Artemis then called Janet to demand that she "talk some sense" into her daughter. Instead, Janet said she applauded Jackie's efforts on behalf of Grand Central. She told her about her father's architectural contribution to New York and said he'd be proud of Jackie. Janet felt Jackie couldn't let down the people she'd committed to help even if it meant waiting a bit before returning to Paris. It was only natural that Artemis's main concern was for her brother, but Janet held her ground and said Jackie was right to stay in New York.

In telling Jackie about the heated call, Janet said something that really surprised her daughter. "That woman acts like she's your mother the way she's always hovering over you. *I'm* your mother, and you need to tell her that." Jackie had never suspected that Janet secretly harbored any jealousy of Artemis. But, then again, as Janet herself always said, "Secrets. That's what we do best in this family."

Janet called Artemis back and said Jackie would stay in New York for now and return to Paris as soon as she could.

"Jackie said she'd do anything she could to help us in the fight," Brendan Gill, president of the Municipal Art Society at the time, recalled to biographer Edward Klein. "She became our great symbol of the struggle, and by far the most powerful person. She went down with us to Washington on a chartered train called the Landmark Express to lobby the Supreme Court to uphold the landmarks preservation law. Hundreds of people got on the train, and Jackie went through the cars and shook hands with every single person."

In 1978, three years after Jackie joined, the society would finally win the fight with the Supreme Court, upholding the building's landmark status. "There would have been no victory at the Supreme Court, no landmarks law, and no Grand Central without Jackie's generalship and carefully doled-out celebrity," said Frederick Papert, of Municipal Preservation Affairs, one of her mentors.

In years to come, Jackie's preservation advocacy would continue, and she'd be instrumental in saving other New York landmarks, such as Lever House and St. Bartholomew's Church. She also managed to block a skyscraper from being built in Columbus Center, two miles away from 1040 Fifth Avenue. However, in terms of architectural preservation, she's really remembered for the saving of Grand Central Terminal. "Maybe it's just a small thing," she said, "or maybe not. I just know that if we all do our part, we can preserve our history. Let's not let it go. It's so important, and it's really all we have."

"HE DIDN'T HAVE MANY FRIENDS"

◇◇◇◇◇◇◇◇◇◇◇◇◇◇

A s promised, a few days after Artemis's call, Jackie was at Ari's side in a Paris hospital. His condition had deteriorated rapidly. He was now on a ventilator.

"Seeing her father so close to death, Christina lost it and called Jackie a witch, saying she'd killed her first husband, she'd killed her brother-in-law, and now was trying to kill poor Ari," recalled Thea Andino, who was in the room at the time. "I felt terrible. As if things weren't bad enough? For Jackie, this was like being struck right across the face. 'Is this how Ari raised her?' she asked me later. I said, 'Yes. I'm afraid so.'"

During the second week of March, doctors said Ari would never recover. They didn't know how long he might linger—a week, maybe a month. Around the time Ari fell sick, Jackie asked her friend Karen Lerner—one of the first women reporters at *Time* and *Newsweek*—to give Caroline a job on a documentary she was producing for NBC about Saudi entrepreneur Adnan Khashoggi. Lerner hired Caroline to work on the crew in Paris.

Because the documentary was set to air on March 16, Jackie planned to host a dinner for the crew in New York at 1040 Fifth Avenue the evening of the broadcast. She left Paris with the intention of returning immediately after the party.

Once back in Manhattan, Jackie telephoned a number of old friends, including Edward Larrabee Barnes. When he arrived at her home about noon on March 12, 1975, Jackie greeted him at her elevator in the foyer. "She had on a cream-colored silk robe, her hair pulled into a little ponytail, no makeup on," he recalled in 1999. "She looked a lot older to me, very drained. As she hugged me, I noticed rosary beads in her hand."

The two went into the library. Jackie lit a cigarette and curled up on a couch. They then spent about a half hour catching up. "He's not doing well, Ed," Jackie said of Ari. "I should've stayed, I know. But I'm so disliked over there by everyone—Christina, his family, his friends." She said she intended to go back to Paris in a week. "I just need time to steel myself for what's coming," she said.

"She also said Rose Kennedy had called that morning concerned about her having returned to the States," recalled the architect. "She feared that if something happened to Ari while Jackie was gone, she'd never forgive herself. 'And she's right,' Jackie said, 'I never would.'"

"She told me she was really at the end of her rope," Barnes recalled. "'It's been one thing after another,' she told me. 'I sometimes feel I need a break from my life, but then I get so mad at myself.' When I asked why, she said, 'Because people in this world have it so much worse than poor, pathetic Jacqueline Onassis. How dare she complain about anything?'"

Jackie told Ed the greatest sense of peace she'd had in recent months occurred the previous night when she and her children enjoyed a quiet night at home watching television and eating Chinese food. "When I'm with them, I remember what matters," she said, "and it's not my own little wants and needs. It's theirs."

Two days later, on March 14, Artemis called. Ari had taken a turn for the worse.

The next morning, March 15, as Jackie packed to return to Paris, Artemis called again to tell her that Ari had died.

Reeling, Jackie reached over to the nightstand, picked up the telephone, and called O Street. When Hugh answered, she told him his friend was gone. He asked how she was doing. Because she'd been so prepared, she said, she thought she'd be able to handle the inevitable. Instead, she felt completely overwhelmed. Why, she wondered, did God want Ari to suffer so? Hugh tried to comfort her as best he could. "God's finger touched him," he said, quoting Alfred, Lord Tennyson, "and he slept. Let's let him sleep."

She thanked him for being Ari's friend. He didn't have many, she added sadly.

He asked if she wanted to talk to her mother. Not in that moment, she told him, but maybe later.

He said he cared about her very much. She said she felt the same way about him.

WHAT REMAINS

⬦⬦⬦⬦⬦⬦⬦⬦⬦⬦⬦⬦

Aristotle Onassis rescued me at a moment when my life was engulfed with shadows. He meant a lot to me. He brought me into a world where one could find both happiness and love. We lived through many beautiful experiences together which cannot be forgotten, and for which I will be eternally grateful."

That was Jackie's statement upon the death of her husband. It seemed controlled, as if she'd analyzed every word for meaning. He introduced her "into a world where one could find both happiness and love"—but, or so seemed the subtext, maybe not with each other. One person close to her claims she wrote the statement fifty different ways before settling on the final version. She wanted it to reflect the true nature of their marriage, but also not expose it.

"I will help you, Jackie," he'd told her before they wed. "I will help and protect you, always." Whatever else had happened in the last six and a half turbulent years, he had kept that promise. She loved him in her own way. And he really had rescued her, for which she was grateful.

"I will miss Ari more than I can say," Rose Kennedy wrote to Jackie on March 17, 1975. She wrote that their "lovely, shared moments together" continued to warm her heart. She was pleased that Janet would be with Jackie in Greece, and "I pray you will call upon your return."

"The sad news, which reached me this weekend, sent my heart winging your way," Lady Bird Johnson wrote on the same day. "The shadow of grief which has pulled at your life seems an unbearable one." She wrote that Jackie's "strength, composure, and courage" had been put to "the severest of tests, always in the public's watchful eye."

"It's not easy to know what to say to one with whom I've shared so much," wrote Ethel Kennedy on March 18.

"Please do not despair," John Warnecke wrote on March 20, "but, instead, be consoled by what remains—your memories."

"God loves you," wrote Joan Kennedy the same day, "and will welcome dear Ari into his kingdom."

Jackie left for Greece immediately after Artemis's call informing her that Ari had died. Her friend Karen Lerner hosted the dinner for Caroline's colleagues at 1040 Fifth Avenue the night of her show's broadcast. Caroline, along with her brother, grandmother Janet, and Marta Sgubin, then joined Jackie in Greece for the funeral. It was hoped that Hugh might also be able to attend. But given the state of his health, Janet and Jackie both decided against his going.

Lee's feelings were mixed. She had recently begun dating an attorney in New York named Peter Tufo. She asked him to contact one of Ari's lawyers to see if any provisions had been made for her in his will, and he was told there were none. Therefore, she decided not to go to the funeral. Instead, she would focus on the launch of the new interior design business she'd just started.

Settling the Onassis estate would take almost two years of wrangling between Jackie and Christina, made even more complicated by Greek law and the absence of a legitimate will, not something written on a piece of paper in the heat of the moment (and there were a number of those). Even the validity of the waiver Jackie had signed fell into question. Taki Theodoracopulos, a friend of both Ari's and Lee's, was one of those encouraging Christina to fight Jackie. "I told her not to give Jackie anything," he said. "I felt Jackie had already profited enough. Emotions were high. You had to choose sides. I chose Christina, and she was clear that she didn't want Jackie to get one thin dime."

Once the dust settled, Jackie ended up with $25.5 million, which, after costs, gave her about $19 million (about $150 million in today's money). She'd also get about $150,000 a year for the rest of her life. Her children would get an annual $50,000 until they turned twenty-one. After that, their total $100,000 a year would go to Jackie for life, and she could give it to them if she wished. Also, she'd have no interest in Skorpios, the *Christina,* or any of Ari's properties.

Even with business reversals of late, Ari was still said to be worth about $500 million when he died, about $4 billion in today's money. Christina was fortunate that the estate was settled in Greece; she never would have gotten away with such a low settlement for her father's widow if they'd been under American jurisdiction. However, Jackie's inheritance still made her exceedingly wealthy. Due also to wise investments in years to come, she'd finally never have to worry about money again.

Immediately, Jackie started trust funds for Lee's children, Tony and Tina, which they could access when they turned twenty-one. As for Lee, Jackie told her through an intermediary that if she had difficulties paying her mortgage or other bills, she should contact a particular lawyer and perhaps something could be worked out for her.

BOOK V

New Horizons

HER THIRD ACT

When Jacqueline Kennedy Onassis began working in the publishing industry in 1975 at Viking Press, the questions she faced were obvious. She hadn't worked since 1953 when she wrote her column for the *Washington Times-Herald.* Why would she start now, especially given her inheritance? "But it's not as if I've just been sitting around for the last thirty years," she told her friend Joan Braden in 1975. "There are many kinds of work. What I did at the White House was work. Lafayette Park was work." Then, with a wry smile, she added, "Being married was work."

The idea of Jackie going into an office to do any kind of job was difficult to comprehend for most of the public. She was famous, wealthy, and seemed to have it all. Why work?

After Ari died, Jackie found herself at a crossroads. "The one thing she'd lacked for many years—and maybe it could be said throughout both her marriages—was sheer contentment," said her friend Dorothy Schiff in 1986; Schiff was the publisher of the *New York Post* for nearly forty years. "I used to wonder, 'When was the last time I saw her smile, really smile, not the mysterious Jackie smile we knew so well. It had been a long time. I also came to believe that one coping method for her was a total rejection of anything untoward. She had a way of blocking out unpleasantness. For instance, I once asked her how she got through some of the more embarrassing things Jack and Ari had done, and she answered, 'What embarrassing things, Dorothy?'" True happiness had been fleeting in her life. She could always relax into her books, her art, her restoration work, and certainly, there was private satisfaction in those endeavors, but after Ari's death, she had a desire to get out into the world and live a different and less complicated life. She told friends she was now looking ahead to "my third act" and was very excited about the possibilities.

Previous biographies of Jackie have claimed that Letitia Baldrige was the first to suggest that Jackie get a job. Actually, it wasn't Letitia who first suggested the idea; it was her stepbrother Yusha Auchincloss.

In September of 1975, six months after Onassis's death, Yusha visited Jackie at her home in New York. She was just getting over the flu and said she was feeling antsy. She wanted to surprise the Kennedys and attend the weeklong celebration of Rose Kennedy's eighty-fifth birthday. The actual day had been back in July, but the party had been postponed until all the family could be together. She wanted Yusha to accompany her. She wished to drive to Cape Cod, a four-and-a-half-hour journey, and thought he could share the driving. The next day, they got into Jackie's green BMW and started off to Cape Cod, via I-95.

During the drive, as they enjoyed Marta's lemon pound cake, Yusha asked Jackie about her plans. She had lately seemed "blue," he later recalled, "or maybe it was restlessness."

Caroline, seventeen, was home for a break while taking art classes in London at Sotheby's, while John, fourteen, was attending the Collegiate School on the Upper West Side. With both children seeming well-adjusted and independent, Yusha wondered about Jackie. Did she think she'd ever remarry?

Before Jackie had a chance to consider the question, he said, "I would hope not. Not for a while, anyway. I think you should work, instead." Jackie was surprised and then, in response, she said those words so often attributed to her during a conversation with Letitia Baldrige: "Who, me? Work?"

"Yusha explained that he'd seen the actress Marlo Thomas with leading feminist Gloria Steinem on television talking about a foundation they'd started—the Ms. Foundation for Women," said his close friend Cybil Wright. "Its purpose was to fund organizations that presented liberal women's voices. He was impressed by it. 'I thought about Jackie,' he told me, 'and thought, yes . . . how good would it be for her to go back to work?'" Later, after learning more about the Ms. Foundation, Jackie would end up donating a significant amount of money to it. As a result, she ended up with a lifetime subscription to Steinem's *Ms. Magazine*; she'd also appear on its cover.

Jackie had already been somewhat influenced by the women's movement. "I have always lived through men," she said in 1975. "Now, I realize I can't do that anymore." In some ways, she was more of a feminist than she realized. When Joan Kennedy was upset over Ted's infidelity in 1961, it was Jackie who advised her to "build a life for yourself outside of this Kennedy world. Don't live through Teddy."

"But, Yush, what would I do?" Jackie asked him, to which he responded, "Try writing for a newspaper again." He was remembering her early days at the *Washington Times-Herald*.

Jackie had often said that if she hadn't married Jack Kennedy, she would've continued to be a writer and photographer. However, he didn't want her to work. He felt a senator's wife shouldn't have a job, especially not be a writer covering politics, as she did, even if indirectly, at the *Times-Herald*. "I always wanted to be some kind of great writer," she had said. "Like a lot of people, I dreamed of writing the Great American Novel." In another interview, she added, "If I hadn't married, I might have had a life very much like Gloria Emerson's. She is a friend who started out in Paris writing about fashion—and then ended up as a correspondent in Vietnam. The two ends of her career couldn't seem further apart and that is the virtue of journalism. You never know where it's going to take you, but it can be a noble life."

"It was Yusha's idea that Jackie call Tom Guinzburg, at the time president of Viking Press," said Cybil. "Perhaps he had some contacts in the newspaper business? Though Tom and Yusha had been friends from Yale, Jackie also knew him through her former brother-in-law, Michael Canfield, Lee's first husband."

At about this same time, Dorothy Schiff had the idea of Jackie entering the race for the U.S. Senate in New York against Senator James Buckley. Jackie said no, that wasn't for her, but after lunching with Schiff, she visited the offices of the *New York Post* and was, again, reminded of her time at the *Washington Times-Herald*. "She said she wanted to get back into publishing in some way," recalled Schiff, "and she was thinking of calling Tommy Guinzburg. I said, 'Yes. You should do it. Call him.'"

As Jackie and Dorothy left the *Post* offices, Jackie saw that a gaggle of photographers had gathered at the entrance waiting for her. She steeled herself. "Okay, here we go," she told Dorothy. "Are you ready?" Dorothy nodded. Jackie then donned her sunglasses and, with her head down, began to walk swiftly to the waiting car with Dorothy struggling to keep up. As they moved, she told Dorothy under her breath, "You can't imagine how many pictures they're taking right now. Literally hundreds."

Dorothy, her voice also low, asked, "Does it bother you?"

Jackie shook her head. "As long as they keep their paws to themselves, it's fine."

A couple of days after her visit to the *Post,* Jackie arranged to meet with Tom Guinzburg for lunch at Le Périgord, a French restaurant on the Upper East Side. They'd last seen each other about two years earlier at a party Truman Capote hosted at the Four Seasons Hotel to interest publishers in a book Lee was writing about her and Jackie's childhood, which she intended to call *Opening Chapters.* Unfortunately, that book would never see the light of day.

"When she told me of her interest in working in publishing, I thought, no, she shouldn't be at a newspaper," Tom Guinzburg said in a 2007 interview. "She should edit books. She'd be a great editor, but not at that moment. She needed more seasoning. I told her I'd bring her into Viking as a consulting editor, meaning she'd be charged with new acquisitions. Maybe she could also work on those books in association with established editors. She had good instincts. She was well-read, obviously, and had a good sense of storytelling. Plus, she knew everyone. She had incredible access, and I knew that would come in handy.

"I gave her a couple of manuscripts and asked her to read them and then talk to me about them. She came back in a week having read all of them, and she was full of great ideas as to how they could be improved. I was impressed. I thought, *Jacqueline Onassis working in an office all day, with normal people, living a normal life? Yes, sure. Why not?* I could see it."

Tom Guinzburg said he wanted to discuss it with his colleagues at Viking, but he seemed fairly certain they would agree with him that Jackie should be offered a job.

A NEW ROMANTIC PROSPECT

∞∞∞∞∞∞∞∞∞∞

At this same time, the fall of 1975, Jackie began dating someone new, the Academy Award–winning Greek director Michalis Kakogiannis—better known in America as Michael Cacoyannis. Jackie was determined to keep this romance out of the public eye. In more than forty years of biographies about her, his name has never, if ever, appeared in any of them.

Born in 1922 in Cyprus, Michael was fifty-three. His most acclaimed work was the film *Zorba the Greek* starring Antony Quinn in 1964, for which he himself was nominated for three Academy Awards, including Best Director. He was also a stage and opera director with critically acclaimed productions in Greece, France, and other countries, as well as known for translating several of Shakespeare's plays into Greek and Euripides into English.

He and Jackie had been friendly in Washington; she respected his opinion and thought he had great taste. After Bobby decided to run for president, Michael told her Bobby came off as cocky and unlikable, so Jackie asked Bobby to meet with him about his image, and Bobby agreed. Michael had just arrived in New York from Greece en route to Los Angeles when he got word of RFK's murder.

After she married Aristotle Onassis, Jackie stopped seeing Michael Cacoyannis. The two men had been good friends but disagreed vehemently on core political beliefs having to do with the Greek junta, the right-wing military dictatorship that ruled Greece from 1967 to 1974. Onassis and the new dictator, Geórgios Papadopoulos, were in league on the Project Omega investment scheme. Their association drove a wedge between him and Cacoyannis.

As Onassis lay dying in a Paris hospital, Jackie called Michael to ask him to visit Onassis and reconcile. By this time, Onassis had come to believe that Papadopoulos had something to do with Alexander's plane crash. Michael did have that deathbed visit with Onassis, with Jackie at his side. It was the first time he'd seen her since the marriage.

Michael never married, though he had a long-term relationship with the novelist Yael Dayan, daughter of the general of Israel, Moshe Dayan. He was also involved with the Greek actress Ellie Lambeti, who'd appeared in his films.

Xenia Kaldara, Michael's friend of thirty years and the president of the board and general director of the Michael Cacoyannis Foundation, recalled, "Back in the 1960s, when Michael first met Jackie, he ran in the same circles as Leonard Bernstein and Rudolf Nureyev. He visited Jackie at the White House several times during the Kennedy administration. He told me they sometimes snuck away for time alone. There was nothing romantic going on between them, though. They were just good friends. He was someone she could confide in and talk frankly to. They had a very soulful kind of rapport."

After Ari's death, Michael and Jackie began talking more frequently. When he had business in New York, he and Jackie went to dinner, and their relationship grew from there. Jackie told intimates that being with him felt familiar and comfortable because of his Greek heritage. He reminded her of Onassis, but without the hard edge. Not an imposing figure like Ari, he was gentle with dark, penetrating eyes, a receding hairline, and a welcoming smile.

JACKIE HAS TO CHOOSE?

◇◇◇◇◇◇◇◇◇

At the time Jackie started seeing him, Michael had recently released his documentary *Attila '74,* documenting the summer 1974 invasion of Cyprus by the Turkish army, which displaced thousands of Greeks and killed thousands more. Supported only by a cameraman and a sound engineer, Cacoyannis traveled across the stricken island and interviewed political leaders, victims, and refugees. Jackie was impressed. As much of his work rooted in classical Greek tragedies, she was able to talk endlessly with Michael about Euripides, Aeschylus, Sophocles, and other tragedians of classical Athens.

After a few dates, Jackie and Michael became intimate. "She was forty-seven and still young," said someone who knew her very well at this time. "It had been a long time, and she wanted to be with a man. He was gentle and sexy, and she enjoyed him. She felt she deserved him." While she may have had a good time, Jackie did have some reservations about Michael after sleeping with him. She often had second thoughts after having sex, as she had when she'd first slept with Jack Warnecke and, later, Lord Harlech. This time was no exception.

Jackie was still in touch with Artemis Garoufalidis, calling her several times a week in Greece to see how she was faring after her brother's death. One day, while Kiki Feroudi Moutsatsos was visiting her, Jackie called Artemis to ask how she felt about Michael. Artemis, who knew the director through her brother, said she approved of any relationship with him. "I want you to see him," she told her as Kiki listened to her end of the conversation. "He's a lovely man and would be good for you."

After that call, Artemis told Kiki, "I think she's looking for someone like Aristo. Of course, there's only one Aristo, but Michalis is a nice man. I've told Jackie in the past, 'Life is all we have, and you've got to live it to the fullest. Aristo would want that for you.'"

While she was dating Michael Cacoyannis, a definitive job offer came from Viking—four days a week, $200 a week.

Two hundred dollars for a woman who'd just come into a windfall of millions after the death of her husband? This made no sense to Michael. Very quickly, the idea of Jackie as a workingwoman became an issue between them. Like many Greek men of his generation, he didn't understand why any woman would want to work when she could either depend on a man to support her or, in Jackie's case, support herself.

For Jackie, this felt familiar. Back in 1973, she was asked by her friend Karen Lerner to narrate an NBC documentary on Angkor Wat and Venice. Ari didn't want her to do it, and the two fought furiously about it. "Greek wives don't work," he insisted. He wore her down, and she eventually declined the opportunity, but she regretted it. Two years later, she'd begin to date Michael in part because he reminded her of Ari—and now he was acting just like him. In other words, her third act was looking an awful lot like her second. "You have to choose," he told her. "Me or the job."

This sent up a red flag she couldn't ignore. "Any time a man asks you to choose, you know what you're in for if you choose him," Jackie later told Artemis. "This may explain why he never married. I told him I needed alignment in my life at this time, not opposition."

Not only was Michael like Ari, he was also like JFK and her father in the sense that he prided himself on being a caretaker. Jackie had wanted to be taken care of, and all three had certainly done just that for her. Her father had doted on her, her first husband gave her status, and her second gave her money. "The main thing for me was to do whatever my husband wanted," she said when she was married to Kennedy. "He couldn't—and wouldn't—be married to a woman who tried to share the spotlight with him. I thought the best thing I could do was to be a distraction." When Ari had businessmen over for dinner, which was almost every night, he'd ask Jackie to leave. She wasn't even permitted to act as a distraction! Ari chose the foods they ate in restaurants. He'd have the meal served to him and then he'd dish out a portion of it on a separate plate for Jackie. While having a partner would be nice, being subservient no longer appealed to her. Jackie told Michael they could remain friends, but the romance was over.

"I actually think there's more to this story," said Xenia Kaldara. "When

Michael directed Katharine Hepburn in *The Trojan Women,* she said she appreciated the way he embraced her spirit, her soul. That's who Michael was—very intuitive as to what a woman needed. He later told me Jackie was very tormented. She'd, apparently, confided some very private things to him. He felt there were aspects of her life she hadn't yet dealt with that were holding her back. He wasn't specific. He'd never betray her. But there was more going on between them than a dispute over a job offer."

"When he said she had to choose, him or her career, she chose herself," recalled Kiki Feroudi Moutsatsos, "and that was a leap ahead for her. She wasn't going to subjugate herself to a man, not the way she had with Aristo, not the way she had with Kennedy. But such were the times we were living in, weren't they? She was influenced by women all around us making similar choices."

∞∞∞∞∞∞∞∞∞∞∞∞∞∞∞

On September 22, 1975, Jackie began work as an associate editor at Viking Press on Madison Avenue. "That first day, it was a zoo," recalled Tom Guinzburg, referring to the mob that had gathered in front of the corporate office. "We snuck her in through a side entrance. But she was fine with walking with her head down through a crowd. 'I never make eye contact,' she told me. 'Once you make eye contact, it's all over. And you have to walk fast,' she said, 'with purpose. They have to think you're late for something and have no time. It's the only way.'"

"I expect to be learning the ropes at first," Jackie said at the time of her new job. "You sit in at editorial conferences, you discuss general things, maybe you're assigned to a special project of your own. It's not as if I've never done anything interesting. I've been a reporter myself and I've lived through important parts of American history. I'm not the worst choice for this position."

SINATRA

◇◇◇◇◇◇◇◇◇◇◇◇◇◇

As soon as she started working at Viking in September 1975, Jackie set her sights on acquiring a big book for the company, one that would distinguish her there, a guaranteed blockbuster that would make it clear she wasn't just a novelty at the company but a real asset. When she and Tom Guinzburg discussed the celebrities she knew or had known who might want to tell their stories, one name kept coming up: Frank Sinatra. Few entertainers were more famous and more controversial. Could Jackie get him to write his memoir for Viking?

Jackie was always conflicted about Sinatra. Back in the 1960s, she felt he and his Rat Pack friends had damaged the image of the Kennedy presidential campaign and were a bad influence on her husband. She'd heard all the stories about Sinatra's illicit relationships and his rumored underworld connections and agreed with Bobby Kennedy that Sinatra should stay away from the White House.

"He only got in to see Jack once," said his daughter Tina Sinatra. When Sinatra sent a white-and-yellow, flowered, covered rocking chair to Kennedy for his forty-fifth birthday, Jackie intercepted the gift and donated it to a children's hospital. "Dad wasn't even invited to JFK's funeral," recalled Tina. But all of that was ancient history. Jackie thought she could separate her personal feelings from what might be best for her professionally.

Sinatra had also been a friend of Jackie's second husband, Aristotle Onassis. Once Jackie and Aristotle were married in 1968, the entertainer would occasionally be on the guest list of the *Christina*. "He was always fun, liked to make jokes and laugh and keep everyone entertained," said Kiki Feroudi

Moutsatsos. "Sometimes, Jackie would ask him to sing, and he'd eagerly oblige, which was marvelous for the other guests. The women would just swoon. Christina and Alexander both always wanted to be on board whenever we knew Sinatra was sailing with us."

In April of 1974, while Jackie was in New York consulting doctors about Ari's autoimmune disease, her friend the bandleader Peter Duchin thought she could use a night of fun. He invited her to a Sinatra concert at the Providence Civic Center in Rhode Island. After the show, he and his wife, Cheray, and Jackie had dinner with Frank. Jackie found it interesting that Sinatra seemed more laid-back and at ease than he had in the sixties, and she figured maybe they'd all just grown up. She was, however, a little put off by how much he drank, but that was just Frank, and she knew it.

Seven months later, in November 1974, Frank called to tell Jackie he was in town and wanted to take her to Jilly's, the nightclub on Fifty-Second Street owned by his friend Jilly Rizzo. "I was bowled over when Frank walked in with her," said Tony Oppedisano, Sinatra's longtime friend and (later) road manager. "I remember she had a sleek, pearl-gray slacks suit on with a few diamonds, looking classy and elegant. She was open and fun, not what I expected, which was a more withdrawn personality. She and Frank held hands and seemed happy to be in each other's company. About a half hour later, Onassis walked in. He seemed unwell. Jackie got up and kissed him and invited him to sit down. It was clear he and Frank had met somewhere else down the line."

They had a good time; Frank dared Jackie to eat the barbecued pork. She said she loved it, and Onassis laughed and said, "Look at her. She's lying. She hates it."

"It was about four thirty when Jackie and Frank left the club," said Oppedisano. "Jackie and Aristotle were walked out by Jilly. Ari said goodbye to everyone and then told Jackie he'd meet her in the car. He walked away and allowed Jackie and Frank to have a few moments to say goodbye. It surprised me," recalled Oppedisano, "that he left her with Frank, but in my opinion, Onassis respected that they had a relationship that predated him. I thought, well, he's not well and maybe he thinks, *I'm not going to be around much longer and Jackie could do a lot worse than end up with Frank Sinatra.*"

Almost a year later and a half after Onassis's death, Frank called Jackie to invite her to his concert at the Uris Theatre with Ella Fitzgerald and Count Basie on September 8, 1975. She was reluctant to go because she'd just had a terrible fright. Someone on her staff discovered that one of her Cape Cod neighbors had rented out his attic to paparazzi. They were actually sleeping there and using a telescope to monitor Jackie's comings and goings. She'd wondered how photographers always knew exactly where she was, and now she knew. Immediately, she called the authorities. They searched the man's home and, sure enough, found three paparazzi nesting in his attic. "The whole thing has made me so sick," she told Frank. "To think they were also spying on Caroline. I actually don't think I can function right now."

Sinatra had been battling with paparazzi for at least thirty-five years, but even he'd never heard of anything so appalling. "Please come to the show," he suggested. "Put this behind you."

That evening, Jilly Rizzo met Jackie at 1040 Fifth Avenue in a black town car, and the two were driven to the Uris Theatre. Joey D'Orazio, a friend of Frank's from Hoboken, recalled going backstage after the performance night. "I noticed that Frank was with this dame, her back to me. She turned around, and Jesus Christ. It was Jackie O., and Frank was hanging all over her. He looked happy as hell, and she had her arm around his waist. She was giddy and girlish, flirtier than I ever imagined of her. When Frank made a joke, she said, 'Oh, Francis, that is just so funny,' flattering him. My wife said, 'My God, she's like a dizzy schoolgirl. That can't possibly be her. Look how she's acting.' I said, 'Oh yeah, that's her, all right.'"

After the show, Frank took Jackie to the popular 21 Club, which was fun if not chaotic due to the bedlam caused by the appearance of two of the most famous people in the world. It was easy to have fun when one was with Frank Sinatra, and Jackie enjoyed herself. However, the next morning, a cascade of troubling events began that would last until the end of the year.

The pictures in the press of Frank and Jackie at the 21 Club concerned Ethel Kennedy enough for her to call Jackie to remind her that he'd been key to bad behavior during the Kennedy administration. Leah Mason, Ethel's personal secretary at the time, placed the call. "Mrs. Kennedy told Jackie she thought being photographed with Sinatra could be problematic for her public image, especially considering that she was newly widowed; Onassis had died six months earlier. Mrs. Onassis told her, 'Ethel, you know me. I stopped caring about what people think the day I married Ari.'"

It was just a few weeks later—on September 22, 1975—that Jackie started working at Viking and began discussions with Tom Guinzburg about a possible Frank Sinatra autobiography. She called Sinatra in Palm Springs and, according to what his attorney, the late Mickey Rudin, said in 1996, "She proposed the idea of a memoir. Frank was for it. When I heard about it, I had my reservations given Frank's predilection for privacy, but we thought with Mrs. Onassis as an editor it might be worthwhile. 'If you do this, you're going to have to level with her about Jack Kennedy and Judy Exner,' I told him. 'Oh, hell no, I'm not doing that,' Frank said. 'That'll just hurt her. I'm not going to do that to her. She doesn't deserve that.' I thought . . . *Okay, well, this is about to get real interesting.*"

JACKIE'S CAMELOT THREATENED

◇◇◇◇◇◇◇◇◇◇◇◇◇

After two more telephone calls with Frank Sinatra about his autobiography, Jackie was genuinely excited about it, as was Tom Guinzburg. They decided to keep the idea to themselves and continue private discussions about specifics such as the advance the company would pay. Things took a surprising turn, though, when Jackie got a call from Dave Powers, who'd been JFK's special assistant and was now chief curator for the John F. Kennedy Presidential Library and Museum in Boston, which was scheduled to open in about four years.

Jackie and Dave had always had a cordial relationship and still saw each other from time to time. She'd been annoyed at him and Kenny O'Donnell for a book they wrote about JFK in 1973, *"Johnny, We Hardly Knew Ye."* It was positive, however, so she decided not to allow it to ruin their friendship.

Powers called to tell Jackie that a committee in Washington called the Church Committee was investigating the government's involvement in assassination plots on foreign leaders. A woman had just been interviewed in September who was said to be a close friend of Sinatra's and of the notorious gangster Sam Giancana. She also had some sort of close relationship to President Kennedy. Her name, Dave said, was Judith Campbell Exner. Had Jackie ever heard of her?

Jackie had at least heard of her. She was one of the many women with whom Jack was rumored to have been involved during the White House years. Unlike Mary Meyer, though, Jackie never saw Judith at the White House and had never met her. After the Kennedy administration, she tried not to think about Jack's many assignations. In fact, according to people who knew her best, by the mid-seventies she wasn't even sure Mary Meyer had been at her dinner table the evening Jack addressed the nation about the Cuban Missile Crisis. She and Janet argued about it in front of family members. Even given her failing memory, Janet would never forget Miss Meyer's presence that night. Apparently, though, Jackie didn't remember or, perhaps, didn't want to remember.

It was during the Kennedy administration that J. Edgar Hoover became alarmed when he learned that Judith Exner, who'd had an affair with Frank Sinatra in 1959, had been calling the president at the White House. According to Exner's later account, not only was she romantically involved with Kennedy, whom she met in 1960, she was being used as a conduit between him and mobster Giancana. Though her account would be disputed, she claimed to be a courier for the president, with money going back and forth between him and the mobster, first to influence the West Virginia primary and later to finance a plot to assassinate Fidel Castro. Whatever was actually going on, just the fact that she was connected to Giancana at all and also in contact with JFK was enough to concern Bobby Kennedy after his brother was finally elected. It was one of the reasons he decided not to allow the president to stay at Sinatra's Palm Springs home in 1962. That's how he ended up at Bing Crosby's, which was where he was intimate with Marilyn Monroe.

Sam Giancana was murdered in June of 1975, the day before he was to testify before the Church Committee.

The Church Committee's findings would not be released until the spring of 1976. But in November 1975—just a couple of months after Jackie proposed her Sinatra book idea—there was a big leak of its work. Judith Campbell Exner, now forty-one, was thrust into national prominence when *The Washington Post* reported what had been one of the Kennedy administration's biggest secrets—that she'd made more than seventy telephone calls in a single year to President Kennedy beginning in March 1961. Several of those calls had originated from the residence of Sam Giancana.

Dave Powers immediately issued a statement saying, "The name doesn't ring a bell to me. The only Campbell I know is Campbell Soup." Other people who'd been around JFK at the time also said they had no idea who Exner was, even though that seemed unlikely. Rose Kennedy saw her on TV while sitting with her secretary Barbara Gibson and observed, "Jack would never be with a woman whose breasts are that big, I'm sorry."

By the end of the year, the Exner story was a jumble of rumor, innu-endo, distortions, and inconsistencies but always with President Kennedy at the center. Her tales of numerous sexual encounters with him—beginning in the winter of 1960 at the Plaza Hotel the night before the New Hamp-shire primary, and ending in the summer of 1962—were the kind of stories Jackie had heard countless times over the years, and which she'd tried to ignore. Now, fifteen years later, these same kinds of tales were being re-ported as news by legitimate outlets like *The Washington Post*. Not only was it personally hurtful and upsetting, it threatened the heroic image of JFK that Jackie had painted for the world after his murder, her portrait of Camelot.

Because Artemis Garoufalidis and her sister Merope Konialidis hap-pened to be in New York on business relating to their brother's estate, Jackie invited them and a few other close friends to her home for dinner. "I have to go to work every day and look those people in the eye while this trash is being reported on," she told them. "I thought this kind of stuff was over, but it's not. It's worse than ever." She told the Onassis sisters she was feeling "very fragile, and I hate that feeling. I've been fighting it ever since Dallas."

Artemis didn't understand why Jackie was putting herself through any of it for the sake of a book. After all, she didn't have to work. She suggested Jackie get away for a while and go back to Greece with her and her sister, but Jackie declined.

Despite all the controversy, Jackie was still interested in acquiring Frank Sinatra's memoir. She felt a responsibility to try to balance her personal con-cerns with what might be best for Viking. "I can't let all of this nonsense affect a decision as to whether or not a book would be a good acquisition," she said. Perhaps the controversy would make the Sinatra book even more marketable and successful.

Tom Guinzburg didn't agree. Considering what was being reported, Frank Sinatra would now be obliged to write in detail about not only Jackie's late husband but also Exner, Giancana—"and all of it," he told her, "and, then, he'll have to promote it on TV and in the press." Guinzburg said he couldn't let Jackie do it. As much as he would love to have the book for Vi-king, he said, "it's not worth it to you. Trust me."

It was bad enough that so much of what was now coming to light could affect Caroline's and John's images of their father. How would it look to them if their mother was at the center of promoting it? Jackie had told Tom that she and Caroline were recently sitting in the living room in front of the television painting their nails together as they often did, when, suddenly, there was Judith Exner talking about having sex with Caroline's father. Jackie jumped up and turned it off.

She knew Tom was right. She couldn't acquire the Sinatra book.

In just a few months (March 1976), Jackie would face further embarrassment upon publication of the *National Enquirer*'s exposé of President Kennedy's affair with Mary Meyer. It was as if the Camelot fable she'd spun that stormy night in Hyannis was being picked apart thread by thread. Still, she refused comment to set the record straight. She knew any statement from her would be like pouring gasoline onto a raging fire. "When every sleazy rumor about Jack Kennedy was treated as fact," Jackie's good friend Pete Hamill later said, "she maintained her silence. And silence, of course, is communication."

Jackie didn't come out and tell Frank Sinatra about her decision. She was worried that if she told him the truth, he'd reveal publicly that she was afraid of what he might write about President Kennedy, or he might use her concerns about the book to promote it.

Bill Stapley, Sinatra's valet of eighteen years, recalled, "Frank was mystified as to why Jackie suddenly gave him the cold shoulder. He thought they'd really hit it off. They were in the middle of a big project. I was in the room when he called her and her housekeeper said she was busy and would not come to the phone. He slammed the phone down. 'She won't take my fucking calls,' he said. He was hurt as much as he was angry. This back-and-forth went on for a couple of weeks until he finally just gave up calling her."

While Jackie didn't acquire the Frank Sinatra autobiography—which he never ultimately wrote—she did bring in some interesting titles for Viking during her tenure there, such as *Remember the Ladies: Women in America, 1750–1815,* a pictorial art and history book about women of the eighteenth century. It was one of the official bicentennial exhibitions by the American Revolution Bicentennial Commission. She also collaborated on two books with Diana Vreeland, former editor in chief at *Vogue*: *In the Russian Style* and *Inventive Paris Clothes 1909–1939. Sally Hemings,* a book about the slave with whom Thomas Jefferson had an affair, was one Jackie championed, her first novel; it would be published after her tenure at Viking was over.

There is one unfortunate side note to the story of Jackie and Frank:

About a year after Jackie's decision to move on from the Sinatra book, Frank was at a party at the home of singers Steve Lawrence and Eydie

Gormé. Everyone was a little drunk and sharing stories. Jilly Rizzo asked Frank about biggest conquests. Frank listed Ava Gardner, Lana Turner, Marilyn Monroe, and . . . Jacqueline Onassis.

A little drunk and feeling boastful, Frank claimed that after his concert at the Uris, he and Jackie went back to his suite at the Waldorf Towers and had sex. His friend Jim Whiting, who was at that party, said, "When Jilly pressed him on it, Frank said he wasn't going to give any more details. He said he wasn't going to brag about it. To my mind, that meant it hadn't happened because Frank was anything but discreet."

Jilly Rizzo later said he suspected Frank was lying. Why? Because Rizzo himself was the one who took Jackie back to 1040 Fifth Avenue that night, after dropping Frank off at the Waldorf Towers.

Jackie in Ravello, Italy, August 1962. Though she tried to have a relaxing vacation, she was secretly shaken by the recent death of Marilyn Monroe. "There's a big difference between wanting to die," she said, "and running out of reasons to live." (© MARK SHAW / MPTVIMAGES.COM)

Twenty-year-old Jackie with
her father, Jack Bouvier, at a
fashion show in East Hampton,
New York, in 1949. Nicknamed
"Black Jack" because of his
ever-present tan, he loved his
daughter unconditionally, and
the feeling was mutual. (JAMIE
AUCHINCLOSS COLLECTION)

When Jackie's mother, Janet
Lee Bouvier, married Hugh
Auchincloss in 1942, he became a
stable influence in Jackie's life.
He would walk her down the aisle at
both her weddings.
(JAMIE AUCHINCLOSS COLLECTION)

Jackie with Jack and their children, John and Caroline, at their home in Hyannis Port—Squaw Island, August 14, 1963. (CECIL STOUGHTON, WHITE HOUSE PHOTOGRAPHS / JOHN F. KENNEDY PRESIDENTIAL LIBRARY AND MUSEUM, BOSTON)

President Kennedy enjoyed many fun times with Jackie's family in Newport. This was taken in July 1962. Behind JFK is Jackie's half sister, Janet Jr. Next to him (in the red shirt) is Jackie's stepbrother, Yusha. Sipping clam chowder is Jackie's mother, Janet, and next to her is Janet Jr.'s date, John Kerry. (CECIL STOUGHTON, WHITE HOUSE PHOTOGRAPHS / JOHN F. KENNEDY PRESIDENTIAL LIBRARY AND MUSEUM, BOSTON)

John Kennedy Jr. at the helm of a speedboat in Hyannis Port on August 25, 1963. "John-John" would turn three in three short months, the day after his father's state funeral. (CECIL STOUGHTON, WHITE HOUSE PHOTOGRAPHS / JOHN F. KENNEDY PRESIDENTIAL LIBRARY AND MUSEUM, BOSTON)

Jackie with Jack at Squaw Island. (© MARK SHAW / MPTVIMAGES.COM)

Jackie and John Jr. in Palm Beach, 1963. (© MARK SHAW / MPTVIMAGES.COM)

During First Lady Jacqueline Kennedy's trip to India and Pakistan in March 1962, she and her sister, Princess Lee Radziwill, visited Rashtrapati Bhavan, official residence of the president of India, Dr. Rajendra Prasad. (CECIL STOUGHTON, WHITE HOUSE PHOTOGRAPHS / JOHN F. KENNEDY PRESIDENTIAL LIBRARY AND MUSEUM, BOSTON)

Jackie and Jack arrive in Dallas on that fateful day of November 22, 1963. In a matter of hours, he would be dead and her life forever changed. (CECIL STOUGHTON, WHITE HOUSE PHOTO-GRAPHS / JOHN F. KENNEDY PRESIDENTIAL LIBRARY AND MUSEUM, BOSTON)

The Dallas motorcade. "So now he is a legend," she said of JFK after his murder, "when he would have preferred to be a man." (WHITE HOUSE PHOTOGRAPHS / JOHN F. KENNEDY PRESIDENTIAL LIBRARY AND MUSEUM, BOSTON)

The procession to St. Matthew's Cathedral during the state funeral, November 25, 1963. Jackie is flanked by Bobby Kennedy and Ted Kennedy. Behind her is her half brother, Jamie Auchincloss, her brothers-in-law Sargent Shriver and Stephen Smith, and Secret Service agent Paul Landis.

Jackie greets dignitaries at the post-funeral reception in the Red Room of the White House. Next to her is Ted Kennedy.

A great president and his First Lady. JFK's murder was so traumatic, Jackie never really got over it. "What a shame," she'd say, "to spend so much time tormented by a thing I could never change."

A DIFFICULT SUMMER

◇◇◇◇◇◇◇◇◇◇◇◇◇◇◇◇

In June of 1976, Lee Radziwill's husband, Prince Stanislaw Radziwill, died of a heart attack at sixty-two. The family happened to be together at Hammersmith Farm for the Newport bicentennial celebration. It was Jamie who took the call from Stas's office in London. He was then charged with telling Lee her ex-husband was gone. Jackie and Stas had been close, and she accompanied Lee to the funeral.

In yet another cruel blow for Lee, Stas's estate was bankrupt. There was no inheritance for her or her children. To help, Janet said she would give her a monthly stipend, but with her own finances so dicey, that effort didn't last long. Jackie helped by setting up trust funds for Tony's and Tina's educations.

Meanwhile, the Auchinclosses continued trying to keep Hammersmith afloat. "Bad investments, bad economy, bad business, all bad," is how Hugh sadly explained it. Janet was annoyed with him, his accountants, his investors, and his lawyers. While she hadn't been keeping track of things, she assumed their money had been invested wisely. By this time, Hugh was almost eighty. He'd been beaten down by the constant stress of trying to keep Hammersmith going, and even though this was the place he'd been born and where he'd always wanted to die, now he wanted to let it go. "I don't fail well," he told Jackie, and she knew that was true. He had always thought of himself as a winner in life and had prided himself on his fiscal responsibility. She knew these reversals were very hard on him.

Jackie wondered if their money had been embezzled. If it had been even a year earlier, she said, she would've opened a thorough investigation. But now, with Hugh's health declining, she felt the best course of action was for them to just cut their losses and sell Hammersmith.

Janet wanted Jackie to purchase it herself to keep it in the family. She could certainly afford it. However, Jackie wanted no part of it.

Losing Hammersmith became a sort of metaphor for the loss of everything Jackie's family had held dear. "The Kennedy years meant everything to Mummy and Daddy," said Jamie Auchincloss, "to all of us. No matter how we felt about Jack from time to time, from year to year, he had brought such wonder to our family. When he was taken from us, it was everything we could do to hold on to whatever was left of the magic. Daddy used to say, 'Where did it all go? It was so great, Jamie. We had such a good life, one adventure after another. What happened?' As he and Mummy aged, it was very difficult to look back and accept that those incredible days of Camelot were behind them.

"It was easier for Jackie," he continued. "She was always the unsentimental type, always one to move forward. And remembering those happy times could be painful for her."

Jamie was right. Jackie didn't want to remember that she and Jack had been married at Hammersmith. She didn't want to remember the president landing on the beach in Marine One with the whole family running out to greet him. She didn't want to remember the parties in the Deck Room. While her family wanted to hold on to all those memories, she'd done everything she could think of to let them go. It was the only way she could survive after Dallas. "So, while finally losing Hammersmith was hard for all of us," Jamie concluded, "it wasn't on Jackie. She'd already let it go many years earlier."

Hammersmith Farm was put on the market for $985,000. The best offer the Auchinclosses got was for $825,000, from a developer who wanted to turn it into a historical museum. Though they'd have to move out of the main house, Janet and Hugh would retain ownership of the Windmill, the Castle, as well as the apartments over its garage called the Palace, and also a surrounding ten acres.

Hammersmith Farm was sold in September of 1976 for $825,000.

THE MOST LOVING THING

<><><><><><><><><><>

On November 2, two months after the sale of Hammersmith, the Auchinclosses made a trip to Washington to vote in that year's presidential election—Hugh for the Republican, Gerald Ford, and Janet for the Democrat, Jimmy Carter. However, once they were at O Street, Hugh's health took a dramatic turn for the worse. Unafraid of dying, he was ready to go. "The life of the dead is placed in the memory of the living," Hugh had told Jackie after JFK died, quoting Cicero. Certainly, that had been the case for her and the rest of the family. Hugh knew he, too, would now live on in their precious memories.

After a week in the hospital, doctors could do nothing more for him. "I don't want him to die here," Janet decided. "I want to take him home." She was told it could be days or even weeks.

Janet's friend Mary Tyler McClenahan recalled, "As he [Hugh] became more and more ill, Janet was infinitely caring. She did everything to make life easier for him. She found sheets that were so soft you didn't feel them. She was wonderfully loving to this man."

As strong as she tried to be for her husband, Janet was filled with sorrow. It was incredibly painful to watch him struggle for breath. After two weeks, a mournful feeling permeated O Street as Hugh continued to linger. Finally, Janet called Jackie and Lee in New York and Janet Jr. in Hong Kong to tell them they should come to Washington to say their goodbyes.

Because relations between Jackie and Lee remained so strained, Lee arranged to go to O Street on Monday, November 15. On November 18, once Lee was gone, Jackie arrived. She spent the night holding an unconscious Hugh's hand and saying the rosary.

The next day, she had to go back to Manhattan for meetings about an important book acquisition for Viking. She promised to return in two days. "Maybe he'll be better," she told Janet.

"Maybe," her mother said, smiling faintly.

The morning of November 20, 1976, Yusha—now forty-nine—pulled aside his half brother, Jamie—twenty-nine.

In a voice so low Jamie could barely hear him, Yusha told him that their father had earlier suggested a way to end to his suffering. Hugh told him, "When you think the time's come, give me some whiskey, put a pillow over my face, and push down until I stop breathing." When Yusha protested, Hugh reminded him that he was his oldest and said he was counting on him. He'd been suffering for almost twenty-five years with emphysema, he said, and it was time for it to end. "The most loving thing you can do for me," he said, "is give me some peace." Then, typical of the history lover he'd always been, Hugh cited the English writer Samuel Johnson: "It matters not how a man dies, but how he lives. The act of dying is not of importance. It lasts so short a time." He had only one other request: he asked Yusha to promise to always care for Janet at Hammersmith. Yusha promised he would.

"Does Mummy know about this?" Jamie asked in disbelief. Yusha didn't answer.

Jamie had to go to the drugstore at his mother's request. Before he left, he went to his father, who was sleeping. He leaned over and kissed him on the forehead.

He was gone for about a half hour. When Jamie returned, the first thing he noticed was the silence. He ran upstairs to the bedroom. There, he found Janet sitting on the bed, holding Hugh's hand. She turned and looked at Jamie with an expression that could only be described as . . . peaceful. She nodded at him and bowed her head.

REACHING OUT TO LEE

◇◇◇◇◇◇◇◇◇◇◇◇

The death of Hugh D. Auchincloss was a big blow for Jackie. He had been an important part of her life for thirty-five years, a true father figure who'd given her away at both her weddings. She could always count on him for reasoned and practical advice and loved him dearly. She grieved for him just as she had her natural father, Jack Bouvier, in 1957. "Daddy's dying left such a hole in our lives," Jamie Auchincloss recalled. "He'd been such a big presence. Jackie told me she'd sometimes pick up the phone to call him, only to then remember he was gone. She recalled to me how much strength he'd given her during Jack's funeral, the things he said to her, the way he was. 'I'd glance over my shoulder, and there he'd be,' she said, 'always focused on me and on how I was, what I was going through. I just always knew he was there.'"

For the next year, Jackie attempted to balance her grief with work and family obligations. Caroline, twenty, was in college, and John, seventeen, was about to graduate high school. They were both smart and mature for their age, and Jackie was proud. She was also determined to give her widowed mother as much of her time as possible, visiting her often at the Hammersmith property in her new residence there, the Castle.

Janet, who hated her new home, was more irascible than ever, often criticizing the ongoing plans to turn the main Hammersmith house into a museum that was to be called Camelot Gardens and which, noted Yusha, "Jackie termed 'tacky.'" Janet's imagination ran wild as she thought about what it might be like to have strangers pay $2.50 for admittance to her and her children's bedrooms and the study once used by President Kennedy. Each time Jackie visited her, they argued about Jackie's decision not to buy

Hammersmith Farm to keep it in the family. Janet was sure Jackie was just getting back at her for her refusal to accept her marriage to Onassis years earlier. Or perhaps for what happened so long ago at her wedding to Jack. "We're known for our grudges in this family," she told a disbelieving Margaret Kearny, who'd worked with Hugh in the Washington office of his brokerage and just didn't think Jackie was that kind of person.

"It was a shame that most of the proceeds from the sale of Hammersmith had to go to pay for death taxes due on my father's estate," Jamie Auchincloss recalled. "Mummy didn't have the money, so it's a good thing we sold the place. They also paid $25,000 for all the furniture, which was a sin, because those pieces had been in the family for generations and were worth ten times that much. I never understood how Jackie let it all go for so little. Her refrain was always, 'It's time for us to move on.'"

One of the biggest decisions Jackie made at this time was to try to repair her relationship with Lee. The fact that Caroline and John were so close to their cousins Tina and Tony made it all the more difficult for the Bouvier sisters to continue their estrangement. After Hugh's funeral, Ethel Kennedy suggested to Jackie that one way to honor him would be to reconcile with Lee. "The biggest mistake we make in this life," Ethel, who lost both parents in a plane crash, said, "is that we think we have more time." Jackie knew she was right. Artemis Garoufalidis had recently told her the same thing. However, Lee was still so angry, she refused to participate in any kind of reconciliation.

Lee told one family member, "Jackie called me and said, 'We have a lot to say to each other,' to which I responded, 'No, actually we don't.' She told me, 'We fight. It's okay,' to which I responded, 'No, it's not.'"

There wasn't much Jackie could do given that Lee was so angry. It was as if she had a tape recording of their past history, and she kept playing it for anyone who would listen. All these years later, she would still tell people about that morning in their mother's bedroom in 1952 when it was decided she should give JFK to Jackie. She'd learned to live with it, she'd say, but then, in 1968, it happened again with Onassis. Her life hadn't turned out as she'd hoped, and she blamed her sister.

After getting nowhere with her, Jackie put $250,000 (about $1.2 million in today's money) in an account for Lee to access at her discretion. She hoped maybe the gesture might help smooth things between them. Lee said she felt the money had only been offered out of guilt, but she accepted it.

FAMILY DRAMA

∞∞∞∞∞∞∞∞∞

At first, Janet Auchincloss tried to be a part of what was happening to her former home at Hammersmith. Janet Crook, who represented Camelot Gardens and Associates, recalled, "It was Mrs. Auchincloss's insistence that it not be turned into a museum that only honored the Kennedys. She wanted it to honor her family, as well. It was difficult for her, though, to stay involved. She missed her husband desperately and felt displaced in the Castle."

She'd call Jackie several times a day at Viking, her emotions swinging from sadness over the loss of her beloved home to anger over Jackie's decision to allow it to happen. Jackie would then telephone Yusha, now living in the Windmill to be near Janet, and the two would often have angry words about Janet's care, unusual for them.

When Jackie asked if Yusha had called Lee to help, he told her she was on the West Coast with a new beau, the wealthy hotelier Newton Cope. Meanwhile, Jamie was working in Washington as a photojournalist. Yusha suggested they take Janet away for a break. Perhaps they could come to 1040 Fifth Avenue and stay with Jackie? Jackie agreed. By the time she got home from the office that afternoon, Janet and Yusha were comfortably settled, and Marta Sgubin was serving them tea.

As the week unfolded, Jackie started to realize something was terribly wrong with her mother. Concern about Janet had been mounting for the last couple of years as she exhibited bouts of forgetfulness attributed to "old age." However, on her first day at 1040, with the emotion of Camelot Gardens weighing so heavily, she was not only forgetful, she seemed to be in a daze. Jackie wondered if she was on new medication, but Yusha said she was only taking her regular blood pressure prescription.

By Tuesday, Janet seemed better. However, on Wednesday morning, while Jackie was preparing to go into the office, Janet asked if Aristotle Onassis might be joining them for dinner. Jackie was so alarmed, she wasn't sure how to respond other than to just remind her that he was gone.

Later that day, Artemis Garoufalidis called. Jackie put Janet on the phone. When Janet spoke to Artemis in fluent French for almost an hour, Jackie was pleased. But then, that same evening, Janet had no memory of having spoken to her.

Jackie loved wearing red and always looked good in it. Suddenly, every time Janet saw Jackie in red, her arms would begin to twitch and she'd become agitated. "Her blood pressure would go up whenever she'd see Jackie wearing that color," said Jamie Auchincloss, "and no one knew why. My theory was that it had to do with Mummy's memory of Jackie covered in Jack's blood. I feared something was definitely off if this memory would still cause her so much distress."

Could it be the onset of Alzheimer's? It was a frightening thought. Jackie and Yusha felt the time had come to consult a doctor.

◇◇◇◇◇◇◇◇◇◇◇◇◇◇◇◇◇◇◇◇

At this same time, the end of 1976, Jackie started appearing in the New York press in photographs with the acclaimed writer and novelist Pete Hamill who, at the time, was a columnist for the *New York Daily News*.

Five years older than Jackie, Pete was a handsome and brusque old-school reporter at the tail end of a six-year relationship with Shirley Mac-Laine. He and Bobby Kennedy had been friends, and he'd worked on the RFK presidential campaign. He was actually one of the men to help disarm Sirhan Sirhan. He met Jackie on the train carrying Bobby's casket from New York's Penn Station to Washington's Union Station.

"Yusha told me there was nothing romantic going on between Jackie and Pete, despite headlines that an affair between them had ended things between him and Shirley," said Yusha's friend Cybil Wright. "When Pete joined Yusha, Janet, and Jackie's children for her forty-seventh birthday dinner at 1040, Jackie made it clear they were just good friends. She was just fascinated by his talent. He was also helpful in introducing her to other writers she might be able to get to sign with Viking."

"I don't know of any public figure whose public image was at greater variance with private reality," Peter Hamill said. "'I picked up the newspaper today,' she told me one evening, 'and read this story about this absolutely horrible woman—and it was me.' She understood that she was the stuff that tabloid dreams are made of, combining in one person the themes of sex, death, and money. But she could be wounded, too."

When Jackie confided in Pete about her mother, he said he had a relative who suffered from Alzheimer's and that he'd be able to get a good reference for a doctor. Jackie took him up on his offer, and that Friday morning, she and Yusha took Janet in for tests and a consultation.

The doctor's diagnosis a few days later was that Janet was probably at the onset of Alzheimer's, but he said it was difficult to know for certain. He was sure that there had been some loss of mental acuity. However, it could be for any number of reasons. Jamie, who wasn't present that day but would learn of the diagnosis from Yusha, recalled, "For the subject of Alzheimer's to even be broached changed our entire world in an instant. We had such panic, this feeling we needed to take immediate action, not understanding the long haul we were all in for."

Always one to strive for as much control over the uncontrollable as possible, Jackie immediately began researching Alzheimer's treatments. She also tasked her friend and former personal secretary Nancy Tuckerman for help.

The day after the doctor's diagnosis, Jackie took Janet and Yusha into the Viking offices to meet her colleagues. As she proudly introduced them to everyone, Yusha noted that he'd never seen Jackie happier than when she was with her colleagues. When she brought him and Janet into Tom Guinzburg's office, Janet knew exactly who Tom was, having met him years ago through Michael Canfield. Somehow, her recognition of a person she hadn't seen since the 1950s felt like a big moment to her daughter and stepson. However, that night over dinner, Janet had no memory at all of meeting Guinzburg. In fact, she insisted it had never happened and even became combative over it.

Meanwhile, Jackie continued to work at Viking. But not for long.

JACKIE O. BAGGAGE

I n October of 1977, a couple of days after Jackie took her mother to Tom Guinzburg's office at Viking, *The New York Times* ran a critical review of a new book the company was publishing by Jeffrey Archer called *Shall We Tell the President?* This write-up was the catalyst for the end of Jackie's tenure at Viking.

The premise of *Shall We Tell the President?* was based on a fictional assassination plot set in the future in 1983, targeting Ted Kennedy. The snarky review from John Leonard of *The New York Times* set off a chain of disturbing events that ended with Jackie's resignation from Viking. "There is a word for such a book," Leonard wrote. "The word is trash. Anybody associated with its publication should be ashamed of herself."

Mortified by the review because, obviously the "herself" Leonard referred to was Jackie, Jackie issued a statement saying she hadn't known anything about the book, was upset about it, and never would have agreed to the book's release. Privately, she was very distraught about it because, not surprisingly, it returned her to her trauma over Dallas. It often happened that when she least expected it something would occur to remind her of Jack's assassination. This book triggered all sorts of bad memories and, it's been said by intimates, caused her to seek Dr. Kris's help with it.

Tom Guinzburg claimed he'd cleared *Shall We Tell the President?* with Jackie in advance and never would've published it without consulting her. Jackie said that wasn't true and now felt she had no choice but to quit her job. She sent a resignation letter to Tom Guinzburg on the night of October 13, 1977.

As with Sinatra, Jackie didn't speak directly to Tom about her decision. She simply removed herself from an awkward situation. She also dropped the many people at the company who thought they'd become her friends. "It was as if none of us had ever existed," said Tom Guinzburg in 2007. "I was filled with regret. All these years later, I remain sad about it. To think there are people who believe I would ever do anything to hurt Jackie over a book of fiction is so upsetting."

Considering the way he'd protected her over the Sinatra matter, it was puzzling to Tom that Jackie would ever think he'd betray her. There was basically nothing he could do. His hands were tied.

October 13, the same night as Jackie's resignation, Janet Jr. and her husband, Lewis Rutherfurd, flew to New York from China for an urgent family meeting, called by Jackie. Mary Wells Forman, Janet's best friend in Hong Kong, recalled, "Jackie telephoned her and asked her and Lewis to come to New York to talk about an important matter relating to their mother. Janet asked me to take her kids while she was gone. I asked what was up and she said, 'Jackie says Mother is slipping and we have to get to the bottom of it as a family.' She and Lewis planned to spend about five days at Jackie's in New York."

The first of several family confabs was tense. "As often happens when relatives are faced with a loved one's serious illness, emotions were heated," said Mary Wells Forman. "Janet Jr. later told me it was suggested that Jackie and Lee alternate weekend visits to Hammersmith to be with their mother in order to give Yusha a break. Lee protested."

Because Lee's romantic interest, Newton Cope, lived on the West Coast, she wasn't willing to commit to anything that would keep her in Manhattan. It wasn't fair to her, she said, and besides, the diagnosis wasn't even Alzheimer's; it was just one possibility.

"When Jackie said she was just being selfish, 'as usual,' the two sisters apparently began to fight," said Mary Wells Forman. "Janet Jr. told me Yusha had to step in to remind them of what really mattered, their mother's well-being and not their ongoing feud. Lee got up and left.

"When Janet Jr. returned to Hong Kong, she was distraught about it," said Mary Wells Forman. "She told me, 'My sisters are so awful to each other. We don't have it in us as a family to handle any kind of crisis, because it always becomes all about them.' She said one of the reasons she'd moved to Hong Kong was to escape their ongoing battles. Now, she said, she felt as if she was being sucked back in, and there was nothing she could do about it."

Something had to give, and Jackie decided it would have to be her job. If anything, it could be said that the Jeffrey Archer book gave her an excuse to leave. "I have to choose Mummy right now," she told Jamie. "That's just the way it has to be."

What happened at Viking was a bigger blow to Jackie than most people knew. "She'd made friends in a workplace and had really proven herself to them," said Jamie. "She loved that job. It was exactly what she wanted to do with her life. She was finally happy and, after all she had been through, she deserved it. For it to end that way shook her. It made her realize, once again, that she wasn't just any woman, she was *Jackie O.,* and that was always going to come with baggage."

MOVING FORWARD

◇◇◇◇◇◇◇◇◇◇◇◇◇

In 1978, Jackie began construction on a new estate on Martha's Vineyard, which she would call Red Gate Farm. With Hammersmith now gone, she decided it was time for her to create her own paradise and purchased some four hundred acres for about a million dollars a few miles across the bay from Newport. Once it was finished, this estate, which overlooked the water, would be spectacular, having been designed to Jackie's exact specifications with the help of her friend Bunny Mellon and the architect Hugh Newell Jacobsen. Besides the main house, there was a separate "barn," which was a large guesthouse with three bedrooms, and a "grain silo," which was John's bedroom, bath, and living quarters. Caroline lived in the main house with her mother whenever she was in residence.

"It seemed as if everyone in Jackie's life was anxious to see Red Gate Farm when it was finished," said Marian Ronan, who worked as a maid there. "However, Madam was selective about her guests. Few Kennedys were invited, for instance. She remained close to Ethel. She invited Rose Kennedy often, but she was just too old to go. There was a wall clipboard in the kitchen covered with a montage of photos of her with JFK, their kids . . . even Onassis. However, she took a dim view of some of the other Kennedys, like Ted, whose infidelity she didn't approve of. She invited his wife, Joan, to Red Gate often, though."

According to what Joan remembered, Jackie always allowed her to vent about Ted as the two pedaled on bicycles through the small, quaint town of Gay Head, or late at night in the kitchen as they dipped into Marta's special deep-dish peach pie. "You're always the best person in the room," Jackie told her. "Don't let your marriage ruin your self-confidence."

Jackie wrote Joan a detailed four-page letter with suggestions as to how to handle Ted's infidelity. Joan had just given her some surprising news about Jack Warnecke. Apparently, Ted asked Jack for a phone that would be charged to Jack's account and billing address so that Joan wouldn't be aware of calls he made to other women. Much to Jackie's surprise, Jack had agreed. She didn't even know the two were friends. She was very disappointed in Jack but seemed resigned. "Sadly, men stick together on these things," she told Joan.

Jackie's letter to Joan is telling. It's as if she was coaching Joan to do what she hadn't done with JFK: confront Ted and insist he change.

Jackie regretted telling Joan to stick it out in her marriage by focusing on herself rather than on Ted's infidelities. While it had been her advice in the 1960s, she felt differently about things by the end of the '70s. She'd grown, becoming much more empowered. She now apologized to Joan and told her she should've advised her to ditch Ted and start life anew. Had she done so, Jackie said, maybe Joan wouldn't have turned to alcohol as she had.

Joan said there was no way in the 1960s she could've walked away from Ted. "Times were different," she said, "and, besides, Grandpa wouldn't have allowed it." They agreed they did the best they could back then.

Jackie's words to Joan in her letter show just how far she'd come since the 1960s, perhaps due to the women's movement, or maybe therapy or perhaps just because of wisdom that comes with age. "Don't be apologetic," she wrote at the top of her letter. "You've had it. This is the 20th Century, not the 19th when little women stayed home on pedestals with the kids and her rosary."

"Forbidden fruit is what is exciting," she continued. "It takes much more of a real man to have a deep relationship with the woman he lives with. The routine of married life can become boring. Don't ask permission," she wrote. "Be a bit mysterious. Then he can't plan things around your absence."

She suggested Joan take vacations with her friends, not Kennedys. She also warned her not to be intimidated by her sisters-in-law. In fact, she suggested making the sisters "scared to death" of her so that they didn't walk all over her. She told her to go to Eunice and Rose with her issues and cautioned her to be sure not to allow them to view her as "a delicate health problem."

"You're no prude or fool," she continued. "If he goes off to a Refugee

Conference in Geneva—you don't like to think about it, but you wouldn't be surprised if he had a big blow-out in Paris with Hooter or someone. But at least he's not home having his phone billed to John Warnecke so that he can talk to Mootsie or Pootsie every night—right in the house with his wife & children. What kind of woman, but a sap or a slave, can stand for that? You want a life of sharing, otherwise why doesn't he just get a Japanese house boy to wait in the other room while he and his aides discuss his problems?" she concluded. "Then, he can have his girls on the side while his sisters can campaign for him."

Jackie suggested Joan divorce Ted and recommended her lawyer Alexander Forger to represent her. The divorce was finally granted in 1982. He was able to get Joan a $5 million settlement.

While Kennedys generally weren't invited to Red Gate Farm, most of Jackie's immediate family was welcome, except for Jamie and Lee.

Her ongoing issues with Lee made Jackie disinclined to invite her to Red Gate. Lee would count on one hand the times she'd see the property.

Where Jamie was concerned, Jackie was upset with him for having cooperated with the author Kitty Kelley on her book *Jackie Oh!*, the first of her successful unauthorized biographies. Jamie gave Kitty a number of interviews thinking he was setting the record straight on things and naive to the fact that what he was really doing was contributing to a book by an author who was hell-bent on toppling Jackie from her pedestal. Though he'd apologized profusely, Jackie couldn't get past it. Janet and Yusha had also cooperated, but it was easier to forgive them. Jackie felt Jamie was, as a professional photographer, more sophisticated and just should've known better. The book was scathing in its tone when published in 1978. It ruined everything between Jackie and Jamie.

In February of 1978, Jacqueline Onassis's brief pause in her publishing career ended when she met with Doubleday & Company's president, John Sargent, and publisher, Sam Vaughan, at 1040 Fifth Avenue and accepted a job offer. It would be almost double her salary at Viking, working three days a week for about $20,000 a year at Doubleday.

While it had only been four months, Jackie had missed working. She also realized that because she could do so little about her mother's illness, putting her life on hold made no sense. "At first, it felt to her as if she had to put everything aside in order to deal with certain important family matters," is how Sam Vaughan put it in 2007. "She soon realized there was nothing she could do about it." Because Janet's illness would be long and protracted, her family would have to figure out how to navigate it while continuing to live their own lives.

Jackie would now join Nancy Tuckerman, still her spokeswoman, who also worked for Doubleday, and a good friend named Lisa Drew, an executive editor at Doubleday. "During our lunches together about it, I assured her it would be a safe place for her," said Drew. "We were excited to have her, she was excited to begin working again. It was a much bigger company than Viking, a huge change for her and one she welcomed."

Jackie's editorial assistant in 1978 and 1979 was Hope Marinetti from Rochester, twenty-four at the time and fresh out of college with a degree in French and Russian Revolution history. She recalled, "After you got to know her, she was nothing like what you'd expect. She was engaging, open, candid, and accessible with a great sense of humor. Though I was very shy, I had an off-color sense of humor myself. Early on, we were discussing a royalty check, and she asked if it had gone out. I doubted it and said, 'Oh yeah, the check's in the mail . . . same way I promise I won't come in your mouth.' She burst out laughing. 'My goodness,' she said, 'I underestimated you! You're not the girl-next-door I thought you were, are you?' That broke the ice between us."

Hope worked on a number of books with Jackie—the novel *Call the Darkness Light* by Nancy Zaroulis being their first—but it's her personal memories of working side by side for two years that show facets of Jackie not always apparent to the public. She has dozens of disparate memories, as one might of a coworker seen every day at the office. She had no idea that, like most people, Jackie compartmentalized her life. She was able to be happy at work, so much so that colleagues had no idea about any of her private struggles.

"It was easy to bond," said Hope. "We'd go to the ladies' room and smoke cigarettes and talk about men. We soon realized we both had a fondness for Jewish men. I invited her to my home for drinks and appetizers so she could meet my best friend, and by 'home,' I mean a little studio apartment in Chelsea with two chairs and a daybed. She made herself at home, sat on the floor as if it were the most natural thing in the world. I made a ricotta pie, and she really enjoyed herself. Then, I went to her home. After the doorman announced me, he said, 'It's the fifteenth floor,' and I said, 'Okay, and the apartment number is . . . ?' and he said, 'It's the whole floor!'

I was so embarrassed. When I got up there, I told her, and she got a real kick out of it. I asked her, 'Is there a back entrance to this place? Because I can never see that doorman again.' I also remember when my own apartment was broken into, she gave me five hundred dollars to get back on my feet. She was that kind of person. We would sit in her office and go through *People* magazine and comment on pictures of her. She'd find one and say, 'My God, look at this outfit. What was I thinking?' One Christmas, I had these really fun rolling papers for making joints. I put them in her Christmas card as a joke. She cracked up and said, 'I'll have to give these to John.'

"In the office, when you'd walk with her to the elevator, she would be one person, very animated and fun and talking about this or that. But once in the elevator, she'd become someone else. A mask would come down over her face. She knew people were coming in, seeing her, and thinking, *Holy shit, it's Jackie O.* So, she'd go into this blank mode and make no eye contact whatsoever, just stare straight ahead. Then, the doors would open, we'd walk out, and she'd instantly be her old self, again—'Now, what were we saying?'

"When I was ready to leave that job, she said, 'Listen, my friend Mike is looking for an assistant, and I think you'd do great.' She set up the interview. It was pouring rain, and she said, 'You'll never get a cab in this weather. Ride with me.' So, I rode with her in a town car to the Carlyle Hotel, and it turned out to be Mike Nichols, the director. He hired me. That was typical of her, just so thoughtful."

Jackie immediately blended with the Doubleday staff, the higher-ups, like the company's president, Sam Vaughan, down to the subordinates like Hope Marinetti. She soon considered it her new home, and it would remain so for the next sixteen years. "She worked hard at editing, reading more manuscripts at home than ever were published, urging people into good work," said Pete Hamill. "And she could write, too. Her notes were models of grace and precision."

Though juggling her work responsibilities with her homelife and her mother's illness was often a challenge, Jackie managed well enough for the first year or so. Then something happened to shake up things once again.

JANET'S NEWS

∞∞∞∞∞∞∞∞∞∞

I n the fall of 1978, Janet and Yusha came to the city to spend the weekend
with Jackie. The pleasant visit took an unexpected turn, however, during
lunch at Le Périgord when Janet mentioned that she'd reconnected with
someone from her distant past. His name was Bingham Willing Morris,
a man she'd known for more than sixty years. She met him when she was
thirteen, and they dated while he attended St. George's School. He was
known to relatives and friends as "Bouch," a nickname derived from the
middle name of his father, John Boucher Morris III. Both Bingham and his
brother, John Boucher Morris IV, were known by the same moniker. He
was now seventy-two and had a home in Southampton.

Janet said Bingham had gone on to marry a friend named Mary Rawlins in 1934, who, six years earlier, had been one of her bridesmaids at
her wedding to Jackie's father. Mary was a year older than Janet, born in
1906; both had attended the Spence School for girls. Morris was now a
widower.

Jackie was confused. "Why did you track this man down?" she asked.
Janet said she hadn't. He'd found her and called her. "After sixty years?" Jackie
asked in disbelief. "When did he call?"

In September.

"When did his wife die?"

August 14; she knew the exact date. It came to her mind quickly.

"His wife dies, and the first thing he does is call you?" Jackie asked. She
didn't like the way it sounded.

When Jackie later asked Yusha if he knew anything about it, he said the mention of it over lunch had been the first he'd heard of it. It must be fiction, Jackie decided, Janet's mind playing tricks on her.

A week later, Jackie drove to Newport for a visit. She walked into the Castle and found Janet sitting in the kitchen having breakfast with a man wearing jeans, a T-shirt, and a straw hat. Janet's chef, Michael Dupree—who'd trained at La Varenne in France and, thus, specialized in French cuisine—was serving homemade *pain au chocolat* and café au lait—chocolate croissants and coffee. It was an odd scene, Janet speaking French to her chef as a stranger slathered butter on a croissant.

"Who are you?" Jackie asked. The man bolted up, extended his hand, and said, "I'm Bouch." He was, Jackie soon learned, the man Janet had earlier mentioned—Bingham Morris.

Upset, Jackie rushed over to the Windmill to find Yusha. He was surprised by her presence; he'd gotten the weekends mixed up and thought she'd be arriving the next Saturday. When she asked about Bouch, he confessed he hadn't told her the truth. Janet had been seeing Bouch from time to time. He'd purposely kept it from Jackie, he explained, because he knew she'd be upset. Her being angry would just upset Janet, he said, "and I'm the one who has to live with her." So, he decided not to tell her.

Jackie went back to the Castle, told Bouch to leave, packed a bag for her mother, and took her back to New York City with her for two weeks.

WARREN BEATTY

I n her mission to secure a big book for Doubleday, Jackie asked Pete Hamill
if he would appeal to his ex-girlfriend Shirley MacLaine for an introduction
to her brother, Warren Beatty. At this time, the autumn of 1978, Beatty was
a massively popular actor thanks to films like *Bonnie and Clyde, Shampoo,* and
the newly released *Heaven Can Wait,* which he produced and for which he'd
be nominated for acting, directing, and writing. Orson Welles had been the
only other person to be so nominated, and Beatty would do it again with
Reds in 1981. He was a longtime supporter of the Democratic Party, and
Jackie felt she'd met him somewhere along the way but wasn't sure. She remembered she wanted him to play JFK in the *PT 109* film of 1963 but wasn't
sure why he hadn't been cast. Actually, President Kennedy had final say over
that role, and he picked Cliff Robertson.

Warren was single, forty-one, and very handsome. He was also rumored
to have hooked up with almost every major female star in show business under the age of fifty. In 2010, his biographer Peter Biskind somehow figured
out he'd had sex with about 12,775 women—how he came to that number
was anyone's guess, but he said the calculation dated from when Warren lost
his virginity in 1956 until he married Annette Bening in 1991 and became
monogamous. The list included stars like Diane Keaton, Joan Collins, Goldie
Hawn, Jane Fonda, Julie Christie, Natalie Wood, and Madonna, though it's
hard to know where legend ended and truth began with Beatty.

After meeting him, Jackie worked hard to convince Beatty to write a
memoir, but he felt it was too soon. He told her to give him ten more years
and he'd come back to her with more enthusiasm for the idea. Jackie found

him interesting and went out on a few dates with him until bringing him back to 1040 Fifth Avenue and having him spend the night. One member of her staff recalls coming into the kitchen one morning to find the actor sitting at the kitchen table talking to John Kennedy Jr. "as if it was the most normal thing in the world."

Adora Rule remembered being tasked with hand-delivering paperwork from one of Janet's doctors to Jackie one morning in the fall of '78, and when she walked out of the elevator, she ran right into Warren Beatty, "who was handsome as all get-out." He was followed by Jackie, who handed him a wallet and said, "You forgot this, honey." When she saw Adora, she smiled and introduced her to Warren as "my mother's secretary." Warren got into the elevator, Jackie kissed him on the lips, and the doors closed. She then looked at Adora and said, "If I were you, I'd probably have some questions right now." Adora said, "Not a one, Jackie." She smiled and said, "Good call, Adora."

Jackie and Warren socialized for a few months, but she found him self-absorbed. He had been an actor for more than twenty years and was at a career peak. It was all he talked about—actors, producers, directors, films, and all in relation to him and to his ambitions. It was understandable. Jackie told intimates they'd spend hours over dinner talking about him and his goals and aspirations, and he never once asked how she was or what was going on in her life. "Then, just before he kisses me good night, he looks at me and says, 'So, how are *you* doing?' and by that time, I'm totally done with him." If the date ended with sex, that was fun, she said, but after a few times, she was "done" with that, as well. When someone close to her asked how Warren was in the bedroom, Jackie said, "Oh, he's fine. Men can only do so much, anyway." She said that had she met Warren ten years earlier, she would have had a lot more fun. Unfortunately, he'd entered the picture "when I had other things I was dealing with and, believe me, having sex wasn't one of them."

Warren told people he was disappointed in Jackie because he thought she'd be more interesting. "She's like a suburban mom," he told Truman Capote. "All she cares about is her kids and whether or not people at her job like her." He said he always thought "Jackie Kennedy would be a lot more exciting."

It ended with Warren Beatty on December 20 after Jackie hosted a Christmas party at 1040. She had many family members present, including her mother, Yusha, and even Lee. Warren showed up with a coterie of people, including Diane Keaton, none of whom Jackie had invited or expected. Jackie normally only invited people she knew into her home. Then, during a conversation with Yusha, Warren said something about sleeping with Jackie. Yusha found it inappropriate. When he told Jackie about it, it was the final straw with Warren.

"It was fun while it lasted," she told one intimate of Warren Beatty, "and it lasted about two weeks longer than it should have."

M T

◇◇◇◇◇◇◇◇◇◇◇◇◇◇

By the beginning of 1979, Janet Auchincloss wasn't the only one with a possible new love interest. Her daughter had become seriously involved with someone her family had yet to meet. Jackie would always be sorry that Hugh hadn't had the opportunity to meet him because she knew they would've gotten along well. His name was Maurice Tempelsman, and he'd play an important role during the rest of Jackie's life.

Fifty-year-old Maurice Tempelsman was born on August 26, 1929, the same year as Jackie—to Yiddish-speaking Orthodox Jews in Antwerp, Belgium. He and his family moved to America during the war when Maurice was about eleven, settling in a refugee community in the Upper West Side of New York. At sixteen, while attending New York University, Maurice began working for his father, a diamond merchant. Soon, they were collaborating in a diamond business known as Leon Tempelsman & Son Inc.

In 1949, when he was twenty, Maurice married Lilly Bucholz, whose father was also in diamonds, but in the mining industry. In the 1950s, Maurice went into business with the U.S. government, stockpiling African diamonds for industrial and military purposes. As a result, he developed strong connections in Africa and, as a major player in his field, made a fortune by the end of the '60s. However, his financial success had been earned at a price. It had affected his marriage. Though they'd go on to have three children and would stay together for them, the union with Lilly was all but over by the beginning of the 1970s.

After Ari died, André Meyer turned to Maurice for advice on how to handle Jackie's inheritance. That's how Maurice began to play a bigger role in her life. When André died in 1979, she felt particularly vulnerable. Though she had never had romantic feelings for him, she always knew André would protect her and be an ally like few others in her life. She'd already been seeing Maurice for occasional dates, and after Meyer's passing, the relationship with him grew more serious as she became more dependent on him for emotional support.

Maurice had always had strong ties to the Democratic Party and had been a friend of the Kennedy family's. Jackie first met him in the 1950s when Jack Kennedy was a senator, having been introduced by Ted Sorensen. She vaguely recalled meeting Maurice at that time but did recall that he and his wife were guests at the 1961 state dinner in honor of Pakistan's president, Mohammad Ayub Khan.

Maurice Tempelsman—whom Jackie and her children always called "MT"—was a stocky man of about five foot eight. He was also a tad overweight, balding, and certainly could never be described as dashing. He was smart and funny, which Jackie said she needed at this time in her life. "I am so tired of serious people," she said, "and Maurice makes me laugh." He enjoyed the ballet and theater, was well read, spoke fluent French like Jackie, had traveled the world, and was an ardent collector of Roman and Greek antiques.

Maurice also happened to be one of a handful of site holders permitted to make direct purchases of diamonds from the De Beers diamond cartel, the internationally based diamond mining and trading company controlling the flow of diamonds in the United States. As a result, his diamond-trading business thrived, and he was a millionaire many times over, which still mattered to Jackie. She didn't need his money, of course, but his affluence was evidence of his success in life, and she wanted to be with someone who was accomplished. With the passing of the years, Maurice would take complete control of Jackie's finances and build her settlement from Ari into a fortune later estimated at between $100 and $200 million. "He always had her back," is how Caroline Kennedy once put it, "and was someone we all grew to love and respect. He was one of the family, almost from the beginning. My mother adored him."

His temperament most attracted Jackie. After her troubled marriages, she never wanted to be in a relationship with someone who sought to dominate her or refused to allow her to grow. Maurice encouraged her in her work in publishing and believed she had a lot to offer. Exceedingly affable and kind, it would never occur to him to tell her how to live her life. He made her feel safe and taken care of. When Artemis Garoufalidis met him in New York, she wholeheartedly approved of him, though she feared Jackie might one day become bored with him. "He's like an old slipper," she said, "very comfortable but, eventually, easily replaced." For the time being, though, she told Jackie to just enjoy him.

People would always wonder about Jackie's relationship with Maurice. Was it sexual? Jackie implied strongly to people close to her that they weren't intimate. "Oh heavens, that would never happen with us," is how she put it in 1982 when a good friend asked if they'd slept in the same bed during a recent stay at a bed-and-breakfast. "That's not us," she said, "and it'll never be us."

She told that same friend something Ari used to say, an aphorism some might've found offensive but which Jackie thought was clever, if cynical. "He used to say, 'A woman is like the world,'" she recalled. "'At twenty years of age, she's like Africa, semi-explored. At thirty, she's India, warm, mature and mysterious. At forty, she's America, technically perfect, but superficial because, deep down, she's troubled. At fifty, she's Europe, completely and utterly in ruins. And at sixty, she's Siberia. Everyone knows where she is, but no one wants to go to her.' After we had a good laugh, I made him promise to tell me that story every ten years," Jackie concluded. She added, "I'm fifty now and, I guess, completely and utterly in ruins."

Almost thirty years after her death, several people who were close to Jackie say she simply wasn't interested in having sex in 1979 when, at fifty, she became involved with Maurice. "It's not disparaging to say that they had an understanding," said one source. "What's wrong with that? Many people in their fifties and sixties and seventies enjoy sex," noted the source, "while many others have different priorities."

With Aristotle Onassis, Jackie got financial security. From Maurice Tempelsman, she wanted emotional security. It would seem she didn't want to have sex with either. "Who knew what they did in the bedroom?" asked Jamie Auchincloss. "More to the point, who cared? Everyone was happy about whatever it was they had."

Everyone, that is, but, at least according to popular rumor, Maurice's wife, Lilly. It's been reported for decades that she refused to give Maurice a divorce. That's not true.

After Maurice began seeing Jackie, Lilly agreed to a Jewish religious divorce, which is called a "get" and the Jewish equivalent to a Catholic annulment. It was obtained through the West Side Manhattan synagogue where the Tempelsmans had worshipped for many years.

According to Orthodox Jewish law, to obtain a get, both parties—Maurice and Lilly—had to petition a tribunal of rabbis. It was Maurice's decision, not Lilly's, that the couple eschew a legal, civil divorce. He and Jackie decided early on they would never marry because a legal union would complicate both their estates. Also, the devout Maurice would have wanted Jackie to convert to Judaism for them to be married under Jewish law, and there was simply no way she would ever abandon her Catholic faith.

For decades, it's been thought and reported that Lilly Tempelsman held Maurice back from marrying Jackie. Her family members say she's always been unhappy with those conclusions but, an exceedingly private woman, she would also never issue any statements to the contrary.

People often remarked on the irony that Jackie's spouses had cheated on her, and now, here she was, the so-called other woman. But, in fact, Maurice was her companion, not her lover. When he moved into her home in 1982, they had separate bedrooms, his being the one once used by Aristotle Onassis. He and Jackie would live together, on and off, for the rest of her life.

"MUMMY'S GETTING MARRIED"

◇◇◇◇◇◇◇◇◇◇◇◇

On a hot summer day in 1979, Yusha called Jackie to tell her he and Janet had just arrived in New York from Newport and were at his part-time apartment at Eighty-Ninth and Park. He wanted to come by later that evening after Jackie's workday for an important family meeting. Though he realized it was last minute, Yusha hoped she would also be able to get Lee to 1040 Fifth Avenue if she was in town. Jackie said she never talked to her sister, and a stranger would have better luck reaching her, but she would at least try. Lee did join the gathering.

When she arrived at 1040, Lee greeted Janet, Yusha, Caroline, now twenty-one, John, eighteen, and Maurice. She even embraced Adora. However, she didn't say a word to Jackie.

Jamie, still at odds with Jackie over the Kitty Kelley book, wasn't invited.

Janet Jr., was, of course, in China with her husband and children.

By this time, Janet was seventy-one and more demanding than ever. Yusha, still living in the Windmill, was having a difficult time keeping staff, many of whom departed due to her mood swings. Her chefs, Michael Dupree and Jonathan Tapper, had their hands full taking on double duties, as did groundskeeper Mannie Faria and his wife, Louise, who'd lived in the Caretakers' House on the grounds since 1968 with their two daughters. Adora didn't live on the property like the others.

Yusha didn't waste any time getting to the point. "Mummy's getting married," he said.

"To whom?" Jackie asked, surprised.

"Bingham Morris—Bouch."

Jackie's response was quick and to the point: "No. She's not."

Janet was clear about what she wanted. "You don't know how lonely I've been without your uncle Hughdie," she said. She said there were days she didn't even want to get out of bed. The minutes ticked away so slowly, she said, that by three o'clock, she'd find herself sitting in a chair in front of the television crying. Two young girls who were being raised on the property, Joyce and Linda, the daughters of caretakers Mannie and Louise Faria, were often the only two people she'd see in an entire week. "All I want is another heartbeat in the house," she said sadly. "Is that so bad?"

Cybil Wright, Yusha's good friend, recalled, "Yusha told me Jackie was brought to tears by her mother's confession. She had no idea. 'What am I supposed to do, call you every time I'm lonely?' Janet asked, to which Jackie exclaimed, 'Yes!' But Bouch was good company, Janet said. He was fun and made her happy. They took long walks, talked about American history, enjoyed music, and even went dancing. Jackie suggested that if she were that lonely, perhaps she should move to an apartment in the city close to her. But Janet wanted her independence and wanted to stay at Hammersmith.

"At first, Yusha had been against the marriage. However, he decided to accept it if it meant someone would be living in the Castle, watching over Janet. He needed a break. It hadn't been easy caring for her. He wanted to spend more time at his own apartment in the city."

Jackie was still dead set against the marriage. John and Caroline wondered if their grandmother was sound enough in mind to make such an important decision. Though Janet's condition hadn't gotten worse, she wasn't the same woman they'd known and loved. Her memory was spotty. Some days, she remembered the past with vivid clarity. On other days, she had no memory at all of important events. Lee sided with Yusha and felt Janet should be able to marry if she wanted to. "You don't get to tell other people how to live their lives," she told Jackie. When Jackie called Artemis Garoufalidis in Greece to ask her opinion, Jackie was pleased to learn that Artemis supported her. A daughter had a responsibility to protect her mother, she said, and if Jackie didn't trust Bingham Morris, she should do everything in her power to prevent him from marrying her mother.

However, in the days and weeks to come, there was simply no talking Janet out of her plans. Maurice finally told Jackie she needed to let her mother do what she wanted to do. While he didn't know Janet well, she seemed mentally sound to him. The times they spent together had been amicable. Maurice felt warmly toward her and felt there was nothing wrong with her wanting companionship. It was Jackie he thought was being unrealistic, not Janet. It became one of their first real arguments, during which he saw a stubborn side of her he'd not seen before.

Should the wedding actually occur, Jackie decided, something needed to be put in place to safeguard her mother's assets—namely, what she still owned of Hammersmith Farm. "Maurice came to understand that Jackie was talking about establishing a conservatorship for Janet's welfare," said someone close to him at that time. "He felt that was a very bad idea and would only cause more dissension. He decided to just call Mr. Morris and ask if he'd sign a prenuptial agreement, which Maurice would draw up with the lawyer Alex Forger. Mr. Morris said he had no problem signing it. Jackie insisted Maurice call Mr. Morris and warn him that if he didn't sign the agreement, there'd be no wedding. But it wasn't necessary, Maurice told her, because Mr. Morris was perfectly willing. Not listening, she told him to threaten any number of legal actions. Again, Maurice told her, none of that was necessary.

"The next thing we knew, Maurice had packed up and moved out of Jackie's apartment. 'Is everything okay?' I asked him. He said all was well; they were just taking a break, a much-needed break."

A JOURNEY AHEAD

◇◇◇◇◇◇◇◇◇◇◇◇◇

Janet's wedding to Bingham Morris took place at the Castle on October 25, 1979, which was about a week after Jackie, Caroline, and John participated in the official dedication of the John F. Kennedy Presidential Library and Museum in Boston. Everyone would be in attendance for the nuptials except for Janet Jr. Also notably missing was Maurice.

An interesting moment occurred as Jackie and Caroline helped Janet get dressed in her bedroom. As Jackie ran a comb through her hair, Janet realized she was wearing a diamond ring. "My God," she exclaimed. "Your wedding ring from Jack. You're wearing it again?" Janet asked.

"I have been, lately, yes," Jackie said.

Seeing this, Caroline's eyes immediately filled with tears. Janet went to comfort her.

"I'm just so happy for you," Caroline told her grandmother.

Lately, Jackie had been remembering her past with Jack Kennedy. She told friends that it was a little less painful to think about him or their marriage than it had been in the past. She believed he had truly loved her, she said, and she felt nostalgic for the Camelot years. In some ways, it felt to her as if things were just a lot simpler back then. "Now, with Mummy and this man," she said, "I just don't know what to expect from life."

Janet's new husband, Bingham Morris, seventy-three, was born on June 25, 1906, in Long Island, New York. He was raised by wealthy parents in Philadelphia and graduated from St. George's School in Newport. He spent his working years as a successful investment banker. He and his late wife had no children and had lived in their home in Southampton. He was half Irish; his late mother, Violet, was born in Belgium, though raised in Philadelphia.

"Bingham was eccentric, not a man anyone could ever imagine at Mummy's side," said Janet's son, Jamie. "He sometimes dressed in straw hats, overalls, and T-shirts. When he was cleaned up, he was good-looking. About six feet tall, maybe one hundred seventy-five pounds, in shape for his age, brown hair, blue eyes. However, he was a dyed-in-the-wool Republican who had a real bias against Democrats, especially the Kennedys."

Jackie felt if she'd just had a little more support from family members, she might've been able to stop the wedding. With Yusha in favor of it, Jamie unsure about it, Lee advocating for it and Janet Jr. away, there wasn't much she could do but just accept it. "I'm afraid we have a real journey ahead of us," she said, "and many of us will be unhappy about it."

At one point, Jackie was having a private discussion with Yusha on the bluestone courtyard behind the Castle. They were talking about Ted Kennedy, who, in two weeks, would enter the 1980 presidential race, challenging the Democratic incumbent, President Jimmy Carter. She said she feared Ted had a subconscious desire to self-destruct because he felt he'd never live up to what people expected of him. "He's not Jack," she opined, "and he's not Bobby. He believes deep down that what he is, isn't good enough."

Bingham overheard Jackie and cracked, "We should thank our lucky stars, then, because the last thing this country needs is another Kennedy."

Jackie's face darkened. "You have a problem with men who honor their principles and values?" she asked.

"No. I just have a problem with you Kennedys," was his response.

THE LONG-OVERDUE APOLOGY

As Jackie was leaving Hammersmith after her mother's wedding, Bingham Morris sidled up to her and whispered in her ear, "Your mummy told me what you did at your husband's inauguration."

Jackie looked at him with confusion.

"You gave her shitty seats. Remember?" he asked.

She told him she had no idea what he was talking about and walked away from him as fast as she could.

"That was low, I admit," said Ivy Rawlins, niece of Mary Rawlins, Bingham's first wife. "But it shows how poisoned things were between him and Jackie, that he would say such a thing to her at his wedding to her mother. When I heard about it, I thought it was going too far."

According to multiple family sources in whom she confided, Jackie said her mother was absolutely right. It had happened exactly as Janet had told Bingham. Jackie had lashed out and given her and Hugh terrible seats at the inauguration in retaliation for the book Janet had helped Mary Van Rensselaer Thayer write. "It was stupid," Jackie reportedly said, "I was stupid. I was just a stupid, stupid little girl acting out and being spiteful. I'm very ashamed." She knew she needed to, once and for all, apologize to Janet for that breach of so long ago.

About two weeks later, according to Donna Lou, Janet's part-time nurse, Janet received a phone call from Jackie. Janet later told the nurse that Jackie had apologized for the mishap at the inauguration. It was fulsome, sincere, and from the heart. Janet gazed at the nurse with a very troubled expression and said, "I don't know what she's talking about. Do you?"

"MY WONDERFUL ARTEMIS"

◇◇◇◇◇◇◇◇◇◇◇◇◇◇◇

By 1981, Jackie's good friend and former sister-in-law Artemis Garoufa-lidis was seventy-nine and not well. Kiki Feroudi Moutsatsos reported to Jackie that Artemis had been having trouble speaking and was unsteady on her feet. Once she was admitted to a hospital in Athens, the diagnosis was liver cancer, advanced and aggressive. Jackie was so distraught by the news, she decided to go to Greece immediately.

The last time she'd talked to Artemis, Jackie confided in her that she'd been having a very bad day. Sometimes, thoughts and memories about Dallas sabotaged things for her, she said, "and once I go down that road, it's all over for me."

Kiki Feroudi Moutsatsos recalled, "Jackie said, 'It's been so many years, and I've tried everything I can to move on, but it feels as if I'll never be truly happy again.' Artemis assured her that these feelings were normal. She often felt the same about her lost daughter, Popi. But life does go on, she told her, and they both had to be strong."

As she was packing for Greece, Jackie got a call from someone in the Onassis organization to tell her Christina had decided to have Artemis transported by Learjet to New York. "Doctors told her there was no hope for her aunt," recalled Thea Andino, "but she wouldn't give up. She wanted to admit her into the Memorial Sloan Kettering Cancer Center in New York and then pray for a miracle. Merope was against it. 'If it's her time, let my sister die here in Greece where she belongs,' she begged her. She said, 'I'm next, and I want to die here in my homeland.'" Merope Konialidis actually lived another thirty-one years. She died in February 2012 at the age of one hundred.

"Once Artemis was checked into Sloan Kettering, Jackie desperately wanted to see her," recalled Thea. "Not surprisingly considering all the bad blood, Christina said, 'Keep that awful woman out of my aunt's room.'"

Preventing Jackie from seeing her good friend wouldn't be easy for Christina, though. Jackie knew many doctors and nurses at the facility who were happy to sneak her into Artemis's room after visiting hours. She would show up at around midnight while Artemis was asleep, heavily sedated on morphine. For more than an hour, she'd sit with her, hold her hand, and pray the rosary.

After about a week of visits, Jackie called one of her hospital contacts to arrange another and was told that Artemis had passed away.

"I was in Greece when Jackie called me, crying," said Kiki Feroudi Moutsatsos. "'I can't believe she's gone,' she told me. 'I don't know why, but for some reason I thought she'd pull through.' She talked about how Artemis would now join Aristo in heaven, 'or at least I like to think that's how things work,' she said. She told me she'd miss her every day for as long as she lived. 'I owe her my whole life,' she said. 'Everything good that's happened to me since the day I met her brother, I owe to my wonderful Artemis.'"

Artemis Onassis Garoufalidis was buried in Skorpios, next to her beloved brother, Aristotle Onassis.

BOOK VI

Challenges

MICHAEL JACKSON

◇◇◇◇◇◇◇◇◇◇◇◇◇◇◇

I n the spring of 1983, John Kennedy Jr. suggested that his mother try to secure the Michael Jackson story for Doubleday. Jackie knew little about the entertainer. He was incredibly talented, John told her, internationally famous and, importantly, very mysterious. Indeed, no one was more enigmatic than Michael, who, at the time, was enjoying the success of what would go on to become the biggest-selling album in history, *Thriller*. Still, Jackie wasn't sure she was interested until John showed her a tape of Jackson's highly acclaimed Motown 25 performance of "Billie Jean." She found him fascinating.

By the time of his Motown 25 performance in 1983, Michael Jackson had been at the top of the recording business for almost fifteen years, carving out his own historical niche first with his brothers in the Jackson 5 and then as a solo star. While she wasn't necessarily a fan, Jackie was convinced a book by Michael would be a big seller for Doubleday, and she wanted to be the one to bring it in. She also figured such a success would give her the freedom to do the kinds of books she really wanted to do, which were more esoteric in nature, having to do with fine arts.

When Jackie pitched the idea of a Jackson memoir at Doubleday's weekly board meeting, the staff was enthusiastic about its potential success. Jackie then contacted Michael's manager, Frank DiLeo.

"I'm sitting at my desk, and I pick up the phone and a voice says, 'Hello, this is Jacqueline Onassis. Do you represent Michael Jackson?'" he recalled in 2005. "I say, 'How do I know this is the real Jackie O.?' She laughs and says, 'Oh, it's the real Jackie O., all right. Is this the real manager of Michael

Jackson?' She said she wanted to come to Los Angeles to talk about Michael writing a book. I told her, 'Good luck with that. I can barely get the kid to write his mother a postcard when we're on tour.' She and an assistant flew out and checked into the Beverly Hills Hotel. I set a plan for her to meet Michael for dinner."

Michael, an avid admirer of Jackie's, had a collection of books about her and the Kennedys. He'd met her once briefly when he was in New York filming *The Wiz* in 1977, but it was in passing. "She's so important to our culture," he once said. "In terms of just being heroic, there's no one like her. I was five when Kennedy was killed, and I remember sitting in front of the television with my mother and watching when John-John saluted. We both thought, *My god, look at Jackie, how strong and brave she is.*"

The dinner with Jackie didn't happen, because Michael became so anxious about it he had a panic attack and wasn't able to leave the house. As big a star as he was, he was incredibly insecure and often felt unworthy of the amazing opportunities that would come his way. "I paced back and forth in my bedroom," he recalled, "and I kept thinking, *No, I'm not ready. This is too big. It's too much. I can't do it. I need more time.*"

Jackie had brought her editorial assistant, Shaye Areheart, to the West Coast with her. The two had a finely tuned working relationship. Shaye did much of the nuts-and-bolts editing, and Jackie was more concerned with broader story points. The meeting was rescheduled for the next day at Michael's home in Encino. "The car drove up to the house, and I was in La Toya's bedroom, looking down," Michael recalled, "and I watched Jackie get out, and I kept thinking, *Okay, she's just a woman, she's just like anyone else, she's human like me.* Once we met, she was just so cool, she put me right at ease."

From the start, Michael made clear his reluctance to write about his life. While he agreed it might be an opportunity to correct some of the many falsehoods about him, he didn't want to write a book that would reveal anything of a personal nature. If he did anything at all, it would have to be a coffee-table book about his life with pictures and extended captions. That was it.

Jackie told him what she really wanted was a full-fledged autobiography, but Michael would not agree to anything of that nature. He wanted no private details about his life in his book.

A FRUSTRATING RELATIONSHIP

◇◇◇◇◇◇◇◇◇◇◇◇◇◇

Even though there was really no consensus as to the kind of book Michael Jackson would ultimately deliver, Doubleday offered him a $300,000 advance—not much considering his wealth, but generous in the publishing business. Doubleday then approved a cowriter for him, Robert Hilburn from the *Los Angeles Times*. It was a good first step and, everyone figured, the details about content could be worked out later. Even though there was no outline or any kind of real plan, Jackie was still thrilled. When Michael called while she was in the middle of yoga with her teacher, Tillie Mia, she put her hand over the phone and whispered to Tillie, "Pick up the extension for a surprise." She wanted her to get a kick out of hearing Michael's voice on the line.

After about a year, Robert Hilburn turned in a first draft, which was only about eighty pages. Now Jackie was disappointed. The book was mostly about celebrities Michael admired, with a few personal anecdotes. The pictures were of him accepting various awards, along with some family shots. There was no way it could be published, Jackie said. She then went to Los Angeles for the first of a number of contentious meetings with Michael as she tried to fashion a true autobiography out of his thin version of his life. It would end up taking four years.

"A writer named Stephen Davis was brought in to replace Hilburn, and we all hoped for the best," said one person who worked closely with Jackie at the time. "But getting Michael to discuss subjects like his sexuality and plastic surgery was like pulling teeth. It just wasn't happening. By about year two, most of us at Doubleday were ready to give up, tell him to keep the advance, and write it off. But Jackie said no; she was determined to see it through. 'I'm not a quitter,' she said, 'and this will happen.' She had dealt with tougher people than this in politics, and she wasn't going to let Michael Jackson get the best of her."

The problem Jackie faced with Michael was that questions she wanted answered about his private life were all questions he hadn't yet asked of himself. He was still in his midtwenties and not at all self-aware.

As she got to know Michael, Jackie had more questions. She couldn't figure out his sexual orientation, didn't understand his eccentric lifestyle, and was clueless as to what motivated him to do what he'd done so success-fully in his career. Every time she asked him a serious question about his life, he answered it as if it were the first time he'd ever given it any thought. "He doesn't really know himself," Jackie told Maurice in the company of friends, "so how can any of us ever hope to know him?" When Maurice said, "Maybe you can bring it out of him," Jackie responded, saying, "Not if he doesn't know what it is."

Whenever he'd open up about something revealing, she'd suggest us-ing it in the book, and he'd say no, it was too personal. It was frustrating and a complete waste of time. It was also ironic. This most famous of women, notoriously private, wanted him to reveal details about his life she'd never reveal about her own. Soon, Shaye Areheart would start dealing with him exclusively.

By about the third year, Michael had lost all interest in the book. Ca-pricious in nature, he moved on, his recordings and tours now more press-ing than his memoir. Despite his lack of attention, a manuscript—largely written by Davis and partly by Areheart—was completed. When Davis submitted it, he was sure it would be rejected. He couldn't believe it when Doubleday decided to move forward with it.

FALLING OUT WITH MICHAEL

B efore publication of Michael's book, which was to be called *Moonwalk,* Jackie balked at writing an introduction to it. Michael telephoned her and threatened to prevent the book's publication if she didn't acquiesce. "I was upset," he recalled in 2000, "because the very first time we met, she said she'd write an introduction. She promised. Then she said no. But a person's word is a person's word."

Reluctantly, Jackie complied—with three banal paragraphs, 115 words, to be exact. It didn't even sound as if she'd written it. Anyone who'd ever read the hundreds of passionate letters she'd written over the years would be hard-pressed to imagine her starting the introduction of an important book about Michael with the words: "What can one say about Michael Jackson?"

Maybe Jackie's apparent lack of enthusiasm made Michael insecure, or maybe he just got cold feet, but shortly before the book was to go to press, he wanted it canceled. John Branca, his longtime attorney, recalled, "He told me to call Doubleday and get him out of it. I said, 'Mike, it's too late and, my God, after four years?' But he was determined. So, I called Shaye Areheart and said, 'Michael wants out.' There was a long pause until she finally said, 'Oh shit!'"

Shaye later called Michael's change of mind "a crisis of faith."

"I just felt it was a bad idea," Michael recalled. "I felt really . . . exposed, I guess. The book was supposed to come out in a week. I was in New York, and Shaye and others at Doubleday met with me at my hotel, but not Jackie. I wished she'd come. Finally, I said, 'Fine, it can come out,' but I wasn't happy about it. I didn't need this. I already had a career. Why did I need this? I only did it for Jackie, and she'd checked out."

Michael was right; in a sense, Jackie *had* checked out. While she did her best to balance her work responsibilities with her personal life, it was difficult. There seemed to always be issues relating to her mother's deteriorating health and controversial marriage. Jackie often seemed anxious and panicked. She was sometimes uncharacteristically testy. While her colleagues suspected problems at home, they knew she was very private and would never ask questions of her.

Moonwalk was published in February 1988 to great fanfare, decent enough reviews, and, eventually, the distinction of being number one on the *New York Times* bestseller list.

Despite any inadequacies, *Moonwalk* still satisfied Michael's audience, giving his fans enough of what they needed. He'd never revealed anything at all in the past, so even the bits that saw light in *Moonwalk*—true and genuinely upsetting stories about his abusive father, fascinating insights into his process as an artist, maybe a fib or two about how little plastic surgery he'd had—intrigued his audience. But it's not what one might hope for if one really wants to understand the true nature of Michael Jackson.

Moonwalk did turn a good profit for Doubleday. As is the custom in publishing, the company intended to release a paperback edition a year after the hardcover. However, Michael refused to allow it. "By that time, I had really had it with the whole thing," he recalled. "For me, it was like . . . a record comes out and it's a success, right? Do you then put it out again a year later? No. That makes no sense. You get one shot. Or a movie comes out, and it's a success or it's a flop. It then doesn't come out again a year later. So, for me, there was no way I wanted the book to come out again. No way."

Jackie was dispatched to try to convince Michael to change his mind. There was a paperback provision in his contract, she reminded him; therefore, Doubleday had every right to publish one. Michael said that if the company went forward with it, he would sue. "I might lose, but I think you would lose more," he said. That sounded like a threat, and Jackie didn't like it. "I dug in. She dug in. Then we stopped talking. I'd call, but she'd never call me back. That was sort of it for us."

No paperback edition of *Moonwalk* was ever released, at least not while Michael was alive. After his death in 2009, a new edition was issued.

Another book by Michael was commissioned in 1992, *Dancing the*

Dream: Poems and Reflections—which was more like the kind of book he originally had in mind. Jackie wanted nothing to do with it, though; it was totally
shepherded by Shaye Areheart.

Despite its commercial success, Jackie viewed *Moonwalk* as a disappointment. She blamed herself, not Michael. She knew she'd never been the
most revealing of celebrities and felt she should've better understood how
challenging it would be to get him to open up.

"It could've been so much more," she told one of her colleagues at Doubleday. In the end, she decided, maybe it was just premature. "We were thirty
years too early," she said. "No one should write their story before they're
sixty. You have to live it first. Then, write it. And even then," she hastened
to add, "maybe not."

JANET'S DIAGNOSIS

◇◇◇◇◇◇◇◇◇◇◇◇◇◇

In January of 1983, Dr. Dennis Selkoe from the Harvard Medical School Center for Neurologic Diseases at Brigham and Women's Hospital in Boston was conclusive in his diagnosis of Janet Auchincloss's condition: she was definitely suffering from the onset of Alzheimer's.

Recently, Janet had been asking her chef Jonathan Tapper what was wrong with her. Though he tried to tell her she was fine and unchanged, she knew better and feared Alzheimer's. Jackie, too, had somehow always known in her heart that her mother had the disease, despite the lack of an official diagnosis.

"It was an early onset," recalled Dr. Selkoe in 2022, "and at that stage, patients are often able to continue with their lives, as was the case with Mrs. Auchincloss. I thought she was lovely, and I felt she would have some time to go before it would be difficult for her. The family, though, I think maybe looked back to review some of the decisions that had been made of late and wondered if she was truly capable of making them."

Now, more than ever, Jackie was sure Janet hadn't been in her right mind when she'd married Bingham Morris. She couldn't help but be upset with Maurice, who was still not living at 1040 Fifth Avenue, for not siding with her in that debate. She knew she needed to get past her anger, however, and focus on what would now be best for her mother. The first thing she did was align herself with the Alzheimer's Disease and Related Disorders Association by giving it a quarter million dollars for research, a donation she'd give annually for the rest of her life. She had several private meetings with one of the association's vice presidents, Yasmin Aga Khan, whose mother, Rita Hayworth, also suffered from the disease. She told Jackie that her mother had taken up painting as therapy and that she'd gotten very good at it. It was still possible to have a life, she said, even when struggling with the disease. Jackie also established a million-dollar trust fund for Janet, which would take care of medical expenses not covered by insurance.

"Mrs. Auchincloss was well enough to go with Jamie to China in the spring to visit her daughter Janet Jr., Lewis, and their three children, Lewis, Andrew, and Alexandra," recalled Janet's chef Michael Dupree. "She could still pull herself together and be the same graceful, elegant lady we all knew. It wasn't as if she changed overnight. There were moments when you wouldn't at all know she was sick."

Janet Jr. had made a satisfying life for herself in Hong Kong, having founded the first overseas chapter of the League of Women Voters in 1979. Lewis was managing director of a venture capital firm and making a very good living. The family lived in an exclusive neighborhood on Victoria Peak; Janet and Jamie were both impressed. "She had finally found happiness," recalled Jamie, "and none of it had anything to do with her famous family or, in particular, her famous sisters. Mummy and I had an enjoyable time. She was so happy seeing Ja-Je and meeting Alexandra, who was a newborn."

"I think Janet's illness affected every member of the family in a different way," said Joyce Faria Brennan, who had lived on the property with her parents, Mannie and Louise, since 1968. "Yusha and Jamie clung more tightly to her as if wanting to savor every minute. Lee distanced herself, saying it was too painful. Jackie took her mother's illness as an opportunity to be closer to her, every moment now more important. As little girls, my sister, Linda, and I loved Mrs. Auchincloss and didn't want her to be sick. I'm not sure we knew exactly what was going on, only that it wasn't good. But what I saw during her older years was a gracious, elegant, and generous woman."

Jack Warnecke called Jackie soon after the diagnosis when he heard about it from a mutual friend. The two had never lost touch and remained close. Sadly, Jack's mother also had Alzheimer's.

When Jack came to New York, Jackie showed him a gold ring Maurice had given her, glistening with emeralds and diamonds and inscribed with the word "Jacks." That was, of course, the nickname Jackie had been given her by her father. She wore it along with the wedding band she'd gotten from Jack Kennedy, so it obviously had special significance even given the present status of their relationship.

Jackie and Jack had dinner one night at 1040 with Ethel Kennedy and Pat Kennedy Lawford. In talking about their mothers, Jackie told a story about her own. During the war, she recalled, trains were often sold out weeks in advance because of pressing military needs. People would stand in line all night at railroad ticket offices, hoping to fill the seats of customers who wouldn't make the trip. However, Janet could always get three tickets from her well-connected father, "and taking a train in the 1940s was such a luxury experience," she recalled, "it was really a big treat." She said she, Lee, and Janet would dress formally for the train ride to Washington, D.C. Sitting on the soft leather divan in the solarium of the Pullman observation car at the end of the train, they'd chatter away for the entire two and a half hours. The windows there were circular, so they could see all around them as they chugged along. Sometimes, they'd go into the coffee shop car and have milkshakes—chocolate for her, strawberry for Lee, and vanilla for Janet. One time, she remembered, Janet paid for a drawing room with its own foam-rubber mattress just so her girls could nap on their return to New York after a long day.

"She recalled a popular advertisement that ran in newspapers and magazines at the time," Jack recalled, "which proclaimed, 'Railroading Is People.' She said, 'In that life, I was just a girl on a train taking a carefree and wonderful journey to Washington with my mother and sister.' She said, 'Who ever would have imagined I'd one day live there as First Lady. And, now,' she concluded, 'I look at Mummy and the way she is today, and I'm so glad I have those memories. I'm just so glad.'"

"TRYING TO CONTROL THE
UNCONTROLLABLE . . ."

◇◇◇◇◇◇◇◇◇◇◇◇◇◇

I n the spring of 1984, Jackie and Maurice reconciled, and he moved back
into 1040. Since they never discussed it with outsiders, whatever agreement they came to is unknown. However, they seemed happy. Feeling that
Jackie needed a break from the stress of her life, he planned a trip for them
to Hong Kong to visit her half sister Janet Jr., Lewis, and the children. They
were proud of the fact that they were able to sneak out of the country, without any fanfare, on Maurice's private jet.

"Janet really liked Maurice when she met him in New York," recalled
Janet Jr.'s Hong Kong friend Mary Wells Forman. "She always said all she
wanted was for her sister to find happiness. She was worried that she'd never
resume her life because of Dallas. I would say, 'But that was so long ago,
Janet,' and she'd say, 'You don't understand. It's always under the surface for
all of us, but especially for Jackie. You don't get over having your husband's
brains blasted out onto your lap. You just don't.' When she met Maurice,
she told me she felt for the first time that Jackie might be okay. 'He's a real
caretaker,' she said, 'and it's usually been the other way around in her relationships.'"

"It was a great trip," Lewis's brother Winthrop Rutherfurd recalled.
"Everyone was so happy, and there was real love in the air. Yes, you knew of
Janet Auchincloss's illness, but you also knew that life had to go on and you
had to go on, too. So, it was a happy time."

There was one problem, however. Janet Jr. confided in Jackie that she'd
been experiencing severe back pain. "She'd been to several chiropractors
and was told there was no solution," recalled Mary Luango, another

of Janet's friends from Hong Kong. "They decided it was sciatica. Jackie thought the pain was too high to be sciatica. Apparently, she'd suffered from it, too, so she knew it well. It sounded more like an upper spinal issue to her. She urged Janet to go back to New York with her to see a specialist."

At the end of the week, the Rutherfurds left their kids with Mary Wells Forman again and boarded Maurice's private plane headed back to the States. When they got to America, Janet Jr. suddenly decided she didn't want to see the specialist, after all. She said she had a premonition he'd give her bad news. In fact, she said she now didn't even want to be in New York; she asked that she and Jackie go to Hammersmith and spend a week there with their mother. She seemed fearful and, though Jackie felt it wasn't warranted, she wanted to calm her and ease her mind. Therefore, she took the week off from Doubleday and went with her and Lewis to Newport. It was then that Janet Jr. met Bingham Morris for the first time. They didn't hit it off. Jackie told her they'd done everything they could think of to get rid of him, but to no avail.

At this same time, in April of 1984, Jackie got news that Ethel's son David died of a drug overdose. David had been troubled for years. She and Janet Jr. took a trip to Hickory Hill in Virginia for the services. "I need to be there for Ethel just as she's always been for me," Jackie said.

"From what her husband later told me, on the flight back to Newport after the funeral, Janet Jr.'s back pain became much worse," recalled Mary Luango. "By this time, Jackie had apparently done her research and didn't like what she'd learned. That kind of pain can be the result of things having nothing to do with the spinal cord. She insisted Janet Jr. see a doctor in Manhattan. Therefore, after one night at Hammersmith, Jackie took Janet to New York for the appointment while Lewis stayed in Newport."

Two days later, while Janet Jr. was at 1040, she got a terrible diagnosis on the telephone: lung cancer.

Jackie called Mary Wells Forman in Hong Kong to give her the news. "My God, I was shocked," she exclaimed. "I asked, 'But how can that be? Janet's never smoked.' I remember Jackie's response. 'When I was in the White House with Jack,' she said, 'the one thing I learned is that asking why things happen is a fool's folly. A better question is: What can I now do about it?' She said they'd all come together as a family and figure it out.

"They decided to keep the news from their mother for as long as they could. Jackie told me she'd heard that a traumatic event in the life of a person suffering from Alzheimer's can make it worse. She told me, 'There are a lot of balls in the air right now, and I just want to be sure to catch them all.'"

After a couple of weeks, the family felt they couldn't keep the news from Janet. She didn't take it well. She said she wished it was she who was so ill, not her daughter. "We immediately thought it had been a bad idea to tell Mummy," said Jamie Auchincloss. "These decisions, what to tell someone who has Alzheimer's and what to keep from them, are tricky. You try to do the right thing, but you seldom do. She was already getting worse, and the timing for this kind of news was not good."

Typical of the way she would take control at difficult times, Jackie sprang into action and arranged for Mary Wells Forman to put her nephews and niece on Maurice's private jet and have them flown to Newport to be with their father. She then consulted with Janet Jr.'s doctor about her treatment.

Janet Jr. told Jackie she wanted to know as little about her cancer and its treatment as possible. She felt the more knowledge she had, the more difficult it would be for her to focus on her recovery because of fear. Therefore, Jackie kept many details from her, including the fact that doctors told her the disease was terminal. "She and Lewis made the decision not to tell Janet Jr.," said Mary Wells Forman. "They took all of that on themselves. All of this, combined with her mother's illness and marriage—it had to be a lot to handle. I once said to Jackie, 'What a struggle this is for you.' She said she didn't look at it that way. 'I don't battle my way through life anymore,' she told me. 'I've done that. But that's not how I choose to live now. It doesn't work. Now I try to stay calm, steady, and centered.' Then, chuckling, she added, 'Oh, and I also drink.'"

Janet's treatment began in the summer of 1984 at the Dana-Farber Cancer Institute in Boston. For the next eight weeks, Janet underwent donated blood transfusions three days a week in an experimental therapy designed to battle the cancer with Jackie's platelets. That, along with chemotherapy, was Janet's only hope.

As doctors expected, Janet lingered for months, never gaining ground, always losing it. Jackie tried to stay optimistic and cheery until, finally, Janet could take it no more. She had begun to come to terms with the inevitable, especially after learning that the cancer had spread to her brain and pancreas. She wanted her sister to also come to terms with it. "It started to upset her to see Jackie trying, trying, *trying* to take care of things and stay in control, as was her way," said Mary Wells Forman. "Finally—and Jackie told me this herself—Janet said to her, 'You've got to let me be scared, Jackie. Can you do that for me?' That was hard. Jackie told me, 'I knew then that I had to let go of any and all hope. I also knew that doing so would be a kind of freedom for both of us. Trying to control this thing that can never be controlled was just so exhausting. So, yes, we let go. We just let it all go.'"

Janet Jennings Rutherfurd died on March 13, 1985, at just thirty-nine. Jackie, Lewis, his brother Winthrop, and Winthrop's wife, Mary, were all at her bedside.

Jamie was with his mother at the Castle when Jackie called to give him the news. "She's gone, Jamie," she said. "Our Ja-Je is gone."

"CROWDS TO DO HER HOMAGE CAME"

◇◇◇◇◇◇◇◇◇◇◇◇

The funeral took place at Trinity Church in Newport on March 19. There was a brief dustup at the Castle when Jackie told Bingham Morris he wasn't invited. "You don't get to decide that," he told her. She said she most certainly did get to decide because "she was my sister, and the decision is made." Seeing that her mother, who was already upset, was becoming even more emotional, Jackie said, "See what you're doing to her?" which he responded to by saying, "*You're* doing it to her, not me."

Finally, Yusha stepped in and asked Bingham to stay home rather than cause his wife more distress. "I am not leaving her side for one second," Bingham said. "She is my *wife,* Yusha. When will you understand that?" Eventually, Yusha was able to convince him not to go, but Bingham was very unhappy about it.

Janet sat with Jackie, Jamie, and Yusha at the service. Lee didn't attend. Caroline was also there with Ed Schlossberg, whom she was dating. It was the first time Jamie would meet the man his niece would eventually marry. John, of course, was also present.

Jackie gave a moving eulogy. After reading a poem Janet Jr. had written, she read a poem she wrote on the occasion of Janet's birth, to the tempo of "The Midnight Ride of Paul Revere."

In part:

Listen my children and you shall hear
of a thing that delighted the hemisphere.
It was nineteen hundred and forty-five when Janet Jennings became alive.

She made all the headlines far and near and became Baby of the
    Year!
Crowds to do her homage came, bringing priceless gifts and rare.
The flower shops all had a boom and Western Union tore its hair.

It ended with the humorous lines:

You'll live a rich, full life, all right
The oppressed you'll always free 'em
and when dead you'll have a statute in Tussaud's Wax Museum.

Jackie noted that she always called Janet "my sister, because Mummy
told us long ago that Auchinclosses don't do anything by halves. She was my
sister," Jackie said, "just as Jamie and Yusha are my brothers."

She spoke about the blood transfusion treatments at Dana-Farber and
said that, during the final one, Janet Jr. told her how much she'd admired her
and wanted to be like her. "That was so funny to me," Jackie said, "because
I felt exactly the same way about her." She added, "The fact that we had the
same blood type made all the sense in the world."

Jackie closed by saying, "Janet was the sweetest sister a girl could ever
have. Knowing her was like having a cardinal in your garden. She was bright
and lovely and incredibly alive. My gosh, how we'll miss her. It won't be the
same without her, but I have a feeling she's with us right now, with me and
Mummy and Jamie and Lee. In fact, she'll always be right here, very close."

WHAT MUMMY WANTS

◇◇◇◇◇◇◇◇◇◇◇◇◇

Janet's chef Michael Dupree was also a registered nurse who'd worked with Alzheimer's patients. He feared Janet Jr.'s death would precipitate a real setback for her mother. Unfortunately, he was right. Jackie noticed it immediately in the Deck Room at the reception after the service. The new owners had allowed it to be used for this sad occasion.

There were moments Janet seemed not to know where she was as she looked around this room where she'd spent so many good years. As mourners approached, she whispered to Jackie to identify them for her. She also kept asking for Bingham Morris, which aggravated Jackie, though she tried not to show it. Bingham was back at the Castle feeling unwelcome. "By this time, we were all worn down," Jamie Auchincloss recalled. "My sister's death, my mother's illness and marriage . . . Jackie had always been a woman who tried to exert control over things, the way she had when Jack died and she orchestrated the funeral. But all of this was too much. By the time Janet Jr. died, I think she felt like she was fighting a losing battle."

A week after the funeral, when Jackie saw her mother again, Janet seemed even worse. One of the servants told her Janet had awakened that morning and asked her to call the White House, saying she needed to "have a word with my daughter." As Jackie sat in the kitchen and carefully doled out her medications, Janet didn't remember that Janet Jr. had passed. "Are Ja-Je and Lewis coming again this summer?" she asked.

"Each time Jackie had to tell her mother that Janet Jr. was gone, it was as if she were hearing it for the first time," said Joyce Faria Brennan. "She would then again be filled with shock and grief—until she forgot about it.

From my understanding, Jackie spoke to Janet's doctors and was told it was best not to contradict her, to just let her believe what she wanted to believe. That had to have been hard to accept. It must have felt as if they were just giving in to the disease. But they agreed it was the thing to do, to have Mrs. Auchincloss continue to believe her daughter was alive and well in Hong Kong."

When her family just went along with her delusions to keep her calm, Janet seemed much better and was often lucid, her personality intact as if nothing was wrong. She and Jackie would take long walks and have detailed conversations. In those moments, it felt like things were better. Jackie would paint her mother's nails, put lotion on her hands, comb her hair, and make her feel like her old, impeccably maintained self.

In her lucid moments, Janet was well aware of the stress and anxiety her children were feeling as a result of her illness. One day, she gathered them together, including Lee, to give them a message. She fought back tears as she spoke. "I won't let you give everything up just to care for me. That's not what I want."

Janet said that not only did she want to maintain the fierce independence she'd known her entire life, Janet wanted her children—she always thought of Yusha as her son—to have lives that would be unencumbered by them having to care for her. "I'm sick and I know it," she said, "but today, on this one day, I am fine. Please don't treat me as if I'm not."

Jackie couldn't help but marvel at her mother's courage in the face of her disease and her determination to see her loved ones go on with their lives despite it. She said she'd always believed that if her mother ever fell victim to a debilitating disease like Alzheimer's, she'd become very needy and maybe even try to guilt her loved ones into taking care of her, abandoning their own lives to do so. That turned out not to be the case. It may have reminded her of something Artemis Garoufalidis used to tell her all the time: "Don't be surprised when people surprise you, or you'll spend most of your time with your mouth wide open."

LILLY

◇◇◇◇◇◇◇◇◇◇◇◇◇

Given the death of her beloved half sister and the ups and downs of her mother's condition, by the time Jackie turned fifty-six in July of 1985, she'd begun to complain of feeling drained or, as she put it one day while talking to Adora Rule's daughter, Janine, "I would have handled all of this so much better in my thirties, but now, with sixty in the offing, I sometimes just feel like staying in bed." She had never been one to sleep that well, anyway, and as she got older, her insomnia became even more pronounced. She still had nightmares about Dallas. They were infrequent, but when they happened, it would sometimes take hours for her to recover. She was still in therapy, but no longer with Marianne Kris. However, she was very much against taking pills, as she once had. She tried to live a cleaner lifestyle with yoga, jogging, and the consumption of healthy foods.

Jackie had fallen into a nice rhythm with Maurice and their friends, with evenings out on the town at the opera or the ballet. On weekends, they'd have company for home-cooked dinners prepared by Marta Sgubin—soft-shell crabs with red new potatoes, perhaps, or a whole poached salmon along with Marta's cantaloupe sorbet for dessert, or maybe eggplant fritters, which Jackie loved—except for the fact that they were so fattening. "Keep it simple," she would always tell Marta, "but delicious and from scratch."

Things took a bit of a dramatic turn in the fall of 1985. Jackie was in a meeting at Doubleday when she was told that Maurice's doctor was on the line for her. A little alarmed, she immediately took the call and learned that Maurice had been rushed to Lenox Hill Hospital with a possible heart attack.

Jackie rushed out of her office with a trusted colleague and hailed a cab. When they got to the hospital on the Upper East Side, they learned that Maurice's heart attack had been mild. It would be treated with an angioplasty procedure, which, at the time, was a relatively new practice. He would be in the hospital for three days, and then there would be a bit of a longer recovery at home. That meant a business trip he planned to Botswana would have to be delayed. He often went to Africa for meetings relating to his diamond business.

As Jackie and her friend waited in a secluded area, a petite woman appeared. Clearly panicked, she rushed over to Jackie. "Is he all right?" she asked. Jackie assured her that Maurice would be fine. Seeing how distraught she was, she offered her a seat next to her. Jackie's friend from work then went to fetch her a glass of water. As she was leaving, she heard Jackie say, "I'm Jackie," offer her hand, and then ask, "And you are?" When she returned with the water, Jackie took the cup and handed it to the woman at her side and said, "Say hello to Lilly Tempelsman, Maurice's wife."

"She was a pleasant-looking woman with short gray hair . . . plain, and I don't mean that in a disparaging way," said Jackie's colleague, "just that, in comparison to Jacqueline Onassis, it was difficult to resist marveling at how Maurice had gone from one to the other."

Jackie and Lilly spoke quietly for about twenty minutes, mostly about the White House state dinner Lilly had attended with Maurice back in 1961. "Do you miss those days?" Lilly asked.

"I do," Jackie said, "but there were also sad times."

Lilly nodded. "Well, as they say," she observed, "sadness flies away on the wings of time."

Jackie was taken aback. "That's so lovely," she said. "Who said that?"

Lilly shrugged. "Maurice always said it, but who knows where he got it from?" There was then awkward silence until a woman in her thirties appeared. "This is my daughter, Rena," Lilly said. "Rena, you know Jackie, don't you?"

Rena stared down at Jackie in her seat. "Yes. We know each other," she said. "Nice to see you again," she added as she shook Jackie's hand without making eye contact. She then curtly said, "I want to see Poppa." Lilly glanced at Jackie.

"Yes, please go back and see him," Jackie offered. "I can later."

Lilly thanked her, said she would tell Maurice she was waiting, and then walked off with her daughter. As they left, Rena turned and glanced at Jackie over her shoulder, giving her a hard look.

Jackie took a deep breath and exhaled loudly. "That was so awkward," she whispered to her friend.

Jackie's friend asked if she'd ever met Lilly before, and Jackie said just that one time twenty-five years ago at the White House. She didn't recognize her. She also joked that "poor Maurice" would suffer another heart attack if he heard they were talking.

Jackie and her Doubleday colleague then passed the time by chatting about Jackie's relationship. When her friend asked if Jackie would like Maurice to divorce Lilly and marry her, Jackie froze up. The colleague was taken by surprise. They'd been so familiar about Maurice up until this point.

"But I just thought . . ." she began.

"No," Jackie said firmly. "I'd prefer that we talk about something else."

CAROLINE

✧✧✧✧✧✧✧✧✧✧✧✧✧

She grew up under the glare of public scrutiny just by virtue of her iconic parents, a father who had been the thirty-fifth president of the United States and a mother who was a former First Lady and, arguably, one of the world's most famous women. The press had dubbed Caroline Kennedy "America's daughter" because of her childhood in the White House from the tender ages of three to six. Often at her parents' side for photo opportunities, she was adorable and precocious, a happy little girl.

Life changed in November of 1963 when Caroline's beloved father was murdered. While historical moments like three-year-old John-John saluting his father's casket during the funeral would always be remembered by all who witnessed them even from afar, for Caroline, who was actually present, they'd remain painful and ever present.

Jackie agonized over Caroline after her father's death because, unlike John, she had such strong memories of him. Jackie had put her in therapy as soon as they got to New York from Washington. "Jackie was torn between showing her daughter her grief so that she'd learn to deal with her own and hiding it from her so as not to further upset her," said Joan Braden. "In the end, she chose the latter, which made Caroline feel she, too, should hide her pain. Doing that proved to be yet another burden for her."

Jackie stopped sending Caroline to a therapist when she was about twelve because she worried that constantly dwelling on sadness might be keeping her from letting go of her grief. As a teenager, though, Caroline never stopped devoting herself to her father, always making sure his photographs had prominent places in her bedroom, always eager to learn more about his legacy.

When the family moved to New York in 1964 and Caroline began attending the Brearley School and then the Convent of the Sacred Heart, Jackie was constantly in touch with Caroline's teachers to gauge her progress and, also, to make sure she didn't receive preferential treatment. While Jackie wasn't always available to her children because of the chaotic nature of her own life, she did at least try, even if, by her own admission, she wasn't always successful at it. She'd always had a reputation of having been the perfect mother. She wasn't. That, however, was between her and her children, and they never publicly criticized her.

"Jackie always wanted to uphold the Kennedy image and wanted both her kids to never desecrate the Kennedy name," said Jamie Auchincloss. "'You are Kennedys,' she used to tell them, 'and must always act like Kennedys, and you must do your father and his brothers proud.' She often had JFK's acolytes, such as Arthur Schlesinger and Pierre Salinger, come to 1040 to talk to them about their father, especially as lurid tales of his relationships with other women like Judith Exner began to be more widely reported in the 1970s."

Though Jackie continued to work out her anger and confusion about Jack's infidelity in therapy, she couldn't help but worry that her children would think less of him if they knew the extent of it. For the most part, Caroline and John disregarded stories about their father that painted him in a negative light. They knew their mother was often mischaracterized by the press and assumed this was also the case with their father.

Some in her life presumed that Jackie didn't want to have the same contentious relationship with Caroline that she had with her own mother. However, there were facets of Janet's parenting that Jackie appreciated and wished to mirror. Janet was always on her side even when she disagreed with her. She was her biggest fan. She always knew, for instance, that Jackie would be a great First Lady. She usually encouraged her in her darkest moments. She wanted the best for her. While Janet was often critical and judgmental, Jackie still knew she was loved.

As supportive as Jackie tried to be, Caroline often said she felt she could never measure up to her standards, or what she called "the Jackie Kennedy yardstick." Jackie tried not to be overly critical of Caroline, but it was sometimes difficult. She disapproved whenever Caroline gained weight, for instance, just as Janet had with her, Lee, and Janet Jr. This picking on her about her diet caused a teenage Caroline to have self-esteem issues that were more apparent to her grandmothers than they were to Jackie.

When Caroline was about fifteen, Rose Kennedy called Janet to tell her she felt Jackie was being too judgmental of her daughter. Janet took umbrage. "Jacqueline knows how to raise her own daughter," she said, "thank you very much." Rose realized she'd gone too far and backed off.

But Janet wasn't easy, either, where Caroline was concerned. If she showed up at Hammersmith with tears or holes in her jeans, for instance, Janet viewed it as a huge sign of disrespect and would make her go to her room and change. She didn't like it, though, when Jackie was critical of Caroline's weight. That had begun when Jackie married Onassis. He would stare with a face of absolute revulsion at his daughter, Christina, as she ate. He thought nothing of calling her a "fat pig." After Jackie married him, she started harping at Caroline, too, about her eating habits. When Caroline would lash out in protest, Jackie was known to slap her in the family tradition—twice, palm of the hand followed swiftly by the back of the same hand.

It was one thing for Janet to have slapped Jackie, quite another, it would seem, for her to witness Jackie doing the same to her granddaughter. She found it very upsetting and insisted Jackie stop. Jackie knew she was right and stopped when Caroline was about sixteen.

ED SCHLOSSBERG

By the beginning of 1986, Caroline Kennedy was twenty-eight years old and had grown into an attractive, intelligent young woman. She was presently attending Columbia Law School, from which she would graduate. As an adult, she had a greater appreciation for all Jackie had gone through in her life. Ten years earlier when Tom Guinzburg was at 1040 Fifth Avenue and told her Jackie was going to work for Viking, Caroline rolled her eyes and said, "What's she going to do there?" Like a lot of teenagers, she didn't give her mother credit for much. By the time she was in her late twenties, though, she appreciated Jackie's struggles. With that appreciation came admiration, especially for what Jackie had experienced during and after the assassination. "Her courage, that's what I see," Caroline said in 1985 to *Good Housekeeping*. "How brave, how courageous she was and is. She's a role model for me and for so many young people."

"By the time Caroline's beau Ed Schlossberg came into the picture—they met while she was working as a research assistant at the Metropolitan Museum of Art—she and her mother were on the same page about most things," said Gustavo Paredes, the only son of Providencia Paredes, Jackie's former White House assistant. He grew up close to Caroline and John. "They wanted the best for each other. Jackie wanted her to marry for love, none of that 'money matters' stuff that had been handed down to her. I'm not sure she thought Ed was right for her, though. Not right away."

Edwin Arthur Schlossberg was born on July 19, 1945. He was twelve years older than Caroline, which was the same age difference between her parents. From an Orthodox Jewish family, he was raised by his parents,

Alfred and Celia Mae Schlossberg, on New York's Upper East Side. His father had his own textile manufacturing firm in New York; the family was well off. Ed attended all the best schools, as did his older sister, Maryann. He received his doctorate in science and literature from Columbia in 1971. Talented, he was an artist who painted in watercolors and used aluminum and plexiglass. He was also an author, a poet, and an architect. He shied away from the limelight, never wanting attention for himself, especially when he began dating Caroline. He quickly became protective of her.

It took time for the Schlossbergs and Kennedys to figure each other out. Ed's mother, known as just "Mae," was an outgoing, expressive person who wanted right away to get to know Caroline and Jackie. It took her a while to understand that neither would be open to long, intimate conversations. Mae—who was twenty years older than Jackie—was off to a shaky start with her when, during their first luncheon, she broached the subject of the assassination. She wanted to console Jackie about it, not that Jackie would ever discuss something so personal with her.

Jackie also didn't know what to make of Ed, who, unlike his mother, was so quiet and introverted it was impossible for her to draw him out. Lisa McClintock, who worked with Caroline at the Met, recalled having dinner with Caroline, Ed, Jackie, and John Jr. early in the courtship. "Jackie was a little distant, not eager to let this new person into the circle. She spent a lot of time studying poor Ed as if he were a museum piece. When he went to the restroom, Caroline asked, 'So, Mother, what do you think of him?' Jackie carefully said, 'Well, dear, he's . . . plausible.'" It's worth noting that this was Janet's exact response twenty years earlier when Jackie asked for her thoughts about John Warnecke.

Jackie spent a few months unclear about what it was Ed did for a living. "He could work for the CIA, for all I know," she said. Actually, he was a successful architect by the time he and Caroline started dating, and he'd remain one for many decades. He was an inward-looking person one really had to work to get to know. Jackie just found him dull and pedantic. "Between the overly familiar mother and the extremely guarded son, she didn't know how to be when she was around them," said Gustavo Paredes. "She got along better with Ed's father, Alfred, who was a mix of his wife's and son's personalities."

Jackie fretted that Caroline would have a boring life with Ed Schlossberg. She'd had such incredible, eventful relationships; she wanted the same for Caroline. Janet was still aware enough to point out to Jackie that she had romanticized her own marriages. "She's not you," Janet told her. "She will not have your life just as you didn't have mine."

Despite her mother's warning, Jackie decided to put her foot down and forbid the marriage. "She said, 'No, Caroline, I'm sorry, I won't allow it,'" said one of her relatives. "She talked about how much she wanted Caroline to experience the world, to travel, to have a wonderful life. With Ed, Jackie predicted Caroline would end up living in a New York suburb and raising a big brood of kids. That would be the end of any hope she'd ever have of living an adventurous life. It's not what she wanted for her. 'Live in Greece,' she told her. 'Live in Paris. Live your life in an exciting way.' It became a big family drama, and, as I heard it, it came between Jackie and Maurice because he didn't agree with her. He was afraid she'd lose Caroline altogether if she took such a position."

Finally, Ed sat down with Jackie and leveled with her, saying, "I love your daughter. She loves me. We can either just run off and elope or you can have the wedding you've always wanted for her. But I'm not going away." He was direct with her, and, apparently, Jackie admired him for it.

"People are scared to death of me," she said, "but not Ed, and I like that." She then reportedly told Caroline, "I love you, I trust you, and I want you to be happy," and that was the end of any disagreement about the marriage.

Caroline and Ed married on July 19, 1986, Ed's forty-first birthday, in Hyannis Port. The wedding was at Our Lady of Victory in Centerville, near the Kennedy compound. Ted Kennedy gave Caroline away; John was Ed's best man. Jackie did what she could to keep it private, even going so far as to ask her hairstylist, Thomas Morrissey, to not speak to anyone about it. It was to no avail. The wedding was bound to be a magnet for press attention.

"I'm filling in for my brother Jack," Ted said in his toast. "First of all, to the mother of us all," Ted said, raising his glass to Rose, who would soon turn ninety-six. To Caroline and Ed, he then said, "We've all thought of Jack today, and how much he loved Caroline and how much he loved Jackie." Then, to Jackie, "that extraordinary woman, Jack's only love. He would have been so proud of you today."

Because Jackie refused to allow Bingham Morris to attend the wedding, it fell upon Yusha to accompany Janet. Hoping to avoid any problems, he told the Schlossbergs, "Caroline's grandmother has Alzheimer's. Don't pay any attention to anything she says." When Jackie learned he'd given out those instructions, she was upset. "Why would you embarrass Mummy like that?" she asked.

Janet had as many good days as bad, and this happened to be a good one. "Your uncle Hughdie would love this day," she told Jackie as guests gathered in front of the church. Jackie agreed. Her uncle Hughdie's presence would have made the day complete. "But, dear, don't forget," Janet said, "the life of the dead is placed in the memory of the living." Jackie looked at her with surprise. That's what Hugh had told her after Jack's assassination, quoting Cicero. It was always astonishing what came so easily to Janet, despite the mental acuity she'd lost.

"How could you possibly remember that, Mummy?" Jackie asked.

"How could I not?" was Janet's answer.

THE OUTSIDER

◇◇◇◇◇◇◇◇◇◇◇◇◇◇

At about the same time Jackie saw her daughter marry, she began another emotional journey with her mother. It started when, during one of her visits to the Castle, she discovered bruises on Janet's arms. Though Janet had no memory of how she'd gotten them, Jackie was certain Bingham Morris was responsible.

A confrontation Jackie had with Bingham turned out to be enlightening. According to a letter he later wrote about it, he denied to Jackie ever having been physically abusive to her mother. Janet was constantly tripping and falling, he explained, and she bruised easily because of blood thinners. Moreover, he surprised Jackie by explaining that the reason he'd married Janet was because she'd asked him to do so. She told him she feared she was losing her mind and said she didn't want to be a burden on Jackie. Anticipating the future, she predicted she'd need someone to care for her, and she knew how well he'd cared for his late wife, Mary. Mary had suffered from diabetes, had her legs amputated, and spent her final years in a wheelchair with Bingham at her side. Janet felt he'd be up for the task of taking care of her, too—that is, if he'd accept the burden. Only the two of them knew how difficult it had been during the time her disease progressed, he told Jackie according to his letter, "and that's between me and your mother," he said.

In closing, Bingham said he wished Jackie, Yusha, Jamie, and the rest of the family would help him care for Janet instead of opposing him every step along the way. "It's hard enough for an outsider such as myself," he wrote, "without all of you ganging up on me every single day. I beg you to give me the benefit of some doubt, and I assure you that you will not regret it."

Jackie didn't know what to think. Was Bingham being honest with her? Did he really love her mother? Maybe she should back off? All of it, especially his version of why they married, sent her into a tailspin. Meanwhile, her mother's denial of abuse and the fact that there were no witnesses to it made it much tougher for Jackie to do anything about it.

"If you knew Bouch, you knew these stories could never be true," said Ivy Rawlins, whose aunt was Mary Rawlins, Bingham's first wife. "Bouch was a caretaker. If he had any fault, it was his savior complex—he wanted to help, and that's why he married Janet Auchincloss."

"Though Jackie tried to force Bingham out, she couldn't do so it if Janet insisted he stay," recalled Ted Page, who was a nephew of Louise Page, who was married to Bingham's brother, John. "She threatened to press charges. 'Do you know what kind of headlines it'll generate if Jacqueline Onassis says you're beating up her mother?' she asked Bingham. 'If you don't want the whole country to hate you, get out.' Bingham agreed to leave until, as he put it, 'the dust settles around here.' Jackie told him, 'It'll never settle as long as you're in our lives.'"

Jackie and Dr. Dennis Selkoe decided it would be best if Bingham Morris wasn't allowed around Janet unsupervised. He would have to stay at his own home in Newport for the time being and visit her for a week once a month until they could figure out what was true of him and what was not.

In early 1987, the situation became even worse when Janet accused Bouch of sexual assault. "He does bad things to me," is how she put it. However, when Jackie questioned her further, she wasn't able to provide details. Thinking perhaps Janet was embarrassed in front of Maurice, she took her for a private walk. "Well?" Maurice asked Jackie when they returned. "Nothing," she said. "She won't discuss it."

"This is a delicate matter, but I think Dr. Selkoe will know how to address it," Jackie wrote to Yusha at the time. "We don't know what goes on in the bedroom, but Mummy has said 'that man wants to do bad things to me I don't like'—and she has moved into the guest room when he is there. Bouch is torturing Mummy and he cannot hide behind the rights of a husband. He has brought things to the point where all find ourselves trying to protect her from him."

Making matters even more complex, after Dr. Selkoe interviewed Janet and Bingham, he doubted her claim of sexual abuse.

"When Bouch met Janet, she was starved for love and affection," said

Ivy. "Her husband had been impotent for their entire marriage. Bouch, even at his age, was virile. On their honeymoon, Janet wouldn't make love. When they returned to the Castle, they started having sex. But a month later, she again wanted nothing to do with him. Every time he tried, she screamed out, 'Rape!'"

One night, Jackie and Yusha searched the Castle for Janet, and she was nowhere to be found. Jackie checked all the rooms and became more frantic. They called out for Bingham. He, too, was gone. Jackie became so upset, she was near tears.

The stepsiblings ran out of the house and walked quickly down a gravel sidewalk toward the beach, all the while calling out for Janet. Then they spotted her, walking along a pathway with her husband, his arm around her. As they ambled along, they spoke softly to one another. Janet put her head on Bouch's shoulder in a moment so tender anyone would've been moved by it. Watching it, how could Jackie and Yusha know what to think?

Coloring everything was Jackie's persistent trauma over Dallas, and it was Lee who recognized it.

In February of 1987, Lee went to Boston to confer with Dr. Selkoe herself. "I told Mrs. Radziwill that I saw no evidence of physical or sexual abuse," he recalled in 2022. "She agreed with me."

In a letter to Yusha (dated March 8, 1987), Lee wrote that they were all well aware of Jackie's "trauma" and that she was afraid her reaction to their mother's new marriage was linked to it, and she wrote that Dr. Selkoe agreed with her.

Indeed, after conferring with Dr. Selkoe, Lee was the only person to make the connection between what was happening now and what had happened in Jackie's past. In some ways, she knew her sister better than anyone else. "Jackie's suffering over Jack emerges whenever she's faced with anything traumatic," she wrote. She added that Jackie hadn't been able to save Jack and couldn't save Bobby, so now she felt "she must save Mummy."

In March 1987, Lee was invited to a family dinner at 1040 Fifth Avenue. Jackie and Maurice were hosting, and their guests included Yusha, Caroline, and John, accompanied by Caroline's husband, Ed, and John's girlfriend, the actress Daryl Hannah. Jamie wasn't invited. Jackie hadn't wanted to invite Lee either, but Janet insisted.

While Jackie had long ago accepted that Lee wasn't going to be helpful at Hammersmith, she couldn't get past the fact that she didn't attend Janet

Jr.'s funeral. Lee explained that her design business was failing, and she was losing her Park Avenue penthouse and being forced to move into a rental. Her finances were upside down, her life was a mess, and no one was willing to help. Therefore, she didn't have it in her to also have to deal with Janet Jr.'s death.

"But she was your sister," Jackie exclaimed. "Are you going to also skip my funeral if it falls at an inconvenient time?"

PRECIOUS MEMORIES

∞∞∞∞∞∞∞∞∞∞∞

While trying to sort out her feelings about her mother's husband, Jackie decided to take Janet back to 1040 Fifth Avenue for a few weeks. Her mother didn't fight it and, in fact, seemed to welcome it.

During this time, Yusha stayed at his own apartment in New York. When Jackie went to work at Doubleday, either John or Yusha watched over Janet. Marta was also in residence. Jackie also decided to hire a nurse. A woman named Sally Ewalt had those duties at the Castle. She didn't want to leave the property and live even part-time in New York, so another nurse, Donna Lou, was hired for when Janet was in Manhattan.

"What I saw was pure, unadulterated love," Donna recalled. "The way Mrs. Onassis doted on her mother, it was hard to believe that they'd ever had a difficult moment. At night, the cook [Marta] would arrange an intimate dinner for them in the library, something simple like a shepherd's pie or a tomato-and-ricotta tart. I remember she'd make a frozen lemon soufflé for dessert because it was Mrs. Onassis's favorite. She and her mother would sit in front of the fireplace and thumb through family scrapbooks while talking about the past."

It was surprising how much Janet remembered, such as the first evening gown she'd ever bought Jackie when she was fifteen. "She could describe it to a tee—full skirted, blue taffeta with puffy sleeves, worn with gold kid slippers," said Donna. "She remembered that Jackie was self-conscious about the slippers because she thought her feet were too big."

Janet also remembered details even Jackie had forgotten about the Kennedy years. "I heard them talk about the presidential campaign and the Cuban Missile Crisis," Donna recalled. "I heard them talk about the president asking Mrs. Auchincloss to judge some kind of horse show right in the middle of the crisis. They told me about the many times she substituted for Mrs. Onassis at the White House. Mrs. Onassis even showed us pictures of a trip she took to Ravello with her sister. It was nostalgic and beautiful. They'd obviously shared so much, a whole lifetime of personal history, happy and sad."

No matter how much Janet's memory had faded, Jackie could tell that many of the puzzle pieces of their life together were still at her fingertips. These incredible, historical moments had all really happened, and there had been nothing like them before or since, so how could Janet ever really forget?

"Do you remember our little dance, Mummy?" Jackie asked one night. She was referring to the routine they always did for guests during parties at Hammersmith. Janet seemed unsure. Jackie went to the record player and put on some music. She turned it up loud. She helped her mother up and started dancing. Slowly, Janet began to join in very haltingly and, yes, she did remember it! She remembered each and every step. It was truly wonderous.

"It is heartwarming to see how happy Mummy can be," Jackie wrote to Yusha. "She could be much happier than she has been in the past few years, were it not for Booch [sic]. The great sadness is that she misses the companionship of a loving husband, watching the evening news together, going to bed and waking up with a beloved companion, all the joys of her years with your father, even when he was in failing health."

In her letter, Jackie equated her mother to a child who fears abandonment, writing, "She clings to the idea of Bouch's company when she talks to him on the phone. She has forgotten how much she wished he would leave during his previous visit, how much he upset and confused her. So, she is vulnerable, invites him again and is tortured by him again." She closed by writing, "I believe that Bouch is a sadist and that tyranissing [sic] everyone in the house and doing worse to her is what gives him pleasure. All the staff think he is sick, and he plays sick games with her."

One night, when Janet came to the dinner table, she found ten matches next to her plate. She smiled at Jackie as she remembered. "Apparently, when Mrs. Onassis and her sister were girls, Mrs. Auchincloss used to take ten matches from a matchbook and place them next to their plates at the dinner table," said Donna. "They would all speak French for the entire meal, and every time one of them used an English word, that person would throw a match away. Whoever held the last match won the game. On this night, Mrs. Auchincloss won, of course. Mrs. Onassis wouldn't have had it any other way."

Another night, Jackie called Janet into the kitchen. On the table were two cups of butterscotch pudding. Jackie had made it herself, and to hear her tell it later, it hadn't been easy. She'd never asked for Janet's recipe; she'd just always loved the results. It had been almost twenty-five years since the last time Janet made the dessert, back in 1963 during the Cuban Missile Crisis. How was that possible? Where had the time gone?

Janet's eyes filled with tears as Jackie squirted Reddi-wip on her special treat.

THE PRINCE

◇◇◇◇◇◇◇◇◇◇◇◇◇◇

Dorothy Schiff of the *New York Post* used to tell a story about Jackie and her son, John, that always raised eyebrows.

It was 1964, and she was scheduled to meet Jackie in the Kennedys' suite at the Carlyle Hotel for lunch and to talk about the *Post*'s possible endorsement of Bobby Kennedy for New York Senate. After being let into the suite by a maid, Dorothy found Jackie in the living room sitting on a sofa with John, who was four, playing *Peter and the Wolf* on a record player. Jackie rose and greeted her. She then turned to John and said, "Make your bow to Mrs. Schiff."

John bolted up, bent himself at the waist, and said, "Nice to meet you."

Jackie told him, "You may leave now," and he said, 'Yes, Mummy," and walked out of the room.

"It was all very royal," Dorothy said, "and I was a little taken aback by the formality."

Dorothy eyed Jackie with amusement. "Why, he's like a little prince, isn't he?" she asked.

Jackie frowned. "No, Dorothy. He's like a little boy," she said. "Nothing more."

"A little boy. Nothing more," was always how Jackie wanted her only son to think of himself when he was young. Yet, how many little boys bow to their mother's friends, at least little boys born in America?

Throughout his life, John Kennedy Jr. received mixed messages about his place in life, from his mother, his grandmothers, his relatives . . . the media . . . the public. But never in his short life would he ever be viewed as just any fellow. As the only son of a beloved slain president whose salute to his father's casket at the age of three had melted the hearts of millions, John would always be "Camelot's only son," which is how *Newsweek* once referred to him. "It will be many years before you understand what a great man your father was," LBJ wrote to him in his own hand on November 22, 1963, the night of the assassination. He wrote that JFK's loss was "a deep personal tragedy" for everyone, and he wanted John, in particular, to know that he shared his grief. "You can always be proud of him," he concluded.

In school, John always stood out because of his famous pedigree. He found the notice to his disadvantage when, in the third grade at the Collegiate School, word got out that he suffered from what would much later be diagnosed as attention deficit disorder. His mother would sometimes go to the school and plead with teachers to be more patient with him; she even did this when he was in college.

By the time he was in his late teens, John had accepted his prominence in our country, which he found had certain advantages: girls flocked to him because of his good looks and celebrity status. He was always better-looking than his cousins, with his square jaw, brown eyes, polished smile, and shock of brown hair so reminiscent of his father's. It was no surprise that he'd have his pick of women. Jackie just hoped he wouldn't take after his father in the dismissive way he treated them.

"John struggled academically, but by the time he graduated from Brown with a bachelor's degree in history [in 1985], he was ready to engage with the public, really put himself out there," said Gustavo Paredes. "He was good at it, too, as evidenced by his moment onstage at the Democratic National Convention in 1988 when he introduced his uncle Ted."

John was twenty-seven when *People* named him Sexiest Man Alive. "By that time, he was a Kennedy through and through, the charm, charisma, good looks all in place, the best of both parents—his father's panache, his mother's dignity—which made him so incredibly popular," said Gustavo. "One thing he and his mother were often at loggerheads over was his choice of women, though, especially when he was in his late twenties. Madonna comes to mind."

MADONNA

◇◇◇◇◇◇◇◇◇◇◇◇

I t was 1988. John was twenty-eight and the pop star Madonna thirty when they began dating. Immediately, the relationship was a source of contention between him and his mother. Thomas Luft, one of John's friends, whose grandmother was a Newport friend of Janet's, recalled being with John and Jackie at Red Gate Farm when the two discussed Madonna. Jackie warned him that "until she's single, she'll be nothing but trouble." John defended her, saying she was an intelligent, empowered woman, the kind of celebrity Jackie, as the editor who'd championed Michael Jackson's autobiography, might actually find interesting.

Jackie really didn't know enough about Madonna to have an opinion about her artistry; she just took issue with antics she viewed as self-serving and attention-seeking. As a public figure who'd spent most of her life trying to control the attention she received, she didn't understand the psychology of a person who'd purposely pursue the public's interest. She predicted that Madonna would one day be sorry she made herself fair game in the media and said Michael Jackson, when she worked with him, had told her he regretted having done the same thing. "He told me the dumbest thing he ever did was pose in an oxygen chamber for publicity," Jackie told a Doubleday colleague, "because it opened the floodgates to an avalanche of ridiculous stories about him."

If Madonna reminded Jackie of Marilyn Monroe—as some writers have speculated over the years—it was only superficially. Peter Beard, in a 2016 email, noted, "Because Jackie wasn't familiar with Marilyn's work, she could make no real comparison [to Madonna's]. All she knew of Marilyn was what she'd done to generate publicity. She once told me she never saw any of her films. She said it would never occur to her to sit through a Marilyn Monroe movie. The only thing she'd ever seen her do was the birthday song to JFK at Madison Square Garden, and she just thought that was sad."

Maybe it was snobbery, but Jackie didn't think Marilyn was that smart, and she felt the same way about Madonna. She knew little about what it took to make it in show business, even after having known Frank Sinatra and Michael Jackson. "It wasn't her world, and she wasn't interested in it," said Peter. "She didn't think it took brains as much as it was maybe just talent and exposure. Where Marilyn was concerned, I told her she was wrong and that Marilyn was smart, an intellectual. "

"There are millions of intelligent women on this planet, John," Jackie told John in front of Thomas Luft. "Why must you go out with the only one who calls herself a 'Material Girl'?"

John countered, "Oh, really, Mummy? Who in this world is more materialistic than you?" At that, Jackie became upset and left the room. John then became a little unglued, running after her and apologizing. For the rest of the day, according to Thomas Luft, he beat himself up about it, muttering about his bad behavior.

That same day, he told Thomas that when he was a little boy, he was so protective of his mother that if they happened across a magazine photo of her in Dallas with his father, he'd put his hand over it and say, "Don't look, Mummy." He knew she'd been through a lot and never wanted to cause her more heartache. "No matter how much they disagreed, he loved her unconditionally and was almost always deferential to her, respectful of her," said Thomas. "I once asked how I should address her. Can I call her 'Jackie'? He said, 'It's Mrs. Onassis, unless she tells you otherwise, and she probably won't.' He had total respect for her and wanted others to have it, too."

The real issue for Jackie where Madonna was concerned wasn't her image or her career. It was that she was Sean Penn's wife. Jackie would never condone John's involvement with a married woman.

When Madonna opened in the play *Speed-the-Plow* on Broadway on May 3, 1988, John was out of town. He convinced Jackie to attend opening night, hoping she'd be impressed. He also made her promise to go backstage and say hello. Jackie went to the show with a colleague from Doubleday. "She was in the middle of something having to do with her mother's husband," said that coworker, "and she said the last thing she wanted to do was see this show, but she did it for John. She put on a red wig so as not to be recognized. In the car on the way to the Royale Theatre, she adjusted it and asked me, 'How do I look?' I said, 'You look exactly like Jacqueline Onassis in a red wig.' No one recognized her, though. She liked the show, thought Madonna was okay."

After the show, Jackie's colleague asked if they were going backstage as promised. Jackie said no, they weren't. She didn't want to give Madonna the opportunity to promote a relationship between them, which she thought was inevitable. "I'm not going to validate the relationship by meeting her," she said.

A CLOSE CALL WITH CAROLYN

◇◇◇◇◇◇◇◇◇◇◇◇

By the time John Kennedy Jr. was in his early twenties, he and Jackie disagreed several times over his choice of career, especially when his heart was set on being an actor. First of all, she felt a man of his pedigree should never "just" be an actor. She felt the Kennedy name would be exploited to promote anything in which he appeared, and there was no way to control the quality of those projects. He eventually went to NYU Law School, which made her happy. He would struggle mightily, though, flunking the bar twice before finally passing in 1989.

Before and after Madonna, there were a string of relationships for John, including one that lasted about six years with Daryl Hannah. His feelings about her vacillated the entire time. So did his mother's, mostly because she believed—as did many—that Daryl was still in love with her former partner, the musician Jackson Browne. Also, Daryl got on Jackie's bad side early on by smoking pot at Red Gate Farm. Jackie and John had many arguments about Daryl, and Jackie would've been happy if he'd ended it with her years before he finally did. "I'm self-aware enough to know there's probably no woman who will ever be good enough for John," she told one of her relatives in 1989. "I can only hope he ends up with someone who treats him well and maybe doesn't smoke dope in my house."

Jackie would never meet the woman John would go on to marry, Carolyn Bessette. The two dated briefly about two years prior to the end of Jackie's life, just before one of John's reconciliations with Daryl. He then started seeing Carolyn again in 1993, but with Daryl still in the picture, he felt the timing wasn't right to introduce her to his mother. He toyed with the idea of bringing her to the opening of the Kennedy Library in October. However, with the entire clan present, he felt too much pressure, especially since he'd been asked to recite Stephen Spender's poem "The Truly Great." Besides, he really didn't want to hear his mother's opinion of Carolyn until he was sure how he felt about her himself. "He told me it wasn't worth a fight with her if Carolyn turned out to just be a fleeting thing," said one of his friends.

There was one close call with Carolyn. It happened in late 1993 when John was dining with her at Keens Steakhouse in Midtown Manhattan. Across the crowded room, he saw his mother, Maurice, Yusha, and his cousin Alexandra (Janet Jr.'s daughter). Though he and Carolyn had just ordered, John tossed back his cocktail and hurried her out a side entrance. Years later, he'd regret it, especially since he was already falling for Carolyn. Jackie later revealed she'd spotted John slipping out of the restaurant with a tall, stunning blonde—"Does he think I'm blind?"—but decided not to mention it to him.

One story often told among family members about John and his grandmother concerns his sister Caroline's graduation from Concord Academy in June 1975. It was one of those rare occasions at which both his grandmothers, Rose and Janet, were in attendance.

While Jackie was proud of Caroline, JFK loomed large over the day. It tugged at Jackie's heart that he wasn't present to see his daughter graduate from his alma mater. She tried to hide her feelings, but Janet could see that she was melancholy. "I just didn't know she would grow up so fast," Jackie said, according to Ted Kennedy's memory. "Her eyes were filled with tears," he recalled in his oral history, "and I thought, whoever thinks their children will grow up? But they do, like it or not, they do . . . I mean, if we're lucky, they do."

At one point, a photographer asked for a picture. Rose called everyone over to pose. Standing from left to right were Jackie, Caroline, Rose, Ted, Janet, and John. As the photographer adjusted his camera, Janet said to her grandson, fourteen at the time, "John, go stand next to your mummy." John nodded and crossed over to Jackie. Maybe sensing her sadness, he reached over, took her hand, and held it tightly. Rose leaned in to Janet and motioned to their grandson with a proud look. Janet smiled and said, "It's like how his mother held his hand the day he was born, and every day since."

TURNING SIXTY

◇◇◇◇◇◇◇◇◇◇◇◇◇◇

On a hot summer day in 1989, Adora Rule's daughter, Janine, arrived unexpectantly at 1040 Fifth Avenue to see her. Marta Sgubin welcomed her as she got off the elevator. "Madam is in her room," she said.

Janine walked down the hallway to Jackie's bedroom and found her sitting in front of a mirror at the vanity. As Jackie stared at herself in the mirror, Janine suddenly felt awkward. Should she announce herself? Or should she just skulk away? As she stood there trying to make up her mind, Jackie raised her head to inspect her neck. She pinched it once or twice. Maybe she didn't like the way it looked because she then took a colorful scarf from the dresser and put it on. Suddenly, she whirled around. "My God! Janine! Why are you standing there?" she exclaimed. Janine said Marta had let her in. "You could at least say something," she told her, upset. "That's so rude. What is wrong with you? Never do that!"

Indeed, Jackie's little moment had been a private one to which many women could probably relate.

Jackie would turn sixty in July. She actually didn't mind aging. She had a standing appointment with her stylist, Thomas Morrissey—who started his career at Kenneth Salon in New York—at his shop, every Monday and Thursday from 1985 until 1994 at 1:00 p.m. for hairstyling and once every three weeks for color—brunette with chestnut highlights, which never once changed. (Morrissey had styled her for ten years prior to that at Kenneth.) Marta would pack a lunch on those days, which Jackie would carry in a baggie in her purse—half a chicken sandwich with the crusts cut off the bread and a Diet Coke. She did not have bodyguards in the '80s, and she also no longer used her own driver; she engaged Big Apple Car, a service owned and operated by all women.

Sometimes, she'd be late for her hair appointment, but she rarely, if ever, apologized. "Accustomed to just walking in and being taken care of, she was oblivious to schedules that had to be shifted or to others being inconvenienced," said Morrissey. "It wasn't thoughtless, really; it just had always been that way for her. People had been accommodating her for as far back as she could remember. That was her life. She was used to a certain way. For instance, once she was in the shop, and Bunny Mellon was in having her hair done. Jackie said, 'Bunny, I just bought this breakfront for my dining room at Martha's Vineyard, and it's so large I'm just betwixt and between as to how to get it up there!' Bunny said, 'Darling, don't be silly! I'll put it on my private jet, of course, and get it right up there for you.' That kind of thing. Of course, Jackie could've had her own private jet, but why bother when you can use your friends'?"

She remained in great shape, jogged around the Central Park Reservoir whenever she had the chance, and still rode her horses at her estate she owned in Peapack, New Jersey. She also did hatha yoga three days a week at 1040. It was always at 5:00 p.m. with her private instructor, Tillie Mia, who'd work with her, in total, for seventeen years, from 1977 to 1994.

Though she didn't think of herself as vain, Jackie did attempt to camouflage the liver spots on her arms with makeup. She made a more dramatic move toward recapturing her youth when she got a face-lift from Dr. Michael Hogan a few months before her sixtieth. She was sorry she'd done it, though. It was much more painful than she'd expected, and she wondered if it had even been worth it. "Who cares about my face, anyway?" she asked Donna Lou, Janet's nurse, whose response was, "Everyone, Mrs. Onassis. Everyone!"

Throughout 1989, Jackie juggled her responsibility to her mother with her duties at Doubleday, her relationship with Maurice, and her devotion to her new granddaughter from Caroline, Rose, born in 1988. "Being a grandmother meant the world to her," said her friend Bunny Mellon in 2012. "She didn't have much time with either of her grandmothers. Her paternal grandmother passed when she was eleven, and Janet's mother died when she was about fourteen. Caroline's grandmothers, Janet and Rose, were both infirm by the time Rose was born. Jackie used to say, 'We're the next generation of grandmothers now, God help us, Bunny.'"

At this same time, Janet's younger sister, Margaret Winifred—known to Jackie as "Tante Win" (*Tante* being French for "aunt")—was also battling Alzheimer's. She would die of it in 1991. With both her mother and her aunt suffering from the disease, as Jackie neared sixty, she worried about her own chances. "I was surprised," recalled Donna Lou, "considering how much research I knew she'd done into Alzheimer's, that Mrs. Onassis told me to get rid of all of her aluminum pans just because someone told her they were linked to the disease. I also recall a day she went to the butcher to purchase a special cut of meat for dinner. The next day, she returned and bought another cut. When she got home and saw the previous day's purchase in the refrigerator, she fretted because she didn't remember buying it. 'I'm all twisted up right now,' she told me. I told her she was just fine. 'We're getting up there, Madam,' I told her. 'We forget. Such is life.'"

Maurice continued to be good to Jackie and care for her and her children. Both Caroline and John were wary of him, however. It would overstate it to say they felt anything but casual warmth toward him. Jackie hoped they'd get closer to him, but something held them back. Though she was generally happy with Maurice, Jackie did stay in touch with Jack Warnecke, who now had an apartment at Sixty-First and Park.

A year after Jackie married Onassis, Jack Warnecke was wed to Grace Kennan, daughter of George F. Kennan, the American diplomat and historian. That marriage ended in 1978.

Nothing untoward ever went on between Jackie and Jack once she was with Maurice. However, she remained conflicted about him and her decision to choose Onassis more than twenty years earlier.

"She came by often, and we had long conversations about our lives," he said in 1998. "We were just good friends sharing, wondering . . . taking stock . . . confronting our flaws. The closer her mother got to death, the more Jackie thought about her own life."

About a week before her sixtieth, Jackie and Jack were talking about the passing of time and remembering their long friendship. When she told him she blamed Janet for some of the poorer choices of her youth, he felt he had to challenge her. It wasn't all Janet; some were her choices, too—it was her, too. He reminded her of a time when they were at the Cape together and she very pointedly told him, "Money is power, and I want both."

Jackie said he was right. It was her character that had made her destiny, not her mother's. Still, Jack said, she lived her life on her own terms. When she disagreed and told him she was "so broken back then," he said she wasn't broken at all, she was just "disassembled." She had to put herself back together after JFK's death. "But after what we had," he said, probably referring to their robust sex life, "I could never see you with someone like Onassis." He asked what she saw in him.

Jackie didn't reveal anything private about her marriage to Aristotle Onassis. Instead, she demurred and said, "Oh, Jack, you know me. I have three lives. Public, private, and secret."

We don't know if she felt her aphorism was her own, or whether she was quoting the Colombian novelist Gabriel García Márquez, who once said, "All human beings have three lives: public, private, and secret." García Márquez did win a Noble Prize for Literature two years prior, in 1982, so it's possible he was her muse.

"I certainly knew what she meant," Jack Warnecke said, "and that was very true of Jackie. Public and private, I knew about. Secret? She let very few people in on that."

THANK YOU

∞∞∞∞∞∞∞∞∞∞

B y the beginning of 1989, Janet Auchincloss had been all but robbed of her precious memories. Still, Jackie continued to enjoy her relationship with her, which was, in many ways, actually deeper and more profound than it had been. "The time had come to find a facility for her," said Donna Lou. "Mrs. Onassis was searching for the right one. I had many brochures and had set a number of appointments for her. She and Mr. Tempelsman told me they wanted Mrs. Auchincloss to be cared for in New York or New Jersey, close by. Money was no object, of course. I figured we'd have her placed in a very good facility by summer."

Bingham Morris, who still lived in the apartment over one of the garages, visited Janet daily, but because she was now so feeble, he seemed less a threat. "He continued to stay even though they never made him feel the least bit welcome," said Ivy Rawlins. "They were horrible to him. He could've abandoned Janet and stayed at his home in Southampton, which was a hell of a lot nicer than the stinking, little apartment Jackie O. put him in. He wanted to be near his wife, though. He said he loved Janet more than he hated Jackie."

On July 22, 1989, Jackie got the call from Yusha she'd dreaded for some time: her mother didn't have much longer. "She needed to go to Newport immediately," said Donna. "Though she'd intended to go to the Cape for a family celebration of Rose Kennedy's [ninety-ninth] birthday, she very quickly changed her plans. Marta and I helped her pack. She was in a sort of daze. Marta gave her a rosary, and as she clutched it, Mrs. Onassis said something like—I can't remember her exact words, but something like, 'Please don't take her from me yet. Not yet.' She was very distraught."

When she arrived at the Castle, Jackie was concerned about Yusha. He'd be sixty-two in a month, and the burden of Janet's illness had been a heavy one for him. He looked tired and older. As soon as Jackie was settled, he went to bed, exhausted.

An hour later, as a brilliant sun set over Narragansett Bay, Jackie held her mother's hand, stroked her hair, and thanked her for their life together. She told her not to be frightened because she was right there, at her side.

She didn't want to let her go. But it was time.

AT PEACE

ooooooooooo

I t was July 27, 1989, the day before Jackie's sixtieth birthday and the morning of her mother's funeral. As she was being driven to the church, Jackie
nervously fingered an antique brooch Janet had given to her as her "something old" in 1953 for her wedding to Jack Kennedy. It was a yellow-and-
gold oval pin with a portrait cameo of Janet's mother, Margaret. Janet had
explained that her mother had given it to her when she married Jackie's
father, Jack Bouvier, in 1928.

Jackie had wanted to give the brooch to Caroline when she married Ed
Schlossberg. Though handing it down seemed like the appropriate thing to
do, she couldn't seem to part with it. The urge to keep it puzzled her and
made her feel selfish. When she sought advice from Janet about it, she understood. "It's a thing between you and me," she said, "and there's nothing
wrong with wanting to keep a thing between you and me." She then rummaged through her jewelry box until she found a similar brooch also given
to her by her mother. She put it in Jackie's hand and clasped her fingers
around it. "Give Caroline this," she said, "from both of us. Her something
old."

Jackie was filled with emotion after her mother's death and, given recent strains on the family, she didn't know what to expect at the service.
Surprisingly, she didn't want Maurice to go with her. All she needed there,
she insisted, were Caroline and John. It promised to be a trying day, and she
wanted to face it on her own, almost as if testing her courage. Maurice, of
course, wanted to be at her side. It felt as if she were casting him aside. Her
mind was made up, though, and nothing would change it. It was as if she

could hear her mother's voice reminding her that she had it in her because, as Janet would always put it, "You are a Lee!"

Jackie said she remembered Janet telling her that when her mother died suddenly of a heart attack in 1943, she went to the funeral alone. At the time, she was newly married to Hugh and, naturally, he'd wanted to accompany her. However, she insisted on facing it by herself. Was this the reason Jackie now wished to go to Janet's funeral without Maurice? It made sense, but if she recognized it as the explanation, she didn't voice it.

Toward the end of Janet's life when she would visit 1040 Fifth Avenue, Jackie always asked Maurice to sleep at a hotel. She said there wasn't enough room at 1040 for the three of them, but that simply wasn't true. Because Maurice got along with Janet, there seemed no reason for Jackie to want to keep them apart—but keep them apart she did.

Jackie had also decided not to have Maurice accompany her to Janet Jr.'s funeral. After that, she said she didn't want him with her at her mother's eightieth birthday party at the Castle. The entire family was present for that occasion, even Lee. Was she purposely keeping Maurice from them? That's how it seemed to many people in her circle.

Now, as she and Yusha pulled up to Trinity Church on Queen Anne Square, Jackie held her mother's brooch tightly as if it might give her the strength she'd need to get through the day. Back in the 1960s, she would sometimes ask Janet what to wear for certain occasions. Janet would always say she couldn't go wrong with "a simple, black shift." A shift dress was a short sleeved, black, knee-length dress popularized at that time, which could be worn anywhere. Jackie's designer Lilly Pulitzer designed about a dozen of them for her, and when she posed wearing it in *Life* magazine, it caused a fashion craze and suddenly everyone was wearing "a simple, black shift." When she put it on the morning of the funeral, Marta felt she'd be chilly wearing short sleeves in the church. Therefore, Jackie changed into what was basically a long-sleeved version of the same dress. It fell in fluid lines around her pencil-thin figure. With her chestnut hair pulled back from her face and cascading to her shoulders, she also wore delicate gold earrings Ari had given her just before their first visit to Hammersmith in 1968.

As soon as her car stopped, Jackie was greeted by more than a thousand onlookers who'd shown up just to get a good look at her and at any Kennedys who might've come to pay their respects. "I remember that she saw Mr. Auchincloss [Yusha] for a moment and embraced him, but then he was quickly lost in the chaos," said nurse Donna Lou. "Ethel Kennedy rushed over to her to rescue her. 'Jackie, come with me,' she said. She put her arm around her and helped her through the crowd. 'Back,' Ethel scolded the onlookers. 'Get the heck back. Give her some room.' She then helped Jackie into the vestibule, where Ted Kennedy and Sargent Shriver awaited. Both hugged her tightly."

The discomfort was palpable as soon as the usher took Jackie to her seat and she realized she would be squeezed into a small box with Lee and Jamie. Jackie had hoped she'd be able to sit with Caroline, Ed, and John, or maybe even Yusha. However, the church had made other arrangements for Janet's three surviving children, and she didn't want to cause a scene. It was too close for comfort, though; she gave Jamie a withering stare as she took her seat. He would later say he caught the faint whiff of her perfume, "light and fresh, like jasmine." She'd only engage in polite but strained conversation with them. Mostly, she held herself very still.

Later, Jackie would ask Jamie to find another car to take to the cemetery, not the family car, because she wanted to have it out with Bingham Morris. Yusha, in the car with Jackie and Bingham, would later say Jackie laid down the law: Morris would get $25,000 from Janet's estate, not a penny more, and he was to leave the Castle immediately and never return. It would be the last time any of them ever laid eyes on him.

Following the service, members of the Auchincloss, Bouvier, and Kennedy families scattered some of Janet's ashes on the grounds of Hammersmith. Jackie and Lee then stood on the property's dock and cast the remaining cremains to the wind.

Lee was now married again, having taken the wealthy director Herb Ross as a husband about a year earlier. Finally, her financial woes were over. She'd live the rest of her life as an exceedingly wealthy woman.

As the sisters spread their mother's ashes, fireworks from the annual Black Ships Festival burst above them in the twilight sky. While the sparkling display was a surprise, it was a welcome and somehow appropriate one. As Jackie and Lee watched the red and golden starbursts with astonishment, it must have felt as if they were sisters again, back when they were little and had just moved to Hammersmith Farm during the war. Hand in hand, they used to walk out to this very dock to gaze wondrously at the battleships, destroyers, and aircraft carriers sailing toward the Newport naval base.

After a few minutes, the fireworks began to subside. Lee abruptly turned to walk back up to the main house as Jackie watched her sorrowfully. Their relationship was just as painful and just as unresolved as ever. Jackie lit a fresh Pall Mall and was taking in the last few color bursts when Adora Rule approached.

It had been thirty-six years since Adora went to work for Janet, helping her prepare for Jackie's wedding to Jack on these same Hammersmith grounds. She was just eighteen. Now, she was fifty-four. She didn't know what to say once she was finally standing before Jackie.

"Did Mummy ever tell you when she first caught me smoking?" Jackie asked, breaking the silence between them. Adora shook her head. Jackie said she was a teenager, and she knew Janet, who also smoked, forbade her to have cigarettes. She was taking the last puff on a cigarette when she heard Janet's footsteps. "I knew she'd kill me," Jackie said, "so I quickly threw the butt over my shoulder." As mother and daughter spoke, they smelled something burning. "The couch was on fire," Jackie exclaimed. "Can you imagine it?" Then, after a beat, she sighed loudly. "I don't have a mummy anymore, do I, Adora?" she asked in a plaintive voice.

Adora was so taken aback, she wanted to hold her. However, they didn't have that kind of relationship. Instead, she took her hand. "Your mummy will always be with you, Jackie," she told her. "She loved you so much."

Jackie nodded. "Thank you for saying that," she said.

By the time Jackie returned to New York that evening, she was physically exhausted and emotionally drained. She decided to take the rest of the week off from Doubleday to recover. For many subsequent days, she was in a bleak mood, taking no calls and seeing few people.

It would take months for Jackie to feel close to Maurice again. She told one intimate she was conflicted because he hadn't been as supportive as she would've liked where her mother was concerned. He hadn't assisted in her effort to try to stop the wedding to Bingham Morris, and if he had done so, Jackie wondered, how different might things have been for all of them?

It would take time for Jackie's relationship with Maurice to heal. She needed time to think. Once again, Maurice moved out of 1040 Fifth Avenue.

Three months later, he moved back in.

BOOK VII

A Sad Farewell

THE ART OF CONTENTMENT

◇◇◇◇◇◇◇◇◇◇◇◇◇

Janet and Hugh. Black Jack. Jack. Bobby. Ari. Janet Jr. Artemis. All gone. Even Rose Kennedy wasn't really in the picture any longer because of her age. So many of the people who'd dominated Jackie's life, who were so vitally important to her, who had comforted her as much as vexed her, had passed on by the beginning of the 1990s.

Thankfully, Yusha remained a touchstone to Jackie's past. After Janet's death, he continued to live in the Castle at Hammersmith Farm and maintain it as a custodian. Though Janet's ownership of the Castle and Windmill and the acres surrounding it had been divided among her heirs, Jackie moved on from the property, as did Lee. Never again would either sister return. But Jackie did appreciate the fact that Yusha cared so much for the place in which she had so many memories. "You are the most thoughtful man and brother in the world," she wrote to him on April 19, 1990. She wrote that being "the patriarch" of Hammersmith Farm could not be easy for him, "but you make such a difference to so many by so lovingly assuming those responsibilities." In 1992, Yusha would run for Rhode Island Senate as an independent. Jackie sent him a generous check as a donation. When he lost, she wrote that she was proud of him and all he did, "with such flying colors." She hoped he would run again, "because Newport needs you."

It was good that Yusha remained such an important fixture in Jackie's life, because Lee was still nowhere to be found. The death of her mother marked a new kind of freedom for Lee, as if finally liberated of her past and of everything she felt had ever held her back. She now worked hard to set aside the insecurity and deep-seated anger that had led to so many years of unhappiness. She was content with her husband, Herb Ross. However, she decided that the only way to ensure that contentment was to marginalize Jackie in her life. She saw her only rarely. That was hard for Jackie, but she understood and, in fact, realized it was probably better for her, too.

Jackie stayed in touch with Jamie with phone calls and letters, but she kept him at arm's distance. It was a shame that this young man whom she loved so much that she wanted him to walk with her, Bobby, and Ted at Jack's funeral was now someone she couldn't open her heart to, but, as Jamie put it, "we figured out a way forward that worked for us, and I had to accept she'd never get past the Kitty Kelley book."

Jackie seldom visited the Cape, though she still owned her house there. It wasn't the same anymore, though, and when she looked back, she realized it hadn't been since Jack's death. Rose was ill and infirm, and seeing her was difficult and often not worth the emotional toll it took. She wasn't even able to acknowledge Jackie's presence because of the onset of dementia, when last they saw each other in the summer of '89. Going back to the Cape periodically when her children were young was a way of keeping them connected to their Kennedy roots. However, Jackie long ago decided they were old enough to return on their own if they wished to do so. John did often, but Caroline almost never.

Red Gate Farm was Jackie's safe haven now, and she loved being there with John, Caroline, Ed, and her granddaughter, Rose. Soon, Caroline would have two more babies, Tatiana in 1990 and Jack in 1993, their eager and shining faces always full of love for their "Grand Jackie."

Happy in her marriage to Ed, the children's mom, Caroline, stayed out of the public eye. She turned down, for instance, an offer to be the chair of the 1992 Democratic National Convention. Some were surprised, but not Jackie. "That's just not who she is," Jackie said, "and one must be true to oneself."

Jackie had only a few friends from the Onassis years. After visiting Skorpios on the first anniversary of Ari's death for a memorial service, she realized it was no longer home. Artemis had been her last link, and with her now gone, there was no attachment to Ari's private island. She did remain friendly with the Greek director Michael Cacoyannis, whom she had briefly dated after Onassis.

Others from Jackie's past continued to hold a place in it by the 1990s. She and Lady Bird Johnson, for instance, remained close and continued a correspondence that lasted more than fifty years. Jack Warnecke remained a fixture in her life. The wealthy Bunny and Paul Mellon were close friends, as were Peter Duchin, the bandleader, and his wife, Brooke Hayward. Ted and Joan—not so much Ted's second wife, Vicki—and Ethel and Eunice Kennedy were a part of Jackie's life; Ted had accompanied Ethel to Janet Auchincloss's funeral.

In April 1993, Ethel turned sixty-five. During her party, the phone rang. "I'll bet I know who that is," she said. When someone handed it to her, she smiled as soon as she heard the familiar voice. "Jackie," she exclaimed, "in all of these years, you've never once forgotten my birthday. How do you do that?" In fact, Nancy Tuckerman made it a point to transfer important birthday dates from one calendar to the next every year so Jackie would remember.

Jackie did have some newer friends, like the performer Carly Simon, a regular visitor to Red Gate Farm, whom she met on Martha's Vineyard in the early 1980s. She also had friends at Doubleday, though she counted few of them as close. She was down to just Tuesdays, Wednesdays, and Thursdays in her office.

Recently, Jackie began working with the writer Dorothy West, the youngest member of the Harlem renaissance of the 1920s and '30s, known to contemporaries—including authors such as Zora Neale Hurston, Langston Hughes, and Richard Wright—as "the kid." When she was on Martha's Vineyard, Jackie met with her weekly at her home in Oak Bluffs, a section long the home of affluent African Americans, on her novel *The Wedding*. The book is set in the 1950s and delves into inter- and intra-racial bigotry.

Abigail McGrath, Dorothy's niece who lived next door, recalled, "One day, Dorothy said to me, 'Abigail! Clean your yard! My editor is coming over.' Later, my son Benson and I looked out the window and we see Jacqueline Onassis getting out of a dark green BMW. What a shock that was. We stood hiding behind the curtains as she walked up to the house with her big sunglasses and colorful kerchief over her hair, very Jackie O. I still wasn't convinced, though, so I sent Benson over to make sure it was her. He went to borrow a cup of sugar and came back and said, 'It can't be her. She's way too young. She looks like she's in her late twenties.' But, yes, it was her, all right.

"Once, we were standing behind the curtain snooping, and Jackie came bolting out of Dorothy's house, slamming the door hard behind her. She was very upset, almost to tears. I thought, *My gosh, Dorothy can be hard to handle.* Benson used to say, 'Dorothy can reduce Mussolini to tears.' She'd even make Jacqueline Onassis cry, and I always thought that could never happen. Come to find out, Dorothy made some promises about finishing chapters and she didn't live up to it, and Jackie was at the end of her rope with her. Dorothy said, 'She stormed out of here, but she'll be back. She always comes back.'"

"She came to see me every Monday to assess my progress," recalled Dorothy before her death at ninety-one in 1998, "driving herself in her blue Jeep, losing her way fairly regularly in the Highlands. We were so different. She was fastidious, I wasn't. She was organized, I wasn't. I had my cats and magazines and [P]ost-it notes and typewriters, but she was patient, loving, and determined. 'Nothing will stop us from finishing your great book,' she told me."

While Jackie's work remained rewarding and she treasured each day of it, privately she no longer wished to surround herself with as many people as she had in her youth. The older she got, the less she needed to depend on others for companionship as long as she had those who mattered most— her children, her grandchildren, and Maurice. She didn't have the interest or even the energy she once had to get dressed up for a late-night dinner, the theater, or the ballet. By the 1990s, curling up with a good book at home with Maurice was, for her, bliss. Perhaps her greatest achievement in life occurred without fanfare and far from the public eye, and that was her mastering the art of contentment. When she and Maurice went to Europe in the summer of 1993, it was a private trip, and few even knew she was there. No fanfare. Just quiet satisfaction.

Because 1993 would mark the thirtieth anniversary of the Kennedy assassination, some in Jackie's life worried that she might fall into a depression because of the media coverage the event was sure to generate. She didn't, though. Of course, she missed Jack just as she missed that time in her life. She tried not to think about any of the darker moments, though. If she gave any of it even a fleeting thought, she could very easily drop right back into that black hole of despair. She knew how to protect herself, never to dwell on it. On the anniversary, she worshipped at St. Thomas More, a small Catholic church on the Upper East Side where, for the last thirty years, she'd asked for a requiem Mass for Jack. Caroline, about to turn thirty-six, and John, thirty-three, were at her side.

John recently disappointed his mother by quitting his job at the district attorney's office in Manhattan so that he could start his own magazine, which he wanted to call *George*. After he'd argued six trials and won six convictions, Jackie thought he'd be a fine lawyer, so she was let down.

John also talked about perhaps being a politician. Of course, Jackie wanted him to serve if that was his dream, but the thought of him doing so was so frightening she couldn't even think about it. She was unsure about his magazine idea because she knew the odds of success in such a venture were slim. However, she liked the fact that he wanted a political voice, and if that was how he planned to serve, she was fine with it. It was a lot better than being a politician, anyway. She looked forward to seeing how it would turn out. There was plenty of time, she decided, to worry about it.

Jackie had found a way to deal with anxiety by just letting it go. She realized that, somehow, she'd still had a marvelous life full of fun and excitement despite its dark moments. She was calmer now than she'd been in recent years.

She was freer, too. With no security detail and no protection, she would walk out of her apartment and eagerly merge with the New York madness she'd so loved since moving back there in 1964. People would stop and stare and wonder if it could really be the former First Lady. Even though she acted as if she didn't notice, she couldn't help but feel their stares. She trusted them not to approach her or ask her uncomfortable questions. Every day, she'd move steadily forward, just as she always had. Pete Hamill put it best: "She hung the celebrity in the closet and lived her life. She could have lived out her days in Icey exile in Europe, hugging some mountain in Switzerland, walled away from the world in some personal fortress on the Riviera. She chose instead to live in New York City, a city as wounded as she was."

While friends like Pete Hamill were well aware of her trauma, as the 1990s unfolded, Jacqueline Kennedy Onassis did seem more at peace with herself, her family, and the world around her. Lady Bird Johnson, who spent a lovely summer day with her at Red Gate Farm in 1993, recalled, "She had just reached this quiet harbor of doing things she wanted to do, and being with people she wanted to do them with, and then . . ."

"WHY HER?"

◇◇◇◇◇◇◇◇◇◇◇◇◇

B y the winter of 1994, Jackie remained one of the most famous women in the world. Her life had been a real adventure. For her and her family, though, she was just Jackie, full of paradoxes like most people. She could be funny and witty with an acid tongue like her mother's. She could be stubborn and petty one day, contemplative and wise the next. In that respect, she was like anyone else. When she was given a diagnosis of cancer, it never occurred to her to ask, "Why me?" It was an anguished world around her that cried out, "*Why her?*"

"Every generation has its defining public figures, the people who tell us who we are," wrote Alice Steinbach for *The Baltimore Sun* after Jackie's diagnosis became public. It was just one of hundreds of tributes to Jackie that month and in the months that followed. "In the last 35 years there have been the obvious ones—John F. Kennedy, Martin Luther King, Robert F. Kennedy, John Lennon and the like," she wrote. "But there are also certain public figures who, though less visible, still serve to remind us of who we are and where we've been. Their very presence adds continuity to our history and serves to link one generation to another. Sometimes we don't recognize them until it's too late. And sometimes we do. I felt this shock of recognition last week when I read that Jacqueline Kennedy Onassis has cancer. Which is to say: the recognition of just how important she is to our brief moment in history."

The heartbreaking journey of Jackie's final months started in November of 1993 when she took a frightening fall from Clown, her show jumper, while fox hunting. She was knocked unconscious for about a half hour. Of course, she'd fallen from horses before, but it's one thing to do so at twenty-four, quite another at sixty-four. She was taken to the hospital, shaken but not terribly hurt. Some minor swelling was detected in a lymph node in her groin. It was thought to be just an infection, and a doctor prescribed antibiotics.

In the weeks after the accident, something wasn't right, and Jackie knew it. She didn't bounce back as she thought she would; she was sore, tired, and felt off. She also felt fluish. A month later when she still didn't feel well, Maurice suggested a Caribbean cruise. During that cruise, Jackie developed a hacking cough. It worried Maurice. One morning, she noticed painful swelling in the lymph nodes of her neck. Then, stabbing pains in her stomach. A doctor told her to return to New York immediately.

Once back in New York, a CAT scan revealed swollen lymph nodes in her chest and abdomen. At the end of January, Jackie got the devastating news: non-Hodgkin's lymphoma. It was a shock. In fact, she would later say she really didn't hear anything that came after the doctor said the word "cancer." She left the doctor's office and went right to church and prayed. On her knees, as she looked up at the enormous crucifix, she began to weep.

"Especially in the last maybe twenty years of her life, she was quite religious," said her friend Niki Goulandris, a Greek philanthropist she'd known from her time with Onassis. "She felt there was something mystical about the way things had unfolded for her, the way she finally found peace in New York after Ari. She'd separated from God after President Kennedy was assassinated, angry at Him, or so she told me. But then after Ari died, then her stepfather and sister [Janet] and mother, she became more spiritual which, she said, was a way of trying to make sense of it all. While art and culture always meant everything to her, especially in her final years, so did religion. She felt all of it was interconnected. She believed in a providential plan."

That night, Jackie told Maurice the news. "I have cancer"—three words she knew would change everything as soon as she uttered them to another person. Maurice took her into his arms, but there was nothing he could say or do to comfort her. That same evening came the terrible task of telling John and Caroline, who took the news as badly as one might expect. The next day, Jackie called Yusha. "It's hard for me to imagine this as being real in my life," she told him, according to his memory, "but it is what it is, Yush, and I have to accept it and I have to deal with it just as I have everything else that's come my way."

Over the next few days, Jackie called a few more friends such as Bunny Mellon to give them the news. She said she felt guilty. She'd done everything right, she said, watched her diet, yoga, meditation . . . everything except one thing—quit her smoking habit of forty years. She said Ari had begged her repeatedly to stop, always fearful it would one day affect her health. He'd beg her to let him throw her pack of cigarettes overboard whenever they were on the *Christina*. Sometimes she let him do it just because it made him so happy. Then she'd race to their stateroom to find another pack. "There was some guilt there," recalled Arthur Schlesinger of his conversation with Jackie at this time. "She said after her stepfather got emphysema, her mother begged her to stop smoking. 'I've done a few things people didn't think I could do,' she told me, 'but to think that this one goddamn thing I couldn't do turns out to be the one thing that kills me is so infuriating.'"

Jackie's cancer was aggressive. The chances for her survival were fifty-fifty.

AN IDIOT'S DANCE

◇◇◇◇◇◇◇◇◇◇◇◇◇

The *New York Times* revealed Jackie's lymphoma diagnosis on February 11. "She is undergoing a course of treatment and there is every expectation it will be successful," said Nancy Tuckerman.

Two days later, on Sunday, Jackie decided she wanted to see Rose Kennedy. It wasn't a good day for Jackie; her joints ached, her head throbbed. However, it had been some time, and she knew Rose hadn't been doing well. She was now 103 and used a wheelchair. She hadn't been seen in public in more than ten years, not since her granddaughter Sydney Lawford's wedding near Hyannis. She suffered a severe stroke a year later and was never the same. Maybe she wasn't surprised at her fate. She always knew happiness was fleeting. Twenty years earlier, in her diary, she wrote that she was often reminded that "there is a destiny that rules over us, because no one whom I know about or whom I read about seems to be completely happy during a long time." She wrote that she had reconciled herself to the fact that she couldn't anticipate "an ideal successful life." She couldn't find anywhere in literature, she wrote, or in life many whose lives she envied. "Most proceed on a middling course, not many great thrills—the normal number of deaths and disappointments," she wrote. She often read Hecuba's "Lament on the Death of Her Grandson," she added, which was written by Euripides, "when she spoke of Fortune—'Here now, there now, she springs back again, an idiot's dance,'" Rose concluded, "and what was true in 550 B.C. is so true now."

Belle-mère was always practical, just like her beloved Jackie, sometimes to a fault. Jackie, though, was always inspired by her stoic realism. She needed to see her one last time.

Jackie, Maurice, and Caroline drove up to the Cape to visit Rose. Ted and his wife, Victoria—whom he'd married two years earlier—welcomed them into the home his parents once owned, which was now his. It looked the same. Nothing ever changed on the Cape; even though Ted and Vicki had remodeled the house, somehow, it still looked exactly as it did the first time Jackie laid eyes on it more than forty years ago.

After catching up with Ted, Vicki, and Ted's sons, Teddy Jr. and Patrick, Jackie spotted Rose out on the green lawn in a wheelchair, a nurse at her side. Though it was freezing cold, Ted said his mother insisted on spending time on the lawn facing the beach every day, bundled up in her warmest wool coat while praying her rosary and gazing out at the rolling sea.

When Jack won the presidency in November of 1960, Rose was seventy. Jackie, who was just thirty-one, marveled at the fact that she still swam in the chilly waters of the Cape every morning. "But why?" she asked her as the two strolled to the beach early one morning, Rose in her black swimsuit. As she quickened her steps toward the rolling waves of Nantucket Sound, Rose said, "One day you'll be old and you'll want to do anything you can to feel alive. Now, don't be a ninny. Come into the water with me." After Jackie begged off, Rose stepped gingerly in and then waded up to her waist. Spotting an oncoming wave, she dived into it. As a shivering Jackie stood on the beach marveling at her mother-in-law, she promised herself that when she turned seventy, she'd be just as fearless and just as eager to feel just as alive as Rose. She fantasized about diving into this same freezing ocean while her daughter watched with admiration. But here she was, just sixty-four, not in a swimsuit but in a heavy, hooded cape, barely able to walk, let alone swim, in icy water. Instead of her daughter looking at her with wonder, Jackie suspected Caroline was watching her with great concern.

Jackie looked out to the lawn and regarded Rose soberly. She walked out of the porch, onto the lawn, and toward her. She then spent some time in an Adirondack chair next to Rose, whispering to her as Maurice and Caroline watched from a distance. At one point, she took the rosary from Rose and appeared to say a prayer with her. Finally, she stood and kissed Rose on the top of her head. She smiled down at her, and, for a moment, it appeared that Rose returned her smile. Jackie then slowly walked back to the house, glancing over her shoulder for one last look.

Rose would be gone in a year, dead at 104 in January 1995. Jackie, much sooner than that.

A MIRACLE CURE?

◇◇◇◇◇◇◇◇◇◇◇◇◇◇

As Jackie was getting ready to leave the house, Ted asked her to wait a moment. He needed to talk to her. He knew of a physician who operated an alternative cancer treatment center in Houston, Texas, the Burzynski Research Institute, run by Dr. Stanislaw Burzynski, a Polish immigrant who'd been treating cancer patients since the 1970s with funding from the National Cancer Institute. He made headlines four years earlier for saving a terminally ill Long Island boy with his injections of "anti-neoplastins" he claimed were part of the body's natural defense mechanisms in fighting cancer cells.

When Jackie asked how Ted knew of this doctor, he explained that a number of Burzynski's patients had reached out to Nancy Tuckerman. Ted may not have known it, but the woman who spearheaded that letter-writing campaign was Mary Jo Siegel of California, in charge, at that time, of a support group of fifty patients of Dr. Burzynski's.

Mary Jo was diagnosed with non-Hodgkin's lymphoma about a year prior to Jackie's same diagnosis. Because the government launched a probe into Dr. Burzynski's methods, he was restricted from using them outside the state. Therefore, she had to fly to Texas for treatments, quite expensive for her but well worth it. She was able to raise her three children to adulthood and credits Dr. Burzynski with saving her life. In 1992, she was given a few months to live. As of 2022, she is still alive in California and now a happy grandmother.

"We loved Jackie," she recalled. "I mean, everyone loves Jackie. There was no reason she shouldn't experience a miracle as I did. We had the same cancer. It didn't have to be terminal. I felt it our duty as a patient support group to bring her attention to my doctor's treatment. So, we faxed or mailed our stories to Jackie in New York."

Because so many of the letters Nancy Tuckerman received cited the same doctor, she decided to forward them to Ted Kennedy for review. He was impressed and, in doing more research, discovered that the first patient the doctor had treated for terminal non-Hodgkin's lymphoma was back in 1980. "This particular patient was radiologically and physically 'cancer-free' in three months," recalled Dr. Burzynski. "He was an American who was treated mostly free of charge. He neglected to change his lifestyle, however, and continued to drink alcohol. About a year later, he went fishing, got drunk, slept out in the cold, got pneumonia, and died . . . cancer-free."

Ted also learned about the FDA's probe into the doctor's unorthodox methods, even though some at the National Cancer Institute thought the doctor's technique was effective. He told Jackie that, in his opinion, special interest groups benefiting from the multibillion-dollar cancer-fighting industry are "threatened by the Dr. Burzynskis of the world." Ted didn't care what the government thought of Dr. Burzynski. If Burzynski could save Jackie, Ted wanted her to be treated by him.

To be treated by the doctor, Jackie would have to go to Texas.

"Texas, Teddy?" she asked with a sigh. "*Texas?*"

Jackie didn't have to say what she was thinking; it was obvious. She was being asked to go to the very state in which Jack's life had been taken for her to now have a chance at a new one. To her, though, it sounded as speculative as it did ironic. She had always been the kind of patient to go with traditional, not experimental, treatments. She trusted her doctors. Ted understood. He told her that most of Burzynski's patients went to him after exhausting every possible conventional method.

"Let's see how your doctors do," Ted suggested, "and, if you decide to, we can circle back to Dr. Burzynski later."

Jackie agreed.

LIFE RUINING

◇◇◇◇◇◇◇◇◇◇◇◇◇◇

The next couple of months were brutal. The chemotherapy treatments Jackie started in mid-January were devastating; she felt terrible nearly every day. Though she tried to stay positive, it was difficult, especially when she'd look in the mirror at her hair loss. During this time, the noted hairstylist Edgar Montalvo, who worked for the Thomas Morrissey Salon, styled Jackie's wig for her every week at her home, in the bathroom, where she had a chair set up. "I brought her $2,000, $3,000 wigs and one $35 wig that looked the best out of all of them," he recalled. Though she tried to keep up with her weekly manicure and pedicure at home from a woman named Natalia Aldea, it was all starting to feel meaningless to her.

Jackie had always been inclined to fall into depression during dark times, and now was no different. She continued doing hatha yoga at home for as long as she could, until she was just no longer physically able. "All I want," she said the last time she saw Tillie Mia, her instructor of seventeen years, "is to ride my horses just one more time." She tried to work with the author Dorothy West, but wasn't able to visit her weekly as she had; *The Wedding* had become her passion project, but Jackie wouldn't live long enough to see it published. (It became a *New York Times* bestseller in 1998 and was optioned by Oprah Winfrey for a television movie starring Halle Berry.)

Seeing his mother so ill, John said, "has been life ruining for all of us." His heart ached for her. He wanted to believe she could fight it, he said, but with each passing day, it seemed less likely. "Still, if we hint that this could be the end, she becomes angry," he said. In truth, as she grew weaker and sicker, Jackie began to despair. She just didn't want her loved ones adding to her fear with their own.

"I feel we must be grateful for all the things we still have," she told Oleg Cassini, with whom she remained friendly all these years. She revealed her illness to him over dinner at the French restaurant Lutèce. She had already begun wearing a wig even though she said it wasn't completely necessary; she was just trying to get used to the idea of it. The biggest challenge for her, she said, was giving in to the limitations of the disease. She wanted to be who she'd always been, she said, but she just didn't have the energy she once had, "and once I accepted that, oddly enough things became easier."

"Even with all the challenges, our lives have just been so great, don't you agree, Oleg?" she asked. He, of course, concurred. With tears in his eyes, he lifted his glass. "To you, my dear Jackie," he said. She touched his glass with hers. "To us," she said, "dear Oleg."

That same day, Jackie wrote to Lady Bird Johnson. "Everything is going wonderfully," she wrote, and she hoped to see her on the Vineyard again next summer.

She wrote to Ethel. "Thank you for the lovely flowers—My goodness, I was floored by their beauty." She wrote that she was thinking of going to the Cape this coming summer and would love to see her. She added that when Caroline told her she had the flu, she was surprised any flu would dare try to slow down Ethel Kennedy, "and I am happy to know it was not successful."

She wrote to Joan that she was sorry she couldn't speak to her when she called recently, but that she was fine, "and I promise to call soon."

She also wrote to Jamie. She was happy to hear he planned to move to Ashland, Oregon, and knew he would enjoy his life there. The reports about her cancer had been exaggerated, she claimed. "I will be just fine," she concluded. "Don't worry about me."

She also wrote to Yusha and told him how much he meant to her. She signed it, "As always—XO—Jackie."

TEN GOOD YEARS

◇◇◇◇◇◇◇◇◇◇◇◇◇

Jack Warnecke picked up the phone and heard that familiar voice. "Hello, Jack. How've you been?"

It had been about a month since the ritual in her apartment during which he and Jackie had burned letters from loved ones in the fireplace.

Jack had never known anyone who enjoyed written correspondence more than Jackie. Recorded history had always been important to her. Whether it was restoring Lafayette Park—which she'd worked on with him in Washington—the White House or Grand Central Station, she considered American history in all its forms vital to our culture. It was one of the reasons she became an editor, to keep alive books about art and culture for future generations.

After her diagnosis, though, Jackie began that surprising ceremony of destroying her own personal history by burning letters from her friends. Every night for a week, she invited a different loved one to her home. That person would find her curled up in front of the fireplace in her pajamas with a chenille sweater, ready for about an hour of duty. Together, they'd reminisce about the past as Jackie reviewed old letters and, one by one, gently placed each on the burning logs.

As he hugged her goodbye that night, Jack Warnecke expected it would be the last time he'd ever talk to her. But then, a month later, he heard her wispy voice on the other end of the phone. "I have a project I think you'll be interested in," she told him. It was a book of architecture being published by Doubleday, and she hoped he'd write its introduction.

When he was interviewed in 2007, John Carl Warnecke asked that some details of this telephone conversation be withheld until ten years after his death. He passed away in 2010 of pancreatic cancer at the age of ninety-one.

As they talked, Jackie told Jack that after four chemotherapy treatments, her tests had come back clean. She thought she'd beaten the disease. She even called her old friend Michael Cacoyannis to tell him she was in remission. Then, unbelievably, an MRI showed that it had metastasized to the membranes of her brain and spinal cord. With that stunning revelation, she and her doctor could do nothing but stare at each other, speechless.

When Jack asked if she was frightened, Jackie said she didn't feel afraid as much as she felt defeated. All hope was not lost, however. She was considering an alternative medicine doctor Ted Kennedy had recommended and was reading up on his successes. Presumably, she was referring to Dr. Stanislaw Burzynski.

She did have a question. If the worst were to happen, was it wrong for her to want to be buried with her late husband at Arlington?

Jack said it wasn't wrong. In fact, he'd always intended that to be the case as far back as his original plans for the grave site. He felt it was where she belonged, especially since her children Patrick and Arabella were also there. "Just as it should be," she said.

Jack asked her if, in reviewing her life, she had any regrets. She wished she could say she had none. However, she said, "if we're honest, we all wish we'd done things differently. Nietzsche's question is a good one." She seemed to be referencing the philosopher's theory of eternal recurrence, which posits that if one had to live his life over again, would he be satisfied with the exact same choices, or would he choose otherwise?

Among any regrets she had, she said there was one big one: she said she wished she hadn't let November 22, 1963, poison the rest of her life.

"But that's not what happened," Jack said, surprised. He said she had gone on after Dallas and, in fact, she had even thrived.

"But I never got over it," Jackie said, sadly, "I got past it maybe, but never over it." Looking back, she wished she'd been able to put the assassination aside entirely and just live her life to the fullest.

It's what she'd always wanted, to move steadily forward, to live a rich life. "One must not dwell only on the tragedies that life holds for us all," she'd said in May 1972 in the rare interview she gave to Maryam Kharazmi while in Iran with Ari, "just as a person must not just think of only the happiness and greatness that they'd experienced. If you separate the happiness and the sadness from each other, neither is an accurate account of what life is truly like. Life is made up of both the good and the bad—and they cannot be separated from each other. It's a mistake to try to do that."

"What a shame, " she now told Jack, "to spend so much time tormented by a thing I could never change." Then again, Jackie mused, maybe that's what her husband deserved—for her to never really get over it. All she knew for certain was that she was still conflicted. She was also sure she could work it all out if only she had, as she put it, "ten good years."

Jack remembered, "I told her I never stopped loving her. When she paused, I thought she was going to say the same to me. Instead, she said, 'That's such a lovely thing to say, Jack. Thank you. I'd like to just leave it there if I may.' I told her, 'Yes, of course.'"

They promised to talk again soon. They never did. "We just left it there," Jack said.

NOTHING TO LOSE

<><><><><><><><><><>

Months had passed since Ted Kennedy mentioned Dr. Stanislaw Burzynski to Jackie, the doctor in Texas who, using unconventional methods, had successfully treated non-Hodgkin's lymphoma. Jackie had agreed that if treatments by her own doctors were unsuccessful, she'd consider going to Texas to consult with him.

At the beginning of May, Ted begged her to let him make an appointment. Jackie felt she had nothing to lose and wanted to go as soon as possible.

"I was notified by my office that Mrs. Kennedy would like to make a consultation at our clinic," Dr. Burzynski said in 2022. "Of course, I was honored by that, and of course, I asked my staff to make an appointment. By this time, we had cured seven patients with similar diseases to the one Mrs. Kennedy had. We had particularly good results with non-Hodgkin's. Some of those patients still survive thirty years later in perfect health without any sign of the disease.

"Unfortunately, the appointment couldn't be made until May 19 because I was traveling overseas. So, it was made for May 19, the day after I was to return to the States, at 10:00 a.m."

The appointment was made for "Jacqueline Kennedy."

"Can you hang on until then?" Ted asked Jackie.

"Of course I can," was her response.

They agreed that they'd go to Texas together.

TIME TO GO ON

◇◇◇◇◇◇◇◇◇◇◇◇◇◇

By the middle of May, Jackie had taken a turn for the worse. She was too weak to travel. In fact, doctors said she had only a short time to live. If she was going to die, she wanted to die at home, not in a hospital.

Throughout Wednesday, May 18, people showed up to be with Jackie and to console Caroline and John and to read passages aloud from some of Jackie's favorite poets, Edna St. Vincent Millay, Robert Frost, and Emily Dickinson.

On Thursday, May 19, Yusha drove as quickly as he could from Newport to New York for one last visit with the woman he had always loved. He had just been in Italy and had prayed hard for either Jackie's recovery or an end to her suffering. He needed to calm himself before he went in to see her, because he knew she wouldn't want him to be upset. He touched her hand. He kissed her goodbye. He whispered to her. "I should have felt sad, but she made me feel very happy and proud to realize how privileged I was to have shared her friendship at the close," he later said. "She could still show that same impatient move-ahead motion in her soft breathing and firm touch that she'd exhibited as a champion equestrienne. She knew it was time to go on, and she would not like to keep her maker waiting. She left without self-pity."

Yusha's friend Robert Westover recalled, "Uncle Yusha told me that as he sat with her and held her hand, all of their firsts came flooding back, their first trip to Europe when they were young, the first time they visited Arlington, their first kiss. He said, 'I looked at her and she was the same girl I'd always loved. If there had ever been a Camelot, I was her knight. And I was proud.'"

Also present were various Kennedys, Shrivers, and Lawfords, such as Ted and Vicki, but not Joan, whom Ted said was just too upset. Friends like Bunny Mellon and Carly Simon also stood vigil.

At about three o'clock, Ethel Kennedy came rushing in with two of her daughters. She saw Eunice and Pat as soon as she got off the elevator. "It can't be," she said, "it just can't be." After embracing one another, the three Kennedy women slowly walked to Jackie's room.

Jackie looked peaceful, lying on her coral-red canopy bed, her head wrapped in a print scarf, her eyes closed and hands folded over her chest. Gregorian chants played softly in the background. Shadows played on the room's pale, lime-green walls from flickering candles. A nurse monitored the morphine drip next to the bed.

"Oh my God," Ethel said as she walked into the room. "It can't be," she repeated. But then, as she got a little closer, she whispered, "Look at her, Eunice. My God. She's so beautiful. Just look at her." As Ethel took Jackie's hand, Eunice and Pat joined her at Jackie's bedside. Maurice then closed the door.

Later that evening, Lee arrived with her son, Tony. There'd been a bit of a reconciliation between the Bouvier sisters when Tony's cancer came back at about the same time Jackie was diagnosed. Maybe if they'd had more time, Jackie and Lee might've been able to find their way back to each other. Or . . . if past is prologue, maybe not. Later, it would be learned that Jackie made no provision for Lee in her will. She'd leave the bulk of her estate, nearly $200 million, to her children. In 2001, Lee would divorce Herb Ross and secure a sizable financial settlement for herself. She'd live in New York and in Paris, surrounded by close friends. "I'm almost happy," she'd say, which was very much like Lee.

As Lee and Tony walked into the hallway, they both embraced Caroline and then John. Then, Lee, her head bowed and her hand to her mouth, walked into Jackie's room. She saw Ethel, Ted, and Vicki gathered around Jackie's bed, praying. She walked to her sister and placed her hand on her cheek. "I love you so much," Lee said, crying. "I always have, Jacks." She kissed her on the lips. "I hope you know it," she whispered.

OLD GRUDGES

〰〰〰〰〰〰〰

On Thursday, May 19, 1994, Jamie Auchincloss drove from his home in Washington, D.C., to the Franklin D. Roosevelt Presidential Library and Museum in Hyde Park, New York, for two days of research for a fiftieth anniversary project relating to Roosevelt's 1944 campaign, the only fourth term and wartime campaign. He wasn't welcome at 1040 Fifth Avenue to say his goodbyes to Jackie, like his brother, Yusha, and sister, Lee. Taking their mother's lead, now Caroline and John considered Jamie a pariah because of that Kitty Kelley book of so long ago, "proving, once again," he quipped, "that, in our family, old grudges don't die, they just get shuffled down to the next generation." It's astonishing to note that Jackie, despite corresponding with Jamie regularly, had never even introduced him to Maurice!

When Jamie arrived at the library, the staff tried to boost his flagging spirits by telling him Jackie had checked herself out of the hospital. "I knew her well enough to know she wished to die quickly without medical fuss among the familiar objects and people she loved," he recalled. "'Control' was a term I applied to her more and more frequently. I predicted to the staff that the controlled morphine drip would take her out that same evening."

Finding himself too distraught to do any kind of research, Jamie, instead, visited Eleanor Roosevelt's grave. "I spoke to her and told her that Jackie was coming to see her," he said. "I also cautioned her that, likely, they'd not be sharing any clothing."

Jackie would have appreciated the humor. "There should never be a wedding without some tears," she had told Jamie when their sister Janet Jr. died, "or a funeral without some laughter."

LAST HOPE

◇◇◇◇◇◇◇◇◇◇◇◇

That morning of May 19, in a final, desperate attempt to save his sister-in-law, Ted Kennedy placed a call to Dr. Stanislaw Burzynski's office in Texas.

Jackie had an appointment that day to see the doctor, who'd just returned from overseas the night before. Ted's call came in just as Burzynski's office was about to telephone to inquire as to her whereabouts.

Ted asked if there was any way the doctor could fly to New York to treat Jackie. "Mr. Kennedy was reminded that Dr. Burzynski was still under grand jury investigation," said his Clinical Trials director, Dean Mouscher. "Treating her in New York would be a crime. Even a patient flying out of Texas with the medication was considered a crime by the FDA."

"My God," Ted exclaimed. "This is Jacqueline Kennedy! Surely, an exception can be made for Jacqueline Kennedy."

No. It just couldn't happen. Ted understood and said he'd have his office call later to make another appointment, for next week. "I'll get her down there," he promised. "Just give us a week."

Meanwhile, a weakened Jackie found the strength to make one last phone call of her own. To a priest. For last rites.

◇◇◇◇◇◇◇◇◇◇◇◇◇◇◇◇

Jacqueline Bouvier Kennedy Onassis died the night of May 19, 1994, with Caroline, John, and Maurice at her side. She was just sixty-four.

Diagnosed in January, gone barely five months later.

"There's something about her that's so unique," Jackie's mother, Janet

Auchincloss, once said of her. "No one I know looks like her, speaks like her, writes like her, or has a better idea of who she's expected to be in the world. She was much too young to be widowed when we lost Jack. It wasn't fair. But somehow, she goes ever forward despite a tragedy so great it would've destroyed most other women. Winston Churchill once said, 'It's the courage to continue that counts.' I believe that's true, and I have so much admiration for my daughter's courage."

Jackie was laid to rest at Arlington National Cemetery, next to her husband John Fitzgerald Kennedy—a president and his First Lady, side by side for all eternity.

Nearby rested their son Patrick and daughter Arabella.

And all was just as it should be.

SOURCE NOTES

More than five hundred friends, relatives, politicians, journalists, socialites, lawyers, celebrities, and business executives, as well as classmates, teachers, neighbors, friends, newspeople, and archivists, were contacted in preparation for *Jackie: Public, Private, Secret*. I and my research team also carefully reviewed, as secondary sources, the many books that have been published over the last fifty years about Jacqueline Kennedy Onassis and her assorted family members, as well as thousands of newspaper and magazine articles written about them. I'm not going to list all of them here, though I will acknowledge those relevant to my research.

As well as new and deep reporting specifically for this work, I also referred to research spanning nearly twenty-five years—1998 through 2022—for my previous histories of Jacqueline Kennedy Onassis and her family. Therefore, I am including in these notes those sources who provided background information during that time, as well as those who offered pertinent detail.

The following notes and source acknowledgments are by no means meant to be comprehensive as much as intended to give the reader a general overview of the depth of my research over a thirty-year span. Also, I've occasionally provided a little more information that didn't make it into the book but may still be of interest.

INTRODUCTION

The story relating to my book *Diana Ross: A Celebration of Her Life and Career*, published by Doubleday, was confirmed by numerous letters from Jacqueline

Onassis to Sam Vaughan, provided to me by an anonymous source. I also interviewed Sam Vaughan in 2007.

In one letter, dated March 11, 1983, Jackie writes, "Irving Lazar called to ask what we were going to do about the Taraborrelli book." She writes that she told him she was going to make available "Taraborrelli's manuscript for Diana Ross to go through," and that she would have "about a month" to do it. She wrote that Lazar said, "But I thought you were going to do her [Ross's] book and not the other one." Jackie told him Doubleday couldn't "simply set aside a book we had under contract without good (or bad) reason." She added that she didn't think "the Taraborrelli book" would preclude Diana from "one day doing her own version of her own truly wonderful story." She noted that Lazar was "quite surprised, not particularly welcoming of the news but reluctantly accepting of it." He said he and Diana Ross looked forward to "reviewing the Taraborrelli manuscript."

In a return letter, Sam Vaughan told Jackie he intended to continue to campaign for Diana Ross's memoir, "and if we are going to keep up the good will between her and us, we have to keep the lines warm." He wondered if they should have another meeting with her and if there was some other writer they could "introduce into the mix" who might appeal to Ross and Lazar.

In an undated letter, which appears to have been written sometime in the spring of 1983, Jackie told Sam Vaughan that she had repeatedly tried to contact both Diana Ross and Swifty Lazar but her calls were not returned. "I think perhaps they are upset with us," she wrote. She added it was "probably bad form" for her to continue to call and that she was going to stop doing so, "at least for now." She noted that she was in talks with Michael Jackson for his own memoir, that it looked "promising," and that she planned to ask Michael to "have a word" with Diana about her. "I feel he has influence over her," she wrote, "and certainly vice versa."

It would be ten years before Diana Ross would write the book she proposed to Jackie. Called *Secrets of a Sparrow,* it was published by Villard in 1993. While it overstates it to say there were "no personal details whatsoever" in the book, there were certainly not many.

FOREWORD: HOW REMARKABLE

Some of the material found here was culled from my interview with John Carl Warnecke in 1998, but the bulk of it comes from our interview in 2007. As Jackie had requested, Mr. Warnecke kept the manila envelope of family photographs. He reviewed them with me as he recalled their special evening together. It's not known what happened to the Louis XV–style giltwood mirror gifted to Jackie by Hugh Auchincloss. It wasn't mentioned in her last will and testament and wasn't found among her estate belongings auctioned off in 1996. Mr. Warnecke said Jackie had indicated to him that she wanted it to be given to Alexandra Rutherfurd, daughter of her half sister, Janet Jennings Rutherfurd.

BOOK I: BECOMING JACKIE

A WORD ABOUT JAMIE AUCHINCLOSS

James Lee Auchincloss is the only son of Janet Auchincloss and Hugh D. Auchincloss, half brother of Jackie Bouvier Kennedy Onassis. He has been so invaluable to my research, there's no way I would've been able to write this book without his memories of his parents and his siblings—his stepbrother, Yusha, his sister, Janet Jr., and, of course, Jackie, as well as his father's other children, Nini and Tommy.

Jamie was interviewed more than thirty times for this book alone and was interviewed at least that many times for my previous work about his mother and stepsisters, *Jackie, Janet & Lee*. He also provided some key photographs for this book.

Most of Jamie's interviews for this book took place in 2021 and 2022. Since he's not yet written his own memoir—someday soon, one hopes!—I feel honored that he has shared so many details of his life with me. The times I've spent with Jamie over the years have been so memorable and important to me. I appreciate his consideration so much.

In 2009, fifteen years after the death of his half sister, Jackie, Jamie got into trouble with the law after admitting to possessing child pornography. He was sentenced to thirty days in jail and three years' probation. I've always maintained that this surprising and unfortunate turn in Jamie's life in no way impacts his standing in history or his memories of growing up during the Camelot years. He paid his debt to society. Today, he lives in Oregon and spends much of his time researching his family as well as those of other presidents and lecturing at presidential libraries across the nation.

"NOBODY KNOWS THE REAL JACKIE" *AND* "THAT BOOK"

While the strange seating situation at President Kennedy's inauguration was alluded to in my book *Jackie, Janet & Lee* (2017), it wasn't until one of Jamie

Auchincloss's many 2022 interviews that the story could be put into context with the explanation of Jackie's decision to seat their mother and her stepfather behind the president.

As a side note, the book in question, *Jacqueline Bouvier Kennedy* by Mary Van Rensselaer Thayer, is worth reading. With a reader's basic knowledge of Jackie's history, it's easy to spot embellishments and fictions if only to better understand Janet Auchincloss's version of history. The book, which had been out of print for many years, can now be purchased or downloaded at Amazon.

I also referenced the text to Jamie Auchincloss's speech "Mud Wrestling with History: Snapshots of My Life as a Brother-in-Law to John F. Kennedy by James Auchincloss."

Interviews: Adora Rule (2016, 2022), Joan Braden (1998), and George Christian (1998).

Volumes: *Jacqueline Bouvier Kennedy* by Mary Van Rensselaer Thayer, *Presidential Wives: An Anecdotal History* by Paul F. Boller Jr., and *First Ladies* by Betty Boyd Caroli.

JACK KENNEDY

I referenced Charles Bartlett's Oral History for the John Fitzgerald Kennedy Presidential Library and Museum. I also referenced "The Kennedys—American Experience," PBS Home Video, DVD, 2003.

Interviews: Betsy Walker (2022), Charles Bartlett (1997), and Senator George Smathers (1999, 2000, 2001).

Volumes: *The Fitzgeralds and the Kennedys: An American Saga* by Doris Kearns Goodwin, *Jack Kennedy: The Education of a Statesman* by Barbara Leaming, *"Johnny, We Hardly Knew Ye"* by Kenneth P. O'Donnell and David F. Powers with Joe McCarthy, *An Unfinished Life: John F. Kennedy, 1917–1963* by Robert Dallek, *Profiles in Courage* by John F. Kennedy, and *JFK: Reckless Youth* by Nigel Hamilton.

THE FIRST FIANCÉ

I referenced the unedited audiotape of Janet Auchincloss's Oral History interview for the JFK Presidential Library and Museum, provided by an anonymous source. I also referred to the diaries of Hugh D. (Yusha) Auchincloss III, 1961, 1962, 1963, and 1964, before they were publicly auctioned in 2019. The diaries were also provided by an anonymous source.

Interviews: Jamie Auchincloss (2021, 2022), Hugh D. (Yusha) Auchincloss III

(1998, 1999), Trina Lloyd (2016), John Husted (1997, 1998), Maud Davis (1998), Gore Vidal (1998), Nina Auchincloss Strait (1998), and Charles Bartlett (1997).

Volume: *Jackie & Janet* by Jan Pottker.

WHAT IF . . . ?

After I wrote *Jackie, Janet & Lee,* I felt deeper reporting was in order to better explain how it was that Jackie ended up with John Kennedy after her sister Lee first expressed interest in him. This chapter is a result of that further reporting.

Janet Auchincloss's morning ritual with her children was described to me by her son, Jamie Auchincloss (2022).

Interview: Cybil Wright (2022).

JACKIE FINDS HER PURPOSE

I referred to correspondence to me from Joan Braden (1990).

Where John Davis is concerned, I also drew from his interview with Joan Rivers on *The Joan Rivers Show* (1992).

For parts of this chapter, I relied on Martin Lacey's 1990 interview with Dorothy Kinnicutt Parish for *Ladies' Home Journal.*

I also referenced J. B. (James Bernard) West's Oral History for the John Fitzgerald Kennedy Presidential Library and Museum, the interview for which was conducted in 1967 by Nancy Tuckerman and Pamela Turnure and released by the library in 1979.

So much has been written about Jackie's White House and Lafayette Square restoration, and, over the last thirty years, I have reviewed at least a hundred handwritten letters and memos from Jackie about it, such as the correspondence to Lady Bird Johnson mentioned in the text. Jackie also discussed her work in depth in her 1964 Oral History with Arthur Schlesinger.

I also referred to "What Price Camelot" by Paul Gray, *Time,* May 6, 1996.

Interviews: Jamie Auchincloss (2022), Adora Rule (2022), James Rowe Ketchum (2000), Gustavo Paredes (2016), John Davis (1999), Liz Carpenter (1998), Nancy Bacon (1998), Hugh D. (Yusha) Auchincloss III (1998, 1999), and Bess Abel (1998).

Volumes: *Designing Camelot: The Kennedy White House Restoration* by James A. Abbott and Elaine M. Rice, and *Jacqueline Kennedy: The White House Years: Selections from the John F. Kennedy Library and Museum* by Arthur M. Schlesinger Jr. and Rachel Lambert Mellon.

"VIVE JAC-QUI. VIVE JAC-QUI."

I referenced Jackie's Oral History for the John Fitzgerald Kennedy Presidential Library and Museum (1964), and Janet Auchincloss's Oral History (September 6, 1964). I also referenced Roswell Gilpatric's Oral History for the Harry S. Truman Presidential Library and Museum (January 19, 1962), as well as his Oral History for the John Fitzgerald Kennedy Presidential Library and Museum (May 5, 1970). I interviewed Mr. Gilpatric in March 1990 for my book about Michael Jackson (relating to Jackie's work with the entertainer), but the interview turned out to be wide-ranging, as were follow-up emails.

Volumes: *Jacqueline Kennedy: First Lady of the New Frontier* by Barbara A. Perry, *The Kennedy Men* by Laurence Leamer, *Mrs. Kennedy and Me* by Clint Hill and Lisa McCubbin, *A Lady First* by Letitia Baldrige, and *"Johnny, We Hardly Knew Ye"* by Kenneth P. O'Donnell and David F. Powers with Joe McCarthy.

ONASSIS

The brief meeting between Hugh D. Auchincloss and the Kennedy brothers at the White House was described to me by an anonymous source.

Interviews: Kiki Feroudi Moutsatsos (2022), Thea Andino (2022), Gustavo Paredes (2016, 2019), Clint Hill (2000), John Davis (1999), and Joe Gargan (1998).

Volumes: *Destiny Prevails* by Paul J. Ioannidis, *Nemesis* by Peter Evans, and *Onassis: An Extravagant Life* by Frank Brady.

"WHAT A LIFE WE'RE HAVING"

Much of the material found here is based on historical accounts of the Kennedy administration in 1961.

Rose Kennedy's note to Jackie was first published in Mrs. Kennedy's autobiography, *Times to Remember.* I also referenced *Rose Kennedy Remembers: The Best of Times, the Worst of Times,* BBC (1974).

Joan Kennedy's memory of Thanksgiving 1961 is from a letter from Mrs. Kennedy to the author, 1998.

I referred to the diaries of Hugh D. (Yusha) Auchincloss III, 1961, 1962, 1963, and 1964.

I also referenced the text of Jamie Auchincloss's speech "Mud Wrestling with History: Snapshots of My Life as a Brother-in-Law to John F. Kennedy by James Auchincloss."

Interviews: Jamie Auchincloss (2022) and Hugh (Yusha) Auchincloss (1998, 1999).

Volumes: *The Fitzgeralds and the Kennedys: An American Saga* by Doris Kearns Goodwin, *Upstairs at the White House* by J. B. West, *The Kennedy Legacy* by Theodore Sorensen, *With Kennedy* by Pierre Salinger, *Diamonds and Diplomats* by Letitia Baldrige; *Power at Play* by Betty Beale; "Ethel Kennedy and Life at Hickory Hill" by Leah Mason (unpublished manuscript), *The Kennedy Women* by Laurence Leamer, *Jack and Jackie: Portrait of an American Marriage* by Christopher Andersen, *All Too Human* by Edward Klein, *The Sins of the Father* by Ronald Kessler, *Seeds of Destruction* by Ralph G. Martin, *First Ladies* by Carl Sferrazza Anthony.

JACKIE'S EARLY DAYS

Jackie's memories of her childhood in New York City are from her essay for the *Vogue* 1951 "Prix de Paris" Competition.

Lee Radziwill's memories of her childhood are culled from an email she sent to an anonymous source in 2012.

I utilized Hugh D. (Yusha) Auchincloss III's sixty-seven-page memoir about his life with Jackie—*Growing Up with Jackie: My Memories, 1941–1953*—which can be found in the Hugh D. Auchincloss Personal Papers of the John Fitzgerald Kennedy Presidential Library and Museum.

I also referenced: "I Remember . . . Reminiscences of Hammersmith Farm" by Esther Auchincloss Blitz, Newport History (Newport Historical Society), spring 1994; "Original Manuscript of Esther Auchincloss Blitz: My Life," Newport Historical Society; "Hammersmith Farm" by John T. Hopf, Camelot Gardens Inc., 1979; "In Living Memory: A Chronicle of Newport, Rhode Island, 1888–1988," Newport Savings and Loan Association, 1988; "How the Remarkable Auchincloss Family Shaped the Jacqueline Kennedy Style" by Stephen Birmingham, *Ladies' Home Journal,* March 1967; and "Rose Kennedy Talks about Her Life, Her Faith, and Her Children," *McCall's,* December 1983.

I referenced various assets of the Auchincloss Family Collection of the John Fitzgerald Kennedy Presidential Library and Museum.

I also referred to the diaries of Hugh D. (Yusha) Auchincloss III, 1961, 1962, 1963, and 1964. I also referenced: "Hugh [Yusha] Auchincloss: Remembering Jackie O," NBC 10 / WJAR, November 20, 2013.

I referenced *One Special Summer* by Lee Bouvier and Jacqueline Bouvier.

Additionally: Birth certificate of James Lee Auchincloss, March 4, 1947,

Doctors Hospital Inc; invitation to Jackie's debutante party and Jamie's christening: "Mr. and Mrs. Hugh Dudley Auchincloss, Miss Jacqueline Lee Bouvier, Master James Lee Auchincloss, At Home on Friday, the first of August from five until seven o'clock, Hammersmith Farm, Newport, Rhode Island"; "Auchinclosses Hold Christening Party" by Betty Beale, *Washington Evening Star,* August 29, 1947; "Auchinclosses Give Party Following Christening," *Washington Evening Star,* January 8, 1946; "Unique Newport Entertainment to Mark Debut and Christening," by Katherine M. Brooks, *Washington Evening Star,* July 30, 1947; "Luncheon with Jamie Auchincloss," by Gwen Dobson, *Washington Evening Star,* December 22, 1972.

I also drew from John Davis's comment to Joan Rivers on *The Joan Rivers Show* (1992).

Interviews: Jamie Auchincloss (2021, 2022), Nancy Tuckerman (2007), Robert Westover (2016), Joe Gargan (1998, 1999), Nancy Bacon (1998), Maud Davis (1999), and John Davis (1999).

Volumes: *Gore Vidal* by Fred Kaplan, *A Woman Named Jackie* by C. David Heymann, and *The Kennedy Women* by Pearl Buck.

JOE'S STROKE, MONEY FOR A BABY? *AND* "DON'T LET THAT BE ME"

New reporting regarding Hugh Auchincloss's meeting with a lawyer to discuss the Kennedy fortune and also the decision to have JFK sleep in the servants' quarters as well as Janet and Hugh's reaction to Joe Kennedy's offer to Jackie was derived from an anonymous Auchincloss family source and corroborated by an attorney who represented the family.

Regarding the deal made by Jackie Kennedy and Joseph Kennedy, I referred to my extensive research about Joe Kennedy's stroke for my book *Jackie, Ethel, Joan* and the subsequent miniseries for NBC of the same name.

Regarding the loss of Arabella and the passing on of an STD to Jackie, I relied on my research on the topic for my book *Jackie, Janet & Lee.*

I referenced my interview with Secret Service agent Joseph Paolella (1998), who witnessed the scenes at Hyannis Port between Hugh Auchincloss and Joseph Kennedy, and then between Jack and Jackie Kennedy.

I also referred to Jacqueline Kennedy Onassis's Oral History at the Lyndon Baines Johnson Presidential Library and Museum (1974).

I also referred to "Life on the American News Front: The Kennedy Family: Nine Children and $9,000,000," *Life,* December 20, 1937.

The letter Jackie wrote to JFK around 1957—it's not dated—was auctioned by RR Auction in 2018. The letter was quoted at that time in *People*: "Jackie Kennedy Told JFK in Rare Love Letter Up for Auction, 'You Are an Atypical Husband'" (October 26, 2018).

Interviews: Jamie Auchincloss (2016, 2021, 2022) and Adora Rule (2021, 2022).

Volumes: *The Patriarch: The Remarkable Life and Turbulent Times of Joseph P. Kennedy* by David Nasaw, *The Sins of the Father* by Ronald Kessler, *The Founding Father: The Story of Joseph P. Kennedy* by Richard Whalen and Joan Whalen, *The Nine of Us: Growing Up Kennedy* by Jean Kennedy Smith, *Jacqueline Kennedy: Historic Conversations on Life with John Kennedy* by Caroline Kennedy and Michael Beschloss, *The Fitzgeralds and the Kennedys: An American Saga* by Doris Kearns Goodwin, and *My Life with Jacqueline Kennedy* by Mary Barelli Gallagher.

JACKIE'S TOUR OF THE WHITE HOUSE

For background on Blair Clark, I referred to "In Memoriam: Blair Clark, 1918–2000" by Marvin L. Kalb in *The Harvard International Journal of Press / Politics of Project,* MIT Press.

I also referenced the television programs *At Home with the Kennedys* (1952, 1958).

Interviews: Jamie Auchincloss (2022), Joan Kennedy (1998, 2001), Leah Mason (Ethel Kennedy's secretary, 2017), James Rowe Ketchum (2000), Perry Wolff (1997), and John Glenn (1997).

MARILYN, WHEN MARILYN CALLS, *AND* THE MADISON SQUARE GARDEN DILEMMA

I referenced my own extensive research of Marilyn Monroe history for my book *The Secret Life of Marilyn Monroe* as well as for the Lifetime miniseries of the same name based on it.

From the Papers of John F. Kennedy at the John Fitzgerald Kennedy Presidential Library and Museum, I obtained the telegram regarding Sardar the horse sent by Jackie to President Kennedy in Palm Springs while he was entertaining Marilyn Monroe. The telegram is: "From: The First Lady To: The President" with the notation (both in type and in handwriting) "Secret Eyes Only." (The word "Secret" is struck through.)

The apparently untrue story that Marilyn called Jackie at the White House and was invited by Jackie to give up her career and move in was first reported by C. David Heymann in *A Woman Named Jackie*. Peter Lawford was the source.

Secret Service agents Larry Newman and Joseph Paolella were both at Hammersmith when Jackie made her decision to absent herself from the Madison Square Garden birthday celebration. Mr. Newman was interviewed in 1999, 2000, and 2012. Mr. Paolella was interviewed in 1999, 2000, 2001, and 2012.

Interviews: Jamie Auchincloss (2022), Adora Rule (2021, 2022), Nancy Bacon (2005), Senator George Smathers (1999), and George Christian (1998).

Volumes: *The Kennedy Women* by Laurence Leamer, *Marilyn Monroe: The Private Life of a Public Icon* by Charles Casillo, *MM—Personal* by Lois Banner and Mark Anderson, *Goddess* by Anthony Summers, *Marilyn: Norma Jean* by Gloria Steinem, and *Marilyn Monroe: The Biography* by Donald Spoto.

"I REFUSED TO RAISE WEAK DAUGHTERS"

I wrote extensively about Mrs. Auchincloss's background and history in my book *Jackie, Janet & Lee*. Some of this chapter is gleaned from my many years of research for that work.

I referenced the extensive transcript of an unpublished interview Mrs. Auchincloss gave to *Ladies' Home Journal* in 1967, provided to me by an anonymous source. I also utilized Mrs. Auchincloss's two Oral Histories for the John Fitzgerald Kennedy Presidential Library and Museum (1964), as well as unedited transcripts of both.

I referred to the diaries of Hugh D. (Yusha) Auchincloss III, 1961, 1962, 1963, and 1964.

I also referenced the text to Jamie Auchincloss's speech "Mud Wrestling with History: Snapshots of My Life as a Brother-in-Law to John F. Kennedy by James Auchincloss."

I referenced: "Bouvier Estate Goes to Widow," *New York Times,* January 19, 1926; "James T. Lee Buys East 48th St. Site," *New York Times,* January 22, 1928; "Dr. James Lee Dies at 75," *New York Herald Tribune,* May 15, 1928; "Mrs. Auchincloss Hit by Propeller," *Washington Evening Star,* July 16, 1929; "Hugh Auchincloss Marries in Capital," *New York Times,* May 8, 1931; "Mrs. H. D. Auchincloss Asks Reno Divorce," *New York Times,* May 24, 1932; "Newport: There She Sits" by Cleveland Amory, *Harper's,* February 1948; "Mrs. Janet Bouvier Weds Lieut. Hugh Auchincloss," *East Hampton Star,* June 24, 1942; "Hugh D. Auchincloss Weds Janet Bouvier at Virginia Estate," *Newport Daily News,* June 23, 1942; "How the Remarkable Auchincloss Family Shaped the Jacqueline Kennedy Style" by Stephen Birmingham, *Ladies' Home Journal,* March 1967.

I also referred to: Marriage certificate, New York City, of Thomas Merritt and Maria Curry, June 6, 1875; Newark, New Jersey, census: 1860, 1870, 1880; St. Patrick Pro-Cathedral, Newark, New Jersey, baptismal records for James Lee, born December 23, 1852; baptism, January 1, 1853.

Interviews: Jamie Auchincloss (2016–2022), Hugh D. (Yusha) Auchincloss III (1998, 1999), and Nina Auchincloss Strait (1998).

Volumes: *Jacqueline Bouvier Kennedy* by Mary Van Rensselaer Thayer and *Janet & Jackie* by Jan Pottker.

"HAPPY BIRTHDAY, MR. PRESIDENT"

Larry Newman and Joseph Paolella were both at Glen Ora the weekend of the birthday celebration, and I relied on their interviews here. Moreover, I interviewed Secret Service agents Bob Foster (2000, 2002) and Lynn Meredith (2005).

Volumes: *The Kennedy Women* by Laurence Leamer, *Marilyn Monroe: The Private Life of a Public Icon* by Charles Casillo, *Goddess* by Anthony Summers, *Marilyn: Norma Jean* by Gloria Steinem.

FEELING OF DREAD, THE TROUBLE WITH LEE, *AND* "HOPE IS THE LAST THING TO DIE"

The letter from Jackie Kennedy to Joseph Kennedy was found in the holdings of the John Fitzgerald Kennedy Presidential Library and Museum.

The letter from Jackie to JFK from Ravello was part of the holdings of an auction held in 2018. It was said to have been given to the late presidential historian and collector Robert K. White by Kennedy's secretary Evelyn Lincoln, who died in 1995. He said that Jackie gave Evelyn the letter, telling her, "If anyone ever questions [the Kennedys' marriage], you can always say this is what our relationship truly was. It was a love relationship." One has to wonder about his claim, however, since Jackie was not that fond of Lincoln since it was she who helped arrange the president's clandestine affairs. However, the letter is authentic, in Jackie's own hand.

While I did not reveal Lee Radziwill's battle with anorexia in my book *Jackie, Janet & Lee* out of respect for her privacy, now that she has passed (2019), I feel it's an important piece of the puzzle of her complex life. I also referenced Mrs. Radziwill's books, *Happy Times* and *Lee*.

Jackie's comment about getting all her opinions from her husband is culled from her Oral History with the John Fitzgerald Kennedy Presidential Library and Museum (1964).

Additionally: "An Exclusive Chat with Jackie Kennedy, by Joan Braden," *Saturday Evening Post,* May 12, 1962; "The Public and Private Lee" by Henry Ehrlich, *Look,* January 23, 1968; "Lee Radziwill's Search for Herself" by John J. Miller, *Column,* December 17, 1972; and "Stay Tuned for the Princess" by Terry Coleman, *New York Post,* June 24, 1967.

Interviews: Annunziata Lisi (1999, 2000, 2015, 2021, and 2022), Terrance Landow (2016, 2022), Gustave Paredes (2016, 2018), Gilbert "Benno" Graziani (2009, 2010), Yancy Newman (1998), Larry Newman (1998), Jacques Lowe (1998, 1999, and 2000), and Clint Hill (1998, 2000).

Volumes: *Mrs. Kennedy and Me* by Clint Hill and Lisa McCubbin, *In the Kennedy Style* by Letitia Baldrige, *The Kennedy White House* by Carl Sferrazza Anthony, *Jacqueline Bouvier Kennedy Onassis: A Life* by Donald Spoto, and *Life in Camelot: The Kennedy Years* by *Life* magazine.

"BLACK JACK"

I referred to correspondence from John Davis (1998) answering questions relating to Jackie's relationship with her father.

I also referred to *Our Forebears: From the Earliest Times to the First Half of the Year 1940* by John Vernou Bouvier Jr., which was privately published.

I had access to an extensive collection of documents, letters, and other correspondence, consisting of more than a thousand pages of research, including legal and estate paperwork related to the Bouvier family, primarily John Vernou Bouvier III and his great-uncle Michel Charles Bouvier, compiled by historian John Davis, Jackie's first cousin. This material is the foundation for stories related to Janet Auchincloss's visit to Jack Bouvier at Jackie's request. The material was provided for my review by a private collector who obtained it at auction.

I also referenced "Daddy Didn't Want His Little Girl to Be a Kennedy" by Harriman Janus, *Photoplay,* May 1969.

Additionally, I interviewed Eva Marie Beale (2016) and had an extensive Q and A on August 29, 2016, about her relatives, the Beales, during which she shared a comprehensive family tree. Please visit her excellent website about her family at https://greygardensofficial.com/.

Interviews: Jamie Auchincloss (2022), Barry Davis (2016), Danine Barber (2016), and Kathleen Bouvier (2000).

Volumes: *The Bouviers; The Bouviers: From Waterloo to the Kennedys and Beyond;* and *Jacqueline Bouvier: An Intimate Memoir,* all three by John H. Davis, *Black Jack*

Bouvier: The Life and Times of Jackie O's Father and *To Jack with Love: Black Jack Bouvier, a Remembrance,* both by Kathleen Bouvier; *Jackie's Newport: America's First Lady and the City by the Sea* by Raymond Sinibaldi, *Palimpsest: A Memoir* by Gore Vidal, *Jacqueline Bouvier Kennedy* by Mary Van Rensselaer Thayer, *740 Park: The Story of the World's Richest Apartment Building* by Michael Gross, *Top Drawer: American High Society from the Gilded Age to the Roaring Twenties* by Mary Cable, *Louis Auchincloss: A Writer's Life* by Carol Gelderman, *Fifth Avenue: The Best Address* by Jerry Patterson, *Smithsonian Stories: Chronicle of a Golden Age 1964–1984* by Wilton S. Dillon, and *The Kennedy Women* by Laurence Leamer.

GREAT MEN AND THEIR FLAWS

Interviews: Jamie Auchincloss (2022), Jack Weston (2021, 2022), and Robert Westover (2016).

Additionally: "Kennedys Come Here for 10th Anniversary," *Newport Daily News,* September 12, 1963; "City, Navy Prepare for Kennedy Vacation from September 22 to October 4," *Newport Daily News,* September 18, 1961; "Kennedy Is Facing a Busy Weekend Before Leaving Newport on Monday," *Newport Daily News,* September 30, 1961; "Kennedy Swears in Customs Official at Hammersmith Farm," *Newport Daily News,* September 29, 1961; "President at Hammersmith Farm for Weekend with his Family," *Newport Daily News,* October 2, 1961; "Mrs. Kennedy in Newport with Caroline and John, Jr.," *New York Times,* June 28, 1961; "Sunset Days of Camelot—An Interview with Cecil Auchincloss" by G. Wayne Miller, *Providence Journal,* September 8, 2013.

SISTERLY CONCERN *AND* JACKIE'S INTERVENTION

Stella Brenton still treasures the 1961 postcard Janet Jr. gave to her as a keepsake.

I had the opportunity to question John Kerry at the 2018 Miami Book Fair in relation to his memoir, *Every Day Is Extra* (2018). His comments about the Kennedys and Auchinclosses were culled from that conversation. Additionally: "John Kerry's Record: One You Can Dance To" by David Segal, *The Washington Post,* February 2, 2004.

I referenced Janet Auchincloss's Oral History for the John Fitzgerald Kennedy Presidential Library and Museum as well as "The Auchincloss Family Collection" at the John Fitzgerald Kennedy Presidential Library and Museum.

Interviews: Stella Brenton (2022), Jamie Auchincloss (2016, 2022), Terrance Landow (2016, 2022), and George Christian (1998).

"WHO'S SHE?"

Ben Bradlee wrote extensively about Mary Meyer and the president's relationship with her in his book *A Good Life.*

When I interviewed Antoinette (Tony) Pinchot Bradlee in 1999, she was not forthcoming about her older sister Mary Meyer's relationship with the president. However, she did provide necessary background. She also said that after Mary's (still unsolved) murder in 1964, she found her diary. Though JFK's name was never mentioned in it, the Bradlees felt certain Mary had written about their affair. Both said they felt betrayed since they had been so close to Mary and the president. Tony gave the diary to the CIA's counterintelligence chief James Angleton, who promised to destroy it. Years later, she learned he'd not kept his promise. Through a friend, she was able to get the diary back and burn it herself.

I referenced the White House visitor logs at the John Fitzgerald Kennedy Presidential Library and Museum to confirm Mary Meyer's many visits.

Interviews: Jamie Auchincloss (2022), Lynn Meredith (2005), Anthony Sherman (2000), Anne Truitt (2000), Larry Newman (1998), Yancy Newman (1998), and Ben Bradlee (1995).

Volume: *A Very Private Woman: The Life and Unsolved Murder of Presidential Mistress Mary Meyer* by Nina Burleigh.

DADDY

It's worth noting here that in July 1952, Jackie wrote a letter to Rev. Joseph Leonard in which she said of JFK: "He's like my father in a way—loves the chase and is bored with the conquest—and once married, needs proof he's still attractive, so flirts with other women and resents you. I saw how that nearly killed Mummy."

Volumes: *The Bouviers: From Waterloo to the Kennedys and Beyond* and *Jacqueline Bouvier: An Intimate Memoir,* both by John H. Davis, and *Black Jack Bouvier: The Life and Times of Jackie O's Father* by Kathleen Bouvier.

HER WEDDING

Hugh D. (Yusha) Auchincloss III discussed Jackie's wedding with his friend Robert Westover, and we drew from his memories of their conversations. Lee Radziwill also discussed the day in depth with Sofia Coppola for *T Magazine / The New York Times* in 2013.

I also drew from many interviews with Jamie Auchincloss (2016–2022), the only living participant in the Kennedy wedding, as well as Adora Rule, who began working for Janet Auchincloss that same day (2016–2022). I interviewed Hugh D. (Yusha) Auchincloss III (1998, 1999).

I referenced "How the Remarkable Auchincloss Family Shaped the Jacqueline Kennedy Style" by Stephen Birmingham, *Ladies' Home Journal,* March 1967.

Additionally: "Kennedy Fiancé Plans Simple, Small Wedding," *Boston Traveler,* June 25, 1953; "Bride Nearly Crushed at Kennedy Wedding," *Atlanta Journal-Constitution,* September 13, 1953; "Jaqueline Bouvier, Senator Kennedy to Wed," *East Hampton Star,* July 16, 1953; "Kennedy-Bouvier License Issued," *Newport Daily News,* September 4, 1953; "What's She Like?" *Brockton (Massachusetts) Enterprise-Times,* June 28, 1953; "Kennedy-Bouvier Nuptials Held at St. Mary's Church Before 700 Invited Guests," *Newport Daily News,* September 12, 1953; "Kennedy-Bouvier Rites Colorful," *Danbury News-Times,* September 14, 1953; "Traffic Curbs Set for Kennedy-Bouvier Wedding," *Newport Daily News,* September 11, 1953; "Wedding Principals Enter St. Mary's Church This Morning," *Newport Daily News,* September 12, 1953; "What Jackie Kennedy Has Learned from Her Mother," *Good Housekeeping,* October 15, 1962; and "Getting Her Due on Doll's Dress: Designer Deserves Credit" by Samson Mulugeta, *Newsday,* January 11, 1998.

Also: Social Files / Senator's Wedding / John Fitzgerald Kennedy Presidential Library and Museum, including letters to Janet Auchincloss from John F. Kennedy (July 28, 1953) and Evelyn Lincoln (August 7, 1953, and September 3, 1953); "Suggested Lists for Jack's Wedding" for "Mrs. Auchincloss and Bobby," August 4, 1953.

THE CUBAN MISSILE CRISIS, GOD'S WILL, *AND* RESOLUTION

I referenced Jackie Kennedy's Oral History with Arthur Schlesinger for the John Fitzgerald Kennedy Presidential Library and Museum (1964).

I also referred to the Oral Histories of Paul B. Fay Jr., Nancy Tuckerman, Pam Turnure, McGeorge Bundy, Louella Hennessey, and Cardinal Richard Cushing (all 1964) and "Roswell Gilpatric's Personal Papers," all at the JFK Library.

Lee Radziwill discussed the Cuban Missile Crisis on *Larry King Live* in 2001. I also referenced "Lee" by Andy Warhol, *Interview,* March 1975.

More information about the Hickory Hill Seminars can be found at the John Fitzgerald Kennedy Presidential Library and Museum.

I referenced "An Exclusive Chat with Jackie Kennedy" by Joan Braden, *Saturday Evening Post,* May 12, 1962, and "What Jackie Kennedy Has Learned from Her Mother" by Stephen Birmingham, *Good Housekeeping,* October 15, 1962.

I also referenced "Hugh [Yusha] Auchincloss: Remembering Jackie O," NBC 10 / WJAR, November 20, 2013.

For the mother-daughters scene in the kitchen with pudding after dinner on October 22, 1962, I referenced the transcript of Janet Auchincloss's interview with *Good Housekeeping,* 1976.

Interviews: Jamie Auchincloss (2022), Terrance Landow (2016, 2022), Helen Thomas (2011), Oleg Cassini (1998, 1999, 2004), Nancy Tuckerman (2007), Chauncey G. Parker III (2005), Clint Hill (2000, 2002), and Ben Bradlee (1995).

Volumes: *Mrs. Kennedy and Me* by Clint Hill and Lisa McCubbin, *The Kennedy Women* by Laurence Leamer, *A Thousand Days of Magic* by Oleg Cassini, and *Designing Camelot* by James A. Abbott and Elaine M. Rice, *Bobby Kennedy: A Raging Spirit* by Chris Matthews, *Bobby Kennedy: The Making of a Liberal Icon* by Larry Tye, *The Kennedy Brothers: The Rise and Fall of Jack and Bobby* by Richard D. Mahoney and David Talbot, *Just Enough Rope* by Joan Braden, as well as *White House Nanny* by Maud Shaw.

PATRICK

I referenced my own extensive research about the loss of Patrick for my books *Jackie, Ethel, Joan* and *Jackie, Janet & Lee,* including Janet Auchincloss's Oral History for the John Fitzgerald Kennedy Presidential Library and Museum, in which she discussed her grandson's death.

Additionally: "2d Son Born to Kennedys; Has Lung Illness" by William M. Blair, *New York Times,* July 12, 1963; "President at Wife's Bedside" by Fred Brady, *Boston Herald,* August 10, 1963, "Family Rejoins Mrs. Kennedy," *Boston Globe,* August 10, 1963; "It Started Out as a Cape Outing," *Boston Globe,* August 9 1963; "Mother Cool, Calm in Crisis," *Boston Globe,* August 9, 1963; "Mrs. Kennedy Awaits News on Discharge," *Boston Globe,* August 13, 1963; "Mrs. Kennedy 'Fine,'" *Boston Globe,* August 8, 1963; "Mrs. Kennedy Gets News of Death from Doctor," *Newport Daily News,* August 9, 1963; "Bibs and Bootees Flood White House" by Blair William, *Boston Globe,* July 12, 1963; "Funeral Mass Said for Kennedy Baby," *New York Times,* August 11, 1963; "President at Wife's Bedside" by Campbell D. Kenneth, *Boston Herald,* August 10, 1963; "Love Letter from Camelot," *New York Daily News,* February 27, 1998; "Janet

Jennings Auchincloss Presented in Newport," *New York Times,* August 18, 1963; "Newport Debut Revelry Carries Over to 2nd Day," *Boston Globe,* August 19, 1963; "John Kerry: A Privileged Youth, a Taste for Risk" by Michael Kranish, *Boston Globe,* June 15, 2003.

Interviews: Jamie Auchincloss (2016–2022), Stella Brenton (2021, 2022), Virginia Guest Valentine (2017), Gustavo Paredes (2016, 2018), Yancy Newman (1998), and George Christian (1998).

Volumes: *Patrick Bouvier Kennedy: A Brief Life That Changed the History of Newborn Care* by Michael S. Ryan and *The Kennedy Baby* by Steven Levingston.

TRYING TO GET ON WITH THINGS

The letters to Jackie from Lady Bird Johnson, Ethel Kennedy, and Hugh D. (Yusha) Auchincloss III were provided by an anonymous source. I also referred to the diaries of Hugh D. (Yusha) Auchincloss III, 1961, 1962, 1963, and 1964.

I referenced "My 8 Years as the Kennedys' Private Nurse" by Rita Dallas with Maxine Cheshire, *Ladies' Home Journal,* March 1971. Additionally, Oral Histories from the John Fitzgerald Kennedy Presidential Library and Museum: Nancy Tuckerman, Pamela Turnure, William Walton, and Maud Shaw. I also referenced, from the JFK Library, "List of John F. Kennedy Visits to Hammersmith Farm," compiled by James B. Hill, February 2000. I also referred to Jacqueline Kennedy Onassis's Oral History at the Lyndon Baines Johnson Presidential Library and Museum (1974).

Interviews: Jack Weston (2021, 2022), Clint Hill (2000), Hugh D. (Yusha) Auchincloss III (1998, 1999), and Nancy Bacon (1998).

LEE'S BAD IDEA

I have written extensively about Jackie and Lee's 1963 trip to Greece in my books *Jackie, Ethel, Joan; After Camelot;* and *Jackie, Janet & Lee,* but with this latest reporting, I think the reader can now fully understand the context of the trip and Ms. Radziwill's motivation behind it. A number of anonymous sources contributed to this chapter.

Interviews: Agnetta Castallano (2020, 2021, 2022), Clint Hill (2000), and John Radziwill (2016).

Volumes: *Yours in Truth* by Jeff Himmelman, *With Kennedy* by Pierre Salinger, *Nemesis* by Peter Evans, *The Fabulous Onassis* by Christian Cafarakis, *The Onassis Women* by Kiki Feroudi Moutsatsos, *Robert Kennedy and His Times* by

Arthur M. Schlesinger Jr., *Maria Callas* by Anne Edwards, *All Too Human* by Edward Klein, *The Kennedy Women* by Laurence Leamer, *The Kennedys: America's Emerald Kings: A Five-Generation History of the Ultimate Irish-Catholic Family* by Thomas Maier.

BLACK JACK'S DECLINE

I referred to a letter John Davis sent me a year earlier, addressing questions relating to Jackie's relationship with her father.

Additionally: "John Bouvier 3rd, 66, Dies," *New York Times,* August 4, 1957; "John V. Bouvier 3rd," obituary, *East Hampton Star,* August 8, 1957; "Opening Chapters: Enchanting Memories and Photos of Her Early Life with Jackie" by Lee Radziwill, *Ladies' Home Journal,* January 1973.

Interviews: Jamie Auchincloss (2016–2022), Kathleen Bouvier (2000), and John Davis (1999).

Volumes: *The Bouviers; The Bouviers: From Waterloo to the Kennedys and Beyond;* and *Jacqueline Bouvier: An Intimate Memoir,* all three by John H. Davis, *Black Jack Bouvier: The Life and Times of Jackie O's Father* and *To Jack with Love: Black Jack Bouvier, a Remembrance,* both by Kathleen Bouvier, *Palimpsest: A Memoir* by Gore Vidal, and *Jacqueline Bouvier Kennedy* by Mary Van Rensselaer Thayer.

EVERY GODDAMN SECOND *AND* JFK'S NEW LEAF

I interviewed Robert S. McNamara in 2008 and referenced his Oral History for the John Fitzgerald Kennedy Presidential Library and Museum (1964) as well as "Staff Memoranda: Maxwell Taylor" (1962) found at the John Fitzgerald Kennedy Presidential Library and Museum.

Much of the material for these chapters comes from the transcripts of interviews Margaret Anne Mossey Kearney gave in 2000 for an Oral History of the Auchincloss family, which was supplied to me by an anonymous source.

Interviews: Jamie Auchincloss (2016–2022) and Adora Rule (2016–2022).

Volumes: *A Good Life* by Ben Bradlee, *Last Lion: The Fall and Rise of Ted Kennedy* by Peter S. Canellos, and *Times to Remember* by Rose Kennedy.

BOOK II: THE TRAGIC HEROINE

FRIDAY, NOVEMBER 22, 1963

In 1964, as one of its 552 witnesses, Jacqueline Kennedy gave her memories of the assassination of President Kennedy in sworn testimony to the Warren Commission. Prior to that, she spoke with Teddy White of *Look* about the ordeal. Of course, she also told the story to many of her friends and family members.

Additionally: Clint Hill interview with C-SPAN, May 2012.

THE VIGIL

Janet Auchincloss spoke in detail about her and her husband's time with Jackie at the Bethesda Naval Hospital in her two Oral Histories for the John Fitzgerald Kennedy Presidential Library and Museum (1964). The account in this book, however, clarifies her comments upon seeing Jackie for the first time by furthering our understanding that they weren't as random as previously thought.

There has always been confusion as to whose idea it was that Caroline and John be taken to their grandmother's home. Maud Shaw had always been blamed for the decision. She said Jackie had passed a message on to her to do so, yet Jackie said she'd never given the instruction. It's now clear that it was actually not Jackie's decision but rather that of Secret Service agents Clint Hill and Bob Foster.

I referenced Robert McNamara's Oral History for the John Fitzgerald Kennedy Presidential Library and Museum and the text to Jamie Auchincloss's speech "Mud Wrestling with History: Snapshots of My Life as a Brother-in-Law to John F. Kennedy by James Auchincloss." I also referred to Jacqueline Kennedy Onassis's Oral History at the Lyndon Baines Johnson Presidential Library and Museum (1974).

Interviews: Cybil Wright (2022, to whom Hugh D. [Yusha] Auchincloss III related his and his family's experiences at Bethesda), James Ketchum (2000), and Hugh D. (Yusha) Auchincloss III (1998, 1999).

SATURDAY, NOVEMBER 23, 1963

I referenced Janet Auchincloss's Oral History for the John Fitzgerald Kennedy Presidential Library and Museum. Hugh D. (Yusha) Auchincloss III wrote about his father Hugh's interest in *Think and Grow Rich* by Napoleon Hill in his 1964 diary. I also referenced the text to Jamie Auchincloss's speech "Mud Wrestling with History: Snapshots of My Life as a Brother-in-Law to John F. Kennedy by James Auchincloss."

Interviews: Jamie Auchinclosses (2016–2022), Cybil Wright (2022), and Robert Westover (2016).

Volumes: *Times to Remember* by Rose Kennedy, *A Good Life* by Ben Bradlee,

White House Nanny by Maud Shaw, *The Death of a President* by William Manchester, *The Kennedys: An American Drama* by Peter Collier and David Horowitz, *The Kennedys in Hollywood* by Lawrence Quirk, *President Kennedy* by Richard Reeves, *A Lady, First* by Letitia Baldrige, *First Ladies* by Carl Sferrazza Anthony, *In Search of History* by Theodore White, *Just Enough Rope* by Joan Braden, *The Dark Side of Camelot* by Seymour M. Hersh, *Palimpsest: A Memoir* by Gore Vidal, *All Too Human* by Edward Klein, *Jack and Jackie: Portrait of an American Marriage* by Christopher Andersen, *The Archbishop Wore Combat Boots* by Rev. Philip Hannan, and *Just Jackie: Her Private Years* by Edward Klein.

UNCLE HUGHDIE'S SAFE PLACE

I referenced Hugh D. (Yusha) Auchincloss III's diaries as well as his memoir, *Growing Up with Jackie: My Memories, 1941–1953*. I also referred to Janet Auchincloss's Oral Histories for the John Fitzgerald Kennedy Presidential Library and Museum (1964).

Additionally, I reviewed a pictorial scrapbook compiled by Janet for Hugh when the Auchinclosses sold Merrywood, entitled *Hugh D. Auchincloss, Merrywood, 1960* and inscribed: "For Hugh D.—A Souvenir of 18 Years Together at Merrywood, with all my Love, Janet, June 21, 1960." I also reviewed *Auchincloss Family Tree* by Joanna Russell Auchincloss and Caroline Auchincloss Fowler (Morgantown, PA: Higginson Book Co., 1957) and "Newport: There She Sits" by Cleveland Amory, *Harper's,* February 1948.

I referenced for this section and others relating to the Auchincloss family: "I Remember . . . Reminiscences of Hammersmith Farm" by Esther Auchincloss Blitz, *Newport History* (bulletin of the Newport Historical Society), spring 1994. I also had access to an original manuscript written by Esther Auchincloss Blitz about Hammersmith, provided by an anonymous source from a private collection. Additionally, I referred to *In Loving Memory: A Chronicle of Newport, Rhode Island, 1888–1988,* Newport Savings and Loan Association, 1988.

Also: "Hugh Dudley Auchincloss Marries Mrs. Nina Gore Vidal in Washington," *Newport Daily News,* October 8, 1935; "Hugh Auchincloss Marries in Capital," *New York Times,* October 9, 1935; "Hugh D. Auchincloss Weds Mrs. Janet Bouvier at Virginia Estate," *Newport Daily News,* June 23, 1942; "Mrs. Janet Bouvier Weds Lieut. Hugh Auchincloss," *East Hampton Star,* June 25, 1942; "How the Remarkable Auchincloss Family Shaped the Jacqueline Kennedy Style" by Stephen Birmingham, *Ladies' Home Journal,* March 1967; "Newport

Summer Residents," *The Newport Directory;* and "Hammersmith Farm" by John T. Hopf (n.p.: Camelot Gardens, 1979).

Interview: Jamie Auchincloss (2022).

Volumes: *America's Secret Aristocracy* by Stephen Birmingham, *Top Drawer: American High Society from the Gilded Cage to the Roaring Twenties* by Mary Cable, and *Louis Auchincloss: A Writer's Life* by Carol Gelderman.

THE ARRIVAL OF A PRINCESS

I referenced Janet Auchincloss's and Nancy Tuckerman's Oral Histories for the John Fitzgerald Kennedy Presidential Library and Museum.

Interviews: Clark Weston (2021, 2022), Nancy Tuckerman (2007), and John Radziwill (2016).

Volumes: *White House Nanny* by Maud Shaw, *True Compass* by Edward M. Kennedy, *Sons of Camelot* by Laurence Leamer, *The Kennedy Women* by Laurence Leamer, *The Kennedy Women* by Pearl Buck, and *Among Those Present* by Nancy Dickerson.

EAST ROOM MASS

I referenced Janet Auchincloss's Oral History as well as *Mrs. Kennedy and Me* by Clint Hill and Lisa McCubbin and *The Death of a President* by William Manchester.

Interviews: Jamie Auchincloss (2022) and Clint Hill (1998).

A SURPRISE GUEST

Interviews: Agnetta Castallanos (2022), Jamie Auchincloss (2022), and Taki Theodoracopulos (2016, 2017).

Volumes: *The Death of a President* by William Manchester and *Five Days in November* by Clint Hill and Lisa McCubbin Hill.

AN ICONIC DRESS

An unedited transcript of Janet Auchincloss's Oral History, provided by an anonymous source, is the source for this chapter.

Interview: Jamie Auchincloss (2022).

JACKIE'S VISITOR

This chapter is based on interviews with two anonymous sources.

SUNDAY, NOVEMBER 24, 1963

I referenced "The Indomitable Mrs. Rose Kennedy" by Eileen Foley, *Philadelphia Bulletin,* June 30, 1964. Also: *Dangerous Minds—The Kennedys,* CNN (1998) and *The Kennedys in Hollywood,* CNN (1998).

Interviews: Jamie Auchincloss (2022), Taki Theodoracopulos (2016), and John Radziwill (2016).

Volumes: *The Death of a President* by William Manchester, *The Hidden History of the JFK Assassination* by Lamar Waldron, *The Kennedy Detail* by Gerald Blaine, *Jack and Jackie: Portrait of an American Marriage* by Christopher Andersen, and *Five Days in November* by Clint Hill and Lisa McCubbin Hill.

ONASSIS GETS A REPRIEVE

I referenced *The Death of a President* by William Manchester.

Interviews: Jamie Auchincloss (2022), Eunice Kennedy Shriver (2002), Agnetta Castallanos (2022), Stanley Levin (2022), Taki Theodoracopulos (2016, 2017), Harry Middleton (1998), and C. Wyatt Dickerson (1998).

MONDAY, NOVEMBER 25, 1963

This chapter is based on Janet Auchincloss's telling of these events to her assistant Adora Rule (2022). I referenced a transcript of Mr. Sorensen's speech at the Charleston School of Law (February 23, 2010). I also referred to Jacqueline Kennedy Onassis's Oral History at the Lyndon Baines Johnson Presidential Library and Museum (1974).

Interviews: Nellie Connolly (1998, 2007), Christopher Lawford (2009), and Ted Sorensen (1998, 2009).

"GRIEF THAT DOES NOT SPEAK"

Interviews: Jamie Auchincloss (2022) and Arthur Schlesinger (1997, 2003, 2006).

Volumes: *Times to Remember* by Rose Kennedy, *True Compass* by Edward M. Kennedy, *Rose Kennedy's Family Album: From the Fitzgerald Kennedy Private Collection* by Caroline Kennedy, *Jacqueline Kennedy: Historic Conversations on Life with John Kennedy* by Caroline Kennedy and Michael Beschloss, *John Fitzgerald Kennedy: As We Remember Him* by Joan Meters and Goddard Lieberson.

CAMELOT POSTSCRIPT

I referenced my own extensive research into this historic evening for my previous books *Jackie, Ethel, Joan* and *After Camelot.* I referred to Jackie's Oral

History for the John Fitzgerald Kennedy Presidential Library and Museum. I referenced Theodore White's unedited notes from his landmark interview with Jackie, which can also be found in the John Fitzgerald Kennedy Presidential Library and Museum. The letter from Jackie to LBJ is found in the LBJ Presidential Library and Museum.

Jackie's 1953 poem was provided by Jamie Auchincloss.

I drew from *In Search of History: A Personal Adventure* by Theodore White. I also drew from Kerry Kennedy at a symposium on Kennedy women at the John Fitzgerald Kennedy Presidential Library and Museum (October 1996).

Note that throughout this book and in particular related to the assassination of President Kennedy, I referenced the CNN documentary series *American Dynasties: The Kennedys* (2018). As well as various Kennedy family members, I, too, was a commentator on each of the six episodes.

BOOK III: REBIRTH

A WORD ABOUT JOHN CARL WARNECKE

The many passages of the second half of this book about John Warnecke's relationship with Jacqueline Kennedy Onassis are culled from my interviews with him in 1998 and 2007. Some of what Mr. Warnecke told me he asked to keep confidential until after his death. He died in 2010, and that material appears here for the first time.

Special thanks to John's daughter, Margo Warnecke Merk, his son Fred Warnecke, his dependable personal assistant Bertha Baldwin, and his trusted business associate Harold Adams.

In 2021, I was asked by Margo to edit her father's autobiography, *Camelot's Architect*. This wonderful book will be published soon. In it, Mr. Warnecke sheds even more light on his relationship with Jacqueline Kennedy Onassis, but what's equally compelling are his vivid memories of his friendship with President Kennedy and the rest of the Kennedy family. It's well worth the read.

THE PASSING OF A YEAR

Tape recordings and transcripts of Jackie's telephone conversations with LBJ can be found in the Lyndon Baines Johnson Presidential Library and Museum. Years of Jackie's correspondence with LBJ and Lady Bird Johnson can also be found in the library. I also referred to "Love, Jackie" by Carl Sferrazza Anthony, AmericanHeritage.com, September 1994.

Interviews: Jamie Auchincloss (2016–2022), Margo Warnecke Merk (2016),

Fred Warnecke (2016), Harold Adams (2016), Liz Carpenter (1998), John Warnecke (1998, 2007, 2008), Joan Braden (1998), Bess Abel (1998), Clark Weston (2021, 2022), and Cybil Wright (2022).

JACK WARNECKE, "TIME QUALIFIES THE SPARK," "NOTHING ABOUT JACKIE IS EASY," AND TOO SOON?

I referenced Jackie's Oral History for the Lyndon Baines Johnson Presidential Library and Museum (1974). I utilized *Growing Up with Jackie: My Memories, 1941–1953* by Hugh D. (Yusha) Auchincloss III. I also referenced the text to Jamie Auchincloss's speech "Mud Wrestling with History: Snapshots of My Life as a Brother-in-Law to John F. Kennedy by James Auchincloss" and "I Should Have Known That It Was Asking..." by Jacqueline Kennedy, *Look,* November 17, 1964.

Interviews: Jamie Auchincloss (2016–2022), Margo Warnecke Merk (2016), Bertha Baldwin (2016), Harold Adams (2016), Robin Chandler Duke (2010), John Warnecke (2007), and Hugh D. (Yusha) Auchincloss III (1998, 1999).

ROSE'S ADVICE

LBJ's correspondence with Jackie can be found in the Lyndon Baines Johnson Presidential Library and Museum. Correspondence from Ethel Kennedy and Joan Kennedy to Jackie can be found in the John Fitzgerald Kennedy Presidential Library and Museum.

Jackie's tribute to President Kennedy appeared in *Look,* November 17, 1964. I also referenced "A Visit with the Indomitable Rose Kennedy," *Look,* November 26, 1968.

Interviews: Fred Warnecke (2016), Harold Adams (2016), Bertha Baldwin (2016), Gustavo Paredes (2016), and John Warnecke (1998, 2007).

Volumes: *Times to Remember* by Rose Kennedy and *The Kennedy Women* by Laurence Leamer.

JACKIE KENNEDY ON A BUDGET?

Janet Auchincloss's meeting with Bobby Kennedy was described by an anonymous source. I referenced John Seigenthaler's Oral History for the Edward M. Kennedy Institute. I also drew from Barbara Gibson's comments to Joan Rivers on *The Joan Rivers Show* (1992).

Interview: Jamie Auchincloss (2022).

Volume: *Life with Rose Kennedy* by Barbara Gibson.

JACKIE, BOBBY, AND ETHEL *AND* JACKIE'S LEDGER

In addition to my interview with Charles Spaulding (1997), I referenced his Oral History for the John Fitzgerald Kennedy Presidential Library and Museum (1968). For the relationship between Jackie Kennedy and Ethel Kennedy, I referred to my extensive research for my book *Jackie, Ethel, Joan.* I referred to a Q and A I conducted with Mary Barelli Gallagher by email (2001) as well as her book, *My Life with Jacqueline Kennedy.*

Interviews: Mona Latham (2010, 2022), Eunice Kennedy Shriver (2002), Clint Hill (1999), Joan Braden (1998), Harry Middleton (1998), C. Wyatt Dickerson (1998), and Andy Williams (2000, 2001).

Volume: *Just Enough Rope* by Joan Braden.

ROSWELL GILPATRIC *AND* STILL SUFFERING?

I referred to my interview with John Warnecke (2007) and Mona Lathan (2020, who recalled the conversation between André Meyer, Hugh Auchincloss, and Jackie, as per André's recollection of it.

I utilized a Q and A I did with Roswell Gilpatric in 1990, follow-up emails with him (1994), as well as his Oral Histories with the John Fitzgerald Kennedy Presidential Library and Museum (#1 and #2, 1970) and his Oral History with the Lyndon Baines Johnson Presidential Library and Museum (1982).

Jackie's letter to Roswell Gilpatric was provided by an anonymous source.

I referred to Kenny O'Donnell's Oral Histories (#1 and #2, 1969) and Joseph Alsop's Oral Histories (#1, #2, 1964) with the John Fitzgerald Kennedy Presidential Library and Museum, as well as "John F. Kennedy on Politics and Public Service," White House Tapes, Miller Center Presidential Recordings Program, University of Virginia.

The Christopher Andersen book mentioned is *Jack and Jackie: Portrait of an American Marriage* (1996).

Volume: *Jackie's Girl: My Life with the Kennedy Family* by Kathy McKeon.

JANET JR.'S CHOICE *AND* THE GRAND GESTURE

These chapters are fundamentally drawn from my interviews with Jamie Auchincloss (2022) and John Warnecke (1998, 2007), as well as Virginia Guest Valentine (2016), Sylvia Whitehouse Blake (2016), Winthrop Rutherfurd III (2016), and Gustavo Paredes (2016).

Jackie's letter to Lady Bird Johnson can be found at the LBJ Presidential Library and Museum.

I also referred to "Jackie Kennedy—World's Most Eligible Widow, Will She Marry Again?" by Lloyd Shearer, *Detroit Free Press,* December 4, 1966; "Jackie A'loha: When Jacqueline Kennedy Lived in Hawaii for Seven Weeks" by Carl Anthony, CarlAnthonyOnLine.com, June 5, 2012.

For more on Jackie's vacation in Hawaii and also Janet Jr.'s wedding, see my book *Jackie, Janet & Lee.*

TRUST ISSUES

I referenced "Clash of Camelots" by Sam Kashner, *Vanity Fair,* October 2009. For more on the bitter William Manchester lawsuit, this terrific reporting is easily searchable on the Internet.

I also referred to "The First Lady as a Leader of Public Opinion," Ph.D. dissertation, Norma Ruth Holly Forman, University of Texas at Austin, May 1971. Jackie's correspondence with LBJ about the Manchester matter is found in the Lyndon Baines Johnson Presidential Library and Museum.

Interviews: Jamie Auchincloss (2022), Harold Adams (2016), Bertha Baldwin (2016), Robert Westover (2016), Margo Warnecke Merk (2016), George Christian (1998), John Warnecke (1998, 2007), Harry Middleton (1998), and C. Wyatt Dickerson (1998).

Volumes: *The Death of a President* by William Manchester, *In Search of History* by Theodore White, and *White House Nanny* by Maud Shaw.

ARTEMIS

I referenced William Davis Ormsby Gore's Oral History for the John Fitzgerald Kennedy Presidential Library and Museum (1970).

Interviews: Kiki Feroudi Moutsatsos (2022), Thea Andino (2022), Joan Thring (1998), and Johnny Meyer (1998).

Volumes: *The Onassis Women* by Kiki Feroudi Moutsatsos, *The $20,000,000 Honeymoon* by Fred Sparks, *Maria Callas* by Anne Edwards, and *The Fabulous Onassis* by Christian Cafarakis.

GRAMPY LEE'S DEATH

I referenced "James T. Lee," *National Cyclopedia of American Biography,* vol. 54, and "James Lee, Ex-Official in City Schools, Dies," *New York Times,* May 15, 1928.

Interview: Jamie Auchincloss (2022).

GREEK MAGIC, ARTEMIS'S ADVICE, *AND* TURNING POINT

Jackie's note to Aristotle Onassis about her allegiance to Bobby Kennedy was provided by an anonymous source. I utilized a Q and A I did with Roswell Gilpatric by email (1994) as well as a follow-up telephone call (1994).

For more on Bobby and Ethel's reaction to Jackie and Onassis, see my books *Jackie, Ethel, Joan* and *After Camelot*.

Interviews: Kiki Feroudi Moutsatsos (2022), Thea Andino (2022), Mona Latham (2022), Nicolas Knoaledius (2022), Stanley Levin (2021, 2022), Acantha Rowe (2022), Frank Mankiewicz (2011), and Richard Goodwin (1998).

Volumes: *Cast a Diva: The Hidden Life of Maria Callas* by Lyndsy Spence, *Maria Callas: Sacred Monster* by Stelios Galatopoulos, *The Fabulous Onassis* by Christian Cafarakis, *Onassis* by Willi Frischauer, *Heiress: The Story of Christina Onassis* by Nigel Dempster, *Onassis: An Extravagant Life* by Frank Brady, and *Destiny Prevails* by Paul J. Ioannidis.

MEETING THE KENNEDYS

I referred to my Q and A with Roswell Gilpatric (1994).

I utilized Jacqueline Kennedy's Oral Histories with the John Fitzgerald Kennedy and Lyndon Baines Johnson Presidential Libraries and Museums.

Jackie's note to Ethel Kennedy after Bobby Kennedy's assassination was provided by an anonymous source. Jackie's note to Roswell Gilpatric after she married Onassis was made public when it was among letters from her to him that were auctioned in 2017.

Interviews: Barbara Gibson (1998, 1999, 2000, 2001), Rosemary Smathers (1999), and Senator George Smathers (1999, 2000).

Volumes: *Times to Remember* by Rose Kennedy and *Life with Rose Kennedy* by Barbara Gibson.

MEETING THE AUCHINCLOSSES

Interviews: Jamie Auchincloss (who was present at his home, Hammersmith Farm, for the Onassis visit; 2016, 2022), Kiki Feroudi Moutsatsos (2022), Adora Rule (2016, 2022), Thea Andino (2022), and Robert Westover (2016).

Volumes: *Destiny Prevails* by Paul J. Ioannidis, *Onassis: An Extravagant Life* by Frank Brady, and *Nemesis* by Peter Evans.

THE DEAL

For more on the arrangement Ted Kennedy made with Aristotle Onassis, see my book *After Camelot.*

Interviews: Alexios Diakas (2022), Mona Latham (2022), and Agnetta Castallanos (2016, 2020, 2021).

THE KENNEDYS SEND THEIR REGRETS

Interviews: Mona Latham (2022), Eunice Kennedy Shriver (2002), Nancy Tuckerman (2007), and Barbara Gibson (1998, 1999).

Volumes: *Times to Remember* by Rose Kennedy and *True Compass* by Edward M. Kennedy.

ONE STEP FORWARD

I referenced "Onassis Mother-in-Law Denies Divorce Claim," *Boston Globe,* April 19, 1975; "Onassis: Memories of an Insomniac," *Washington Evening Star,* March 17, 1975; and "A Dream Realized" by Jacqueline Kennedy Onassis, *Ladies' Home Journal,* September 1971.

It was always very illuminating perusing the "Jackie's Wedding to Onassis" file (Box 4) of the Rose Fitzgerald Kennedy Papers of the John Fitzgerald Kennedy Presidential Library and Museum, as well as "Diaries 1959–1970" (Box 4), in which Rose writes about Jackie's marriage to Onassis. "Comments and Corrections on the *Times to Remember* Manuscript" (Box 19) is also interesting in that Rose seemed uncertain as to how she wanted to frame her opinion of Jackie's marriage and, ultimately, decided to be very magnanimous. I also referenced my interview with Cybil Wright (2022), to whom Hugh D. (Yusha) Auchincloss III related his father's moments with Jackie before her marriage to Onassis.

Interviews: Adora Rule (2016, 2022), Kiki Feroudi Moutsatsos (2022), and Thea Andino (2022), Robert Westover (2016), and Marie-Hélène de Rothschild (2016).

Volumes: *Jackie's Girl: My Life with the Kennedy Family* by Kathy McKeon, *Rose Kennedy and Her Family: The Best and Worst Times of Their Lives and Times* by Barbara Gibson and Ted Schwarz, *Jack Kennedy: Elusive Hero* by Chris Matthews, and *Nemesis* by Peter Evans.

BOOK IV: DECISIONS AND CONSEQUENCES

A WORD ABOUT KIKI FEROUDI MOUTSATSOS

I am so honored to have had the cooperation of Kiki Feroudi Moutsatsos. Without her, I never would've been able to bring to life her close friend Artemis Garoufalidis, Aristotle Onassis's sister and the matriarch of his family. I wanted to acknowledge Artemis in this book because I felt she was undervalued in other accounts of Jackie's life. Kiki made that goal attainable. As Aristotle Onassis's personal assistant, Kiki had a front-row seat to so much amazing history, and I'm grateful for all the interviews she gave for *Jackie: Public, Private, Secret.*

Kiki has a terrific book of her own, *The Onassis Women,* and I highly recommend it. It's riveting and can be purchased on Amazon.com.

MRS. ONASSIS

Clark Weston (2022) and Garrett Johnson (2022) both provided information relating to Hugh Auchincloss's health challenges at this time and the hospitalization paid for by the Onassises.

Lee Radziwill's late biographer, Diana DuBois (1998), provided information about her anorexia and treatment. I also referenced Ms. DuBois's book *In Her Sister's Shadow.*

Aristotle Onassis's comments about his marriage to Jackie—"She can do exactly as she pleases"—were widely quoted at the time.

I also referred to "Meet Marta: The Nanny Who Cared for the Kennedys" by Max Barbakow and Cristina Costantini, ABC News, March 12, 2013; and "Why My Sister Married Aristotle Onassis—An Exclusive Interview with Lee Radziwill," *Cosmopolitan,* June 1969.

Interviews: Kiki Feroudi Moutsatsos (2022), Agnetta Castallanos (2022), Thea Andino (2022), Jamie Auchincloss (2022), Gustavo Paredes (2016, 2018), John Radziwill (2016), Robert Westover (2016), and Janine Rule (2022, relating to the hiring of Maud Shaw and her early relationship with Janet Auchincloss).

RUTH AND NAOMI

I referred to "Rose Kennedy at 80," *Life,* July 1970.

For this section and others in this book, I referenced Rose Kennedy's diaries, which can be found in the Rose Fitzgerald Kennedy Papers of the John Fitzgerald Kennedy Presidential Library and Museum along with perhaps more than a hundred letters from her. Her writings can be difficult to understand, however, because of her often illegible handwriting. It's a problem I also faced with Hugh D. (Yusha) Auchincloss III's diaries—as well as those of his father, Hugh D. Auchincloss Jr.—all of which are extremely difficult to decipher.

Interviews: Kiki Feroudi Moutsatsos (2022), Agnetta Castallanos (2022),

Benedict Fitzgerald (2004, 2014), Barbara Gibson (1998), and Edward Larrabee Barnes (1998, 1999).

Volumes: *The Kennedy Women* by Laurence Leamer, *Times to Remember* by Rose Kennedy, *True Compass* by Edward M. Kennedy, *Life with Rose Kennedy* by Barbara Gibson, *Rose Kennedy* by Barbara A. Perry, *Rose: A Biography* by Gail Cameron, and *Iron Rose* by Cindy Adams and Susan Crimp.

PETER BEARD

I referenced "The Complicated Sisterhood of Jackie Kennedy and Lee Radziwill" by Sam Kashner, *Vanity Fair,* April 2016.

Interviews: Agnetta Castallanos (2022), Kiki Feroudi Moutsatsos (2022), Barbara Allen Kwiatowska (2016), Peter Beard (1998), and Diana DuBois (1998).

Volumes: *In Her Sister's Shadow* by Diana DuBois, and *Happy Times* and *Lee,* both by Lee Radziwill

"SOME THINGS YOU JUST DON'T TALK ABOUT"

The material relating to Janet Auchincloss's discovery is based on interviews with anonymous sources. Regarding Jackie's nudes, I interviewed the photographer Settimio Garritano's widow, Katia Bede Garritano (2016).

Interviews: Jamie Auchincloss (2022), Kiki Feroudi Moutsatsos (2022), Thea Andino (2022), and Jack Warnecke (1998, 2007).

Volume: *Palimpsest: A Memoir* by Gore Vidal.

JACKIE'S THERAPIST *AND* MONTAUK

I referenced "Jacqueline Kennedy Onassis in Tehran" by Maryam Kharazmi, *Kayhan,* Iran, May 1972.

Jackie described her near drowning in a letter to Thomas T. Hendrick, special assistant to the secretary, Department of the Treasury, Secret Service detail on August 7, 1967. "The water was so cold that one could not hold one's fingers together," she wrote. "I am a very good swimmer and can swim for miles and hours but the combination of current and cold were something I had never known. There was no one in sight to yell to. I was becoming exhausted, swallowing water and slipping past the spit of land, when I felt a great porpoise at my side. It was Mr. Walsh [Jack Walsh, her Secret Service agent]."

For more on Dr. Marianne Kris, see my book *The Secret Life of Marilyn Monroe.*

Jackie's letter to Pat Nixon can be found in the holdings of the Richard Nixon Presidential Library and Museum. I also referred to "Inside Jackie Kennedy's Secret Visit to the White House," by Jennifer Boswell Pickens, *Town & Country,* February 3, 2021.

Peter Beard's comment—"Lots of loyalty . . ."—is culled from an email by him (1998).

I also referenced "Nobody Needs a Part Time Marriage—Interview with Prince Stanislaw Radziwill" by George Carpozi Jr., *Photoplay,* April 1973.

Interviews: Jamie Auchincloss (2022), Stanley Levin (2022), Adora Rule (2022), Dawn Morris (2022, along with a Q and A by email), Patricia Atwood (2022), Jay Mellon (1998), and Karen Lerner (2015).

"MUTUAL WAIVER & RELEASE" *AND* GIVING UP A FORTUNE

I reported on Jackie's meeting with Janet Auchincloss at the Colony Club relating to Hammersmith in my book, *Jackie, Janet & Lee.* For this book, Jackie's meeting with Hugh Auchincloss regarding the same subject is culled from interviews with his associate Garrett Johnson (2022).

I also referenced: "Auchincloss Says He Isn't Surprised on Farm Rejection," *Providence Journal-Bulletin,* May 8, 1976; "Auchincloss Tells of Wish to Save Family Estate," *Newport Daily News,* April 23, 1976; "Exclusively Yours: Historic Hammersmith," by Betty Beale, *Washington Evening Star,* November 28, 1971; "Committee Endorses Plan," *Providence Journal-Bulletin,* March 27, 1977; "Cultural Center Proposed for Hammersmith Farm," *Providence Journal-Bulletin,* August 10, 1977.

Interviews: Jamie Auchincloss (2022), Kiki Feroudi Moutsatsos (2022), Leah Mason (2015, regarding Jackie's loan to Ethel), Stanley Levin and Mona Lathan (both 2022 regarding Jackie's meeting with Onassis and her signing of the "Mutual Waiver & Release").

THE BEGINNING OF THE END

The correspondence from Lady Bird Johnson to Jackie can be found at the Lyndon Baines Johnson Presidential Library and Museum.

I drew from Hugh D. (Yusha) Auchincloss III's auctioned diaries (1964) and his *Growing Up with Jackie: My Memories, 1941–1953.*

Interviews: Kiki Feroudi Moutsatsos (2022), Jaimie Auchincloss (2022), Gustavo Paredes (2016, 2018), Garrett Johnston (2016, 2022, who was present and an eyewitness to the Onassis visit to Hammersmith Farm in July of 1973), Karen Lerner (2009, 2015), and Letitia Baldrige (2000).

Volumes: *In Her Sister's Shadow* by Diana DuBois and *Jackie & Janet* by Jan Pottker.

A HOLLYWOOD KISS

I referred to the Auchincloss Hammersmith guest book.

Interviews: James Redford (2010) and George Christian (1998).

Volumes: *Robert Redford: The Biography* by Michael Feeney Callan, *The Outlaw Trail: A Journey Through Time* by Robert Redford and Jonathan Blair, *Filming* The Great Gatsby by Bruce Bahrenburg, *The Sundance Kid: A Biography of Robert Redford* by William Schoell and Lawrence J. Quirk, and *F. Scott Fitzgerald at Work: The Making of* The Great Gatsby by Horst H. Kruse.

"WILL WE EVER GET OVER IT?" MARITAL TENSIONS, *AND* PRENEZ BIEN SOIN

I referenced an email exchange with Patricia Atwood (2022). I also drew from an email exchange with Peter Beard (2018).

Interviews: Jamie Auchincloss (2022), Kiki Feroudi Moutsatsos (2022), Acantha Rowe (2022), Thea Andino (2022), Adora Rule (2016, 2022), Janine Rule (2022), Leah Mason (2012), Noelle Bombardier (2012, 2015), Stelio Papadimitriou (1999), and Frank Mankiewicz (1998).

Volumes: *Greek Fire* by Nicholas Gage, *Onassis: An Extravagant Life* by Frank Brady, and *Capote* by Gerald Clarke.

OUTSIDE OF HERSELF

I referenced a Q and A email with Joan Kennedy (1998). I also referenced Jackie's February 24, 1975, letter to Mayor Abraham Beame.

I referred to a transcript of Jackie's press conference in the Oyster Bar of Grand Central Station as well as "The Surprising Role Jackie Kennedy Onassis played in Saving Grand Central Station" by Tina Cassidy, Bloomberg, February 3, 2013. I also referenced to "Love, Jackie" by Carl Sferrazza Anthony, AmericanHeritage.com, September 1994; "Part of the Family" by Paula Span, *New York Post,* May 30, 1994; "Jackie's Manifesto" by Liz Smith, *New York Newsday,* June 17, 1994.

Interviews: Jamie Auchincloss (2022), Thea Andino (2022), R. Couri Hay (2018), Frederick Papert (2008), and Dave Powers (1997).

Volumes: *When Jackie Saved Grand Central* by Natasha Wing, *America's Queen* by Sarah Bradford, *Jacqueline Kennedy Onassis* by Donald Spoto, *Just Jackie: Her Private Years* by Edward Klein.

"HE DIDN'T HAVE MANY FRIENDS" *AND* WHAT REMAINS

Rose Kennedy's letter to Jackie can be found in the John Fitzgerald Kennedy Presidential Library and Museum. Lady Bird Johnson's letter can be found in the Lyndon Baines Johnson Presidential Library and Museum. John Warnecke provided his letter in 2007, and Ethel Kennedy's was provided by an anonymous source.

Interviews: Jamie Auchincloss (2022), Stanley Levin (2022), Thea Andino (2022), Taki Theodoracopulos (2016), Karen Lerner (2009), Bess Abel (1998), Edward Larrabee Barnes (1998, 1999), Dave Powers (1997), and Liz Carpenter (1994).

Volumes: *The Fortune Hunters* by Charlotte Hays, *Just Jackie: Her Private Years* by Edward Klein, and *America's Queen* by Sarah Bradford.

BOOK V: NEW HORIZONS

HER THIRD ACT

I referenced "Dorothy Schiff—the Real Woman" by Rona Barrett, KABC, Los Angeles. Additionally, I referred to transcripts of the symposiums "The Kennedy Women" and "The Literary Life of Jacqueline Kennedy Onassis" at the John Fitzgerald Kennedy Presidential Library and Museum, October 4, 1996, and January 23, 2012, respectively.

Interviews: Captain Buddy Vanderhoop (2022), Cybil Wright (2022), Robert Westover (2016), Tom Guinzburg (2005, 2007), Dave Powers (1997), Frank Mankiewicz (1998), and Joan Braden (1998).

Volumes: *Men, Money & Magic* by Jeffrey Potter and *The Lady Upstairs* by Marilyn Nissenson.

A NEW ROMANTIC PROSPECT *AND* JACKIE HAS TO CHOOSE?

I referenced Jackie's Oral History for the John Fitzgerald Kennedy Presidential Library and Museum.

Interviews: Xenia Kaldara (2022), Christos Siafkis (2022), Kiki Feroudi Moutsatsos (2022), Thea Andino (2022), Tom Guinzburg (2005, 2007), and Karen Lerner (2009),

Volume: *Jackie as Editor* by Greg Lawrence.

SINATRA *AND* JACKIE'S CAMELOT THREATENED

I referenced "The Dark Side of Camelot" by Kitty Kelley, *People*, February 29, 1988; "The Last Act of Judith Exner" by Gerri Hirshey, *Vanity Fair*, April 1990; and "The Exner Files" by Liz Smith, *Vanity Fair*, January 1997. I authored two books about Frank Sinatra: *Sinatra: A Complete Life* and *Sinatra: Behind the Legend*. Some of the material in this book relating to him has been culled from that research.

Worth noting: Judith Exner died on September 24, 1999. On September 30, after publication of its obituary of her, *The New York Times* wrote an addendum to it: "An obituary on Monday reported the death of Judith Campbell Exner." It quoted assertions she had made over the years that she had had an affair with John F. Kennedy before and after he was elected president. The article reported that aides of President Kennedy's, including Dave Powers, denied the affair. But it should also have reflected what is now the view of a number of respected historians and authors that the affair did in fact take place. The evidence cited by various authorities in recent years has included White House phone logs and memos from J. Edgar Hoover.

Interviews: Thea Andino (2022), Joey D'Orazio (2022), Kiki Feroudi Moutsatsos (2022), Tony Oppedisano (2018, 2020), Barbara Gibson (1998), Leah Mason (1996, 1998), Bill Stapley (1997, 1998), Jim Whiting (1997, 2022), Micky Rudin (1996), and Jilly Rizzo (1991, 1992).

Volume: *The Dark Side of Camelot* by Seymour M. Hersh.

A DIFFICULT SUMMER

Interviews: Jamie Auchincloss (2022), Garrett Johnston (2022), and Robert Westover (2016).

THE MOST LOVING THING

Interviews: Jamie Auchincloss (2022), Stanley Levin (2022), Mary Tyler McClenahan (2000), and Hugh D. (Yusha) Auchincloss III (1998, 1999).

REACHING OUT TO LEE

Interviews: Jamie Auchincloss (2022), Stephen Rockewell (2022), Isabel Williams-Black (2022), Jillian Miles (2022), Janet Crook (2016), and Leah Mason (2015).

FAMILY DRAMA

I referenced "A Private Life Defined by Wit, Compassion" by Pete Hamill, *New York Newsday,* May 22, 1994.

Interviews: Jamie Auchincloss (2022), Cybil Wright (2022), Adora Rule (2022), Janine Rule (2022), Robert Westover (2016), Janet Crook (2016), and Hugh D. (Yusha) Auchincloss III (1998).

JACKIE O. BAGGAGE

I referenced "The Bright Light of His Days" by Jacqueline Kennedy On-assis, *McCall's,* November 1973, and also various articles and essays found in "Jacqueline Kennedy Onassis 1929–1994," *People Tribute,* summer 1994.

Interviews: Mary Wells Forman (2022), Tom Guinzburg (2005, 2007), and John Leonard (1998, 2008).

Volumes: *The Kennedys: An American Drama* by Peter Collier and David Horowitz and *The Kennedys: America's Emerald Kings: A Five-Generation History of the Ultimate Irish-Catholic Family* by Thomas Maier.

MOVING FORWARD

I drew from "A Fascinating Peek at the Jackie You Never Knew" (inter-view with Marian Ronan), *National Enquirer,* June 21, 1994; and "Jackie's Style," *People,* May 7, 2001.

Jackie's in-depth, four-page handwritten letter to Joan Kennedy ("Forbid-den fruit is what's exciting") was auctioned in February 2007 by Alexander Historical Auctions for $7,500. The founder of Alexander, Bill Panagopulos, said it was discovered in an abandoned storage unit locker in Hyannis Port.

An example of how random such auctions can be, at this same sale, Pana-gopulos auctioned seven of Aristotle Onassis's gold-filled molars, which had been removed by his dentist Dr. H. Justine Ross, in approximately 1950. Also auctioned were thirteen pages of Onassis's dental records, two sets of his x-rays, and a letter from the dentist, strongly suggesting he take better care of his teeth. The molars, extracted to make way for a bridge, totaled one troy ounce of gold and were contained in a glass jar. They sold for $1,300.

I also referred to "Letters Show Jackie Kennedy's Other Side," CBS News, February 24, 2007.

Interviews: Hope Marinetti (2022), Bill Panagopulos (2007), Sam Vaughan (2007), Marian Ronan (2000), Marta Sgubin (1998), and George Christian (1998).

Volumes: *Cooking for Madam* by Marta Sgubin, *The Kennedys: An American*

Drama by Peter Collier and David Horowitz, and *The Kennedys: America's Emerald Kings: A Five-Generation History of the Ultimate Irish-Catholic Family* by Thomas Maier.

JANET'S NEWS

Interviews: Cybil Wright (2022), Robert Westover (2016), Michael Dupree (2016), and Hugh D. (Yusha) Auchincloss III (1998, 1999).

WARREN BEATTY

Except for Adora Rule, all other sources relating to Jackie's relationship with Mr. Beatty asked for anonymity.

Interview: Adora Rule (2022).

Volume: *Star: How Warren Beatty Seduced America* by Peter Biskind.

MT

Because of the sensitive nature of Jackie's relationship with Mr. Tempelsman, all sources, except those noted below, asked for anonymity.

Interviews: Jamie Auchincloss (2022) and Mona Latham (2022).

Volumes: *A Woman Named Jackie* by C. David Heymann, *Jacqueline Bouvier Kennedy Onassis: A Life* by Donald Spoto, and *Just Jackie: Her Private Years* by Edward Klein.

"MUMMY'S GETTING MARRIED"

Interviews: Cybil Wright (2022), Isabel Fritz Cope (2016), Gustavo Paredes (2016, 2017), and Marion Cope (2016).

A JOURNEY AHEAD

I referred to "Jackie Spots Paparazzi at Mother's Wedding," Associated Press, *Baltimore Sun,* October 27, 1979; "Hot Blood—and Gore, Chapter Two" by Sally Quinn, *Washington Post,* June 7, 1979; "Mrs. Auchincloss to Marry for the Third Time," *New York Times,* August 21, 1979; "Mrs. Onassis is the Witness at Her Mother's Wedding," *New York Times,* October 26, 1979; "The Kennedys Gathered for Ceremony" by Gloria Negri, *Boston Globe,* September 20, 1980; "Her Famous Family Gathers at Wedding of Mrs. Auchincloss" by Marialisa Calta, *Providence Journal-Bulletin,* October 26, 1979. I also referenced correspondence between Hugh D. (Yusha) Auchincloss III and Bingham Morris (undated).

Interviews: Jamie Auchincloss (2022), Adora Rule (2022), Jonathan Tapper (2017), and Michael Dupree (2016).

Volume: *Janet & Jackie* by Jan Pottker.

THE LONG-OVERDUE APOLOGY *AND* "MY WONDERFUL ARTEMIS"

Interviews: Donna Lou (2022), Marlene Brody (2022), Kiki Feroudi Moutsatsos (2022), and Thea Andino (2022).

BOOK VI: CHALLENGES

MICHAEL JACKSON, A FRUSTRATING RELATIONSHIP, *AND* FALLING OUT WITH MICHAEL

As Michael Jackson's biographer (*Michael Jackson: The Magic, the Madness, the Whole Story*, 1958–2009) and longtime friend (from 1970 until his death in 2009), I had many conversations with him about his time at Doubleday with Jacqueline Onassis. With this book, I am revealing his true feelings about this complicated time as told to me in recollections from 1983 until approximately 2005. All of his quotes found here were to me.

Interviews: Michael Jackson (1983–2005), Frank DiLeo (2005, 2010), and John Branca (1997).

JANET'S DIAGNOSIS, "TRYING TO CONTROL THE UNCONTROLLA-BLE . . ." *AND* "CROWDS TO DO HER HOMAGE CAME"

I referenced a transcript of Jacqueline Kennedy Onassis's eulogy to Janet Auchincloss Rutherfurd, March 19, 1985. I also referred to "A Private Life Defined by Wit, Compassion" by Pete Hamill, *New York Newsday,* May 22, 1994; and "Like Cleopatra, Jackie's Legend Will Not Whither" by Liz Smith, *New York Newsday,* May 22, 1994.

Interviews: Jamie Auchincloss (2022), Mary Wells Forman (2022), Michael Dupree (2022), Dawn Luango (2022), Donna Lou (2022), Cybil Wright (2022), Dr. Dennis Selkoe (2016, 2022), Jonathan Tapper (2016), Joyce Faria Brennan (2016), John Warnecke (1998, 2007), Winthrop Rutherfurd (2018), and Oatsie Leiter Charles (1998).

WHAT MUMMY WANTS

Interviews: Jamie Auchincloss (2022), Joyce Faria Brennan (2018), Eileen Slocum (1998), and Chauncy Parker III (1998).

LILLY

The Doubleday colleague with Jackie while at the hospital asked for anonymity.

Volume: *Cooking for Madam* by Marta Sgubin.

CAROLINE, ED SCHLOSSBERG, *(AND LATER)* THE PRINCE, MADONNA, AND A CLOSE CALL WITH CAROLYN

I drew from an email exchange with Peter Beard (2016). I also drew from Ted Kennedy's Oral History at the UVA Miller Center (2004) as well as the following Oral Histories from the Edward M. Kennedy Institute: Robert Shriver III and Maria Shriver (2019), Victoria R. Kennedy (2010), and Caroline Raclin (daughter of Victoria Reggie Kennedy) (2008).

Additionally I referred to "Story of JFK Jr.: A Profile of Courage" by Michael Kilian, *Chicago Tribune,* July 22, 1999; "How Caroline and John Remember Their Father" by David E. Powers, *McCall's,* November 1973; "Ted Kennedy's Memories of JFK" by Theodore Sorensen, *McCall's,* November 1973; "Crazy for Carolyn" by Tessa Namuth et al., *Newsweek,* October 20, 1996; "JFK Jr.'s Final Journey" by Evan Thomas, *Newsweek,* August 1, 1999; "John-John Caught Running Away from Home" by Leslie Valentine, *Silver Screen,* October 1971; "Caroline Kennedy: A Little Girl in Turmoil" by Lester David, *Good Housekeeping,* January 1969; "How Caroline Kennedy Plans to Break Out of Her Mother's Jet Set Prison" by Sharon Willson, *Silver Screen,* August 1974; "My Mother—The Queen of Camelot" by Elizabeth Castor, *The Australian Women's Weekly,* November 2001.

I also drew from my extensive research for the two-part series I authored "The Life and Loves of the Prince of Camelot," *Woman's Day,* July 26, 1999, as well as my three-part series "JFK Jr.—Golden Child," *Star,* August 1999. I drew from reporting for my three-part series on Caroline Kennedy, "Camelot's Daughter," *Woman's Day,* March 2000, as well as reporting for my series of features on Ms. Kennedy for *Entertainment Tonight,* November 2000.

I reported extensively about Caroline Kennedy and John Kennedy Jr. in my book *The Kennedy Heirs.* I also wrote comprehensively about John Kennedy Jr.'s relationship with Madonna for my book *Madonna: An Intimate Biography.* I drew here from my research for both of those works, including one of my many interviews with Madonna (June 1989).

Interviews: Jamie Auchincloss (2022), Thomas Morrissey (2022), Cybil Wright (2022), Lisa McClintock (2022), Thomas Luft (2022), Randy Beattie (2018), Robert Westover (2018), Josefina "Fina" Hardin (2017), Sean Penn

(2003, 2005), Gustavo Paredes (2016, 2017, 2018), Taki Theodoracopulos (2016), Stephen Styles Cooper (1998, 2005, 2010, 2015), Tammy Holloway (2010), Bryan Holloway (2010), Richard Bradley (2010, 2017), Holly Safford (2010), Christopher Lawford (1998, 2009, 2017, 2018), John Perry Barlow (1999, 2015, 2017), Marta Sgubin (1998), and Joan Braden (1998).

Volumes: *Times to Remember* by Rose Kennedy, *Sweet Caroline* by Christopher Andersen, *Fairy Tale Interrupted: A Memoir of Life, Love, and Loss* by RoseMarie Terenzio, *The Good Son* by Christopher Andersen, *American Legacy* by C. David Heymann, *John and Caroline* by James Spada, *Prince Charming* by Wendy Leigh, *Forever Young* by William Sylvester Noonan, *The Men We Became* by Robert T. Littell, *Men, Money & Magic* by Jeffrey Potter, *The Kennedys: An American Drama* by Peter Collier and David Horowitz, *The Kennedys: America's Emerald Kings: A Five-Generation History of the Ultimate Irish-Catholic Family* by Thomas Maier, and *The Lady Upstairs* by Marilyn Nissenson.

THE OUTSIDER

The letter from Bingham Morris to Jacqueline Onassis was provided by an anonymous source from a private collection. Jackie's letter to Hugh D. (Yusha) Auchincloss III regarding Bingham Morris and Lee's letter to Hugh D. (Yusha) Auchincloss III regarding "Jackie's trauma" were both provided by anonymous sources from private collections.

Interviews: Ivy Rawlins (2022), Ted Page (2022), and Dr. Dennis Selkoe (2022).

PRECIOUS MEMORIES

Jackie's letter to Hugh D. (Yusha) Auchincloss III was provided by an anonymous source from a private collection.

I referenced *The Kennedys: America's Emerald Kings: A Five-Generation History of the Ultimate Irish-Catholic Family* by Thomas Maier.

Interviews: Donna Lou (2022) and Robert Westover (2016).

TURNING SIXTY

Interviews: Jamie Auchincloss (2022), Thomas Morrissey (2022), Tillie Mia (2023), Janine Rule (2022), Donna Lou (2022), R. Couri Hay (2016, 2019), Bunny Mellon (2012), and Jack Warnecke (2007).

THANK YOU *AND* AT PEACE

Interviews: Donna Lou (2022), Ivy Rawlins (2022), Jamie Auchincloss (2022), and Adora Rule (2022).

BOOK VII: A SAD FAREWELL

THE ART OF CONTENTMENT

Jackie's two letters to Yusha are from *Growing Up with Jackie: My Memories, 1941–1953*. I also referenced "A Private Life Defined by Wit, Compassion" by Pete Hamill, *New York Newsday,* May 22, 1994.

Interviews: Jamie Auchincloss (2022), Victoria Meekins (2022), Abigail McGrath (2022), Leah Mason (2013), and Hugh D. (Yusha) Auchincloss III (1998, 1999).

Volumes: *America's Queen* by Sarah Bradford, *Jacqueline Bouvier Kennedy Onassis: The Untold Story* by Barbara Leaming, and *Touched by the Sun* by Carly Simon.

"WHY HER?" AND AN IDIOT'S DANCE

I referenced "Her Graceful Silence Has Spoken Louder than Many Words" by Alice Steinbach, *Baltimore Sun,* February 15, 1994; "My Mother, Rose Kennedy" by Ted Kennedy, *Ladies' Home Journal,* December 1975; and "Portrait of a Lady" by Elizabeth Gleick, *People,* February 28, 1994.

I also referenced Rose Kennedy's diaries, which can be found in the Rose Fitzgerald Kennedy Papers of the John Fitzgerald Kennedy Presidential Library and Museum.

Interviews: Cybil Wright (2022), Joyce Newton (2022), Blythe Coleman (2022), Abigail McGrath (2022), Robert Westover (2016), Arthur M. Schlesinger Jr. (1997, 2003, 2006), and Niki Goulandris (2010).

Volume: *Times to Remember* by Rose Kennedy.

A MIRACLE CURE?

In addition to the interviews listed below, I also relied on an anonymous source in Ted Kennedy's family.

Interviews: Dr. Stanislaw Burzynski (2022), Dean Mouscher (2022), and Mary Jo Sigel (2022).

LIFE RUINING

I drew from Edgar Montalvo's "Hair Apparents," Post Staff Report, *New York Daily News* (April 2, 2013). Jackie's letter to Lady Bird Johnson is found in the Lyndon Baines Johnson Presidential Library and Museum, and her letters to Ethel Kennedy and Joan Kennedy can be found in the John Fitzgerald Kennedy Presidential Library and Museum. Her letter to Jamie was provided by him, and her letter to Yusha is found in his manuscript *Growing Up with Jackie: My Memories, 1941–1953.*

Interviews: Tilly Weitzner (2022), Thomas Morrissey (2022), and Oleg Cassini (1998, 2004).

TEN GOOD YEARS

Interview: Jack Warnecke (1998, 2007).

NOTHING TO LOSE

Interviews: Dr. Stanislaw Burzynski (2022) and Dean Mouscher (2022).

TIME TO GO ON

I referenced *Growing Up with Jackie: My Memories, 1941–1953* by Hugh D. (Yusha) Auchincloss III and *What Remains* by Carol Radziwill. I also referenced research for my book *Jackie, Janet & Lee.*

Jackie's last moments with her friends have been widely described by all who witnessed them.

Interviews: Robert Westover (2018), Thomas Morrissey (2022), and Tilly Weitzner (2022).

OLD GRUDGES

I referenced the text to Jamie Auchincloss's speech "Mud Wrestling with History: Snapshots of My Life as a Brother-in-Law to John F. Kennedy by James Auchincloss."

I also referenced "Portrait of a Lady" by Elizabeth Gleick, *People,* February 28, 1994; "A Great First Lady" by Bill Hoffman, *New York Post,* May 20, 1994; "Dying with Dignity" by Gale Scott, *New York Newsday,* May 21, 1994; "A First Lady Who Charmed a Nation" by Lars-Erik Nelson, *New York Newsday,* May 21, 1994; and "A Quiet Life with 'M.T.'" by Bill Turque, *Newsweek,* June 6, 1994.

Interview: Jamie Auchincloss (2022).

LAST HOPE

I referenced "America's First Lady" by Peggy Noonan, *Time,* May 30, 1994; and "The Jackie Mystique" by Anemona Hartocollis, *New York Newsday,* May 22, 1994.

I referenced the extensive transcript of an unpublished interview Janet Auchincloss gave to *Ladies' Home Journal* in 1967, provided to me by an anonymous source.

Interviews: Dr. Stanislaw Burzynski (2022) and Dean Mouscher (2022).

SPECIAL THANKS

I would also like to thank the following people who assisted me in tangible and intangible ways: Alexander J. Forger, Alexandra Georgopoulou, Elaine Vanderhoop, Elizabeth DuBose, Brenda Connors, Diana Clemente, Efraim J. Rotter, Alexandra Zaroulis, David Fahey, Kevin Lee, Colleen Townsend Pilat, Greg Donahue, Jack Moderner, Jan Fishman, Juli Vanderhoop, Karen Pranschke, Mary Hopkins, Nikki Haskell (re: Peter Beard), Seamus McKeon, Sarah Hutson, Theodore Ginsberg, and Carolyn Powers (re: Dr. Burzynski).

Thanks also to the fine people at the Martha's Vineyard Museum (Linsey Lee, Bonnie Stacy, Heather Seger, and Bow Van Riper); the *Martha's Vineyard Times,* the *Montauk Sun* (Kenny Giustino), the Michael Cacoyannis Foundation, *The Newport Daily News,* Newport Historical Society (Ingrid Peters), Mary Hopkins, Ossabaw Island Foundation, Rapp Funeral Home, the *Savannah Morning News,* the *Martha's Vineyard Gazette* (Hillary Wallcox), Thomasville County Historical Foundation and the Georgia Research Center and the Sixth Floor Museum at Dealey Plaza (Stephen Fagin), and, also, Vince Palamara, one of the world's leading experts on the Kennedy Secret Service detail, who has written several books about the subject and who assisted me in many ways for my books about the Kennedys. I urge you to visit his fascinating blog at http://vincepalamara.blogspot.com/.

Thanks also to: Academy of Motion Picture Arts and Sciences; Ancestry .com; AP Images; Associated Press Office (New York); Beverly Hills Library; *Boston Herald* Archives; Corbis Gamma Liaison; Corbis Getty Images Globe Photos; Hedda Hopper Collection in the Margaret Herrick Library,

Academy of Motion Picture Arts and Sciences, Beverly Hills; Heritage Auctions, Hong Kong; League of Women Voters; Lincoln Center Library of the Performing Arts, Lincoln Center, New York; Los Angeles Public Library; *Los Angeles Times;* Louis B. Mayer Library of the American Film Institute; Margaret Herrick Library; MPTV Images; Museum of Broadcasting, New York; MyRoots.com; Natchitoches Parish Tourist Commission; Natchitoches Tourism Bureau; *New York Daily News; New York Post; New York Times;* New York University Library; Newport Chamber of Commerce; Newport Country Club; *Newport Daily News;* Newport Garden Club; Newport Historical Society; *Newport Mercury;* Occidental College, Eagle Rock, California; *Philadelphia Daily News; Philadelphia Inquirer;* Philadelphia Public Library; Preservation Society of Newport County; Rex Features; *Shreveport Times;* Southampton Historical Museum; Southampton Press; St. Clare–Newport Senior Center; Time-Life Archives and Library, New York: Tour Natchitoches; University of California, Los Angeles.

Special thanks to the staffs of the John Fitzgerald Kennedy Presidential Library and Museum, in particular Maryrose Grossman, Nadia Dixson, and Kyoko Yamamoto, for all their amazing assistance. Thanks also to William Johnson, Ron Whealan, June Payne, Maura Porter, Susan D'Entrement, Allen Goodrich, and James Hill.

I am also grateful to Marianne Masterson and Delores DeMann for assisting me in the reading and analyzing of these many transcripts.

As I do with all my Kennedy-related books, I must also acknowledge David Powers, former special assistant to President John F. Kennedy, the first curator of the John Fitzgerald Kennedy Presidential Library and Museum. I was lucky enough to interview him back on January 11, 1997. Certainly, no mention of the John Fitzgerald Kennedy Presidential Library and Museum is complete without a nod to Mr. Powers, who died March 27, 1998, at the age of eighty-five.

Thanks also to the staff of the Lyndon Baines Johnson Presidential Library and Museum.

A WORD ABOUT CATHY GRIFFIN
AND OUR SOURCES

I've been so fortunate to work with the same private investigator and chief researcher, Cathy Griffin, for the last thirty-three years, an incredible run of success for us as a team. Cathy has always managed to find people to talk to for our books who have never before talked about our subjects. Moreover, she has a way of encouraging those who have talked to other biographers to be more candid with us and put into new context stories that have been told in the past. Since Cathy was also the primary researcher for my other bestselling books about the Kennedys—*Jackie, Ethel, Joan; After Camelot; Jackie, Janet & Lee;* and *The Kennedy Heirs*—she has a great grasp of the subject matter and knew exactly where to go for *Jackie: Public, Private, Secret* to get the deeply reported stories we needed to tell Jackie's history in a new and exciting way.

Cathy and I value our sources. After all, my books would be nothing without them. We cultivate each one to make sure he or she knows how much we appreciate the cooperation and how we never take it for granted. Sources sometimes risk a lot to cooperate, and so we make it a point to never let it be regretted.

Many of our sources approve their stories before publication—all they have to do is ask. I have no problem granting that approval, because I understand how important it is to them that they be accurately portrayed. If someone says something they may later regret, we go back to that source to make sure it was said in earnest. Sometimes, the source wishes to rephrase it—and that's fine, too. Whatever it takes to be accurate while at the same time compassionate and empathetic, that's what we do. As a result, in all these years of working together, never have we had a single disgruntled source. Never has there been a person who wanted to retract his or her story or has been unhappy about the way it was told, and that's a tribute to Cathy and her rapport with our sources.

With the conclusion of every book, I always say, "That's it. I'm done now." Inevitably, though, I go back for just one more, and it's because Cathy Griffin makes it all worthwhile. So, once again, as always, I thank her from the bottom of my heart.

PERSONAL ACKNOWLEDGMENTS

I want to thank my terrific editor, Charles Spicer, for all his encouragement over the years. This is our fourth book together, and the third Kennedy-related title—along with *Jackie, Janet & Lee* and *The Kennedy Heirs*—while the fourth, *Grace & Steel,* is about another of America's royal families, the Bushes. Charles is such a great editor in so many ways, not the least of which is his commitment to the job at hand. I know I am in great hands with him, and I'm sure we'll do many more books together at St. Martin's Press.

Thanks also to Charles's ever capable assistant, Hannah Pierdolla. My appreciation, as well, to production editor Cassie Gutman, and Sara Robb and Chris Ensey with ScriptAcuity Studio, who did a wonderful job copy editing this manuscript.

I would also like to acknowledge my late domestic literary agent, Mitch Douglas, who passed away on November 5, 2020. Mitch represented me for more than twenty years, and I am sort of lost without him, I admit. He was a good friend as well as my agent, and I know he would've loved this book.

I would also like to acknowledge my foreign agent, Dorie Simmonds of the Dorie Simmonds Agency in London, who not only has represented me for more than twenty years but also is a trusted friend.

Thank you to my television agent, Judy Coppage, of the Coppage Company, who read the first draft of *Jackie: Public, Private, Secret* and gave me some much-needed encouragement. I'd also like to thank her assistant, Sydney Sterling.

I would like to thank my amazing attorney, Laurie Megery, of Myman Greenspan Fineman Fox Rosenberg & Light. She specializes in making deals the right way—without angst and drama—and believe me, I've had plenty of that in the past and know how draining it can be. I thank her and her team, and that includes her assistant Greg Maxey, for such good and fair representation.

Special thanks also to Jo Ann McMahon and Felinda Adlawan of McMahon Accountancy Corporation.

I also want to acknowledge one of my television-producing partners and very good friend, Keri Selig, as well as Hannah Reynolds of Intuition Productions.

I'd also like to acknowledge another television-producing partner of mine, Tucker Tooley. He and his team at Tucker Tooley Entertainment are assisting me in bringing this book, as well as two others of mine, to television. I thank them for the partnership, and that includes Greg Renker, Christian Parent, and Aaron Schmidt.

I would also like to thank my close friend Jillian DeVaney, who read this book in manuscript stage, as she does all my books, and offered invaluable insight.

My thanks to Jonathan Hahn, a brilliant writer, my personal publicist, and good friend. Thanks also to his wife, Lindsay Brie Mathers, for her love and support.

Special thanks to my good friends Andy Hirsch, Andy Steinlen, George Solomon, Richard Tyler Jordan, John Passantino, Linda DiStefano, Hazel Kragulac, Andy Skurow, Brad Scarton, Brian Newman, Scherrie Payne, Freda Payne, Susaye Greene, Barbara Ormsby, David Spiro, Billy Masters, Kac Young, Susan Kayaoglu, Barb Mueller, Mark Mussari, Peter Dillard, Susan Batchelor, Park Messikomer, and Donna McNeill.

I have always been so blessed to have a family as supportive as mine. My thanks and love go out to Roslyn and Bill Barnett and Jessica and Zachary; Rocco and Rosemaria Taraborrelli and Rocco and Vincent; and Arnold Taraborrelli. A big smile, also, for Axel Taraborrelli.

I must also acknowledge those readers of mine who have followed my career over the years. I am indebted to each and every reader who has stuck by me. I am eternally grateful to anyone who takes the time to pick up one of my books and read it. Thank you so much.

All my books are written with my late parents, Rocco and Rose Marie Taraborrelli, in mind at all times. I miss them.

J. Randy Taraborrelli
June 2023

INDEX